The Life Story of

PRESLEY MARION RIXEY

Surgeon General, U. S. Navy

1902-1910

Biography and Autobiography

Biography by

REAR ADMIRAL WILLIAM C. BRAISTED, M. C., U. S. NAVY

AND

CAPTAIN WILLIAM HEMPHILL BELL, M. C., U. S. NAVY

WASHINGTON, D. C.

1910

SHENANDOAH PUBLISHING HOUSE, INC.

STRASBURG, VIRGINIA

1930

Rear Admiral Presley Marion Rixey, U. S. Navy

DEDICATED TO

HIS FAMILY

AND

THE MEDICAL CORPS OF THE UNITED STATES NAVY

IN MEMORY OF

PRESLEY MARION RIXEY

DOCTOR OF MEDICINE

WHOSE SERVICES EXCITE A JUST PRIDE

IN THE ONE AND A GRATEFUL APPRECIATION

IN THE OTHER, AS THEY WERE

OF VALUE TO HIS

COUNTRY

What other things I hitherto have done
Have fallen from me, are no longer mine;
I have passed on beyond them, and have left them
As milestones on the way. What lies before me,
That is still mine, and while it is unfinished
No one shall draw me from it, or persuade me
By promises of ease, or wealth, or honor,
Till I behold the finished dome uprise
Complete, as now I see it in my thought.

Longfellow's "MICHAEL ANGELO."

PREFACE

WHILE it is appreciated that a degree of perspective is desirable in the truthful estimation of the position which any public life deserves in history, it is also believed that much of importance in the review of such a life is inevitably and hopelessly lost if the biographer delays his task too long.

Conscious of our limitations as biographers, we have aimed only to make these pages a fair memorial of a remarkable man, though keeping in view our principal purpose to record the events and experiences of his interesting life before time had veiled their distinctness or actually carried all knowledge of them beyond reach with the passing of contemporaries. When the undertaking was first suggested, Dr. Rixey was in the zenith of his picturesque career, and it seemed desirable to all who were concerned that some effort should be made, even if with no better success than would result in the compilation of a memorandum, to place the innumerable incidents of this period beyond any uncertainty of the mind to recall.

Had it not been for our personal knowledge of Dr. Rixey and had we not enjoyed friendly relations with him or possessed some share of his confidence, this sketch of his life could not have been written. Nor could we have made an interpretation of the fragmentary mass of his private papers or of "that notable supplement, for biographical purposes—the record of the times" in which he occupied a prominent place, preserved in the daily papers and periodicals of many parts of the country which he had accumulated, unless we had been able to consult him personally. In addition to these sources of information, we have obtained the material utilized in this sketch from the files of the Bureau of Medicine and Surgery of the Navy Department, and from his family.

We commit this result of our self-imposed and pleasant labor to the charitable judgment of those best able to measure the difficulties of the task. If the facts herein related serve as a considerable foundation upon which future and more competent biographers may build, and if, moreover, the perusal of these pages is a source of satisfaction to his family, and a lesson to rising generations in the medical service of the Navy, our object will have been fulfilled.

He was too much engaged at this time to aid his biographers by his personal reminiscences, nor could he turn over to them the diary of his cruises nor the personal letters received from President Roosevelt and others in official life.

PRESLEY MARION RIXEY

Surgeon General, U. S. Navy, from 1902 to 1910

Rank of Rear Admiral from 1902

Retired from Active Duty 1910

Called for Active Duty for the World War

and

Served Until Its Close

Part I

Biography by

Rear Admiral William C. Braisted, M. C., U. S. Navy

Captain William H. Bell, M. C., U. S. Navy

1909 and 1910

Part II

Autobiography

CONTENTS

Part I

CONTENTS *(Continued)*

Part II

Autobiography

LIST OF ILLUSTRATIONS

BIOGRAPHY OF PRESLEY MARION RIXEY

INTRODUCTION

"Seest thou a man diligent in his business, he shall stand before kings."

THIS simple little text, which Franklin's father was in the habit of quoting to the future statesman, philosopher and diplomat, while working in the old candle shop in Boston when a boy, could not be resurrected and employed to better purpose than as an introductory retrospect to a consideration of the subject of this sketch and as a hint to the secret of the success of his career. Dr. Rixey has devoted himself diligently to the affairs which have fallen to his lot; his life has been full of responsibilities of small and great magnitude; and he has stood beside the highest in the nation, enjoying their utmost confidence and warmest friendship.

His inspiring example should not perish with the lives of those who now know him, for he was a maker of history, albeit a humble one. Macaulay truly tells us "that he who takes no pride in the achievements of his ancestors will do nothing worthy the remembrance of his descendants." It is firmly believed that this warning may be taken in a metaphorical sense and in such wise holds true as regards the deeds and accomplishments of our predecessors, whose lives were noteworthy in various channels of endeavor and deserves attention irrespective of blood ties as an incentive to study and profit by their records.

CHAPTER I

ANCESTRY AND YOUTH

PRESLEY MARION RIXEY was born in the town of Culpeper, Culpeper County, Virginia, July 14, 1852, the second son and third of his generation in a family of nine children, only five of whom lived to maturity. His father was Presley Morehead Rixey, born in Culpeper County, a few miles from Culpeper, June 7, 1812, where he became a well known, respected and prosperous farmer in the community, distinguished for his intelligence, integrity, and business ability. He was a tall, spare, fine looking man and those who knew him remember him as a striking figure of the community in the picturesque garb of his period. For many years—indeed, as far back as Dr. Rixey's recollection reaches—his father was blind, having gradually lost his sight by the development of cataracts. In spite of this fact, he led an active life and supervised his farm through the eyes of his boys who rode over the property on horseback in company with him and kept him advised of existing conditions. He lived to an advanced age—81 years. This infirmity probably had a material influence toward softening his nature, though with all his stern business qualities he was natively of a gentle and kindly disposition, and he was of course unable to take a large part either in the conduct of his affairs or the rearing of his family. He married twice—the first wife soon died leaving this union without issue, and his second wife, whom he also survived, and the mother of the subject of this sketch, was Mary Frances Jones, of Culpeper, Va., and in her he must have found the greatest comfort as a helpmeet, capable of assuming that part of his business and domestic responsibilities which he was obliged to relinquish on account of his infirmity. In stature she was well above the average height of her sex yet more heavily proportioned than her husband. By nature she was a loving, loyal hearted wife, and mother, with great force of

MRS. PRESLEY MOREHEAD RIXEY
Rear Admiral Rixey's mother

character, and her children owe much to her influence, for she governed them in a firm though eminently just manner and sought to develop the best in them. In these traits of character she exhibited her stolid English heritage. The Rixey side of the family it is believed is of hardy Scotch descent. Certainly the rugged health, sterling qualities, never ceasing energy and bright and scintillating intellects of the children indicate Scotch blood. The line of descent from the earliest American ancestor, Richard Rixey, of Prince William County, Va., to the present generation was physically and morally of sturdy stock, ethically of high standing and comfortably circumstanced. The political affiliations of the family were Democratic and its sympathies Southern, and during the Civil War it was identified with the Confederate Cause. As stated above, up to this time the family had been well to do for those days, but its income was greatly curtailed by the war in common with so large a proportion of our old Southern families, and it took effort and sacrifice to properly educate the children. During the rebellion, Dr. Rixey was in his early teens and thus recalls many incidents connected with this long and terrible conflict. The schools were closed much of the time and his youthful energies were, therefore, turned to land tilling and other useful occupations about the farm and home, as was the case with most boys in those trying days, particularly throughout the South, who found themselves suddenly raised to manhood's estate as far as concerned contributions to their families' welfare and the assumption of many of the responsibilities of the men who had gone to the front.

Culpeper was the center of a good deal of fighting and many of the raids back and forth between the "Confederate and Yankee forces" were made through the town, in the streets of which firing was often active. The Rixey boys were, of course, excitedly interested and, though their mother tried to keep them in the cellar, protected from harm at such times, they were an irrepressible brood, hard to control, and they frequently evaded her vigilance and made their way to the front of the house—even to the front yard, where they could see what was going on, ignorant—or at least unappreciative—of the real danger to which they were exposing themselves. On one such occasion when desultory long range firing was going on from the neighboring heights and the bullets were whizzing by and striking in various places nearby, these boys stole out and, conscious of wrongdoing, tried to conceal themselves from their mother by lying, out of sight, on the porch beneath the windows. For some time they escaped discovery, but finally they were ignominiously drawn from their hiding-place and warmly chastized.

The Rixey home with its famous hospitality was twice abruptly demanded as Headquarters by high officers of the contending armies—once by General Siegle and once by General Grant. Even though the household was in sympathy with the South and opposed to the North, the Rixeys were not blind to the difference in the personalities of these

two men and, in contrast to their feeling for the brusque, overbearing Siegle, they learned to like the calm, generous, self-reliant Grant. Some years later, Grant, as President of the United States, appointed young Rixey to the Navy, but much was to happen before this turn in his life.

Through his early boyhood he was small and slight, giving no promise of attaining the height which, judging from his parents, it was natural to expect, but he was active and wiry, and, though not regarded a bad boy, was brimming over with the masculine pranks common to his years—always ready for anything and, when not occupied in the hay field or elsewhere on the farm, or at school, always on the go, either riding or hunting, fishing, or in games of one sort or another with his youthful associates. A fox hunt was his particular delight and he was in the saddle and off behind the pack at every opportunity. It was not until seventeen years of age that he began to shoot up in stature and soon after that he became the tall, slender boy that those who know him today can imagine him. He was, however, always strong and he engaged in every task and every amusement with tremendous energy and intensity of interest. An incident in his boyhood is related which shows the early development of a marked determination of character. His brother had been bullying him or had done something else that had aroused his anger and he picked up an old lock and threw it at him, striking him on the shin with considerable force and resultant injury. In spite of the fact that the brother was in the wrong, his mother regarded the act as unwarranted and reprehensive and, therefore, took him in hand for punishment. As was her wont, she carefully explained her judgment in the affair and called upon him to say that he was sorry or accept the alternative of restriction for a certain period. He, however, disclaimed any sorrow for his act of retaliation and refused to express a regret that he did not feel, whereupon his mother carried out her intention of locking him in a room, to which he submitted, though not without a protest and some argument upon his part as to the justice of the discipline imposed. This was a new phase in the boy's evolution. He had reached a stage in his development when he was beginning to weigh the right and the wrong of things on his own account and he felt that in this case he was improperly bearing the brunt of and being made to suffer disproportionately for an offense for which he was not in the first instances responsible. He apparently regarded the disagreement with his mother as a reasonable difference of opinion and when he refused to say that he was sorry it was with the conviction that he was availing himself of a legitimate means of expressing rebellion. For the first time the mother realized that this son had arrived at an age beyond the propriety of such discipline and, in thinking over this evidence of his determination and reasoning, came to the conclusion that in the future he must be dealt with by a different method, more in accordance with his apparent greater maturity. She never again attempted to inflict corporal punishment, but contented herself with appeals to his sense of right. Thus she employed her abundant intelligence in the rearing of her children, and the broad wisdom and rare discretion which she exercised in their management laid the foundation for the achievement of her ambition that her sons should be capable and upright men. It was under the moral and psychic influence of a wise mother; with the ever present example of a noble, high principled father; with the training to industry which he received on the farm; and in the midst of such an environment as a healthful, open, and beautiful country that young Presley's character was formed as he developed to manhood.

He received his early education in the public schools of Culpeper and Warrenton, Va., where he was sent after the Civil War. But now the question of higher education confronted the parents and like the gentlemen landowners of the post-bellum days, the father thought it necessary to educate his boys in the professions.

Young Presley, from his early youth, evinced a great passion for medicine and surgery and playmates tell of several whippings that came to him for catching his father's chickens and dissecting them. He was called doctor when only a boy in knee breeches, and it was not surprising, therefore, that, upon the completion of his preliminary schooling, he should have turned a hopeful attention to the medical profession. His family was not able to be of great assistance to him, but, undaunted by difficulties, he sought and achieved his aim. It was the custom in those early days for young medical aspirants to begin their studies in the office of some physician, usually a friend of the family, who had consented to assume the role of preceptor, and it was in this wise that Presley began reading medicine in Culpeper with his cousin, Dr. Samuel Rixey, thus fitting himself for college.

In due time he entered the University of Virginia, where he continued his professional education and from which institution he was graduated with the degree of Doctor of Medicine in June, 1873, at the age of twenty-one—all but one month. Money was a serious consideration at this time, and though it was all wrong, he had to press forward with such energy that he obtained his degree in nine months. Indeed, so hard did he work that he would stand up and study, with the book resting on the mantel-piece, in order that he might not fall asleep from exhaustion.

After a month's rest leading the outdoor life the young doctor regained his accustomed vigor and it was absolutely necessary for him to make a decision of how he should make a living. A young neighbor of his, Dr. Charles Yancey had, a few years before Dr. Rixey, graduated from the University of Virginia in nine months, after which he went to Philadelphia, Pa., took a quiz course under Dr. J. Ewing Meers and matriculated at the same time at Jefferson Medical College. Fortunately at this time he was at home and Dr. Rixey went to call on him and obtain information how Dr. Yancey had managed to get into the Navy and how he liked it. The information was very satisfactory and after viewing Dr. Yancey's new uniform Dr. Rixey's mind was made up and he was satisfied that what had been done before could be done again. He wrote at once to Dr. Meers and in another month he was in Philadelphia following in Assistant Surgeon Yancey's footsteps. Dr. Meers was a

Assistant Surgeon PRESLEY M. RIXEY, U. S. NAVY, 1873
Age 21 years

very excellent quiz master and he had a number of students taking the quiz for either the Army or Navy, among them Drs. Harmon, Gaines, and Ambler, all dear friends of his from that date. All of these gentlemen, including his friend Dr. Boyd, went before the medical board of Naval Examiners in December, a little more than a month before Dr. Rixey who did not go up until January.

One of his greatest pleasures in Philadelphia was the clinics of the elder Drs. Gross, Dacosta, Pencost, and many others most celebrated in Medicine and Surgery in 1873. Their teachings were most instructive, especially to him who had thus far no clinical experience. He speaks of these teachers and of his professors at the University of Virginia with the greatest affection which was only equaled by his admiration of their skill which made a lasting impression upon him. Early in January Dr. Meers advised Dr. Rixey to go before the Naval Board of Examiners in Washington,

Assistant Surgeon PRESLEY M. RIXEY, U. S. Navy, 1876
Age 24 years

D. C. The sessions of the Board at that time were held at the S. E. corner of K and 18th Streets, N. W.

He and a friend, who was also trying for a commission in the Medical Corps of the Navy, took a room in a boarding house together and these two young men spent the time pending the approaching ordeal in reviewing the subjects upon which they were to be examined. They were both keenly alive to the importance of measuring up to the standard of requirement in the coming inquiry into their eligibility, for it meant a fair start in their chosen life work, and they were obsessed by an anxiety lest they should fail. When the appointed day arrived, the subject of our sketch presented himself full of hope, yet not without misgivings, but the only embarrassment which he experienced, though the examination was hard and he did not make a brilliant showing, was the question, when asked to write his full name, as to the significance of the initial "M" in his signature. He had always signed himself "Presley M. Rixey," never having given a thought to his middle name, and to his shame, for the life of him he could not remember what "M" stood for, much to the astonishment of his mother when he told her of the incident. It appears that the "M" was the initial of Marion, the masculine form of Mary, which was the name of his mother and after whom he had been named; but in the early Naval registers following his admission into the Navy, he was officially recorded as "Presley M. Rixey," and it was not until years afterward that the error was corrected and his middle name written out.

CHAPTER II

EARLY SERVICE IN THE NAVY

DR. RIXEY was commissioned assistant surgeon in the Medical Corps of the United States Navy January 28, 1874, his commission being signed by President Grant, and set out upon that long period of service which has been crowned with the highest honors attainable in the medical Corps. In his service of thirty-six years he has succeeded to a place in all the grades of his branch of the Navy, viz; Passed Assistant Surgeon (April 18, 1877); Surgeon (November 27, 1888); Medical Inspector (August 24, 1900) and Medical Director (May 7, 1907)—the latter of which grades he attained while occupying the office of Surgeon General, to which he was appointed February 5, 1902.

He was first assigned to duty on the *Sabine*, which was at that time the receiving ship at the Navy Yard, Portsmouth, N. H., and this assignment he recalls as one of the most agreeable and profitable in his whole service, for it was there that the acquaintance between him and his future wife began, and it was there, also, that he was able to accomplish a great deal of telling medical reading. This was during the first half of the year 1874.

Dr. Rixey has always been a diligent student, and his high standing in the medical profession is the result of the habit of earnest industry which he formed in those early days. At the same time he did not shun society or other means of diversion, such as skating and sleighing, and he was counted one of the lights of the younger element of the small but charming circle at that station. He was attentive to all of the young ladies and, though feeling a distinct partiality for the society of Miss Earlena English, he was discouraged in his contemplated courtship by learning of her engagement to another man. These two young people first met at a hop on the *Sabine*, where the English girls, owing to the illness of their mother, were chaperoned by Mrs. Roderick McCook, wife of Captain McCook, U. S. Navy. Mrs. McCook presented them to each other and has ever since been a close friend.

In the summer of 1874 he applied for assignment to the *Plymouth,* which was fitting out to go to the Asiatic Station, but she proved an unhappy ship and, while disappointed at the time, he was afterwards glad that his request was not granted. Such is the common history of individuals of the Navy, and events have often proved that an officer may broadly shape the course of his life but he cannot always arrange the details of the future or anticipate what is best for him. In the spring of 1874, Captain Earl English, U. S. N., the father of the same Miss English who had infatuated Dr. Rixey, was detached from duty as Captain of the Portsmouth Navy Yard and ordered to command the *Congress,* then on the European Station, and, as fortune would have it, Dr. Rixey, instead of securing assignment to the *Plymouth,* was also ordered, August 18, 1874, to join the *Congress.* This he did at Spetzin, Italy, either in the latter part of 1874 or early in 1875, for it took several months to reach her, and it was in this way, while serving on this ship in the Mediterranean, that his acquaintance with Miss English was soon renewed. As was and still is often the case with the daughters of Naval officers, Miss English spent a great deal of time abroad. Her education was commenced in her native country, but was finished in the schools of France, and, during the stay of the *Congress* in European waters, she was at a private school in Paris. Her mother and sisters were also abroad, moving from place to place in Southern Europe, and, frequently, she would join her family at some Mediterranean port where the *Congress* was for the time at anchor. On these occasions Dr. Rixey, of course, saw much of Miss English, and, when he learned that her engagement had been broken he lost no opportunity to press his own suit. At this period of our Navy, commanding officers of cruising ships were allowed to take their families on board, so that, when the *Congress* was ordered home, Captain English brought his family, including Miss English, with him, a circumstance which was greatly to Dr. Rixey's advantage, as is shown by the fact that, soon after the *Congress* had arrived at Port Royal, South Carolina, Dr. Rixey and Miss English became .engaged. She was a charming, high-spirited, accomplished girl, and the success of Dr. Rixey's courtship was the cause for sincere and hearty felicitations from all sides. The *Congress* was then ordered north to Philadelphia, to be in attendance at the opening of the Centennial Exposition, and here Dr. Rixey was present on the platform with distinguished men of the day, when the great Corliss engine, which turned all the machinery at the Exposition, was first put in motion. From here, after a two weeks' stay, the *Congress* was ordered to Portsmouth, where Captain English, now become Commodore, was detached and ordered again to the Navy Yard at that place, though this time as Commandant. In the meantime, his family was on their way north overland from Port Royal to join him in Portsmouth, but, before they had arrived, Dr. Rixey was detached and ordered (August 1, 1876) to the Naval Hospital, in Philadelphia.

The date when Dr. Rixey would be due for examination for promotion (April 18, 1877) was approaching, and, though he occasionally visited his fiancee in Portsmouth, he employed his leisure hours industriously in preparing himself professionally. He felt so confident of success in this examination, however, that the wedding day had been set to immediately follow it. The wedding invitations had been engraved at Drekas in Philadelphia, but strict instructions had been given that they were not to be sent out until after the examination, fearing the appearance of presumption which such an announcement might have in the eyes of the Naval Medical Board, and he was, therefore, rather startled when one of the members of the board, Dr. Spear, picked up what looked suspiciously like his wedding card and casually remarked that that was the sort of thing he was constantly receiving. Fortunately for Dr. Rixey's peace of mind, it proved not to be the invitation he was interested in, but this was not ascertained until after his face had flushed and he had exhibited a nervous manner or otherwise exposed a guilty conscience. This incident occurred the first day and was a bit of fun at the expense of the candidate which was quite characteristic of Dr. Spear, who suspected the young man's tender interests; but nothing more happened to upset Dr. Rixey's equilibrium, and he completed the examination with a creditable margin in his marks. The wedding invitations were, thereupon, promptly dispatched and he and Miss Earlena E. English, daughter of Commodore (later Rear-Admiral) Earl English, U. S. Navy, were married on April 25, 1877, in the home of the Captain of the Yard, at the Portsmouth Navy Yard. This house Admiral English had elected to occupy in preference to that regularly assigned to the Commandant. No children have blessed the union of Dr. Rixey and Miss English.

Congress adjourned this year (1877) without having appropriated sufficient money for the expenses of the Navy, but this, it will be recalled, was not due to any malicious intent, for other departments of the government suffered similarly. It is said to have been directly attributable to the depletion of the United States Treasury, following the crisis of 1873, and the unwillingness of Congress to plunge the nation further into debt by the issue of bonds. However, that may be, the fact remains that, about the time Dr. Rixey and his bride were starting on their honeymoon, the whole naval personnel was put on furlough pay for three months, and Dr. Rixey, in common with all other naval officers, was obliged to borrow money for current expenses until the Government was able to pay arrearages.

It is a tradition in the Navy that, during this trying period, the *Monocacy* then on the European Station, was the only ship which was being fully paid off, and at the time this created a widespread feeling of discontent. But it was afterwards learned that the ship's paymaster, Edward N. Whitehouse, was a man of large private means and that he was dipping down in his own pocket and securing funds for the purpose on his personal bills of exchange. This existing state of affairs was a hardship to all, but particularly to the young couple. Nevertheless they took a short trip up through Maine and ended by returning to the home of Mrs. Rixey's family at the Portsmouth Navy Yard, for a short visit and the balance of the doctor's leave of absence was spent at Culpeper, Va., with his father and mother. It was during this short visit at the English home that the line and staff squabble, then prominent in the naval service, was finally settled, as far as concerned the English household and its new son-in-law. They were gathered at dinner when a younger sister, who was hardly old enough to reason about such things herself and probably only repeated the opinion she had somewhere heard, brought up the old question of line and staff differences, which had swelled and ebbed for many years in the past, with the line side emphasized in her remarks. She had not said more than enough to show the trend of her thoughts, when the head of the table interrupted with the reminder that, as far as his household was concerned, there was no such thing as a line and staff difference, and that thereafter the subject would not be referred to in his family, which now united both line and staff.

Not duly heeding her father's injunction or the sincerity of his prohibition, however, this young woman once more on the same occasion ventured upon the forbidden subject, but she promptly came to grief by the firm order of the Commodore to leave the table, and it is said that never again was he called upon to enforce his will in this matter within the circle of his family. While on leave at this time, Dr. Rixey was detached from the Philadelphia Hospital and placed on waiting orders, and thus the first few months of his married life (May, June, July, and part of August) were joyously spent in the undivided companionship of his young wife. This is practically the only period of his official life which was unemployed. In August of 1877 he was ordered to the United States Navy Yard, Norfolk, Virginia, and there he remained for about one and one-half years. There were no quarters available for him at that station, so that, during this period, he and Mrs. Rixey occupied a small suite in the old Atlantic Hotel, across the river from the Navy Yard, in Norfolk, Va. The assurance that theirs was a happy union is vouchsafed as we listen to the reminiscences of Mrs. Rixey and picture them many nights sitting under a lamp in their meagre, but sufficient, quarters—he poring over his professional books and she sitting quietly and patiently by busying her dainty fingers with sewing or embroidery, comforted in the realization of his presence and the thought that he was making important use of his time and storing up for that great event in the indefinite future. Men are, most often, what their wives make them, and we can well imagine, indeed, we know that this wife gave many lessons in the art of diplomacy and did much to modify rugged characteristics. She was determined that he should not do less well than was within his capabilities, if she could prevent it, and she brought every power and her best judgment to bear with the highest attainable position as her objective. It is not to be inferred, however, that their sojourn in Norfolk was lacking in bright and pleasant diversions, for it was not their natures to apply themselves unreasonably to the serious concerns of life, and they were too sensible not to realize the truth in the old adage, as to the consequences of "All work and no play * * *." Besides, Mrs. Rixey's delightful personality was not to be lost to the society of the community in which she was living, and she and the doctor made a popular addition to the gay young set of Norfolk and in Navy circles. Thus it has ever been wherever Mrs. Rixey has lived—her simple dignity and grace of manner, her tact, her quiet sincerity, her broad information and acquaintance, and her interesting conversational abilities, have made her welcome and given her a prominent position among the leading people of different cities, particularly Washington, where she has resided so long.

On February 21, 1879, their happy life at Norfolk was broken up by orders assigning the doctor to sea duty, on the *Tallapoosa*, Mrs. Rixey returning to Washington to stay with her parents while her husband was away. Her father was Chief of the Bureau of Equipment at this time. The *Tallapoosa* was at that time performing the same special service, though of a more democratic character, as that performed in the recent past and now by the *Dolphin*, and later by the *Mayflower*. This cruise was full of interest and brought him in contact with many in public life, especially the Secretary of the Navy, Mr. Richard Thompson. He was his family physician and consequently at the expiration of the cruise he was ordered to the Naval Dispensary, Washington, D. C.

On February 21, 1872, having completed a tour of three years at sea, the doctor was relieved and ordered to duty on shore as assistant to the attending physician in Washington, and now once more he and Mrs. Rixey were able to enjoy the comfort of home life, which is of necessity so intermittent in the Navy.

Dr. Rixey continued on this duty at the Naval Dispensary for two and one-half years and then again he was ordered to sea, reporting for duty on the *Lancaster* on Sept. 18, 1884. This cruise was of three years, one month, and seventeen days duration and covered many thousand miles, starting from Southampton, England and going thence on a cruise in the Mediterranean Sea, West Coast of Africa, St. Helena, East Coast of South America, East Coast of Africa, Madagascar, Zanzibar, returning to the East Coast of South America—transferred to the *U.S.S. Trenton*, West Indies, and New York, N. Y.

Here again we must quote Dr. Rixey's own account of the incidents of this cruise; November 7, 1887, Dr. Rixey was again detailed for duty at the Naval Dispensary, and following this he once more went to sea (February 6, 1893), this time as surgeon of the *Dolphin*, on which ship he remained for two years, ten months and four days, the experiences of which duty were, in certain striking features, a repetition of his service on the *Tallapoosa*.

The underlying reason for his assignment to the *Dolphin* is connected with a sad incident in the Tracy family.

CAPT. B. H BUCKINGHAM
U S Navy

Briefly, a fire broke out in the home of Secretary of the Navy Tracy, and his wife and one daughter lost their lives. His married daughter and granddaughter, Mrs. and Miss Wilmerding, had jumped from upper windows of the house and, sustaining injuries, were carried to the home of Commander T. B. M. Mason, where Dr. Rixey was called to attend them. He also attended Mr. Tracy on this occasion and they became such staunch friends that the Secretary kept him in Washington as long as possible and then detailed him to the *Dolphin*.

During his service on the *Dolphin*, he became a warm friend of its Commanding Officer, Captain B. H. Buckingham, and later when this officer became seriously ill, Dr. Rixey had an opportunity to express his kindly regard by prolonged and devoted service to the invalid—not only those of a physician, but of a friend as well, and in this latter capacity, Mrs. Rixey joined her husband in giving him tender care. Captain Buckingham had been placed in the Naval Hospital, but, as he had repeatedly asked to be taken out and placed where he could be near the doctor, Mrs. Rixey suggested that he be brought to their own house in Virginia. Accordingly, he was cautiously taken out in an ambulance (a two-hour ride) by Dr. J. D. Gatewood, and there the doctor and Mrs. Rixey watched over their patient with a persistent hope and nursed him back to many years of active life in spite of the fact that the consulting doctors had told Secretary Herbert that he could not possibly live.

On December 10, 1895, Dr. Rixey was once again assigned to special duty in Washington, and there he remained, except for 1 month and 7 days on the *Solace*, without change to other stations—with what results he was kept in Washington shall be told hereafter.

This short tour of duty on the hospital ship *Solace* (from July 26, 1898, to September 2, 1898) came about in this way: When the Spanish-American war broke out, Dr. Rixey applied for active sea duty on one of the battleships, but at that time he was treating Secretary Long for an intractable condition of one of his knees, and his services

HON. JOHN D. LONG
Secretary of Navy, 1897 to 1902

were deemed so essential at the Capital, in order that the Secretary might be kept up and about to discharge the increased and pressing work of his office consequent upon naval hostilities, that the doctor could not be spared. We know with what reluctance Mr. Long had accepted the resignation of Mr. Roosevelt, as Assistant Secretary of the Navy, who desired to go to the front, and Mr. Long was naturally unwilling to deprive himself of all those upon whom he depended for help of one kind or another in this important crisis. As time passed, however, Dr. Rixey became more and more impatient in the fear that hostilities would be ended before he would be given an opportunity to see active service and he, therefore, repeated his application and urged its approval.

This time Mr. Long agreed to send him to sea, but was vague as to the time orders might be expected, and before he could fulfill his promise, the battle of Santiago, which, as events proved, practically ended the war, was fought. It was then that Mr. Long realized the approaching conclusion of the conflict of arms, and in his desire to accede as far as possible to Dr. Rixey's wishes, ordered him to the ambmulance ship *Solace* which was the only sea duty at that time open to him. On this ship he made one brief trip to Cuba, and thus became identified with the naval operations of the war in what to him was an unsatisfactory capacity though in the only service permitted him. He, of course, appreciated the importance of the responsibility of keeping Secretary Long physically able to bear the burdens of his office during that exacting period, but he never ceased to regret that he was permitted such a small part in the active campaign.

Dr. Rixey recalls his eleven years of sea duty and the associations incident to this service with the greatest pleasure, and he got on exceptionally well with his shipmates. His anger was quickly aroused by any slurs upon the profession and Corps which he represented, and his associates soon learned to respect him and to avoid irritating him so unnecessarily. He had and still has many good friends among these old shipmates in all branches of the service, and his brother officers of the Medical Corps, while speaking highly of his professional ability, "are, if possible, even warmer in their praise of his uniform courtesy and kindness of manner. He is recognized as an officer of unusual executive ability, jealous for the traditions of the medical service, and yet particularly gracious to younger physicians just entering upon their careers."

So says the Saturday Evening Post, Philadelphia, of October 19, 1901, and in the same article Dr. F. S. Nash is quoted as saying: "I shall never forget the first time I saw the Doctor. It was in 1877, while he was stationed at the Norfolk Navy Yard. I was a beardless youth, and had never seen a ship nor met a naval officer. Having passed my examinations and received my certificate as a surgeon, I was ordered to report for duty on board the U. S. Receiving Ship *Franklin*, then lying at Norfolk. After learning how to get aboard the vessel, I sent my baggage to the launch ignorant of the fact that even the seats in that little boat were subject to Naval rules. There were a number of officers in the boat, but none of them paid the least attention to me. I was lonesome and felt like whistling to keep up my courage, and the future did not look very bright at that time. In a few moments, however, an officer approached me, introduced himself as Doctor Rixey, and asked if I were not Dr. Nash. His genial, yet dignified manner put me at ease at once. He introduced me to some of the other officers and on reaching the ship presented me to her commander, and by quiet and unobtrusive attention smoothed the way for my first plunge into naval life. He kindly instructed me as to my duties, and his conduct made the deeper impression upon me as it was in contrast with that of some others.

"This refinement, quiet dignity and consideration for others is the reason why, when it became necessary to inform Mrs. McKinley of the grave condition of her devoted husband, Dr. Rixey was selected to perform that painful duty, and his manner no doubt aided Mrs. McKinley in bearing up so bravely under the shock which might well have crushed a stronger person."

CHAPTER III

SERVICE LEADING UP TO APPOINTMENT AS PHYSICIAN TO THE PRESIDENT

AS previously stated, Dr. Rixey performed a tour of special duty in Washington, D. C., at the Naval Dispensary, from February 21, 1882, to September 18, 1884, and again from November 15, 1887, to January 5, 1893, during which periods he made many staunch friends and gained an experience in general practice which was to stand him in good stead in later years. On December 10, 1895, after an interim of nearly three years duty on the *U. S. S. Dolphin*, he was again detailed in charge of the Naval Dispensary in Washington, D. C., and during this last tour of special duty was assigned as physician to the Executive Mansion, as will be related hereafter. He quickly picked up the old threads which had not been entirely broken while serving on the *Dolphin*, as that ship was then, as it has been since, much at the Navy Yard in Washington, D. C., and from the very beginning his professional activities, both in official and private practice steadily increased. The importance of this detail in finally shaping his character and professional capabilities in the broadest sense cannot be overestimated, and his success in winning and holding the confidence of his patients testifies in large part to his discernment, mental alertness, quick, and sound professional judgments, tact and gentle courtesy in his sick-room relations, for his calls were to the bedside of a widely varied clientele, including the humblest and the best families in Washington and vicinity—among the latter patients being many public and otherwise prominent men. With a practice of this character it is not possible to live through many mistakes or serious ones, and the fact that he survived those exacting requirements for years with credit speaks volumes in his favor. The need for agility in adaptation to changing circumstances was constant, but he was by nature suited to meet this peculiar demand; and his early training in the

Navy served him well to this same end, for he had happily not been affected by the hardening influence of professional relations with the enlisted personnel of the old Navy.

The danger that young medical officers may grow gruff and suspicious and thus compromise their usefulness is today, and was in his time even more imminent, in view of the well-known practice of malingering. His attitude in regard to that tendency is best expressed in his own words when he attempted to reach the officers of his department with a word of advice through the medium of his last annual report. In this publication he said:

> " * * * * Malingering could be made an interesting and an amusing subject by the narration of various cases, and it is important to remember, throughout all that which may be said hereafter, that a sense of humor is an important asset in the preservation of one's balance and equanimity when confronted by a case of this sort. But the subject has, depending upon the circumstances surrounding each case, a more or less serious aspect as regards the perpetrators of this deception, the medical officers concerned, and the service broadly. It involves far-reaching, subtle effects, and should not, therefore, be discussed lightly.
>
> "Its deep significance to the Navy as an organization lies in the uncertainty with which it surrounds the efficiency of men for the service of the country in times of peace, and, particularly, of war, and the immediate and prospective expense to the Government in the management and disposition of cases and in pensions for unsolved cases. Malingering has been a common subject of consideration in military medical circles for many centuries, and there are, no doubt, upon the pension rolls of our Government hundreds of cases of pensions which owe their origin to malingering. That this expresses the truth is a matter of common suspicion, and daily effort is being made to reduce this number. It is just here that medical officers are playing their part as diagnosticians and working single handed in the campaign of elimination, for from the legal point of view the proof of such offenses, which must precede punishment, is usually not a matter of direct and positive evidence, but of judicial conclusion, and therefore insecure. The types of afflictions which this character of impostor attempts to simulate are innumerable—both medical and surgical in nature—and vary somewhat with the special object sought and the resourcefulness of the individual. * * * *

"Some are easily exposed, others are exposed with difficulty, and others, though suspected, cannot be proved; but all are annoying and perplexing. Their discovery and punishment have a wholesome effect upon the morale of all those cognizant of the affair, and failure to detect threatens discipline. The detection of impostors of one form or another has tested the ingenuity of naval surgeons, and though the zeal of these officers and the generally better class of men now being enlisted have combined to reduce malingering, cases are continually arising and are still far too numerous. The field for this sort of imposition has been greatly extended by the application of the principle of employers' liability to navy yards and stations. It is partly this fact which has led the bureau to discuss the question. Though among the Midshipmen at the Naval Academy the honor system with respect to intentionally misrepresenting the condition of health is being successfully tried, it is without doubt too much to expect that throughout the broad range of government service there will not be many examples of imposition by misrepresentation. Medical officers, as is to be expected, now and again err in their judgment and occasionally accuse an innocent man, and it is in this regard that caution and advice are indicated.

"This prevalence of malingering and the constant liability that cases of it may be encountered unconsciously creates a suspicion in the minds of medical officers, and the whole service should recognize that this may at any time, unintentionally, react unjustly in exposing the innocent to suspicion and reproof and depriving a bona fide case of needed attention. This is a danger to which the skulkers most certainly expose honest men, and those responsible for such consequence therefore constitute an enemy to society, and the crime is all the more flagrant because of them. With this idea clearly represented there can be no use for the entertainment of a false sense of fraternal loyalty or the protection of offenders. They should be hunted down by all as a matter of self-protection.

"On the other hand, the medical officers are cautioned to fight against the development of suspicious attitude of mind in the exercise of their professional work. If allowed to gain an ascendance, it will surely ruin that perspective so necessary in the study of cases, will warp proper judgment, and lead to regrettable mistakes. It will not do for a medical officer to be too jealous of his amour propre—too fearful, in other words, of being deceived and made use of. It will not do to view such individual attempts too seriously or to lose that oftentimes saving sense of humor in the management of suspected cases. It is far better to give unnecessary care to several cases of what might be feigned illness than to neglect one real sufferer."

HON. JOHN FRANKLIN RIXEY
Congressman from the 8th Congressional District of Virginia and brother of Admiral Rixey, whose assistance as a member of the Naval Committee of the House was most valuable, 1905

This period of Dr. Rixey's career was but the beginning of his friendship with the distinguished personages of the past decade, yet before the opportunities which his subsequent identification with the White House gave him to broaden such acquaintance, his practice and social intercourse among national and civil government officials and other prominent people was extensive. Among the friends and patients in official life was the Chairman of Naval Affairs Committee of the House, Honorable C. A. Boutelle. Dr. Rixey was anxious to have his brother, a member of Congress, on the Committee of Naval Affairs, and asked him if he thought he could arrange it, and in a short time received the following:

House of Representatives
Committee on Naval Affairs
Washington, D. C.

August 4, 1898.

Dear Dr. Rixey:

I am very glad that I succeeded before the adjournment of Congress in getting Speaker Reed to appoint your good brother a member of the Committee on Naval Affairs. There was a great deal of pressure for this vacancy but I made it a personal matter and shall be glad to have your brother as a colleague. In these whirligig times I do not know whether you are still in Washington, but I send this note at a venture.

With best regards to yourself, Mrs. Rixey, and Miss English, I am,

Always sincerely yours,
(Signed) C. A. Boutelle.

This enabled him to be of service to the Navy for almost four years before he was Surgeon General, and after that, up to the time of his brother's death, he was most helpful in all work when legislation was required.

Some of those recorded as his patients at this time were: Senator Eugene Hale, Vice-President Hobart, Secretary John Hay, and other Cabinet Officers, Senator Hanna and other senators, the Speaker of the House of Representatives, Chairman of the Naval Committee of the House, many other Congressmen, and several of the diplomatic corps and the secretaries of the Navy, in all the recent administrations, including Secretary of the Navy, John D. Long, who was a warm friend, admirer, and an ardent supporter of Dr. Rixey. As will be remembered, Mrs. Long was in delicate health and not able to really bear the social burdens of her husband's conspicuous official position, so that she and her daughters were also patients and friends. Later it was at the special instance and request of President McKinley that Dr. Rixey was one of the late Vice-President Hobart's physicians.

It is interesting to our purpose to relate that, in most cases, his professional relations developed into close friendships, which have continued to the present day. The

Hon. John Hay
Secretary of State, 1898 to 1905

defections were for various causes—generally misunderstandings, such as are likely to arise between high-spirited personalities, though in some cases the doctor admits his own mistakes in judgment through impulsiveness as a responsible factor. It is the mark of a good mind to recognize one's own faults and the recognition is the forerunner of their control. This tendency of his character to impulsiveness, which developed so early and was manifest in the quarrel with his brother, is the besetting defect lying at the bottom of his various missteps, for his mature judgment was always good, and it is this trait that his devoted wife has studied and labored so faithfully to correct, and that has given her many moments of anxiety with respect to his public life. In speaking of this, Mrs. Rixey said: "I have always believed that a wife could make her husband nearly, if not entirely, what she desired him to be, but I have come to think either that his impulsiveness was too deeply inborn or that I began my corrective efforts too late to eradicate it." However, it is well to remember that it takes steel to strike fire on flint and a record of so many enduring intimacies serves to indicate that the other parties to the defections were not without fault. Nobody can honestly claim that there is but one side to any situation, and as for tempers that are a little too quick, remember that we all have the vices and virtues of our temperament: that which makes us hasty makes us also active, vigilant, eager for the success of what we undertake and sensible to the least opposition.

Dr. Rixey's management of important cases was always attended by a display of kindly professional interest and support on the part of medical men throughout the country and he was the recipient of many letters at different times offering pertinent suggestions and otherwise showing a disposition to be of assistance. One such letter was addressed to him by Dr. Alfred T. Livingston, of Buffalo, N. Y., under date of February 12, 1904, during Senator Hanna's illness. His personal consultations with members of the profession were always agreeable and of this Dr. Rixey says: "Of course, there were frequently differences of opinion, but my relations with members of my profession have always been most satisfactory." Coming in constant contact with such learned members of his profession as William Pepper of Philadelphia, Osler, Welch, Halstead, Kelly, and Young of Johns Hopkins, Baltimore, Janeway, McBirney, Bryant, Kelsey of New York, and Maurice Richardson of Boston, and hosts of others gave him the advanced thought of his profession in those days and his reminiscences of his associations with such eminent men are most agreeable.

It was in the fall of 1898 that Dr. Rixey, much to his surprise, and at the instances of Secretary Long, received an order to accompany President McKinley and party, in a professional capacity, to Atlanta, Ga., where he was going to review the troops before they were disbanded at the conclusion of the Spanish-American War, and this occasion marks the origin of his appointment as physician to the Executive Mansion. In anticipation of this trip, Secretary of the Navy Long, who, with his daughter, was to be of the party, went to the President and asked if he (the President) was planning to take a physician with him. "No," said the President, "but why do you ask?" Then Mr. Long reminded him that his daughter had not been well and that, on her account particularly, he thought it desirable that some physician should accompany them. Upon consideration, the President expressed himself as also of the opinion that it would be desirable for many reasons to identify a medical man with the party, and, having no one in mind himself, asked Mr. Long to suggest some doctor. Dr. Rixey had long been the Secretary's esteemed physician, and it was, therefore, natural that he should have been his first thought in the selection of an attending physician. The President quickly assented to the proposition and, as it later developed, was so pleased with Dr. Rixey's personality and professional capabilities and the manner in which he performed his services during the trip that he did not forget him. Indeed, this temporary duty incident to the Atlanta trip was most important in determining his whole future active career. It is characteristic of him that he always discharged his duties the very best that he knew how and was jealous of his position as a representative of a learned profession which he believed was to be upheld with dignity and pursued with fidelity to its highest traditions. This guiding principle and the conviction that a man's manner of conducting his daily life is the record which counts in preparing him to meet emergencies and in leading to opportunities were the underlying causes of his acceptability to the President. Dr. Rixey entertained no undue foresight of the possibilities of the trip as an incentive. His efforts were no more zealous than usual or than the circumstances required, and he returned to his regular duties after the trip without thought of any consequences of his recent association with the Presidential Party or the remotest idea of following it up. He was greatly surprised, therefore, at the events which transpired about a week later. While walking on 15th Street, he encountered President McKinley, also walking, with two of his cabinet officers. Dr. Rixey saluted and was about to pass on when the President exhibited a desire to speak to him, and as the doctor approached, opened the conversation by the inquiry—"Why did you not accompany me on my recent trip to New York?" "Mr. McKinley," said the doctor, "I had no idea that my presence was desired." And so the matter was left until a few days later, when, in obedience to the President's invitation, the doctor called upon him at the Executive Mansion. In the course of this interview, Mr. McKinley told Dr. Rixey that he wanted him to continue to be his attending physician and also take medical charge of Mrs. McKinley who had been an invalid many years. General George M. Sternberg, who had succeeded General Wood when that officer left Washington to go to Cuba as Colonel of the Rough Riders, was at that time physician to the White House, so that, by his expressed wishes, the President was all unwittingly creating an embarrassing situation between Dr. Rixey and his esteemed colleague of the sister service. Dr. Rixey was aware of Dr. Sternberg's existing relation to the White House, and, while rightfully pleased by the compliment conferred and humanly desirous of accepting the distinction, his sense of honor and his fidelity to the unwritten ethics of his profession, served at once to turn his thoughts to Dr. Sternberg with solicitations for the feelings of this friend who would certainly be placed in a trying position by virtue of his own proposed elevation. It is a great distinction in the medical fraternity to be the physician at the Executive Mansion—yet, he put all thought of this aside and expressed his consideration for Dr. Sternberg in no uncertain terms to the President and protested the propriety of displacing him; but the President, knowing that the frequent trips from Washington obligatory upon Dr. Sternberg in the capacity of White House physician were interfering with his duties as Chief of the Medical Department of the Army, insisted that the difficulty could be satisfactorily arranged and indicated, moreover, that it was his unalterable intention that it should be arranged. Dr. Rixey, therefore, immediately sought a conference with Dr. Sternberg, and, though it was manifestly impossible to disregard the wishes of the President and decline what was tantamount to an order, it was Dr. Rixey's aim to, as tactfully as possible, adjust the awkward situation amicably and preserve a valued friendship which seemed in all human probability and according to precedent to be unavoidably placed in jeopardy. Before Dr. Rixey found opportunity to carry out his purpose, however, Dr. Sternberg called on him and then were exchanged the remarks—on the one hand of a man stung by the sense of having suffered an injury which he credited perhaps naturally, though wrongfully, to the insinuation of another, and on the other hand of a man regretful of the part he was forced to play in a friend's discomfiture, yet increasingly resentful of the implication that he had designedly and by unfair means gained the succession. The picture of this interview need not be enlarged upon; suffice it to make the fair assumption that, had the man with whom Dr. Rixey had to deal been less generous, less broadminded, less familiar with the controlling impulses of honest men, less charitable in viewing the ambitions of others, and less willing to see and give weight to the practical side of the circumstances before him, an insuperable barrier would have unfortunately arisen between these two estimable men. As a matter of fact, they came to an amicable understanding. President McKinley himself was influential in effecting this happy result, and at Dr. Rixey's suggestion Dr. Sternberg was asked to continue his visits to the White House as consulting surgeon. Dr. Sternberg accepted the invitation and accordingly the two doctors met in consultation at the White House every Sunday morning, a practice which was continued until Dr. Sternberg went to the Philippines on a tour of inspection. It was during General Sternberg's absence that Mr. McKinley died. This intercourse warmed the friendship of the older and the younger man and savored their relationship with a feeling of mutual respect and admiration which has endured to this day.

It was Dr. Rixey's frequently expressed belief that, in spite of the many distinctions that had been bestowed upon General Sternberg, his merits and great work have never been accorded the full measure of recognition which they deserved. At a dinner given June 8, 1908, to General Sternberg by distinguished members of the medical profession, who wished to do him honor on the occasion of the 70th anniversary of his birth, Dr. Rixey was given opportunity to offer a tribute to "The guest of the evening," and in responding to the toast said:

> "It gives me great pleasure to say a few words in personal appreciation of our distinguished guest, General Sternberg, whom I have known and been associated with so many years. The work that he has accomplished and is still doing is so well known to us all that it seems unnecessary to dwell on the many brilliant successes that have marked his long and honorable career and that has made him a marked figure in the medical and military life of our nation.
>
> "My personal acquaintance with him began at Rio de Janiero, Brazil, where he had been sent by our Government to investigate yellow fever. I was attached to the Flagship *Lancaster* and spent considerable time in that port. There I had opportunity to meet our guest of the evening frequently. I was deeply interested in his work, especially so as the flagship was visited by

Passed Assistant Surgeon PRESLEY MARION RIXEY, U. S. Navy, 1886
Attached to U. S. Flagship *Lancaster*

the disease, of which he was making a special study. The bandmaster and chief musician of the ship, contrary to the rule, had been allowed to remain on shore over night and had, no doubt, been inoculated by infected mosquitoes there.

"On my return from this cruise, I was ordered to duty in Washington, and in due time Dr. Sternberg was ordered home and appointed Surgeon General of the Army. His work as the head of this branch of the War Department, together with his great work in the Civil and Spanish-American Wars and up to the time of his retirement, is now a part of the history of our country.

"The medical world knows, and is to be congratulated upon, his continued active participation in professional interests and here, in his home city we all are familiar with his philanthropic work in the betterment of health and the extension of happiness.

"In conclusion, I wish to express my sincere congratulations to my friend upon this, his 70th birthday, and to wish for him many years of unimpaired usefulness and happiness."

CHAPTER IV

THE MCKINLEY ADMINISTRATION

THUS began Dr. Rixey's official connection with the Executive Mansion, as President McKinley chose to call it, which continued ten years and which was so full of interest and incidents—both pleasurable and otherwise. Splendid as Mr. McKinley was as a statesman, inspiring as a political leader, magnetic as a man, great as was his public career, the finest and noblest side of his character was the devotion he showed as a husband. His tenderest solicitude was constantly going out to Mrs. McKinley who had long been in a condition of semi-invalidism, and he could not, therefore, be insensible to Dr. Rixey's thoughtful and painstaking professional care of her or to the change for the better in her health following the complete charge of her case which Dr. Rixey quickly assumed. While Mrs. McKinley's invalidism was due to an irremedial condition, Dr. Rixey believed that her general health was susceptible of great improvement and that *pari passu* with progress in this direction the periodic attacks from which she suffered would become less frequent and severe. Based on this assumption, his efforts were attended with most gratifying success, but the first requisite to his purpose was information as to the ingredients of a compound which Mrs. McKinley was in the habit of taking. This formula was not easily ascertained, however, for the medicine in question was compounded personally by a New York practitioner who was disposed to hold the prescription a secret, but Dr. Rixey told the President that he could not be expected to work thus in the dark nor take the responsibility of a case which was being treated by administrations unknown to him, and the desired information was, therefore, obtained. It is unnecessary to the narrative to here set down the various ingredients as learned—suffice it to say its use was at first restricted and then interdicted with the beneficial results so quickly observed by those intimately

Wm McKinley

associated with her, and, most of all, by Mr. McKinley. From this time on Dr. Rixey was a daily visitor at the Executive Mansion, sometimes calling several times a day to inquire about his patient, and he was from now on, also, a regular member of the Presidential party on all of Mr. McKinley's trips to different parts of the country and an invited guest on all special occasions, such as receptions and dinners, etc., at the Executive Mansion. Dr. Rixey's professional relation to the President frequently took him out of Washington and during his absence his assistant, Surgeon Stone carried on the work of the dispensary while his private patients were turned over to other friends. Dr. Rixey's public life is so intimately associated with that of the McKinley administration and President's movements, that a recitation of the latter serves well to indicate the more important movements and events in Dr. Rixey's life during this period. The first of these trips upon which the doctor attended was in December (13-20) of 1898, when the President, with members of his cabinet and invited guests, went to the Atlanta Peace Jubilee and then visited Tuskegee and Montgomery, Alabama, and Savannah and Macon, Ga. During this trip there were a number of entertainments of one kind or another by the citizens or institutions of the several cities visited, and among others a banquet by the Savannah Board of Trade and Associated Citizens of Savannah to President McKinley (Dec. 17, 1898).

On all of the President's tours to be mentioned in the course of this biography, it is to be remembered that time was crammed to overflowing with events of more or less moment. Often, breakfast, lunch, and dinner would be taken in as many different cities during a single day and the people prominent and otherwise in the community who were met at each place were in number far beyond memory to recall.

The winter of 1898 in Washington was gay and during this season the warm friendship between President and Mrs. McKinley and Dr. and Mrs. Rixey was established and the

President McKinley With Dr. Rixey, Starting on His Customary After-Breakfast Morning Stroll

The President's Favorite Walk Through The Woods

attachment waxed in cordiality and strength during the succeeding years.

In June (16-29) of 1899, Dr. Rixey accompanied the President on his trip through New England, and the summer months following were spent by the President and Mrs. McKinley and Dr. and Mrs. Rixey at Hotel Champlain, on Lake Champlain. Here Dr. Rixey urged Mrs. McKinley to walk and ride as much as possible and usually he would call for the President to take his walks while Mrs. McKinley was resting after luncheon. These short walks were usually cut short by his anxiety to get back before his wife would be up and dressed for a drive in the immediate vicinity of the hotel.

In October (4 to 19), 1899, Dr. Rixey was again off with the President and members of the Cabinet for a tour to Chicago and the northwest. The President's party was regally feted all along the line and they enjoyed a hospitality which rivaled the South in warm hearted expressions. The event of the trip was the ceremony of laying the corner-stone of the U. S. Government building in Chicago on "Chicago Day," October 9, followed in the evening by a banquet "tendered to the President of the United States and distinguished guests by the people of Chicago." Among the other entertainments which were given in honor of the President at Chicago was the "Autumnal Festival," October 10, and a banquet of the Commercial Club that same evening. The most noteworthy occasion of the trip at other points along the route of travel was a banquet in honor of President McKinley and party, given under the auspices of the Merchants' and Manufacturers' Association of Milwaukee, at the Hotel Pfister, October 16, 1899.

The winter of 1899-1900 at the National Capital was marked by nothing unusual as far as the doctor was concerned, though he and Mrs. Rixey were frequently at the Executive Mansion on the occasion of State Affairs and also informally. Indeed, it rarely happened that they were not included among the especially esteemed guests whatever the entertainment at the Executive Mansion—whether the season's regular receptions and dinners or special functions. Among the latter, during 1900, was a reception in honor of the 26th Annual Session of the Mystic Shrine for North America, May 23, and an informal luncheon following the exercises arranged by the joint committees having charge of the Centennial Celebration of the Establishment of the Seat of Government in the District of Columbia, December 12.

The summer of 1900, during the political campaign, was spent at Canton, Ohio.

The second Inauguration of President McKinley (Mr. Roosevelt Vice-President) occurred March 4, 1901, and during the ceremonies of this occasion Dr. and Mrs. Rixey sat on the Inaugural platform in the Senate wing of the Capitol. They were members of the President's immediate party and, as such, as on previous occasions, had a card of admission to the exclusive entrance of the Executive Mansion and were otherwise commended to the courtesy of those in charge of the various Inaugural ceremonies.

As soon as arrangements could be made, April 29, following the Inauguration, the President, with members of his Cabinet and other invited guests, among whom Dr. and Mrs. Rixey were included, started on his long tour through the South to the Pacific Coast. In Dr. Rixey's words, "The trip to the West was a veritable triumphal procession and at every point along the route where Southern hospitality was given opportunity for expression, the ovations tendered reflected the popular sentiment for Mr. McKinley and the complete approval of his administration which was so fully demonstrated by the overwhelming majority accorded him by almost every section of country at the polls in the fall of 1900."

In Tennessee a banquet was given by the citizens of Memphis, "in honor of the President of the United States and his Cabinet," April 30; in Mississippi a reception was given by the citizens of Vicksburg to "His Excellency, William McKinley, President of the United States, and his party," May 1 (Dr. and Mrs. Rixey occupied the 9th carriage in the procession, with Dr. J. H. Purnell and

Captain C. L. Longley, M. N. G.); in Louisiana a banquet was given by the citizens of New Orleans on May 1, and the following day, May 2, a reception was given by the Louisiana Historical Society in New Orleans in honor of the President and his Cabinet; in Texas the President and his party were entertained at dinner by the Governor of the State in his mansion at Austin, May 3; in Arizona a collation was given in honor of His Excellency, President McKinley and party at Hotel Adams, Phoenix, May 7; in California numerous festivities had been arranged in honor of the President and his party, and all those that were attended proved to be most interesting and pleasant. The souvenirs of the trip and the lavish hospitality which was enjoyed from almost the moment they entered the State tell a delightful story, and the reader must envy them their opportunity to see all that this wonderful State has to show under such agreeable and superior auspices. Each member of the party was introduced to the Pickwick Club, the California Club, the Olympic Club, the Union League Club and others, and the Los Angeles Driving Club and Bohemian Club of San Francisco arranged the distinctive entertainments for which they are renowned, known respectively as "Fiesta Matinee" (May 10) and "High Jinks" (May 15). One of the most enjoyable entertainments which the party was able to attend was a reception at the City of Santa Cruz, followed by a delightful drive to and luncheon at the "Big Trees." It would be almost impossible to describe the floral decorations of the train on this wonderful trip. Such profusion of flowers and fruit are rarely seen.

The program for the President's visit in California contemplated many other features of entertainment and otherwise of interest, among them a banquet to President McKinley at the Palace Hotel, San Francisco, and the launching of the *U. S. S. Ohio* at the Union Iron Works, Calif., but the festivities were curtailed and the balance of the tour home via the Northern States was interrupted by the illness of Mrs. McKinley. She was a patient whose condition was always doubtful at the best. She had been an invalid

MRS. WILLIAM McKINLEY
The Beloved Wife of President McKinley

for years, but a sweet-faced, uncomplaining and self-denying one, whose health fluttered constantly and rarely for a few hours remained stationary. It was only by the most heroic fortitude of her own, supplemented by the skilled attentions of Dr. Rixey, and the self-effacing devotion of her husband that she was enabled ever to endure the shortest journey. In earlier times, these journeys were never long—ending, for the longest, at Canton, and always made under tolerable conditions. These successes encouraged her to undertake the trip to the Pacific Coast.

Night and day, on this trip, as on others, Dr. Rixey was within call. He had made Mrs. McKinley's health a special study; it was his study to the end of her life, and he knew every symptom of her never-quiet system. It was by this knowledge, applied with unflagging and unceasing vigilance, that her strength was sustained when she was deemed in danger of collapse—an occurrence far more frequent than is generally known. It was his knowledge that was always available—in Washington or elsewhere—and that lightened the burden of Mr. McKinley's care, always grave under the pressure of public duties. Those who read the name of Dr. Rixey had only a vague conception of his laborious duties—duties made all the more exacting by reason of the extremely sensitive condition of Mrs. McKinley's health. Her illness in San Francisco in the spring of 1901 threw a pall of depression over everybody and, as said before, put a stop to everything but deep concern for the beloved and stricken First Lady of the Land. Indeed, she was seriously ill, a characterization which portends much in a life so frail, and for days her life hung in the balance with the President and every member of his party waiting anxiously and supplicating earnestly for a favorable change in her condition. Mrs. Rixey was also of the Presidential party on the trans-continental trip, and during all this trying period, she and Dr. Rixey occupied a room adjoining that of Mrs. McKinley, so that the doctor could be close at hand to watch the progress of the case and attend Mrs. McKinley at every change in her condition.

Besides Dr. and Mrs. Rixey, Secretary and Mrs. Cortelyou remained in the Scott residence with the President during Mrs. McKinley's illness there. The doctor was untiring in his devotion to her slightest need, alert to employ every measure which gave the least promise of benefit, and unhesitating in calling to his side any assistance which he felt was needed to strengthen his resources in the care of such a precious life—not only to the President, but to her friends and the people of the country at large. He called in consultation the best medical talent of San Francisco among them Dr. Hirschfelder, Dr. Gibbons, and Dr. Cushing;—but he was in unfailing attendance and bearing—not only the responsibility of the central figure in the management of the case, but the unremitting wearing anxiety of a warm friend. Mrs. Rixey was constantly near to give him moral strength and encourage him during those commonly experienced fleeting periods of apprehension as to the outcome. As is well known, Mrs. McKinley finally rallied and brought joy to the hearts of all by a progressive, though protracted, convalescence.

The apparent recovery of Mrs. McKinley from an attack of illness which seemed to doom her to inevitable death was a marvel to all who were cognizant of her frail system, and it was more particularly and generally appreciated, perhaps, by reason of the victim's station in life. The press at the time was liberal in its praise of Dr. Rixey and among other tributes The Philadelphia Times of June 16, 1901, may be quoted as follows: "Much comment has been made over the devotion of Mr. McKinley to his invalid wife, but little has been said about Dr. Rixey, who has been her constant and tireless attendant, and to whose unfaltering exertions her present hopeful condition is largely attributable."

In the evening Post of San Francisco, Calif., under date of May 22, 1901, appeared the trite tribute from the pen of Hugh Hume: "Good evening, Dr. Rixey. Others, besides your patients, appreciate your skill as a physician."

It is not surprising that, by his tender devotion to this patient and by the efficient management of her case, Dr.

Rixey endeared himself beyond measure to the President—nor is it to be wondered at that, during the trip East, in the latter part of Mrs. McKinley's convalescence, the President voluntarily promised the doctor that, upon the first occurrence of a vacancy in the Office of the Surgeon General of the Navy, he would appoint him to that vacancy. Secretary of the Navy Long and Secretary of Agriculture Wilson were present on the occasion of this unsolicited and surprising announcement by the President, and Secretary Long immediately asked his pleasure as to the publicity or otherwise of the determination to appoint Dr. Rixey to the position. The President replied that it was to be regarded as confidential, but, turning to the doctor, said that the secret might be confided to Mrs. Rixey. It was most natural that she should be deeply concerned with and proper that she should be allowed to rejoice in such a prospect. It would have been an unnecessary restraint to have denied or withheld that concession, and the unfailing humanity of Mr. McKinley helped the decision just as the same potent influences came to the rescue of the judicial Solomon in reaching his determination as to the real mother of a certain babe.

The feelings of Dr. Rixey are best described in his own words, and they deserve to be set down, for the Surgeon-Generalcy had been the ambition of Mrs. Rixey for years, though she had not expected its realization so soon. Dr. Rixey says: "The announcement took me so much by surprise that I could only imperfectly express my appreciation. Mr. Long, noting my confusion, in his own peculiar happy voice said: 'Now don't go and tell Mrs. Rixey.' The President spoke up at once and said: 'You go and tell her at once.' You may rest assured I lost no time in obeying this order of my Commander in Chief."

In private intercourse with the doctor, subsequent to the return trip across the continent, the President occasionally referred to this promise, but he did not live to fulfill it himself, nor did he make any mention of it during the last days of his life. His wishes, however, came to Mr.

Roosevelt as a legacy borne by and through the kindly interest and friendship of Secretary Long and Secretary Wilson who were auditors on the occasion when Mr. McKinley first elected to inform the doctor that he would make him Surgeon General of the Navy. These two gentlemen took it upon themselves to acquaint Mr. Roosevelt with Mr. McKinley's desire in the matter before leaving Buffalo after the death of the martyred President. Mr. Roosevelt respected that legacy and fulfilled the promise in memory of his beloved predecessor, though, long before the opportunity occurred, he had recognized the merits of Dr. Rixey, continuing him as attending physician of the White House, and they and their families had become warm friends, so that his appointment of Dr. Rixey to be Surgeon General of the Navy in deference to Mr. McKinley's wishes was not without substantial reason on his own account. His appointment and the circumstances attending it will be mentioned in their proper places.

The delicate undertaking of bringing Mrs. McKinley east from San Francisco was decided upon only after a most searching inquiry into her condition and fortitude, though even then the proposition met with much opposition at the hands of those physicians whom Dr. Rixey had called in consultation. Dr. Rixey's intimate acquaintance with Mrs. McKinley's physical stamina led him to insist that she would be able to endure the trip, and his opinion finally prevailed and was given the support of his professional associates. The physicians had held their last consultation on May 25, and after they had announced their decision that Mrs. McKinley was strong enough to endure the transcontinental journey, preparations were rapidly made. Mrs. McKinley enjoyed a refreshing night's rest and the next morning seemed elated at the prospect of soon being at home. She was conveyed from the Scott residence to the Oakland ferry in a closed carriage over a circuitous route, which was chosen so that the invalid might pass over only smoothly paved streets, the jarring basalt rocks which are laid on many blocks being avoided. She was accompanied by the President, Dr. Rixey and a trained nurse, the rest of the party proceeding to the starting point in a more direct way. The streets were packed with people, yet there was absolute silence.

The start was made on May 26 and events justified the undertaking, for as is well known, the doctor, with the assistance of two excellent California nurses, brought his patient back to Washington without untoward incident. For several months her health continued to be such that few entered her sick room or saw her, and thus passed the spring months at the White House in sad contrast with the gaiety of the year before and an absence of the usual happy observance of her birthday in June. However, there is always something to be thankful for, and to quote the Philadelphia Times of June 9, 1901—"It is extremely doubtful whether Mrs. McKinley would have been able to pass another June anniversary at all had it not been for the constant attention and professional skill of the White House physician, Dr. Rixey, whose ability the President esteems most highly."

The summer of 1901 was passed by the President and Mrs. McKinley at their home in Canton, Ohio, and there Dr. Rixey also spent most of the summer. He made occasional visits to Washington to see that the work of the Naval Dispensary was being properly conducted, but his principal charge was Mrs. McKinley, who was still in a precarious condition, and by his watchfulness during this period of convalescence, succeeded in nursing her back to her ordinary health, by the early fall, so that she was able to accompany Mr. McKinley to the Pan-American Congress in Buffalo. Her health, in fact, was then better than it had ever been in recent years, and sitting on the "celebrated porch" at their Canton home the night before they left for Buffalo, the President spoke of the marked improvement with joy and looked forward to her being able to participate in the entertainments in Washington.

It was in early September that President McKinley and his party, of which Dr. Rixey was a member, started from Canton for Buffalo to be the guests of the Pan-American

Exposition. The reception of this distinguished party was noteworthy and the hospitality extended it could not be surpassed. Everyone was in high spirits and enjoying the hearty evidence of supreme goodwill which everywhere met their gaze, but all this fades in memory as we contemplate, even from the softening perspective of the years elapsed, that appalling tragedy which, on September 6, marked the Pan-American Exposition distinctive among such affairs. It was at about four o'clock on this date, while standing on the slightly elevated platform in the Temple of Music, that President McKinley was shot. The details of this shocking incident are too well known to need repetition here. Dr. Rixey was not a witness of this memorable event. The President and party had returned from Niagara Falls, where they had been entertained at luncheon, and Dr. Rixey had been detailed by the President to accompany Mrs. McKinley to the Milburn residence, where he and Mrs. McKinley were domiciled, so that the doctor was not immediately on hand when the President was shot, but was promptly summoned and arrived at the Emergency Hospital in the exposition grounds at the beginning of the operation. This was about 5:30 p. m., and Dr. Mann, with a full corps of assistants, was ready to begin a laparotomy which all the consulting surgeons deemed imperative. In his report, Dr. Rixey says:

> "Being satisfied with the completeness of the preparation and the ability of the operating surgeon, I made ready to assist and watched every step of the operation. The wounds having been closed and the President's condition being good, I requested Dr. Roswell Park, the Medical Director of the Pan-American Exposition, to send nurses and a surgical bed to the Milburn house and to take personal charge of the removal of the President, as I had to inform Mrs. McKinley of her husband's condition and make ready a room for his reception."

Mr. Milburn gave up his entire home in Buffalo and devoted his whole time and energy to the needs of the President. At 7:30 p. m. the President was removed from the hospital to the home of his host, John G. Milburn, and from now on Dr. Rixey took official charge of the case.

"Here," says Major Pilcher, "he displayed in the highest degree those qualities which evidenced not only professional acquirements of an extensive range, but executive ability and diplomatic faculties of a remarkable character. The skill and devotion which he displayed in the management of the case of the President and the almost equally exacting case of the President's invalid wife, won for him the admiration and affection of the entire country."

He, of course, continued the valuable association of Dr. M. D. Mann, Dr. Roswell Park, Dr. Herman Mynter, Dr. Eugene Wasden, Dr. Charles McBurney and Dr. Charles G. Stockton, all of whom signed the official bulletins with Dr. Rixey, the President's physician. These bulletins tell a story of alternating hope and despair and the end is described by Dr. Nelson W. Wilson in the Buffalo Medical Journal of October, 1901:

> "Outside the wind rustled the leaves of the trees the President loved so well. In the adjoining room slept the wife mercifully unconscious of the agony of the scene which was being enacted so near her. The respirations became gasps; slower and slower, then halting. Dr. Rixey leaned far over the President and raised his hand in warning. A sob broke the awesome silence of the room—a sob which was stifled. The gasping of the President had ceased. Dr. Rixey straightened up, his face drawn with the agony of his suffering. A faint sigh fluttered at the President's lips, and his head sunk into the pillows like that of a man falling into a deep sleep."

The self-sacrificing devotion to duty shown by Dr. Rixey during the long painful days that elapsed between the shooting and the death of President McKinley, Sunday, September 14, 2:15 a. m., offers one of the most striking features of the historic tragedy. During this distressing time the only rest he took was in brief periods of rarely over two hours duration. It seemed he must become exhausted, but he continued with iron endurance. Fatigue did not impair his clear judgment or alter the poise of his personal bearing. His personal affection for the martyred President was deep and complete, and the death was a grievous shock to him.

"In the line of duty, while receiving the people, was shot by Leon Czolgosz"—is the official statement filed with the Surgeon General of the Navy by Dr. Rixey as the introduction to his report upon the wounding, illness, and death of the late President McKinley. The cause of death was stated to be "Gangrene of both walls of stomach and pancreas, following gunshot wound."

The Washington Post of October 27, 1901, says:

> "The report itself is remarkable for its exhibition in the closest possible detail of the exact state of the patient during his mortal illness (and all symptoms were faithfully set forth.) It is in the shape of a ship's log almost, showing at intervals of a very few minutes, rarely more than an hour, the patient's progress toward the end. Perhaps the most valuable data contained, from a medical point of view, is the accurate registering of the medication of the case—not a single morsel of food nor a dose of medicine, nor a bath is omitted in this account. Included in the running story at the proper intervals are the bulletins which were given to the public as the case progressed."

Following is the report in full.

MEDICAL AND SURGICAL REPORT OF THE CASE OF THE LATE PRESIDENT OF THE UNITED STATES

By PRESLEY M. RIXEY, Medical Inspector, U. S. Navy

William McKinley, President of the United States. Born January 29, 1843. Native of Ohio. Gunshot wound of abdomen. Wound received at 4:07 p. m., September 6, 1901, in the Academy of Music, Pan-American Exposition, Buffalo, N. Y. In the line of duty, while receiving the people, was shot by Leon F. Czolgosz.

FIRST DAY—September 6, from 4:07 p. m. to midnight.

Report made to Dr. Roswell Park, medical director, Pan-American Exposition, fixes the time of shooting at 4:07 p. m., and the President's arrival at the Emergency Hospital 4:18 p. m. Immediately upon being undressed an examination revealed upon the surface of the body two wounds, the one to the right of the sternal line being an abrasion 1 cm. in diameter. Measuring from the suprasternal notch the distance was 5½cm., from the right nipple 10 cm. and from the line of the right nipple 8¼ cm. The second wound was a penetrating wound of the abdomen 15½ cm. from the left nipple and 16½cm. from the umbilicus, being 1 cm. from the right of a line drawn from the umbilicus to the nipple, and made by a .32 caliber bullet.

All those present agreed that an immediate laparotomy was demanded, and preparations were made accordingly. Dr. Eugene Wasden, of the Marine Hospital Service, administered the anesthetic. The administration of the ether was begun at 5:20 p. m., and the President was under its influence at 5:29 p. m. Dr. M. D. Mann was the operator, Dr. Herman Mynter first assistant, Drs. Parmenter and Lee sponging, Dr. E. C. Mann at sutures, and Drs. Hall and Rixey assisting with the lights. Miss Walters was in charge of the nurses—Miss Morris, Miss Barnes, Miss Baron, Miss Shannon, Miss Dorchester, and Miss Simmons.

5:30 p. m. Dr. Mann made a vertical incision 8 cm. in length, passing through a bullet wound, and in a few minutes enlarged it to 10 cm. A piece of cloth, carried in by the bullet, was found and removed.

5:38 p. m. 0.002 grams strychnine administered hypodermically.

5:41 p. m. The stomach was exposed and a perforating bullet wound found in the anterior wall midway between the orifices of the stomach about 1 cm. in diameter and about 1½ cm. from the line of the omental attachment. The wound was examined and enlarged so as to admit the finger.

5:43 p. m. The wound of the stomach was secured with a double row of silk sutures.

5:55 p. m. Respiration, 33; pulse, 84; both of good character.

5:58 p. m. Incision increased to 14½ cm. Abdominal cavity carefully explored and all bleeding points tied off.

6:05 p. m. Respiration, 36. Intestines examined; omentum ligated and divided after which perforation in posterior wall of stomach was readily found. It was about 1½ cm. in diameter. The wound was carefully sutured. Pulse 88, and of good character.

6:20 p. m. Pulse, 102; only fair in character; respiration, 39; 1.6 c. c. of brandy given hypodermically.

6:23 p. m. Dr. Roswell Park, medical director Pan-American Exposition, arrived in the operating room.

6:31 p. m. Abdominal cavity irrigated with sterile salt solution and abdominal opening sutured.

6:40 p. m. Pulse, 120; fair; respiration, 36.

6:48 p. m. Pulse, 124; tension good; respiration, 36.

6:50 p. m. Abdominal sutures in place; 7 silk-worm gut sutures, with catgut between.

6:51 p. m. Anesthetic stopped.

7:01 p. m. Bandaging completed. Pulse, 122; respiration, 32.

7:17 p. m. Hypodermic of morphine, 0.004 gram administered.

7:32 p. m. Removed from the hospital to the ambulance, Drs. Park and Wasden accompanying the President. At this time his condition was good, but he was still under the influence of the anesthetic.

8:20 p. m. Arrived at the Milburn house and put to bed in fair condition. Pulse, 127, temperature, 100.6; respiration, 30. The nurses on duty were Miss K. R. Simmons and Miss A. D. Barnes, from the Emergency Hospital.

8:25 p. m. Morphine sulphate, gm. 0.016, administered hypodermically.

8:30 p. m. Pulse improved in character; slight nausea.

The first bulletin issued by the President's physicians, dated at 7 p. m., was as follows:

> "The President was shot about 4 o'clock; one bullet struck him on the upper portion of the breastbone, glancing and not penetrating; the second bullet penetrated the abdomen 5 inches below the left nipple and 1½ inches to the left of the median line. The abdomen was opened through the line of the bullet wound. It was found that the bullet had penetrated the stomach. The opening in the front wall of the stomach was carefully closed with silk sutures; after which a search was made for a hole in the back wall of the stomach. This was found, and also closed in the same way. The further course of the bullet could not be discovered, although careful search was made. The abdominal wound was closed without drainage. No injury to the intestines or other abdominal organs was discovered.
>
> The patient stood the operation well. Pulse of good quality, rate of 130. Condition at the conclusion of the operation was gratifying. The result cannot be foretold. His condition at present justifies hope of recovery."

8:43 p. m. Pulse, 132. Rested quietly for eight minutes.

9:15 p. m. Vomited a small amount of partly digested food and a small clot of blood. No fecal odor.

9:40 p. m. Vomited small amount of undigested food.

10:25 p. m. Pulse, 128; temperature, 100.4; respiration, 24.

10:40 p. m. The following bulletin was issued:

> "The President is rallying satisfactorily, and is resting comfortably. Temperature, 100.4 degrees; pulse, 124; respiration, 24."

10:45 p. m. Slight discoloration of dressings and occasional twinge of pain.

11:00 p. m. Pulse, 122; temperature, 101; respiration, 24.

11:10 p. m. Voided urine, 90 c.c.

12 midnight. Pulse, 128; temperature, 101; respiration, 24. Slept quietly 20 minutes. Saline enema retained.

SECOND DAY--September 7, 1901.

12:40 a. m. Passed urine, 60 c.c.

1:00 a. m. The following bulletin was issued:

> "The President is free from pain and resting well. Temperature, 100.2; pulse, 120; respiration, 24."

2:00 a. m. Pulse, 126. Passed urine, 30 c.c.

3:00 a. m. Pulse, 110; temperature, 101.6; respiration, 24. The President continued to rest well.

3:20 a. m. Passed 15 c. c. urine.

4:10 a. m. Pulse, 100. Sleeping.

4:55 a. m. Pulse, 108; temperature, 101.8; respiration, 24. Large amount of gas expelled.

5:05 a. m. Pulse 104. Pain severe on deep inspiration.

5:20 a. m. Saline enema, 1 pint; retained. Restless.

6:00 a. m. The following bulletin was issued:

> "The President has passed a good night. Temperature, 102; pulse, 110; respiration, 24."

6:15 a. m. Morph. sulph., gm. 0.016, administered hypodermically.

6:50 a. m. Pulse, 125. Passed urine, 60 c.c.

8:00 a. m. Pulse, 123, temperature, 102.2; respiration, 24.

The nurses, Miss Simmons and Miss Barnes, returned to the Emergency Hospital, having been relieved by Miss Maud Mohun and Miss Jane Connolly.

9:00 a. m. The following bulletin was issued:

> "The President passed a fairly comfortable night, and no serious symptoms have developed. Pulse, 146; temperature, 102; respiration, 24."

Acting Steward P. A. Eliot and Private Jack Hodgins and Ernest Vollmeyer, all of the Hospital Corps, United States Army, have been detailed as orderlies.

12:00 noon. Pulse, 136; temperature, 102.2; respiration, 28. Hypodermic of morph. sulph. gm. 0.01 administered.

1:15 p. m. Saline enema 500 c.c.

3:30 p. m. Pulse, 140; temperature, 102.2; respiration, 24.

4:30 p. m. Pulse, 127. Hypodermic digitalis. Passing much gas by the mouth.

5:30 p. m. Pulse, 124. Passed urine, 60 c.c. Sponged with alcohol. Sleeping. Passed gas by mouth.

6:30 p. m. Complains of intense pain in pit of stomach. Gave morp., 0.008 gm. hypodermically. No pain but restless. Sponged with alcohol, and rested quietly for half an hour. The following bulletin was issued:

> "There is no change for the worse since last bulletin. Pulse, 130; temperature, 102.6 degrees; respiration, 29."

7:35 p. m. Pulse, 133. Saline enema, 500 c.c., retained.

7:40 p. m. Hypodermic digitalis. Passed urine, 45 c.c.

8:50 p. m. Pulse, 132; temperature, 102.5; respiration, 28.

9:30 p. m. The following bulletin was issued:

> "Conditions continue much the same. The President responds well to medication. Pulse, 132; temperature, 102.5; respiration, 25. All temperatures reported are taken in the rectum."

10:30 p. m. Has slept quietly for 15 minutes. Saline enema, 500 c.c., with 4 gm. somatose. Rejected 60 c.c.

10:40 p. m. Gave hypodermic digitalis.

10:55 p. m. Pulse, 140. Very restless. Gave morph. 0.008 gm., hypodermically.

11:15 p. m. Passed from the bowels 240 c. c. greenish-colored fluid and two particles of fecal substance. Passed gas by the mouth.

First Urinalysis

Quantity	30 c.c.
Color	dark amber
Reaction	strongly acid
Urea	0.028 gm. per 1 c.c. of urine
Albumin	a trace
Phosphates and chlorides	normal
Sugar	none
Indican	very small amount

Microscopical Examination

The sediment obtained by centrifuge shows a large amount of large and small epithelial cells, with some leucocytes and occasional red cells. There is a comparatively large number of hyaline casts principally small, with some finely granular ones; also an occasional fibrinous one. The amount of sediment is large for the quantity of urine submitted. There were no crystals in the sediment.

THIRD DAY—September 8, 1901.

12:30 a. m. Pulse, 138; temperature, 102.6; respiration, 28. Restless during sleep. Limbs sponged with alcohol. Voided urine, 60 c.c. Quiet, and slept from 2 to 3 o'clock.

3:20 a. m. The following bulletin was issued:

> "The President has passed a fairly good night. Pulse, 122; temperature, 102.4 degrees; respiration, 24."

3:30 a. m. Saline enema, 500 c.c. Somatose, 4 gm.

4:00 to 4:30 a. m. Confused and very restless.

5:00 a. m. Pulse, 120; temperature, 102.2; respiration, 26. Complains of feeling chilly, but it passed in a moment.

5:35 a. m. Voided urine, 45 c.c. Restless and talkative from 5 to 6 o'clock.

5:50 a. m. Expelled a small quantity of brown fluid and gas by rectum.

6:00 a. m. Expelled small quantity of brown fluid. Gas by mouth. Sleeping.

6:55 a. m. Hypodermic digitalis. Passed gas by mouth.

7:45 a. m. Pulse, 132; temperature, 102.8; respiration, 24. Hypodermic of strychnine 0.001 gm.

8:20 a. m. Wound dressed. Urine voided, 90 c.c.

9:00 a. m. The following bulletin was issued:

> "The President passed a good night and his condition this morning is quite encouraging. His mind is clear and he is resting well. Wound dressed at 8:30 and found in a very satisfactory condition. There is no indication of peritonitis. Pulse, 132; temperature, 102.8; respiration, 24."

9:30 a. m. Sleeping.

10:15 a. m. Pulse, 132. Hypodermic digitalis.

10:25 a. m. High enema; epsom salts, glycerine, and water.

10:40 a. m. Small dark-brown fluid stool with gas.

11:00 a. m. Voided urine, 90 c.c.

12 noon. The following bulletin was issued:

> "The improvement in the President's condition has continued since last bulletin. Pulse, 128; temperature, 101; respiration, 27."

Hypodermic strychnine. Small dark-brown fluid stool.

12:30 p. m. Saline enema with somatose; not retained. Alcohol rub. Sleeping. Dr. Charles McBirney of New York, joined the surgeons.

3:00 p. m. Voided urine, 90 c.c. Pulse, 130; temperature, 101; respiration, 30.

4:00 p. m. The following bulletin was issued:

> "The President since the last bulletin, has slept quietly, four hours altogether—since 9 o'clock. His condition is satisfactory to all the physicians present. Pulse, 128; temperature, 101; respiration, 28."

Hypodermic strychnine. Sleeping.

4:45 p. m. Restless and talkative. Water, 4 c. c., by mouth; first taken by mouth.

4:55 p. m. Water, 4 c.c., by mouth. Enema of sweet oil, soap, and water. Passed some gas and 270 c.c. slightly colored fluid with a few particles of fecal substance and a very little mucus.

5:10 p. m. Water, 4 c.c. Sponged with alcohol. Mouth washed with peroxide solution.

5:35 p. m. Water, 8 c.c. Gas passed by mouth.

5:50 p. m. Gas and water discharged by rectum.

6:10 p. m. Water, 8 c.c.

6:20 p. m. Water, 8 c.c. Nutritive enema of egg, whisky, and water, partly rejected.

7:15 p. m. Hypodermic digitalis.

7:30 p. m. Hypodermic strychnine.

7:40 p. m. Pulse, 130; temperature 101.6; respiration, 28.

8:00 p. m. Water discharged from the bowels. Very restless.

8:20 p. m. Passed a great deal of gas and some fluid with particles of fecal substance.

9:00 p. m. The following bulletin was issued:

> "The President is resting comfortably and there is no special change since last bulletin. Pulse, 130; temperature, 101.6; respiration, 30.

Restless. Voided urine, 45 c.c.

9:45 p. m. Gas by rectum. Quiet only a few minutes at a time.

10:00 p. m. Pulse, 128; respiration, 28.

Second Urinalysis

Quantity	450 c.c.
Color	amber—slightly turbid
Reaction	strongly acid
Specific gravity	1.026
Urea	0.038 gm. per 1 c.c. of urine
Albumin	mere trace
Sugar	none
Indican	abundant
Sulphates	increased
Phosphates	somewhat increased
Chlorides	somewhat increased

Microscopical Examination

Microscopical examination of sediment obtained by centrifuge shows fewer organic elements. Some large and small epithelial cells and some leucocytes. Casts are not so abundant as yesterday and are principally of the small finely granular variety. There is a marked diminution in small renal epithelial cells.

Quite a quantity of large crystals of uric acid and bacteria are present.

FOURTH DAY—September 9, 1901.

12:01 a. m. Pulse, 124; temperature, 101.4; respiration, 28. Gas by mouth. Sleeping.

1:25 a. m. Water, 8 c.c. Restless from 1 to 1:30 o'clock.

2:00 a. m. Quiet and sleeping. Gas by mouth and by rectum.

2:20 a. m. Took water, 12 c.c. Voided urine, 120 c.c.

3:15 a. m. Very restless and mind much disturbed. Codeia phos. 0.015 gm. hypodermically.

3:20 a. m. Nutritive enema. Sponged legs and arms with alcohol.

4:10 a. m. Quiet and resting. Pulse, 120; temperature, 101; respiration, 28.

5:15 a. m. Water, 12 c.c. Expelled small quantity of fluid, faecal odor, with particles of faecal substances and gas.

6:00 a. m. The following bulletin was issued:

> "The President passed a somewhat restless night, sleeping fairly well. General condition unchanged. Pulse, 120; temperature, 101 degrees; respiration, 28."

Slept at intervals from 5 to 6 o'clock. Water, 12 c.c.

7:09 a. m. Water, 15 c.c. Gas by rectum. Voided urine, 150 c.c. Mind clear. Feels chilly. Water, 24 c.c.

8:00 a. m. Water, 24 c.c.

9:00 a. m. Pulse, 112; temperature, 100.8; respiration, 28. Restless from 8 to 9 o'clock. Passing gas by mouth and rectum.

9:20 a. m. The following bulletin was issued:

> "The President's condition is becoming more and more satisfactory. Untoward incidents are less likely to occur. Pulse, 112; temperature, 100.8 degrees; respiration, 28."

The following memorandum was issued to the nurses:

Nurses' Hours

Miss Mohun	8 a. m. to 4 p. m.
Miss Connolly	4 p. m. to midnight
Miss McKenzie	12 midnight to 8 a. m.

The nurse going off duty must not leave the sick quarters until she has satisfied her relief that all dressings are prepared and the relief understands the instructions of the physicians. The instructions will be in writing. Nurses on tour duty must not leave the sick room without proper relief (some one of the staff at the bedside of the patient), and then only for five minutes, unless relieved by a trained nurse.

Miss Hunt will be in the house and will be the relief for meals and also the special nursing of Mrs. McKinley.

Dr. Rixey will write out the instructions of the physicians and be accessible at all times. Any change demanded must be reported to him at once.

9:35 a. m. Water, 30 c.c.

10:00 a. m. Calomel, 0.015 gm., dry on the tongue. Nutritive enema of egg, whiskey, and water.

11:00 a. m. High enema, olive oil and castor oil.

11:15 a. m. Calomel, 0.015 gm., dry on the tongue. Water, 30 c.c. More quiet.

12 noon. High enema, 2,000 c.c. soap and water with 8 c.c. or gall. This was followed by a large, light brown, partly formed stool with gas.

12:15 p. m. Calomel, 0.015 gm. Water, 60 c.c. Voided 240 c.c. urine. Sleeping.

1:15 p. m. Calomel, 0.015 gm., dry on the tongue. Alcohol rub. Sleeping.

2:15 p. m. Calomel, 0.015 gm. Water, 24 c.c. Sleeping.

3:00 p. m. The following bulletin was issued:

"The President's condition steadily improves and he is comfortable, without pain or unfavorable symptoms. Bowel and kidney functions normally performed. Pulse, 113; temperature, 101; respiration, 26."

Wound dressed.

3:20 p. m. Calomel, 0.015 gm. Dry on the tongue.

4:20 p. m. Spit up 15 c.c. greenish bitter fluid.

4:30 p. m. Voided urine, 120 c.c. Nutritive enema given; part rejected.

5:50 p. m. Hot water, 16 c.c.

6:15 p. m. Pulse, 112. Considerable gas by mouth, and feels nauseated.

7:10 p. m. Hot water, 16 c.c. Slept 15 and 20 minutes.

8:00 p. m. Slept 20 minutes. Pulse, 112; temperature, 101; respiration, 27.

9:30 p. m. The following bulletin was issued:

"The President's condition continues favorable. Pulse, 112; temperature, 101; respiration, 27."

Voided urine, 180 c.c. Gave codeia, 0.015 gm.

10:00 p. m. Nutritive enema. Complains of feeling full and very uncomfortable.

11:30 p. m. Hot water, 16 c.c.

Third Urinalysis

Quantity received	540 c.c.
Color	amber—slightly turbid
Specific gravity	1.026
Albumin	a trace
Indican	not so abundant as yesterday
Urea	0.047 gm. per 1 c.c. of urine
Chlorides and phosphates	about normal
Sulphates	still somewhat high
Sugar	none

Microscopical Examination

Microscopical examination of sediment obtained by centrifuge shows a decrease in the amount of organic elements and an increase of amorphous urates, but fewer crystals of uric acid. Casts are fewer and only the small granular and large hyaline varieties. The proportion of large casts is greater. There are very few epithelial cells, mostly of renal type. A large number of cylindroids are found.

FIFTH DAY—September 10, 1901.

12:05 a. m. High enema of soap and water. Expelled part of the enema with light-brown stained fluid with dissolved fecal substances. Slept quietly for 25 minutes.

1:46 a. m. Uncomfortable; turning frequently.

1:50 a. m. Very quiet and slept 35 minutes.

2:30 a. m. Pulse, 108; temperature, 100.4; respiration, 26. Voided urine, 180 c.c. Gave hot water, 24 c.c.

3:00 to 4:00 a. m. Sleeping. Hot water, 30 c.c.

4:10 to 5:05 a. m. Sleeping.

5:20 a. m. The following bulletin was issued:

"The President has passed the most comfortable night since the attempt on his life. Pulse, 118; temperature, 100.4; respiration, 28."

Has passed much gas by mouth and rectum.

6:00 a. m. Wakened and feels very comfortable. Water, 60 c.c.

7:05 a. m. Nutritive enema. Alcohol rub. All previous temperatures by rectum; all following by mouth unless otherwise noted.

8:40 a. m. Pulse, 109; temperature, 99.8; respiration, 25.

9:00 a. m. The following bulletin was issued:

> "The President's condition this morning is eminently satisfactory to his physicians. If no complications arise a rapid convalescence may be expected. Pulse, 104; temperature, 99.8; respiration, 26. The temperature is taken by mouth and should be read about 1 degree higher by rectum."

9:20 a. m. Water, 60 c.c. Voided urine, 60 c.c. Sleeping.

10:45 a. m. Nutritive enema; expelled a portion.

11:40 a. m. Pulse, 112; temperature, 100.3; respiration, 26. Water, 60 c.c. Complains of some distress in abdomen.

12 noon. Expelled a quantity of light yellow fluid, fecal odor.

12:30 p. m. Hypodermic codeia phos., 0.015 gm. Resting more quietly; sleeping. Voided urine, 150 c.c.

2:00 p. m. Lime juice for the mouth. Water, 30 c.c. Oozing visible on bandage.

2:45 p. m. Pulse, 120; temperature, 100; respiration, 28. Gas by mouth.

3:20 p. m. The following bulletin was issued:

> "There is no change since this morning's favorable bulletin. Pulse, 110; temperature, 100; respiration, 28."

3:35 p. m. Wound dressed. Water, 24 c.c. Voided urine, 150 c.c. Sleeping.

4:15 p. m. Resting. Alcohol rub. Sleeping. Water, 90 c.c.

6:10 p. m. Nutritive enema. Slept half an hour and expelled 180 c.c. light yellow fluid, fecal odor, with gas.

9:20 p. m. Pulse, 114; temperature, 100.6; respiration, 28. Some of the stitches removed from the abdominal wound and dressing done by Dr. Mann. Much exhausted, tired, and very restless.

10:30 p. m. The following bulletin was issued:

> "The condition of the President is unchanged in all important particulars. His temperature is 100.6; pulse, 114; respiration, 28.
>
> "When the operation was done on Friday last it was noted that the bullet had carried with it a short distance beneath the skin a fragment of the President's coat. This foreign material was of course removed, but a slight irritation of the tissues was produced, the evidence of which has appeared only tonight.

It has been necessary on account of this slight disturbance to remove a few stitches and partially open the skin wound. This incident cannot give rise to other complications, but it is communicated to the public as the surgeons in attendance wish to make their bulletins entirely frank. In consequence of this separation of the edges of the surface wound, healing of the same will be somewhat delayed. The President is now well enough to begin to take nourishment by the mouth in the form of pure beef juice."

SIXTH DAY—September 11, 1901.

12:05 a. m. Beef juice, 4 c.c. First food taken into the stomach since the operation. Tasted good.

1:15 a. m. Beef juice, 4 c.c. Water, 90 c.c. Urine voided, 240 c.c.

2:00 a. m. Starch and laudanum enema followed by nutritive enema. Alcohol rub.

3:00 a. m. Wound dressed by Dr. Rixey. Expelled from rectum 90 c.c. light yellow fluid, fecal odor.

4:50 a. m. Has slept about 40 minutes. Beef juice, 4 c.c. Water, 90 c.c.

5:15 a. m. Gas by rectum. Feels chilly. Voided urine, 150 c.c.

6:00 a. m. The following bulletin was issued:

> "The President has passed a very comfortable night. Pulse, 120; temperature, 100.2; respiration, 26."

Beef juice, 6 c.c. Sleeping.

7:00 a. m. Beef juice, 8 c.c. taken with a relish.

8:00 a. m. Beef juice, 8 c.c. Resting comfortable since 12 o'clock. Sleeping more than usual.

8:30 a. m. Pulse, 116; temperature, 100.2; respiration, 28. Voided urine, 180 c.c. Took beef juice, 12 c.c.

9:00 a. m. The following bulletin was issued:

> "The President rested comfortable during the night. Decided benefit has followed the dressing of the wound made last night. His stomach tolerates the beef juice well, and it is taken with great satisfaction. His condition this morning is excellent. Pulse, 116; temperature, 100.2."

10:10 a. m. Wound dressed. Remaining stitches removed. Starch enema followed by nutritive enema. Beef juice by mouth, 12 c.c.

11:00 a. m. Water, 120 c.c. Expelled small amount light yellow fluid, fecal odor. Sleeping.

12 noon. Sleeping.

12:40 p. m. Beef juice, 16 c.c. High enema soap and water.

12:50 p. m. Hypodermic strychnine. Restless.

1:15 p. m. Albumin water, 16 c.c. Alcohol rub. Slept quietly for 1 hour.

2:15 p. m. Pulse, 120; temperature, 100.2; respiration, 26. Complains of headache.

2:30 p. m. Beef juice, 16 c.c. Voided urine, 240 c.c.

3:00 p. m. Camphor applied to head. Albumin water, 16 c.c.

3:30 p. m. Wound dressed by Dr. McBirney. The following bulletin was issued:

> "The President continues to gain and the wound is becoming more healthy. The nourishment taken into the stomach is being gradually increased. Pulse, 120; temperature, 100.2."

4:00 p. m. Beef juice, 16 c.c.

4:50 p. m. Water, 180 c.c. Voided urine, 120 c.c.

5:00 p. m. Starch and laudanum enema.

5:20 p. m. Nutritive enema of egg, whiskey, and water. Sleeping.

6:15 p. m. Albumin water, 16 c.c.

7:30 p. m. Slept three-quarters of an hour. Complains of bandage being too tight.

7:35 p. m. Beef juice, 16 c.c. Pulse, 120; temperature, 100.4; respiration, 30.

8:00 p. m. Lower strap loosened by Dr. Rixey. Sleeping.

8:45 p. m. Albumin water, 16 c.c. Rubbed with alcohol. Complains of bandage being uncomfortably tight and it is loosened by Dr. Rixey. Blood count by Dr. Wasden shows absence of blood poisoning.

9:40 p. m. Beef juice, 16 c.c. Wound dressed by Dr. McBurney.

10:00 p. m. The following bulletin was issued:

> "The President's condition continues favorable. Blood count corroborates clinical evidence of absence of blood poisoning. He is able to take more nourishment and relishes it. Pulse, 120; temperature, 100.4."

10:40 p. m. Beef juice, 16 c.c. Changed to fresh bed.

11:00 p. m. Starch and laudanum enema.

11:20 p. m. Nutritive enema of whiskey, egg, and water.

11:40 p. m. Beef juice, 30 c.c. Strychnine hypodermically, 0.002 gm. Pulse, 126; temperature, 100.4; respiration, 32. Sleeping.

12 midnight. Beef juice, 30 c.c. Voided urine, 240 c.c.

Fourth Urinalysis

Quantity ------------------------------------ 82 c.c.
Color ------------------------------------ amber—clear

Specific gravity	1.027
Reaction	strongly acid
Albumin	a trace
Indican	abundant
Urea	0.04 gm. per 1 c.c. of urine
E. phosphates and chlorides	normal
Sulphates	still a little high

Microscopical Examination

Microscopical examination of sediment obtained by centrifuge shows a marked diminution in amount of organic elements, but a great increase in uric acid crystals.

There are very few epithelial cells—mostly of renal type.

There are fewer casts—small and large hyaline—some finely granular.

Cylindroids are more abundant.

SEVENTH DAY—September 12, 1901.

1:00 a.m. Beef juice, 30 c.c. Very restless. Alcohol rub.

1:45 a.m. Has been sleeping. Water, 90 c.c. Complains of pain in the abdomen.

2:00 a.m. Beef juice, 30 c.c. Whiskey, 8 c.c. Water, 60 c.c.

3:10 a.m. Chicken broth, 60 c.c. Water, 120 c.c.

4:00 a.m. Beef juice, 30 c.c. Sleeping.

4:35 a.m. Water, 16 c.c.

5:00 a.m. Pulse, 122; whiskey and water; chicken broth. Voided urine, 270 c.c.

6:00 a.m. Beef juice, 30 c.c. Upper part of body quite moist from 5:30 to 6 o'clock. Sleeping.

6:20 a.m. The following bulletin was issued:

> "The President has had a comfortable night. Pulse, 122; temperature, 100.2."

7:00 a.m. Whiskey and water. Sleeping.

7:35 a.m. Hypodermic strychnine.

8:00 a.m. Voided urine, 150 c.c. Whiskey and water. Comfortable night; sleeping more than usual.

8:30 a.m. Chicken broth, piece of toast, and small cup of coffee.

9:15 a.m. Wound dressed and doing well. Washed with iodine solution and peroxide.

9:20 a.m. Castor oil, 30 c.c.

9:30 a.m. The following bulletin was issued:

"The President has spent a quiet and restful night and has taken much nourishment. He feels better this morning than at any time. He has taken a little solid food and relished it. Pulse, 120; temperature, 100.2 degrees."

10:00 a. m. Pulse, 122; temperature, 100.2; respiration, 29. Whiskey and water.

10:30 a. m. Beef juice, 45 c.c. Slept at intervals. Bathed head and hands with camphor. Passing much gas by rectum and mouth.

11:30 a. m. Pulse, 124. Infusion of digitalis, 8 c.c. Restless and depressed. Alcohol rub and sponge.

12:05 p. m. Hypodermic strychnine, 0.002 gm.

Dr. McBirney returned home.

12:30 p. m. Whiskey and water. Chicken broth. Sleeping.

1:15 p. m. Voided urine, 240 c.c.

1:30 p. m. Small piece of toast and one soft-boiled egg. Did not relish it and ate very little. Quieter and more cheerful since having last strychnine.

2:00 p. m. Pulse, 128; temperature, 100.2; respiration, 28. Water, 90 c.c. Infusion of digitalis, 8 c.c. Skin moist and cold.

2:30 p. m. Complains of headache and nausea. Whiskey and water. Beef juice, 45 c.c. Drowsy; feels very tired.

3:05 p. m. Pulse, 134; temperature, rectum, 101; respiration, 32. Hypodermic strychnine, 0.003 gm. Dr. Stockton called in consultation.

3:00 p. m. The following bulletin was issued:

"The President's condition is very much the same as this morning. His only complaint is of fatigue. He continues to take a sufficient amount of food. Pulse, 126; temperature, 100.2."

3:30 p. m. Infusion digitalis, 15 c.c. Hypodermic codeia phos. 0.015 gm. Water, 150 c.c. Whiskey and water. Beef juice, 30 c.c. Resting and sleeping at intervals.

4:45 p. m. Pulse, 128; respiration, 28. Mind wandering and restless.

5:00 p. m. Infusion digitalis, 15 c.c. Chicken broth, 90 c.c. Skin moist and cold.

6:00 p. m. Pulse, 130; respiration, 31. Sleeps at intervals. Complains of feeling very tired and headache.

6:30 p. m. Voided urine, 210 c.c. Whiskey and water. Sleeping.

7:00 p. m. Hypodermic strychnine, 0.003 gm. Calomel, 0.18 gm. Dry on tongue.

7:30 p. m. Whiskey and water. Quiet and sleeping at intervals.

8:00 p. m. Pulse, 130; temperature, rectum, 101; respiration, 28. Wound dressed by Dr. Mann.

8:30 p. m. Resting very quietly. Upper part of body quite moist; cold. The following bulletin was issued:

> "The President's condition is not quite so favorable. His food has not agreed with him and has been stopped. Excretion has not been properly established. The kidneys are acting well. His pulse is not satisfactory, but has improved in the last two hours. The wound is doing well. He is resting quietly. Temperature, 100.2; pulse, 128."

9:30 p. m. Castor oil. 30 c.c.

9:35 p. m. High enema, soap and water and ox gall. Water, 120 c.c. A large, dark, semifluid stool. Urine voided, 180 c.c.

10:00 p. m. Whiskey and water. Hypodermic strychnine, 0.002 gm.

10:30 p. m. Seems much exhausted after the enema. Whole body moist and cold. Pulse weak and thready. Slept quietly 20 minutes.

11:00 p. m. Whiskey and water. Normal salt solution, 420 c.c., subcutaneously.

12 midnight. Whiskey and water. Infusion digitalis. Oxygen inhaled. The following bulletin was issued:

> "All unfavorable symptoms in the President's condition have improved since the last bulletin. Pulse, 120; temperature, 100.2."

Fifth Urinalysis

Quantity	132 c.c.
Color	light amber, very turbid
Specific gravity	1.025
Reaction	acid
Albumin	mere trace, if any
Indican	less
Urea	0.044 gm. per 1 c.c. of urine
Sulphates	about normal
E. phosphates	much increased
Chlorides	normal

Microscopical Examination

Microscopical examination of sediment obtained by centrifuge shows fewer organic elements than the last examination. There is less uric acid and a large amount of amorphous phosphates. Renal casts, about as in the last examination, with very few cylindroids.

EIGHTH DAY—September 13, 1901.

12:20 a. m. Voided urine, 240 c.c. Restless and complains of headache. Pulse fairly good.

1:00 a. m. Pulse, 132. Whiskey and water. Perspiring; body warmer. Very restless and wants to get up; tired.

1:45 a. m. Hypodermic strychnine, 0.002 gm.

2:00 a. m. Whiskey and water, camphorated oil hypodermically.

2:15 a. m. Clam broth, 45 c.c.

2:45 a. m. Hypodermic camphorated oil.

2:50 a. m. The following bulletin was issued:

> "The President's condition is very serious, and gives rise to the gravest apprehension. His bowels have moved well, but his heart does not respond properly to stimulation. He is conscious. The skin is warm and the pulse small, regular, easily compressible, and 126; respiration, 30; temperature, 100."

3:00 a. m. Hypodermic of camphorated oil. Whiskey and water. Clam broth.

3:30 a. m. Quiet. Pulse, 124, volume fair; respiration, 32. Water 16 c.c. Hypodermic camphorated oil. Condition of skin better. Sleeping.

4:00 a. m. Whiskey and water. Essential oil of camphor hypodermically.

4:30 a. m. Chicken broth, 60 c.c.

5:00 a. m. Whiskey and water.

5:20 a. m. Pulse, 122, volume not good. Infusion digitalis, 15 c.c. Whiskey and water. Mind clear. Sleeps for 5 to 10 minutes at a time.

5:55 a. m. Hypodermic strychnine, 0.003 gm. Skin slightly better.

6:30 a. m. Liquid peptonoids; whiskey and water.

7:00 a. m. Coffee, 45 c.c. Clam broth, 60 c.c.

7:40 a. m. Pulse, 128; temperature, 100.8; respiration, 32.

8:00 a. m. Whiskey and water. Passed urine, 270 c.c.

8:30 a. m. Hypodermic of adrenalin. Chicken broth.

8:45 a. m. Hypodermic camphorated oil.

9:00 a. m. Wound dressed with balsam of Peru. Whiskey and water. Liquid peptonoid, 15 c.c. The following bulletin was issued:

> "The President's condition has somewhat improved during the past few hours. There is a better response to stimulation. He is conscious and free from pain. Pulse, 128; temperature, 99.8."

Sixth Urinalysis

Color	Amber—turbid, with phosphates
Quantity	252 c.c.
Reaction	acid
Specific gravity	1.023
Albumin	mere trace, if any
Urea	0.047 gm. per 1 c.c. urine
Indican	a trace
E. phosphates	increased
Chlorides	normal
Sulphates	a little high

Microscopical Examination

Microscopical examination of sediment obtained by centrifuge before and after clearing shows no change from yesterday's sample. Casts, hyaline and granular, both large and small, comparatively few. Cylindroids, a few. Crystals, large amount of uric acid, some sodium urate, and in the untreated specimen a large amount of amorphous deposit, principally of phosphates. There are a few epithelial cells, small granular. Occasional red cells and leucocytes. Spermatozoa.

9:40 a. m. Hypodermic of strychnine, 0.002 gm. Hypodermic adrenalin, 1.4 c.c.

10:00 a. m. Salt solution subcutaneously. Whiskey and water.

10:20 a. m. Clam broth, 60 c.c.; refused one half.

11:00 a. m. Whiskey and water.

12 noon. Whiskey and water. Sleeping at intervals; slept 15 minutes.

12:30 p. m. Chicken broth, 60 c.c.; took only half of it. The following bulletin was issued:

> "The President's physicians report that his condition is practically unchanged since the 9 o'clock bulletin. He is sleeping quietly."

1:00 p. m. Whiskey and water. Called for bedpan but bowels did not move. Quiet and sleeping.

1:45 p. m. Pulse, 123, not good; temperature, 100.4; respiration, 26. Liquid peptonoids 15 c.c. A little difficulty for the first time in swallowing. Hypodermic strychnine, 0.002 gm. Hypodermic brandy, 2 c.c.

2:00 p. m. Whiskey and water.

2:15 p. m. Clam broth, 30 c.c.; refused more. Wound dressed and doing well.

2:30 p. m. Voided urine, 240 c.c. The following bulletin was issued:

> "The President has more than held his own since morning, and his condition justifies the expectation of further improvement. Pulse, 123; temperature, 99.4."

Hypodermic of brandy, whiskey, and water. Liquid peptonoids.

3:30 p. m. Hypodermic brandy. Pulse very weak. Hypodermic camphorated oil.

4:00 p. m. Whiskey and water. The following bulletin was issued:

> "The President's physicians report that he is only slightly improved since the last bulletin. The pulse and temperature remain the same as at that hour."

4:30 p. m. Hypodermic of brandy. Chicken broth, 60 c.c.

4:36 p. m. Hypodermic essential oil camphorated.

4:40 p. m. Hypodermic strychnine, 0.002 gm.

4:55 p. m. Adrenalin hypodermically. Brandy and water.

5:00 p. m. Oxygen. Urinated involuntarily.

5:15 p. m. The following bulletin was issued:

> "The President's physicians report that his condition is grave at this hour. He is suffering from extreme prostration. Oxygen is being given. He responds to stimulation but poorly. Pulse, 125; respiration, 40."

6:00 p. m. Oxygen continued. Normal salt solution subcutaneously. Whiskey and water. Hypodermic nitroglycerine; hypodermic brandy.

6:15 p. m. The following bulletin was issued:

> "The President's physicians report that his condition is most serious in spite of vigorous stimulation. The depression continues and is profound. Unless it can be relieved the end is only a question of time."

6:25 p. m. No response to stimulants. Very restless. Hypodermic morphia, 0.015 gm., and atropine, 0.00045 gm.

7:40 p. m. Oxygen continued; almost pulseless. Morphia hypodermically, 0.015 gm.

9:00 p. m. Heart sounds very feeble. Oxygen continued. Slight reflex movements, and at 2:15 a. m., September 14, 1901, the President died.

In addition to those already mentioned, there were present in the operating room, Emergency Hospital, at the time of the operation:

Mr. Simpson, medical student, who was at the instrument tray.
Dr. Charles G. Stockton, of Buffalo.
Dr. P. W. Van Paymen, of Buffalo.
Dr. Joseph Fowler, of Buffalo.

Dr. D. W. Harrington.

Dr. W. D. Storer, of Chicago.

Dr. Nelson W. Wilson, sanitary officer of the exposition and in charge of the hospital until the medical director's arrival. Dr. Wilson made the report of the operation to the medical director.

P. M. Rixey,
Medical Inspector, United States Navy.

5:00 p. m., September 14, 1901, the following bulletin was issued:

"The bullet which struck over the breastbone did not pass through the skin, and did little harm. The other bullet passed through both walls of the stomach near its lower border. Both holes were found to be perfectly closed by stitches, but the tissue around each hole had become gangrenous. After passing through the stomach the bullet passed into the back walls of the abdomen, hitting and tearing the upper end of the kidney. This portion of the bullet track was also gangrenous, the ganrene involving the pancreas. The bullet has not yet been found. There was no sign of peritonitis or disease of other organs. The heart walls were very thin. There was no evidence of any attempt at repair on the part of nature, and death resulted from the gangrene, which affected the stomach around the bullet wounds as well as the tissues around the further course of the bullet. Death was unavoidable by any surgical or medical treatment and was the direct result of the bullet wound."

The physicians and surgeons present at the autopsy and signing the above 5 o'clock report of September 14, were:

Henry D. Gaylord, M. D.
Herman G. Matzinger, M. D.
P. M. Rixey, Medical Inspector, United States Navy.
Matthew D. Mann, M. D.
Herman Mynter, M. D.
Roswell Park, M. D.
Eugene Wasden, surgeon, United States Marine Hospital Service.
Charles G. Stockton, M. D.
Edward G. Janeway, M. D.
W. W. Johnston, M. D.
W. P. Kendall, surgeon, United States Army.
Charles Carey, M. D.
Edward L. Munson, assistant surgeon, United States Army.
Hermanus L. Baer, M. D.

Notes on the Autopsy on President McKinley

September 14, 1901

Ordinary signs of death; ecchymosis in dependent portions of the body. Rigor mortis well marked. Upon the surface of the chest to the right of the midsternal line a spot 1 cm. in diameter, dark red in color, with a slight scab formation covering it; measuring from the supersternal notch the distance is 5½ cm.; from the right nipple, 10 cm.; from the line of the right nipple, 8¼ cm. Surrounding this spot, at which point there is an evident dissolution of the continuity of the skin, is a discolored area of oval shape extending upward and to the right. In its greatest length it is 11 cm., and in its greatest width, 6 cm. It extends upward in the direction of the right shoulder. The skin within this area is discolored; greenish yellow and mottled. The surface of the abdomen is covered with a surgical dressing which extends down to the umbilicus and upward to just below the nipples. The innermost layer of cotton is covered or stained with balsam of Peru and blood. On removing this dressing a wound is exposed. Inserted in the wound are two layers of gauze, likewise impregnated with balsam of Peru. The wound has been packed with gauze saturated with the same substance. The wound is 14½ cm. in length and is open down to the abdominal muscles. The layer of abdominal fat is 3¾ cm. in thickness. The appearance of the fat is good, a bright yellow in color. No evidence of necrosis or sloughing. In the left margin of the surgical wound, lying 1 cm. to the right of a line drawn from the umbilicus to the left nipple, 15½ cm. from the nipple and 16½ cm. from the umbilicus, is a partly healed indentation of the skin, and an excavation of the fat immediately beneath it. This extends down to the peritoneal surface. The base of the surgical wound is formed by folds of omentum. On making the median incision, starting from the supersternal notch and extending to a point just below the symphysis, the subcutaneous fat is exposed, which is of bright yellow color and normal appearance, except in an area which corresponds superficially to the area of discoloration described as surrounding the wound upon the chest wall. In this area the fat is of a red color, the connective tissue structure is infiltrated with dark red pigment. The subcutaneous fat is firm and measures 4¾ cm. in thickness. On opening the sheath of the right rectus muscle it is seen to be of dark red color. (Culture taken from ecchymotic tissue under the upper bullet hole and from between the folds of the small intestine.) (Three tubes from each locality on agar and gelatine.)

On opening the abdominal cavity the parietal surface of the peritoneum is exposed and is found to be covered with a slight amount of bloody fluid; is perfectly smooth and not injected. The great omentum extends downward to a point midway between the umbilicus and the symphysis. It is thick, firm; its inferior border is discolored by coming in contact with the intestines. Below the umbilicus a few folds of intestines are exposed.

These are likewise covered with discolored blood, after the removal of which the peritoneal surface is found to be shiny. On the inner aspect of the abdominal wound the omentum is found to be slightly adherent to the parietal peritoneum, and can be readily separated with the hand from the edge of the wound. (Culture taken at this point, the surface of the wound.) At this point the omentum is somewhat injected. This adhesion to the omentum is found to extend entirely around the abdominal wound. The peritoneum immediately adjacent to the inner aspect of the abdominal wound is ecchymotic. In the omentum immediately beneath the abdominal wound is an incision, 5 cm. from the medial line and extending downward from the margin of the ribs 8 cm. On removing the subcutaneous fat and muscles from the thoracic wall, the point which marks the dissolution continuity of the skin upon the surface is found to lie directly over the margin of the sternum and to the right side between the second and third ribs. There is no evidence of ecchymosis or injury to the tissues or muscles beneath the subcutaneous fat. On making an incision through the subcutaneous fat directly through the wound upon the surface a small cavity is exposed about the size of a pea just beneath the skin, which is filled with fluid blood. (A section of tissue, including the lower half of the wound and extending through the subcutaneous fat, is taken for examination. The upper portion of the wound is removed for chemical examination.) The subcutaneous tissue underlying the area of discoloration on the surface of the chest wall shows hemorrhagic infiltration.

On removing the sternum the lungs do not extend far forward. A large amount of pericardial fat is exposed. Pleural surface on both sides is smooth. There are no adhesions on either side within the pleural cavities. The diaphragm on the right side extends upward to a point opposite the third rib in the mammary line. No perceptible amount of fluid in either pleural cavity. On opening the pericardial cavity the surface of the pericardium is found to be smooth and pale. The pericardium contains approximately 6 c.c. of straw-colored, slightly turbid fluid (some taken for examination).

On exposing the heart it is found covered with a well-developed paniculus. The heart measures from the base to the apex on the superficial aspect 10½ cm. The right ventricle is apparently empty. The heart feels soft and flaccid. On opening the left ventricle a small amount of dark red blood is found. The muscle of the left ventricular wall is 1½ cm. in thickness; dark reddish brown in color; presents a shiny surface. The average thickness of the pericardial fat is 3½ mm. (Blood taken from the auricle for examination.) The left auricle contains but a small amount of dark, currant-colored blood. The mitral valve admits three fingers. The right ventricle, when incised in the anterior line, is found to be extremely soft; the muscular structure is 2 mm. in thickness. The paniculus measures 7 mm. The muscle is dark red in color; very shiny.

On opening the right auricle it is found to be filled and distended by a large currant-colored clot which extends into the vessels. The tricuspid orifice admits readily three fingers. The coronary arteries were patulous and soft; no evidence of thickening.

On unfolding the folds of intestine there is no evidence of adhesion until a point just beneath the mesocolon is reached, when, on removing a fold of small intestine a few spoonfuls of greenish gray thick fluid flows into the peritoneal cavity. On the anterior gastric wall is an area to which a fold of the omentum is lightly adherent. On breaking the adhesion there is found a wound about midway between the gastric orifices, 3½ cm. in length, parallel with the greater curvature of the stomach, 1½ cm. from the line of omental attachment. This wound is held intact by silk sutures. The cardiac end of the stomach is free. There is no evidence of adhesion at any other point on the anterior wall. The gastric wall surrounding the wound just mentioned, for a distance of 2 or 3 cm., is discolored, dark, greenish gray in appearance, and easily torn. On exposing the posterior wall of the stomach from above along the greater curvature of the stomach the omentum is found to be slightly adherent, a line of silk ligatures along the greater curvature of the stomach marking the site where the omentum had been removed. On throwing the omentum downward the posterior gastric wall is exposed. On the posterior wall of the stomach, a distance of 2 cm. from the line of omental attachment, is a wound approximately 2 cm. in length, held intact by silk sutures. The gastric wall surrounding this wound is discolored. On the surface of the mesocolon, which is posterior to the gastric wall at this point, is a corresponding area of discoloration, the portion coming directly in contact with the wound in the gastric wall being of dull gray color. The remainder of the surface of the posterior wall of the stomach is smooth and shiny. Beyond the surgical wound in the posterior wall of the stomach is found an opening in the retro-peritoneal fat large enough to admit two fingers. This opening communicates with a tract which extends downward and backward as far as the finger can reach. The tissues surrounding this tract are necrotic. On removing the descending portion of the colon a large irregular cavity is exposed, the walls of which are covered with gray, slimy material, and in which are found fragments of necrotic tissues. Just at the superior margin of the kidney is located a definite opening which forms the bottom of the tract traced from the stomach. On stripping the left kidney from its capsule, it is found that the superior portion of the capsule is continuous with the cavity. The weight of the left kidney is 5 oz., 1 gr. The kidney is readily stripped from its capsule; is dark red; the stellate veins are prominent; and along its greater curvature are numerous dark red depressions. On the superior aspect of the kidney is a protrusion of the cortex, dark-red in color, and in this protrusion is a laceration 2 cm. in length, extending across the superior border approximately at right angles to the periphery of the kidney and from before backward. On incising the kidney, the cortex and medulla are not easily distinguishable from one another; both are of rose-red color, the cortex measuring approximately 6 mm. in thickness. The vessels in the pyramids of farriem are very prominent. Beneath the protruding portion of the surface the cortex is dark red in color. This discoloration extends downward in pyramidal form into the medulla. The laceration of the surface marks the apex of the protrusion of the kidney substance. Between the spleen and the superior aspect of the kidney is a necrotic tract which extends down and backward and ends in a blind pocket. The tract, which includes the superior aspect of the kidney, can be traced into the perinephritic fat to a point just above the surface of the muscles of the back. The necrotic cavity, which connects the wound on the posterior wall of the stomach and the opening adjacent to the kidney capsule, is walled off by the mesocolon and is found to involve a considerable area of the pancreas. A careful examination of the tract leading down toward the dorsal muscles fails to reveal the presence of any foreign body. After passing into the fat the direct character of the tract ceases and its direction can be traced no farther. The adjoining fat and the muscles of the back were carefully palpated and incised without disclosing a wound or the presence of a foreign body. The diaphragm was carefully dissected away and the posterior portion of the thoracic wall likewise carefully examined. All fat and organs which were removed, including the intestines, were likewise examined and palpated without result.

The great amount of fat in the abdominal cavity and surrounding the kidney rendered the search extremely difficult.

The liver is dark red in appearance, the gall bladder distended. The organ was not removed.

The right kidney is embedded in a dense mass of fat; capsule strips freely; it weighs 5 ounces; measures 11½ cm. substance is soft; cortex is 6 mm. in thickness. There are a few depressions of the surface, and the stellate veins are prominent.

The pancreas at its center forms part of the necrotic cavity. Through its body are found numerous minute hemorrhages and areas of gray softening, the size of a pea and smaller. These are less frequent in the head portion of the pancreas.

The cause of death having been established and the autopsy having lasted nearly four hours, it was discontinued, as a further search for the bullet could serve no useful purpose.

There is no evidence of organic disease in any organ examined.

* * * * * *

In regard to the chemical and bacteriological report, I have just received, under date of September 24, from Dr. Metzinger, the following:

There was no bacterial or chemical source of poison found on either cartridge or weapon.

From the outer wound there was obtained a gas bacillus with the ordinary pyogenic organism, but no streptococcus.

The chemical examination of the necrotic cavity showed that the material was alkaline and no free hydrochloric acid; microscopically showed only tissue material that was disorganized and unrecognizable.

The rest of the work as it relates to the autopsy is still in an incomplete condition, and there is little prospect of arriving at any definite results within the very near future.

In Dr. Metzinger's report submitted later he says the clinical examination of the empty shells and cartridges were negative, and closes his report with the following paragraph:

The absence of known pathogenic bacteria, particularly in the necrotic cavity, warrants the conclusion that bacterial infection was not a factor in the production of the conditions found at the autopsy.

A copy of Dr. Gaylord's report, received by me on October 16, gives the following anatomical diagnosis:

> "Gunshot wound of both walls of the stomach and the superior aspect of the left kidney; extensive necrosis of the substance of the pancreas; necrosis of the gastric wall in the neighborhood of both wounds; fatty degeneration, infiltration, and brown atrophy of the heart muscle; slight cloudy swelling of the epithelium of the kidneys.
>
> "The piece of retro-peritoneal fat, where it forms part of the necrotic cavity, is seen on section to be covered with a thick gray deposit, which has an average thickness of from 4 to 6 mm. Beneath this, and separating it from the fat, is a well-defined area of hemorrhage from 1 to 2 mm. in thickness. The appearance of this piece of tissue is characteristic of the fat tissue surrounding the entire cavity. A section, made perpendicular to the surface and stained with haematoxylineosin, shows the infiltration between the fat cells or of fat necroses. The surface of the tissue which, in the microscopic specimen was covered by a layer of grayish material, proves, under low power, to consist of a partly organized fibrinous deposit. At the base of this deposit is evidence of an extensive hemorrhage, marked by deposits of pigment. The surface of the membrane is of rough and irregular appearance and contains a large number of round cells with deeply stained nuclei. Under high power the organization of the membrane may be traced from the base toward the surface. The portion immediately adjacent to the fat tissue consists of a network of fibrin inclosing large numbers of partly preserved red blood corpuscles. In many areas the red blood corpuscles are broken down and extensive deposits of pigment are found. Extending into the fibrin structure of the

membrane are numerous typical fibroblasts and round cells. In some regions pigment is evidently deposited in the bodies of large branching and spindle cells. Here and there included in the membrane are the remains of fat cells, and toward the surface of the membrane a large number of round cells, scattered through the interstices of the membrane. There are but few polymorph nuclear leucocytes. Here and there in the membrane are fragments of isolated fibrous connective tissue, with irregular contours and an appearance suggesting that they are fragments of tissue which have been displaced by violence and included in the fibrin deposit. The fibrin in the superficial layers of the membrane is formed in hyaline clumps. The organization along the base of the deposit is comparatively uniform.

"Sections stained with methylene blue, carbo-thionin, and Gram's method, were carefully examined for the presence of bacteria, with negative results. Even upon the surface of the membrane there are no evidences of bacteria.

"The section of the left kidney, including the triangular area of hemorrhage described in the macroscopic specimen, reveals the following appearances; (Section hardened in formalin with haematoxylin-eosin). Examined macroscopically section represents a portion of kidney cortex made perpendicular to the surface of the cortex and including an area of hemorrhage into the substance of the cortex 1 cm. in length, measured from the capsular surface downward, and presenting a width of from 5 to 6 mm. The capsular surface has evidently been torn.

"Under low power the margins of the preparations are found to consist of well-preserved kidney structure. There is a slight amount of thickening of the interstitial tissue and occasional groups of tubules are affected by beginning cloudy swelling. The glomeruli are large and present a perfectly normal appearance. As we approach toward the center of the preparation occasional glomeruli are met with in which capillary loops are engorged, and the adjacent tubules contain red corpuscles. A short distance farther the kidney structure becomes entirely necrotic. Here and there the remains of tubules may be made out, and these are infiltrated with cells. The necrotic area presents a rough, net-like structure. As we approach toward the surface of the kidney we find that the necrosis becomes more marked. There is the merest suggestion of kidney structure, its place being taken by disintegrated red blood cells and leucocytes embedded in a well-defined fibrinous network. There is great distortion of the kidney structure about the periphery of the necrotic area. In this region a considerable amount of pigment is also found in the necrotic tissues.

"Under high power the characteristics of the necrotic tissues may be better observed. The kidney structure is broken up and torn into irregular fragments, infiltrated by red blood corpuscles and leucocytes. In the portion of the necrotic mass beneath the capsule the kidney structure is practically obliterated and is replaced by a network of fibrin which includes large numbers of red blood cells and leucocytes. Scattered through the entire necrotic area are frequent deposits of pigment. In the deeper portions of the necrotic area the margins of the fibrin deposit are invaded by fibro-blasts from the connective tissue structure of the kidney. The organization in these areas is, however, slight.

"Sections stained with methylene blue and Gram's method and carefully examined under oil immersion fail to reveal the presence of any organisms. In preparations stained with methylene blue the deposits of pigment may be readily observed. Section of the same tissue hardened in Hermann's solution and examined for fat shows the presence of numerous fat droplets, within the epithelium of the tubules which are adjacent to the area of necrosis. In the portions of the preparation more widely distant from the area of necrosis no fat is present.

"Section of the right kidney, hardened in formalin and stained with haematoxylin-eosin, reveals the presence of areas in which slight parenchymatous degeneration of the epithelium in the uriniferous tubules may be noted. These areas are not extensive, and are confined to single groups of tubules. The interstitial connective tissue of the organ seems to be slightly increased in amount but there is no well-defined round-celled infiltration. An occasional hyaline glomerulus is to be met within these cases, surrounded by increased connective tissue. The epithelium of the kidney tubules, aside from those in which the parenchymatous degeneration is present, is well preserved. The nuclei are well stained, protoplasm finely granular.

"A fragment of the stomach wall taken from the immediate neighborhood of the anterior wound, is in a condition of complete necrosis. The nuclei of the cells are scarcely demonstrable. The epithelial surface is recognized with difficulty. At its base are apparently a few round cells. Examination of the blood vessels reveals nothing characteristic. There is apparently no evidence of thrombosis. A section made through the gastric wall at some distance from the wound reveals the well-preserved muscular structure of the gastric wall, which presents no characteristic alterations. Superficial portions of the epithelium have apparently been affected by post-mortem digestion. However, in one portion of the preparation the epithelium is intact and shows distinct evidence of marked round-celled infiltration between the granular structures. The blood vessels contain red blood corpuscles with the usual number of leucocytes.

"The fragments of heart muscle which were removed from the right and left ventricular walls were examined in the fresh state and exhibited a well-defined fatty degeneration of the muscle fibers, and in the case of the right ventricular wall an extensive infiltration between the muscle fibers of fat was apparent. Sections from these fragments of muscle hardened in Hermann's solution are taken for examination. A fragment of muscle from the right ventricular wall was removed at a point where the fat penetrated deeply into the muscular structure, the ventricular wall at this point showing an average thickness of 2½ millimeters. Under low power the muscle fibers are separated into bundles by masses and rows of deeply stained fat cells. The muscle fibers are seen to contain groups of dark-brown granules lying in the long axes of the cells. Under high power these are resolved into extensive groups of dark-brown pigment arranged around the nuclei. The muscle fibers are slender; the cross and longitudinal striation is well defined. Examined near the margin of the preparation, where the osmic acid fixation has been successful, all of the muscle fibers are found to contain minute black spherical bodies extending diffusely through all the muscle fibers about the entire margin of the preparation. These fine fat droplets are present in sufficient amount to speak of an extensive diffuse fatty degeneration of the muscle fibers. Where the large fat cells have separated the muscle fibers, these are found to be more atrophic than those in the central portions of the larger bundles.

"The examination of the section through the healed bullet wound on the chest wall reveals nothing of importance. The dissolution of continuity is filled in by granulation tissue, and there is evidence of beginning restoration of the epithelium from the margins. Stains for bacteria give negative results.

"In summing up the macroscopic and microscopic findings of the autopsy, the following may be stated. The original injuries to the stomach wall had been repaired by suture, and this repair seems to have been effective. The stitches were in place and the openings in the stomach wall effectually closed. Firm adhesions were formed both upon the anterior and posterior walls of the stomach, which reenforced these sutures. The necroses surrounding the wounds in the stomach do not seem to be the result of any well-defined cause. It is highly probable that they were practically terminal in their nature and that the condition developed as a result of lowered vitality. In this connection there is no evidence to indicate that the removal of the omentum from the greater curvature and the close proximity of both of these wounds to this point had any effect in bringing about the necrosis of the gastric wall, although circulatory disturbances may have been a factor. The fact that the necrotic tissue had not been affected by digestion strongly indicates that the necrosis was developed but shortly before death. The excavation in the fat behind the stomach must be largely attributed to the action of the missile. This may have been the result of unusual rotation of a nearly spent ball or the result of simple concussion from the ball passing into a mass of soft tissues. Such effects are not unknown. The fact that the ball grazed the superior aspect of the left kidney, as shown by the macroscopic investigation of that organ, indicates the direction of the missile, which passed in a line from the inferior border of the stomach to the tract in the fat immediately superior to the kidney. There was no evidence that the left adrenal gland was injured.

"The injury to the pancreas must be attributed to indirect rather than direct action of the missile. The fact that the wall of the cavity is lined by fibrin, well advanced in organization, indicates that the injury to the tissues was produced at the time of the shooting. The absence of bacteria from the tissues indicates that the wound was not infected at the time of the shooting and that the closure of the posterior gastric wound was effectual. The necrosis of the pancreas seems to us of great importance. The fact that there was no fat necroses in the neighborhood of this organ indicates that there was no leakage of pancreatic fluid into the surrounding tissues. It is possible that there was a leakage of pancreatic fluid into the cavity behind the stomach, as the contents of this cavity consisted of a thick, grayish fluid containing fragments of connective tissue. In this case the wall of fibrin would have been sufficient to prevent the pancreatic fluid from coming into contact with the adjacent fat. The extensive necrosis of the pancreas would seem to be an important factor in the cause of death, although it has never been definitely known how much destruction of this organ is necessary to produce death. There are experiments upon animals upon record in which the animals seem to have died as a result of not very extensive lesions of this organ. One experiment of this nature, reported by Flexnor, Journal of Experimental Medicine, Volume II, is of interest. The fact that concussions and slight injuries of the pancreas may be a factor in the development of necrosis is indicated by the researches of Chiari, Zeitschrift fur Heilkunde, Volume XVII, 1896, and Prager medicinische Wochenschrift, 1900, No. 14, who has observed (although a comparatively rare condition) extensive areas of softening and necrosis of the pancreas, especially of the posterior central portion, which lies directly over the bodies of the vertebrae, where the organ is most exposed to pressure or the effects of concussion. The wound in the kidney is of slight importance except as indicating the direction taken by the missile. The changes in the heart, as shown by the macroscopic inspection and the microscopic examination, indicate that the condition of this organ was an important factor. The extensive brown atrophy and diffuse fatty degeneration of the muscle, but especially the extent to which the pericardial fat had invaded the atrophic muscle fibers of the right ventricular wall, sufficiently explain the rapid pulse and lack of response of this organ to stimulation during life."

The cause of death of the President has been made plain by the autopsy. It was due primarily to a gunshot wound by a .32 caliber bullet fired at close range, devitalizing the tissues immediately surrounding its tract, so that gangrene of those parts injured, involving the stomach, pancreas, kidney, and other tissues were absorbed, and with the degenerated condition of the muscular tissue of the heart caused death, the final symptoms being those of exhaustion.

Report of Death

Name of deceased: McKinley, William.
Office: President of the United States.
Date of death: September 14, 1901.
Time of death: 2:15 a. m.
Place of death: 1168 Delaware avenue, Buffalo, N. Y.
Date of burial: September 19, 1901.
Place of burial: Canton, Ohio.
Cause of death: Gangrene of both walls of stomach and pancreas following gunshot wound.

I hereby certify that McKinley, William, President of the United States, died while at Buffalo, N. Y., as set forth in the record of his case, as follows:

The President was holding a public reception at the Academy of Music, Pan-American Exposition, Buffalo, N. Y., on September 6, 1901, and whilst shaking hands with the people was shot at 4:07 p. m. through the stomach by Leon F. Czolgosz.

There is good evidence that the disease (or injury) causing death was in line of duty, the facts being as follows: The President was shot by an assassin whilst receiving the people.

P. M. Rixey,
Medical Inspector, United States Navy.

* * * * * *

I must mention here the giving up by Mr. John G. Milburn of his entire home in Buffalo and the devoting of his whole time and energy to the care of the President.

In concluding this report I must also refer to the untiring and devoted services of Mr. George B. Cortelyou, secretary to the President, who, with Mr. Nelson P. Webster, Mr. M. C. Latta, members of the Executive staff, and Mr. C. A. Conrad, of the Post Office Department, were on duty night and day. Executive Mansion Steward William Sinclair and Messengers Charles Tharin, Thomas Lightfoot, and Harry Mickie were also on duty at the Milburn house during the President's illness.

In obedience to the Department's orders, I was with the President's party at Buffalo, N. Y., on September 6. Upon arrival at the railroad station on its return from Niagara Falls, about 3:30 p. m., the President directed me to escort Mrs. McKinley to the Milburn house.

As soon as I learned of the attempt on the President's life, I hastened to his side at the Emergency Hospital on the Exposition grounds and was in the operating room with him at about 5:30 p. m. The President was under the influence of the anesthetic administered by Dr. Eugene Wasden of the United States Marine Hospital service. Dr. M. D. Mann, with a full corps of assistants, was ready to begin a laparotomy, which all deemed imperative.

Being satisfied with the completeness of the preparation and the ability of the operating surgeon, I made ready to assist and watched every step of the operation. The wounds having been closed, and the President's condition being good, I requested Dr. Roswell Park, the Medical director of the Pan-American Exposition, to send nurses and a surgical bed to the Milburn house and to take personal charge of the removal of the President, as I had to inform Mrs. McKinley of her husband's condition and make ready a room for his reception.

On his arrival I assumed charge of the case, having as consultants Dr. M. D. Mann, of Buffalo, N. Y.; Dr. Roswell Park, of Buffalo, N. Y.; Dr. Herman Mynter of Buffalo, N. Y.; Dr. Eugene Wasden, of the U. S. Marine Hospital Service. Dr. Charles McBirney, of New York, joined the consultations at 3 p. m. September 8, and left for home after the 9:30 a. m. bulletin of September 12. Dr. Charles G. Stockton, of Buffalo, N. Y., joined the consultations at 5 p. m. September 12. Dr. Edward G. Janeway, of New York, and Dr. W. W. Johnson, of Washington, D. C., arrived and Dr. McBirney returned after all hope had departed. All were present at the autopsy. Dr. H. G. Matzinger of Buffalo, N. Y., made all the urinalyses and also had charge of the chemical and bacteriological work. The histological examination of the tissues were made by Dr. H. R. Gaylord, who, with Dr. Matzinger, performed the autopsy.

In addition to the nurses mentioned, Miss Grace McKenzie, of Baltimore, Md., was employed after her arrival, and Miss Evelyn Hunt, of San Francisco, Cal., Mrs. McKinley's nurse, assisted as required.

* * * * * *

The Medical News of September 28, 1901, contained an editorial which deserves to be published here as showing the temper of the medical profession of the country toward the traducers of Dr. Rixey and his eminent colleagues with respect to their management of the President's case. It is a rebuke none too severely administered and should be included as an important item in the narration of the circumstances surrounding this event.

"Immediately following the death and autopsy of the late President, there appeared signed articles in the daily press from several prominent physicians in this city, and an editorial in a leading medical journal, openly criticising the physicians who attended President McKinley in a manner that has stung the whole medical fraternity into expressions of shame and scorn—shame that the editor of a journal that has always upheld the honor and dignity of the profession should have stooped from his high position to traduce, by innuendo and covert criticism, the medical men who attended the late President; scorn that any physician should have sunk to the level of the scandal-mongers of the sensational press and deliberately suggest to an excited and believing public weapons of suspicions to be used at random against the men who have handled this famous case.

"It can be readily imagined that it must have been trying to the yellow journals that the X-ray apparatus was not used, and that they were defrauded of a skiagram of the dying President; but that any physician should sneer at the conscientious conclusions reached by the anxious surgeons to dispense with the X-rays and should state concerning this opinion that 'it seemed safer to guess than to be sure' is, we feel, little short of an insult. 'What excuse', is asked, 'must be offered to the public for the utter inability to find the bullet even in the dead body?' But why, we ask, should the sympathetic, overwrought public think of demanding excuses from the medical men who, by their strenuous efforts, prolonged, for a week. the life of a doomed President, unless the idea had been suggested? To hint to the public that they are aggrieved and that they have a right to ask the surgeons to explain 'Why they allowed a lost ball to be buried with the victim's body?' is little short of trying to make the Nation's tragedy a popular spectacle.

"It is not, however, this gallery play that deserves the severest condemnation. It is the subtle way in which many of these articles have been worded so that, while they seem to mingle praise for the surgeons with lamentations over the inevitable, they nevertheless convey to the reader a startled sense of suspicion and alarm that all was not done that might have been done. We are ashamed of this utter violation of professional standards, of the manifest unfairness of making charges when the accusers could not possibly be in possession of the full details of the case, of the lack of charity in dealing treacherous, underhand blows to the few and of this holding up to public criticism a vicious cartoon of medical men so prominent that the entire medical profession must bear the scoffs. It is these things that have amazed, pained, and angered the American medical brotherhood.

"To so cruelly and maliciously hint that a 'fatal blunder in diagnosis had been made,' especially after the autopsy had demonstrated the necessarily fatal character of the wound, is evidence of a very low standard of professional ethics, and it is not to be wondered at that the attending surgeons and the medical profession of the country should feel the affront and demand an apology."

As a matter of fact, Dr. Rixey achieved national—and, indeed, international fame through his devoted service at the bedside of President McKinley during his mortal illness, as well as on previous occasions, when the President was sick, and the family and more intimate friends of Mr. McKinley know and often expressed their conviction that the complete recovery from a most virulent attack of grippe from which he suffered in January, 1900, was due to the excellent advice given and the care exercised by his private medical attendant, Dr. Rixey. The doctor was vigilance itself in the management of the case, and not the least important item in his success on this occasion was his insistence that his patient should be entirely exempt from those irritating labors to which Mr. McKinley was in the habit of lending such patient attention. His success as the medical advisor of Mrs. McKinley is also well-known. But Dr. Rixey was more than a trusted medical advisor—he was an esteemed friend and companion, and the attachment which is widely known to have existed was not without foundation. He was always at the call of his eminent patients and his record as their attending physician shows that, on every occasion, when Mr. and Mrs. McKinley left Washington, Dr. Rixey was with them. Often Mrs. Rixey was a member of the President's parties. Many times, however, she remained at home, though the doctor went as usual. This separation was, of course, unpleasant to both, but, as a naval surgeon, he and Mrs. Rixey were accustomed to separation, and it could scarcely be avoided. Besides, as physician to the Executive Mansion, he was fully alive to the responsible duties he had undertaken and was always cheerful, fresh and vigorous—at least, he always looked so, whether tired or not. We can well imagine how appalling his responsibilities must have looked sometimes, and he is to be congratulated most heartily upon the creditable manner with which he supervised the physical well-being of the occupants of the White House—not only in the McKinley Administration, but through the Roosevelt Administration. In this connection, The Texas Medical News of September, 1901, very aptly says:

> "If, in a case of so important a patient (as the President of the United States or one of his family or any prominent government official, such as were frequently under Dr. Rixey's care), anything goes wrong by mere chance, the public has an unpleasant propensity to criticize. The public cannot be blamed for this, for it knows no better, but its criticism is galling all the same, and the stoutest-hearted of us all might well recoil before the chance of having it visited upon him."

There was an element of the heroic, therefore, in his performance of this duty with such tenacity and determination.

In his desire to serve the President's family to the best of his ability and with such promptness as would insure the greatest possible control of any disease he might be called upon to treat, Dr. Rixey was influenced to select a Washington residence as near the Executive Mansion as a suitable home was obtainable. A private telephone connected his home with the Executive Mansion and his calls at the latter were daily and regular whether he had been sent for or not. Other doctors had been on duty at the White House before, but none entered so completely into the lives of his patients there as did Dr. Rixey, and while he did not have the faculty which has been so often credited to him of "never getting tired," he did have, fortunately, a tremendous amount of endurance. Moreover, he did what few men can do successfully—he forsook his own desires, wishes, and pleasures in the fulfillment of duty. Washington and many throughout the country know this and admire him. As to Mr. and Mrs. McKinley, those in a position to know declare that they considered him almost essential to their lives in and out of Washington.

After the awful suspense just before the President's death, during which the world stopped work at the dreaded announcement—"The President is dying," and couriers were searching the wilderness of the Adirondacks for the Vice-President, all eyes and hearts turned to that devoted wife who had said her last good-bye to a devoted husband. Can we imagine the utter desolation of the one who had lost the guiding, protecting hand that she had leaned so confidingly on and upon which she had depended so much for many years? She was alone, save one—her doctor, Presley Marion Rixey, in whom she reposed such affectionate confidence, and he counts it one of the blessings of his life that he was able to bring some little comfort to her at this hour of greatest sorrow. No person can hope to be so close to a soul in bitterest distress over a death as the doctor who has striven to save the life of the beloved one, and this was Dr. Rixey's compensation, as it is the compensation of the profession which he graces. To be of service at such a time is a privilege accorded the elect and Dr. Rixey's faithful and tender care of Mrs. McKinley at this time and until her own death won for him the affection of the American people who hung on his words as to her condition and outlook.

After Mr. McKinley's death and obsequies, Dr. Rixey escorted her to Canton, Ohio, and there he remained the gentle and wise medical counsellor, regulating her life and striving to bring her through the acute period of her trying ordeal of sadness and to a normal state of mind.

The hardest task Dr. Rixey and the relatives and attendants of Mrs. McKinley had was to get her away from the idea that she must die and join her husband. Dr. Rixey had learned that driving tended to promote repose of mind and sleep for the distinguished patient, so, in order to supplant this morbid idea, he prescribed frequent drives, and often drove with her.

In the Oregonian of Sept. 28, appeared the following comment:

> "The judgment of Dr. Rixey that Mrs. McKinley would rally, if anywhere, from the shock of her husband's tragical death in her old home in Canton, is being verified from day to day by a slight but steady increase in the strength of the sorely afflicted woman. It is not improbable that she will regain the full measure of strength that has been her portion for some years, and perhaps pass through serene, gentle invalidism down to old age."

On October 1, Dr. Rixey returned to his regular duties in Washington, leaving Mrs. McKinley under the care of Drs. Phillips and Portmann, but he was continually advised of her condition and made trips to Canton whenever his services were needed. Before the departure from Canton, Dr. Rixey is quoted as issuing a statement for the relief of all anxious friends to the effect that "Mrs. McKinley's condition is such that all her friends may be very hopeful that no change for the worse will occur. I entertain no apprehension for the near future and the general health of Mrs. McKinley may be said to be as good as it was a year ago."

When Mrs. McKinley was on her death bed, in July, 1902, Dr. Rixey was summoned to her side and there remained until she had passed from this world to join her martyred husband. Thus was completed the severance of associations which had been beneficial and happy alike to the McKinleys and the Rixeys. Between the death of Mr. McKinley and that of Mrs. McKinley much of importance had happened in the life of the doctor; but of this, in another chapter. Suffice it to say, that before Mrs.

McKinley died, she received from President Roosevelt, through Secretary Cortelyou, the gratifying information that her physician, Dr. Presley Marion Rixey, "in pursuance of the intentions of the late President McKinley, and in recognition of devoted services as well as because of eminent fitness would be appointed Surgeon General of the Navy upon the expiration of the term of office of Surgeon General Van Reypen." At the same time the Secretary of the Navy was requested by the President to "instruct Dr. Rixey to make such arrangements as will enable him to continue, if needed, his care for Mrs. McKinley between now and the time of his appointment to his new position."

Leslie's Weekly, in commenting upon this action, under date of Oct. 24, 1901, says

> "President Roosevelt's action in notifying Mrs. McKinley * * * was an eminently proper and graceful (manner of announcing his) recognition of devoted and valuable services rendered during a most critical and trying period. * * *"

This chapter of Dr. Rixey's life cannot be properly concluded without some reference to his and Mrs. Rixey's intimate personal relation with the President and Mrs. McKinley. As previously remarked, there existed between these two families the warmest and closest possible friendship and the doctor and his charming wife were not only included among those invited to all official functions at the Executive Mansion, but were very frequently there, at dinner informally or in the private parlors of the McKinleys for a quiet evening of cards or music. There was always the most delightful conversation on these occasions for members of the cabinet and other distinguished men were among those present, and the gentlemen talked upon broadly interesting topics and about public affairs unreservedly before the ladies. The doctor and Mrs. Rixey, as well as others who were fortunate enough to have known the McKinleys "en famille" attest their simple charm and, on such informal occasions when the social atmosphere was unrestrained, Mrs. McKinley's cleverness and wit was given free play and she proved a most interesting hostess. The

President, too, at these times was full of fun, and when Secretary Wilson was among the guests, would call upon him for the old Scotch folk-songs which he sang so well and always to the great amusement of the assembled company. The doctor tells of these enjoyable occasions with an expression of face and tone of voice which indicate the pleasantest recollections and, indeed, it must have been the greatest possible privilege to be a party to such associations under such delightfully unconventional circumstances.

It was the habit of the McKinleys and Rixeys to exchange gifts on Christmas and other fete days or anniversaries, and many such souvenirs, among others a chair sent on Christmas of 1900, are cherished by the Rixeys and are to be seen in their home. But these were not the only tangible expressions of friendship between them, for Mrs. McKinley and Mrs. Rixey frequently sent flowers to each other and many cordial informal notes passed between these two ladies.

CHAPTER V

THE ROOSEVELT ADMINISTRATION

APPOINTMENT OF SURGEON GENERAL OF THE NAVY

AS will be well remembered, Mr. Roosevelt began his administration abruptly with the taking of the oath of office at Buffalo, N. Y., in the library of the residence of Mr. Ansley Wilcox, immediately upon his arrival after the death of President McKinley. The news of the impending death of the President reached him in the north woods, where he had gone on a hunting trip, as soon as Mr. McKinley was pronounced out of danger by the doctors, and the story of his hurried return is as exciting as his arrival in the hour of deepest gloom, which the terrible national bereavement had thrown over everything and everybody, was affecting. Of all that immediately followed the death and funeral of President McKinley, enough has been said to indicate the movements and grief of the subject of this sketch.

He was continued as the physician to the White House by President Roosevelt, and as soon as he thought Mrs. McKinley's condition such that he could reduce his attendance upon her to occasional visits, he returned to Washington and resumed his duties as director of the Naval Dispensary and at the White House, where, for the next seven and one-half years, he was as much a friend and trusted medical advisor as he had been during the latter part of the previous administration. He had never been Mr. Roosevelt's advisor up to this time, but the President soon learned his personal and professional worth and valued him not only for his ability but as a congenial companion. Contrary to the usual naval traditions, he was an excellent horseman and he was also a fine shot, with a fondness for hunting, so that, in this respect, the President found him much to his liking and they enjoyed many an outing together. Indeed, in many other respects, Dr. Rixey was of the same mettle as

Surgeon General Presley Marion Rixey, U. S. Navy
Chief of the Bureau of Medicine and Surgery, 1902

President Roosevelt. The warm friendship which grew up between them was, therefore, most natural and we can well imagine the pleasure with which Mr. Roosevelt anticipated the opportunity to place in office a good man who gave promise of "doing things."

Fortunately for all concerned, he had not long to wait, as Surgeon General William K. Van Reypen's term of office was due to expire on December 18, 1901, and on this date the vacancy awaited would occur. As a matter of fact, it was perfectly understood that advantage would be taken of this opportunity to make the appointment indicated; but, in deference to Dr. Van Reypen's interest and natural wish to be allowed to enjoy the benefits of retiring under the 40 years' law from the office of Surgeon General, Dr. Rixey courteously consented to the proposition that his nomination be temporarily deferred, and that Surgeon General Van Reypen be reappointed, in order that he might complete his 40 years' service in the Navy while in office. It was, however, distinctly understood that Surgeon General Van Reypen was to voluntarily retire when the purpose of his reappointment had been accomplished, as it would be early in January, yet when this time arrived, Surgeon General Van Reypen, contrary to the understanding and in disregard of the courtesy extended by Dr. Rixey, and of the moral obligation imposed at the time of his reappointment, exhibited a disposition to postpone his application for retirement and prolong his tenure of office indefinitely, on the plea, among other things, that his services were needed in the preparation of the Bureau's estimates for appropriation. Dr. Rixey patiently waited for Surgeon General Van Repyen to take the promised voluntary step, and it was when Dr. Rixey finally called his attention to this promise that Surgeon General Van Reypen offered the above excuse for deferring compliance. Dr. Rixey promptly and in no uncertain terms informed Dr. Van Reypen that he most emphatically objected to the preparation of estimates for his (Dr. Rixey's) own administration by another, that he was fully capable of doing that himself and prepared to do so, and moreover, that he would regard his (Dr. Van Reypen's) further continuance in office as a disposition to break faith. Surgeon General Van Reypen seemed unmoved by these representations, and it actually became necessary for Dr. Rixey to appeal to the Secretary of the Navy to secure his rights in the case. Dr. Van Reypen went on the retired list, therefore, nominally, at his own request, on January 25, 1902. That Dr. Rixey should have been forced into the annoying and unpleasant position of a complainant did not reflect creditably upon Dr. Van Reypen who, but a few weeks before, had been the recipient of a benefit which he owed to the courtesy of Dr. Rixey, and no one else, for the decision as to whether or not the concession of reappointment should be granted had been left entirely within Dr. Rixey's pleasure to say "yes" or "no."

In Army and Navy circles it had been freely predicted that there was a rapid rise in store for Dr. Rixey and this prophecy was in process of realization when, on January 21, 1902, President Roosevelt nominated him to be Surgeon General of the U. S. Navy, to succeed Dr. Van Reypen. Two or three weeks passed and nothing had been heard from the Senate. It seemed that, for some unknown reason, the confirmation was being delayed, but, upon inquiry, it was found that the appointment had merely been overlooked on the desk of the Chairman of the Senate Committee on Naval Affairs and, when brought to light, it was quickly confirmed, though not before many amusing speculations as to reasons for the delay had been published by the press. Owing to this delay, Dr. Rixey did not assume the duties of his new office until February 10, 1902, and, during the interim between Dr. Van Reypen's retirement and Dr. Rixey's installment, the assistant to the Bureau, Surgeon J. D. Gatewood, administered its affairs, so that no embarrassment resulted from the failure of the Senate to act on Dr. Rixey's nomination. A similar condition existed in the Bureau at the expiration of the term of office of Surgeon General Wales, when Dr. Van Reypen, then assistant to the

Bureau, acted as chief for a period of about two months, pending the appointment of Surgeon General Gunnell.

Dr. Rixey was the 17th Surgeon General and the 2d of his grade to have been thus distinguished. At the time of his appointment, he had been 28 years in the Navy and was number 13 on the list of Medical Inspectors and 28 in lineal rank. His advancement, therefore, was over the heads of 27 who were then senior to him. Although the appointment was rather disappointing, from a personal point of view, to the officers who ranked Dr. Rixey, they appreciated the fact that the President was assuming no prerogative and not establishing a precedent, for it had been done previously in both the Army and Navy, and it was realized that his appointment was a tribute to his ability and an expression of the esteem in which he was held by those who had had an opportunity to test his professional capacity. Indeed, his appointment was generally approved, as evidenced by contemporaneous comment.

The "Mirror" of Washington, D. C., gave place to the following editorial expression:

> "Word comes to me that the appointment of Dr. Rixey to be Surgeon General of the Navy is most satisfactory to the people of the Bureau of Medicine & Surgery, for they all know him to be a courteous and considerate officer, and his knowledge of the civil and professional routine of the Bureau will enable him to at once conduct the affairs of the office on business principles."

And again, in the "International Journal of Surgery" of March, 1902, we read

> "The appointment of Dr. Rixey as Chief of the Medical Department of the U. S. Navy must be a cause of general congratulation in the medical profession, of which he is a valued member. In his position as medical adviser to President McKinley, Dr. Rixey demonstrated his executive abilities at a time when they were put to the severest test, and his constant devotion endeared him to the American people. We are sure that his promotion will contribute materially to the greater efficiency of the service, in which such qualities as he has shown himself to possess are so desirable."

It may be seen that Dr. Rixey did not owe his advancement altogether to the fact that he was President McKinley's and President Roosevelt's physician, and that he enjoyed their highest esteem and confidence. He was equally high in the estimation of the profession generally and was destined to become more firmly fixed in its regard as time passed, though and because he could not and did not conform to the prediction at the end of the following editorial comment which appeared in a St. Louis paper, Jan. 23, 1902:

> "No fault will be found with the President for appointing Dr. P. M. Rixey as Chief Surgeon of the Navy. His record is that of a competent and faithful surgeon and physician, and his characteristics, as shown to the American people within the last year, are a guarantee that he will strictly attend to his own duties, carefully refraining from taking part in the squabbles of naval officers."

This prophecy was all very nice, and, as a matter of fact, nobody was more anxious to have the concerns of the Medical Department run smoothly than he, but there were certain reforms necessary to the proper evolution of the medical service which did not come easily and in the attainment of these he spared no effort and fought also, as will be seen in the subsequent review of his administration. He had previously given considerable study to the needs of the service and besides being fully prepared to enter upon the duties of his new office he entertained a high ambition for the Medical Department of the Navy.

The doctor's objection to having the estimates for the first fiscal year of his administration prepared by his predecessor was justified by later developments, and in his report for 1902, we find the following pertinent reference to his prompt request for an increase of the appropriation for material improvements:

> "Immediately upon assuming charge of the conduct of the business of the Bureau, I was confronted by the fact that insufficient estimates for the year ending June 30, 1903, had been submitted to Congress. The enlarged expenses incident to the increase of the personnel of the Navy and to the increase of the establishment of new naval stations outside of the continental

limits of the United States, had caused a deficiency of $40,000, for the fiscal year 1902, but the estimates for 1903 had not been increased in keeping with this growing demand on the Bureau, as evidenced by this large deficiency—a deficiency of more than one-third of the original estimates for 1902. It became necessary, therefore, to recommend at once that Congress be asked to increase the appropriation for the Bureau for 1903 over those for 1902 to the extent of this deficiency, and an estimate was submitted raising the amount from $95,000 to $125,000, under the head of "Medical Department," and from $20,000 to $30,000 under that of "Repairs, Medicine and Surgery." Congress, recognizing the necessity for this increase, granted it."

When Dr. Rixey, in the course of his European cruise, visited the British Navy Medical School at Netley, he formed the determination that, if ever the opportunity offered, he would make similar provision for the Medical Corps of the U. S. Navy. True to this long-cherished determination, he now, as one of the first acts of his administration, took steps to establish those educational facilities for the instruction of recent appointees and for the periodic professional refreshment of older medical officers which he regarded as so important to individual proficiency and the efficiency of the Medical Department as a whole. How well this conceived need was met and with what measure of success the purpose in view was pursued, is best depicted by the remarks of Secretary of the Navy, George von L. Meyer, in his address before the graduating class of the U. S. Naval Medical School, in the spring of 1909. His review of the history of the institution ran as follows:

"The origin of the Naval Medical School was an interesting and noteworthy step in the evolution of the medical department of the Navy toward higher standards in keeping with the spirit of scientific medical progress which has been so marked during the past ten years. It may be said to have had its inception in the realization that the career of a naval surgeon involves much of a peculiar nature and requires a more perfect general rounding out than is obtainable in the various medical schools of the country.

"Fleet Surgeon Ninian Pinkney, presumably from his observations during the Civil War, was among those to suggest the advisability of the Naval Medical School, but in his day, it failed of accomplishment. Surgeon General Tryon entertained the same idea and put it into successful operation on a small scale as the 'department of instruction' at the U. S. Naval Laboratory, Brooklyn, N. Y., in 1893, from which time it continued until the outbreak of the Spanish-American war. That crisis terminated the operation and eventually the existence of the school at that place and the educational provision was not begun again until the present surgeon general was appointed in 1902. At this time, nearly ten years after the first effort to find some lodgment and start a course of instruction considered so absolutely necessary to qualify the young graduate from civil life, Surgeon General Rixey took up the work. It remained for him to revive the idea and give it practical form. Today the school stands on firm ground; its function is clearly defined, and its good work is recognized by all. It is the excellent organization under which it has been conducted, the careful, discriminating selection of the presidents of the school, and its staff of instructors and the untiring watchfulness and supervision that has been given by the Surgeon General of the Navy in the development of the course which have made the present high standing of the school possible and finally given it an unquestioned and permanent place as an institution of the naval establishment and one contributing incalculably to the efficiency of the Navy in a vital direction. * * * * *

"Nowhere else in this country is it possible to obtain the special training demanded by the naval service, which is given at the Naval Medical School, and the work of this institution, therefore, is a continual and valuable benefit to the government. The benefit of these courses, originally intended solely for the instruction of those just entering the service, has now been extended to those older officers who, returning from sea service or from duty at some isolated station, are in need of professional refreshment."

Through the interest and untiring efforts of Surgeon General Rixey, the succeeding years of its operations were characterized by splendid improvement in every feature of equipment and curriculum. Before his retirement it had reached a proud pinnacle of excellence and of unquestioned value to the individual, the service, and the profession, and was given a respected place among the best post-graduate schools—not only of this country, but of the world. He is to be congratulated upon this one inestimable achievement, but there are many others which redound to his credit and the record of his official life is written in these achievements.

It is only possible, in a biographical sketch such as is here contemplated, to give the mere outlines and dwell only upon the striking incidents of this distinguished officer's career. As the prelude to his long and eventful tenure of the post of Surgeon General of the United States Navy, a position which he held to the great benefit and advancement of the medical department, it is desired to proclaim the deep debt owed to him by the service he worked for so faithfully and well. He raised the medical service in every respect from a deplored state of backwardness to a plane such as it never seemed likely to attain—a position fully in accord with the scientific standards of the times. He made it a participant of the high honors of the medical profession by virtue of the excellent character of medical practice in naval circles and of research work by his medical officers whom he was continually inspiring to an interest in the scientific side of their duties and whom he unstintingly equipped with all the instruments of precision and other standard appliances of the age. This was in striking contrast to some of his predecessors in whom he had noticed a disposition to be more interested in questions of economy than in subjects of professional importance—a guiding policy under which medical officers were degenerating, and from the first he determined to redress the balance so far as lay in his power. In consequence, a bond of fellowship sprang up in his branch of the service and the Medical Corps worked in harmony for the common objective. Like Sir James McGrigor, for a long time Director General of the Royal Army Medical Service, "He realized to the full that the efficiency and fighting value of * * * (a military service) were closely interwoven with the efficiency of its medical branch, and he labored incessantly, and not without success, to perfect this branch and to bring its true function home to the minds of those in authority." From the day he first entered office, the great work began, and slowly, but steadily, through the past eight years his efforts bore fruit; all important reforms were

MRS PRESLEY MARION RIXEY, 1902

accomplished and epoch-making improvements were established.

Dr. Rixey's position carried with it the rank of Rear Admiral and he was frequently addressed by this title by officers of the line as well as officers of the staff corps of the Navy. Frequently, also, he was addressed as "General" (an abbreviation of "Surgeon General") by members of other government services or acquaintances in civil life. But he always preferred to be addressed as "Doctor," which was evidenced by the fact that his intimate friends employed that title, knowing the pride he felt above everything else in his identification with the medical profession.

Dr. Rixey made his record at the head of the Medical Department of the Navy in spite of the demands upon his time incident to his professional relations to President Roosevelt and family, though, on the other hand, many of his splendid ideas could not have been carried into effect without the friendship and strong support of Mr. Roosevelt. It is to the doctor's credit that such an uncompromising advocate and industrious worker for the betterment of things in specific directions and in general, as Mr. Roosevelt was, should have seen fit to endorse his projects, and it is also to the doctor's credit that he displayed such rare discretion in the legitimate advantage which he took of Mr. Roosevelt's kindly feeling for him and sincere interest in the success of his policies. Dr. Rixey never asked the President to consider trivial matters and as a consequence, when the doctor did appeal to him officially, he willingly gave his attention, confident that an important question was at issue. Moreover, the doctor respected the friendship which the President so heartily accorded him and he never attempted to interject official matters upon their social intercourse, though frequently the President would himself initiate conversation upon some matter which he knew was absorbing the doctor's attention at the time. His self-restraint in this respect was all the more commendable, for the President was always approachable and ready to discuss official problems, and there was ample opportunity for it during their many trips

Theodore Roosevelt

and outings together. Indeed, their personal relations were most intimate and on every occasion which savored of an outing of any duration, the President showed a distinct predilection for Dr. Rixey's companionship.

The President, with Mrs. Roosevelt and their children, were often the guests of Dr. and Mrs. Rixey at their home, either in the city or in the country, and the following letter will serve to indicate the appreciation of this hospitality:

THE WHITE HOUSE
WASHINGTON

March 18, 1907.

My dear Mrs. Rixey:

In the confusion of Archie's sickness, I doubt if I ever thanked you for the sausage. And let me now, my dear Mrs. Rixey, thank you for the many, many kindnesses which you have shown over and over again to my children. They are all your debtors, and Washington would have been a very different thing for all of them had it not been for the Virginia farm and the two dear people who own it.

Faithfully yours,

(Signed) THEODORE ROOSEVELT.

Mrs. P. M. Rixey,
1518 K Street,
Washington, D. C.

Dr. and Mrs. Rixey in turn were informal guests at the White House for luncheon or dinner, and at other times. They were, of course, always among those invited to official entertainments at the White House, and have been entertained at Oyster Bay, where Dr. Rixey was frequently called also in a professional capacity. Surgeon R. M. Kennedy, one of his assistants in attendance upon the President's family, tells of Dr. Rixey's professional alertness. Indeed, his mind was always remarkably quick of comprehension, grasping the true inwardness of a situation almost by intuition. This faculty was particularly observed when, on one occasion, he was called to see Master Archie Roosevelt. He immediately diagnosed the boy's disease as diphtheria, and then, before anybody else had time to take in the gravity of the situation, had given his direction for isolation, nursing, and general management of the case, with a thoroughness which showed a perfect familiarity with the needs and a comprehension of his responsibilities. Dr. Kennedy, who is himself not slow witted, regarded it as remarkable—not, of course, that Dr. Rixey knew what was required, but that the details should have been so completely at his tongue's end, even when taken unawares, as it were. So it was in all of his professional relations, and, at the White House, in order to have ready facilities for the handling of any condition that might arise in the Executive Family, he thoroughly equipped a small operating or dressing room, which, among other things, included a medical case of liberal therapeutic range. On his trips with the President he carried a generous armamentarium calculated to meet any emergency, and he was equally cautious whether preparing for a hunting trip or a political tour, and there were many of each.

The hunting trips which they took together are too numerous to mention. Many of them were arranged by the doctor to be taken in Virginia for quail or wild turkeys, and the doctor accompanied the President on a number of his hunts for big game in Louisiana and the far west. The turkey hunting always took place just before Thanksgiving, and the doctor took an especial pleasure in securing as many shots as possible for the President. On one occasion they had gone down to Albemarle, Virginia, and had hunted three days without a kill. There were plenty of turkeys to be seen all about, but they were very shy and the President had not been able to get within gun range. Finally, however, about sunset of the last day, a fine turkey flew toward the hunters. Dr. Rixey, standing on a knoll, saw him start and was in position to shoot him, but he withheld his fire and sung out a warning to the President, who in this way brought down the only prize of their outing. It proved to be a magnificent bird and the President was so appreciative of Dr. Rixey's deference to his gun that he had the wings handsomely mounted and decorated with a silver plate, bearing the date, and sent them to the doctor.

Concerning another of their hunting trips, the doctor tells rather an amusing story. Secretary Root and Mr. Cortelyou were among the party and Dr. Rixey, in giving instructions to his brother about the preparation, laid particular emphasis upon the need of a good team and a reliable driver, who was familiar with the country, to meet the party upon its arrival at Brandy, Virginia, and drive his distinguished guests to Representative John F. Rixey's country estate, "Beauregarde," which was their destination. The train did not arrive until the late evening, so that the drive was in the dark; but after they had gone a short distance, the doctor's keen eye observed a lack of familiarity of the land marks, and, leaning forward, asked "Jim" (the driver) if he knew whether or not he was on the right road. To his surprise and much to the amusement of his guests, the reply came: "Lor', Boss, I dun'no! I ain't trabeled dis here road since 'fo' de war." Thus the doctor's stipulation for a driver "who was familiar with the country" miscarried, and it was a long time before he heard the last of it. The party, however, reached its destination safely in ample time for a good dinner and a good night's rest in preparation for an early start the next morning. The preparation for the reception of this distinguished party and its entertainment during the days of the hunt were made by Mrs. Rixey and Dr. Rixey's sister, assisted by "Old Jacob," the family chef, and the many details of the arrangements included a menu for every meal—breakfast, lunch, and dinner. The house at "Beauregarde" had not been occupied for sometime, and the task of making it habitable and providing for the table on short notice was tremendous. Their efforts, however, were attended with great success, and this was Mrs. Rixey's reward, as it is a substantial reward for any undertaking.

One amusing incident connected with this preparation is told by Mrs. Rixey. It seems that, as arrangements were being completed, two men, strangers to Mrs. Rixey, approached the house and made inquiry as to which room the President was to occupy. Mrs. Rixey met them on the front porch and not only refused to answer their question, but refused their admission to the house for the reason, as she explained, that she did not know them and could not, therefore, accept their statement of friendly intentions. These two individuals happened to be secret service men and Mrs. Rixey's attitude struck them as admirable. Then they showed their credentials and orders, and the information sought was cheerfully given.

During the Washington season of 1901 and 1902, effort was made to rise out of the gloom which Mr. McKinley's death had thrown over the country, and though many and various entertainments were given at the White House, the Capital's social atmosphere lacked its erstwhile spirit and the social leaders had an uphill task in their endeavor, more especially because they themselves were laboring under the same depression that they were trying to dispell.

In the spring of 1902, two particularly important international events took place and they are mentioned here, as other official events will be mentioned in their proper places, because of Dr. Rixey's customary identification with the President's immediate party at the time of their occurrence.

In February, 1902, his Royal Highness, Prince Henry of Prussia, visited the United States as the representative of the Emperor of Germany, and on February 24, a large dinner was given in his honor by the President of the United States at the White House. The next day, February 25, the launching of the Schooner-Yacht "Meteor," which was being built in this country for His Majesty, the Emperor of Germany, took place at Shooters Island, N .Y., and following this ceremony a luncheon in honor of the President of the United States and Prince Henry of Prussia was given by the Townsend-Downey Shipbuilding Company.

On May 22, there was a reception to the French guests visiting Washington to unite with the Government in the dedication of the monument to Marshal de Rochambeau.

The elaborate ceremony attending the unveiling took place in the afternoon and was followed by a dinner at the White House in honor of the French guests. Dr. and Mrs. Rixey attended all of these functions.

President Roosevelt's first great tour was in 1903, and this year was, also, with respect to small trips, celebrations and social functions, a busy one, so that Dr. Rixey had much to do outside of the duties of his office. Among the events which he attended (sometimes accompanied by Mrs. Rixey), as the friend or medical advisor of Mr. Roosevelt, were: A concert tendered by the German Liederkranz and Arion Singing Societies of New York, to the President of the United States and Mrs. Roosevelt at the White House, February 24; and the Methodist Mass Meeting in Commemoration of the 200th Anniversary of the birth of John Wesley and the success of the Twentieth Century Thank Offering Movement at Carnegie Hall, N. Y., February 26.

On April 1, President Roosevelt started on his grand tour to the Pacific Coast (Dr. Rixey accompanying him), on which he was to be absent until June 5 (the second and third of April of this period being devoted to a detour from his direct route). In these two days the President and his party made a hurried trip from Chicago, Ill., to Madison and thence to Milwaukee, Wis. Before leaving Chicago, a banquet was given in the President's honor at the Auditorium Hotel, and in Milwaukee also a banquet at the Plankington Hotel of that city in honor of the President was tendered by the Merchants and Manufacturers' Association. All across the continent at every stop the President and his party were feted, another banquet being tendered by the Commercial Club of Minneapolis, at the Hotel Nicollet, and there were many interesting as well as amusing occurrences which the doctor recounts, much to the entertainment of those friends who catch him in a leisure hour, and who give promise of being a sufficiently sympathetic audience to draw him out.

The President took no other long tour until after his second Inauguration, March 4, 1905, when, between Oct. 18 and 31, 1905, he traveled through the South, returning from New Orleans to Washington by water. Among his papers, the doctor possesses one amusing souvenir of the visit to New Orleans, in the form of a cartoon which appeared in a Louisiana paper and was sent to him on the eve of the departure for the South as a hint in safeguarding the President against infection with yellow fever. The trip was made soon after the suppression of the yellow fever epidemic which occurred in that section of the country during the summer of 1905, and the cartoon in question represented a mosquito-proof perambulator in waiting for the President at the New Orleans depot.

As has been indicated, the President made no long tours between the one to the west in 1903 and that to the south in 1905, but between these dates he took a number of short trips upon which Dr. Rixey accompanied him, as usual, to attend various celebrations at different points outside of Washington. Among these were the anniversary of the Battle of Gettysburg, at Gettysburg, Pa., May 29-30, 1904, and Founders' Day, at the Union League Club of Philadelphia, Pa., January 30, 1905.

But to return to the progress of Dr. Rixey's administration as Surgeon General of the Navy and the improvements which he was able to effect during his first term: At the outset of the resumption of this question of his accomplishments, it is proper to remark that he had not only the support of Mr. Roosevelt in bringing about reforms; but, in his success at the hands of Congress in furthering his aims for the betterment of the medical service, he enjoyed the interest and active influence of his younger brother, Representative John Franklin Rixey, who was a Member of the House Committee on Naval Affairs. This backing was undoubtedly of the utmost help to him, yet, he himself exhibited untiring energy and industry in pushing matters of public importance—a fact which stirred Senator Eugene

Hale, on Feburary 16, 1909, to a caustic utterance on the floor of the Senate.

It was during the Second Session of the Sixtieth Congress, when an effort was being made to secure provision for a Dental Corps for the Navy, that Senator Hale referred to the subject and to Surgeon General Rixey in the following words: "* * * The Navy has never suffered because there has not been a dental corps. It is the agitation for another corps. It is urged by the Surgeon General of the Navy, who is perhaps the most persistent man in drumming at Congress early and late, for things in his bureau, of any man in the Navy Department." The next morning, when Surgeon General Rixey read this in the Congressional Record, he was not blind to the true intent of the words, but he nevertheless regarded them, and all others who heard or read must also have regarded them, as in a certain sense complimentary and an endorsement of his efforts in the interest of the medical branch of the Navy. It led him, however, to consider making a statement of his attitude in regard to those projected improvements in the attainment of which he was dependent upon the favorable action of Congress, and, on Feb. 18, 1909, he addressed a letter to Senator Hale, which, in part, ran as follows:

> "From your reference to me in the debate on the Naval Appropriation Bill, you appear to think that I am more persistent than I ought to be. I am very sorry to have been compelled, by my sense of duty as I see it, to work so hard and for so long a time for what I and all others, who have taken the time to look into the requirements of the physical condition (of the personnel) of the Navy, have found to be necessary, if the needs of the sick and injured * * * are to be cared for in accordance with modern methods.
>
> "The question of dental surgeons has been urged before Congress by me from a sense of duty, in order to prevent and relieve physical suffering and to conserve the strength of those in the service for purposes of duty * * . So also with the Hospital Corps Bill."
>
> * * * * * * *
>
> "I am sorry that, for seven years, I have had to work for these two bills. If they had become laws the first year, the

Bureau would have been saved an immense amount of labor and much physical suffering would have been prevented among the sick and injured of the Navy.

"I shall have to go over the whole matter again next year if nothing can be done this session. No one would regret the necessity of this more than I."

It seemed appropriate to mention this incident in this place, though it is a wide anticipation of events as the date indicates. The object in view was to show that "won't be-downed" spirit which typified Dr. Rixey's conduct of the affairs of the medical department during his tenure of office and which was the underlying reason for and explanation of his many accomplishments. It would be almost impossible to satisfactorily enumerate the reforms and improvements which were effected during his first term of four years in office, for many were of a continuous nature and the process of evolution along several lines extended over into his second term. Reference to special and definite changes will, therefore, be postponed to the next chapter, where a complete review of the achievements of the whole administration will be given. Suffice it here further to say that, early in the first year of his incumbency he began to work energetically for the elevation of the medical department in many directions, taking up such questions as: An increase in the number of medical officers; educational opportunities for medical officers; the efficient training of the Hospital Corps; the improvement of sick quarters on shipboard; ambulance and hospital ships; medical equipment for field service; medical department representation on important organized naval boards; women nurses for naval hospitals; a sanatorium for the treatment of the tubercular sick of the Navy; and the renovation and modernizing of all naval hospitals, as well as the building of new hospitals where required. Valuable lessons had been taught by the experiences of the Spanish-American war and these, together with other conceived needs, Dr. Rixey determined should not be neglected. During the succeeding three years of his first term, numerous other reforms and improvements—material and otherwise, were instituted, as shown by his annual reports, and, among these, was a book of instructions for medical officers, the authorization of dentists for the Navy and the question of command in the Medical Corps. To have won the recognition of the authorities to the right of medical officers to command, a prerogative which had been jealously monopolized during the previous history of the Navy by officers of the line, was an important victory. The steps in and the circumstances attending Dr. Rixey's successful contention for the principle involved in this question are interesting and will be dealt with more fully in the following chapter.

CHAPTER VI

ROOSEVELT ADMINISTRATION (continued)

SECOND TERM AS SURGEON GENERAL, U. S. NAVY

THE continuous evolution of the medical service of the Navy toward a high standard under Dr. Rixey's capable guidance was attracting general attention and the President being fully cognizant of his ability and the good work he was carrying on reappointed him February 5, 1906, for a second term as Surgeon General of the United States Navy. Thus, happily, was made possible the continuation of his excellent policies and, to a noticeable extent, the complete realization of his ambitious projects and high ideals. He had earned and was still further to merit the esteem in which he was held by the Medical Corps as a whole, by the medical profession at large, by other branches of the service, and by the authorities of certain foreign medical services who were acquainted with the great work he was accomplishing for military medicine and the enhancement of the dignity of the medical profession in military circles and, hence, the dignity of the medical profession generally. His reappointment, therefore, was, if possible, more widely applauded than his original appointment and furnished the occasion for congratulation on all sides that there was to be no change, no interruption of that progress in which he was the central force and for which there was such great need.

The second term of his administration was perhaps more active in building up his branch of the service than was the first term, though this is expressing almost the impossible. It was, however, natural that it should have been so, for he was by that time well in harness and fully in touch with the various outlying responsibilities of his office, save that he lacked the desirable personal familiarity with the conditions and naval hospitals in the far east. This one long regretted deficiency in a proper acquaintance with the constituent elements of his department he now found opportunity to correct and in the fulfillment of his determination to visit the east for the purpose of inspecting the property of the medical department, of inspecting the sanitary conditions of the several stations and of ascertaining the health conditions in that part of the world he completed a circumnavigating trip. During his absence he entrusted the care of the President and his family to his assistant Surgeon W. C. Braisted, U. S. N., and Surgeon James C. Pryor, U. S. N.

But before speaking of this trip at greater length, it seems timely to say that in taking up new projects on behalf of medical department efficiency he never lost sight of the old or dropped a single thread until its place in the fabric he was weaving was fully worked out and contributing its usefulness and strength to the whole.

Early in May of 1906, he left Washington under orders for Cavite, P. I., via Honolulu and Yokohama, for the special temporary duty above indicated and was instructed upon completion of this duty to "return to Washington, D. C., via Europe, if deemed advisable in the best interests of the service." Mrs. Rixey accompanied him, as did also Mrs. Julian James, whose delightful personality added greatly to the charm of the trip, and in obedience to his orders they sailed from San Francisco on the *Manchuria* about May 25, the doctor having first inspected the hospital at Mare Island, Calif., the Mare Island Navy Yard and the San Francisco Training Station. From the point of view of enjoyment, this trip from beginning to end could not have been more delightful and Mrs. Rixey cherishes a carefully and chronologically complete souvenir and diary record which tells the story of the interests which engaged their attention from point to point, the entertainments which were extended to them at almost every stop, and the varied experiences which punctuated their progress around the world.

As regards its official and real purpose, this trip proved eminently successful, instructive and profitable to the doctor personally and indirectly to the service, for the information which he gathered by his close observation and searching inspections were applied to useful ends, in some cases immediately and in others as soon as practicable. Nothing apparently was overlooked and nothing forgotten, for Surgeon General Rixey and his aides (Dr. E. H. H. Old en route out and Dr. G. F. Freeman en route home), made detailed notes of all defects and requirements as well as useful professional data learned at every institution or station inspected. Those inspected after leaving San Francisco were: The Naval Station, Hawaii; the Naval Hospital, Yokohama, Japan; Naval Station, Cavite, P. I.; Naval Hospital, Canacao, P. I.; Naval Station, Olongapo, P. I., and a number of naval vessels, including the *Ohio*, *Galveston*, *Chattanooga*, *Rainbow*, *Cincinnati*, and *El Cano*. During his sojourn in Japan he visited the English hospital at Yokohama and the Charity and Red Cross hospitals, the Imperial Japanese Navy Department, and the Naval Medical School—all at Tokyo. Here a lunch was given in honor of Dr. Rixey and the ladies of his party at the celebrated "Maple Club" by Surgeon General Suzuki, of the Imperial Japanese Navy. A short stay was also made in the cities of Kobe and Nagasaki, where the inspection of two of the ships was made. From Japan he went to Shanghai, where the inspection of two of the ships was made, and then he went to the Philippines. Here besides inspecting the hospital and station above mentioned, he visited the following institutions at Manila: Belibid Prison, San Lagaro Hospital, Civil Hospital, Government Laboratories, St. Paul's Hospital, and the First Reserve Hospital (U. S. Army).

Before leaving Manila, he addressed a letter to Rear Admiral Train, commanding the Asiatic Station, in regard to matters requiring attention prior to the date of his (Dr. Rixey's) arrival home, and in his final report to the Secretary of the Navy he not only went exhaustively into the various needs of the several Government institutions and stations inspected, but made valuable comment upon the diseases peculiar to them and a running reference to the character, the excellent work and the administration of other institutions which he visited along his route of travel. His report concludes: "On the 7th of July I took a steamer for Hong Kong; arrived on the 9th, visited Canton, China, on the 10th, and on the 11th took the *S. S. Roon,* via Singapore, Penang, Colombo, Aden, Suez, Port Said, and Naples for Genoa, arriving there August 11th, and finding that I had ten days before sailing from Southampton for New York, I took a train for Paris, visiting the Pasteur Institute Laboratory and Hospital, all of special interest in connection with the investigation of tropical diseases. I also visited the old hospital Hotel Dieu. In London I visited the Naval Medical School at Haslar and the large Naval Hospital at that station.

"I left Southampton on the 22d of August, arriving at New York on the 28th and at Washington, D. C., the same day."

The foregoing gives a general view of the ground Surgeon General Rixey covered, but it does not convey an adequate idea of the fund of information which he acquired during this trip extending over about three and one-half months. Samoa and Guam he was unable to visit, but except for these two stations he had now completed his acquaintance with the important isolated divisions of his department and had materially enlarged his understanding of the sanitary and medical problems of the Navy and broadened his outlook upon ways and means as seen in the practices of the other services and establishments which he investigated. He has always been ready to consider suggestions for improvement and has sought assistance to this same end in every promising direction, so that it may be taken for granted that he made good use of all the considerable points that he picked up.

Hardly had he returned to his duties in Washington when he was made President of a board of which Medical Director George E. H. Harmon and Surgeon James F. Leys, U. S. Navy, were appointed members, "for the purpose of examining such existing laws relating to the personnel of the Navy as affect the officers of the Medical Corps, and to determine whether, in the judgment of the board it would be desirable in the interests of efficiency and economy to make any changes in, additions to, or omissions from such laws, having due regard for justice and for the interests of the officers of the Corps." It was directed that the report of the board, embodying conclusions, was to be made to the Department as soon as practicable, but not later than Oct. 1, 1906.

The organization of this board as a sub-board was largely due to the representation which the Surgeon General had repeatedly made in his annual reports relative to the needs of the Medical Corps for increased numbers, rank and pay and authority for the employment of military titles. Applications for admission to the Medical Corps of the Navy were falling off and, there being at the time some 50 vacancies with a prospect of more in the near future, Surgeon General Rixey was urging reforms in these directions as of the utmost importance to the efficiency of the medical service. The same question, about the years 1872, 1873, and 1874, confronted the British Admiralty, who were deaf to the appeals of the medical officers of their navy, as well as to those of the medical schools and societies of Great Britain, until the dearth of candidates compelled the notice of the authorities and they were constrained to meet the demands in behalf of their medical service, when the flow of surgeons into the Navy was restored. In the full realization of the probable importance of its recommendations the preliminary report of the Board was strong and direct as to existing needs and remedies. In the meantime, Dr. Rixey had been ordered to accompany President Roosevelt to the Isthmus of Panama and, as during his absence the members of his sub-board had been convened to consider and express opinion upon the proposed recommendation of the Personnel Board, Dr. Rixey upon his return took advantage of his prerogative to submit a supplementary expression of opinion, which, though in the main supporting his colleagues, was in certain particulars a minority report. He presented his objections to the proposed recommendations of the Personnel Board, and urged the original recommendations of his board in strong and convincing terms, but in spite of this fact and the importance of the matter, and notwithstanding the modest nature of remedies suggested, no action was taken beyond the publication by Congress in document form of all the correspondence, and Dr. Rixey was obliged to seek to compensate this inaction by strengthening the effectiveness of his Corps by such resources as were at his command. Though he, of course, could not directly supply the numerical deficiency in the higher grades, he did succeed in immeasurably raising the professional standing of the medical department of the Navy and thus offering a legitimate advertisement of its attractiveness to young physicians of the country as a theatre for their careers. Moreover, Surgeon General Rixey conducted an effort to bring the opportunities for an honorable career offered by the naval medical service directly to the attention of young physicians, especially at the various medical centres, by personal interview and by the distribution of literature. The services of the medical press were enlisted to publish and disseminate detailed information, and the medical service of the Navy in its general aspects was made the subject of addresses by Dr. Rixey himself before a number of representative medical societies. One address entitled "The Medical Profession as Represented in the United States Navy" was delivered by him, by invitation, before the Thirty-ninth Annual Session of the Medical Society of Virginia at Richmond, Va., and another entitled "The Development of the Navy Medical Corps to Meet the Modern Requirements of Specialization in Medical Practice" was delivered by him, also by invitation, before the Essex County Medical Society of New Jersey.

During his second term of office, Dr. Rixey was frequently asked to prepare articles for different publications or to address various organizations, and though his time was already fully occupied and though public speaking was not to his taste, he usually accepted such invitations in the belief that their acceptance was one of the unwritten obligations of his office and that as the representative of the medical department of the Navy, he would be benefitting this branch of the service by thus bringing it occasionally before the medical public—both in his person as Surgeon General and in the form of carefully prepared, telling references to it. He, however, confined himself in public discussions strictly to subjects of medical bearing or other matters that came within his proper concern only with respect to the naval service, so that when in 1909 he was asked by the editor of the Delineator to write an article for that publication on "The Sociological Progress of America" he replied in part as follows:

> "While I am more or less interested in the sociological progress of America, as all good citizens must be, my active interest in this direction has been only insofar as that progress affects the United States Navy."

This sentence expresses one of the subtle, though distinctive, features of his administration, for his interest was actually very broad as regards the welfare of the personnel of the Navy, including considerations of mental and moral as well as physical hygiene, and he worked continually for the improvement of conditions surrounding them as may be learned by reading his annual reports, particularly those of the last few years. He was the recipient of many congratulatory letters upon the excellence and breadth of these reports and it was a common thing to read in the medical and lay press such comments as this which appeared in the Army and Navy Register of Nov. 21, 1908. "One of the most interesting, as it is one of the most important of the annual reports of the year, is that of the Surgeon General of the Navy."

And again in the same periodical—"This unusually interesting report of Surgeon General Rixey shows the results of the untiring efforts of that Bureau Chief to raise the efficiency of his department to the highest standard, and, together with previous reports, bespeaks his devotion to the cause of humanity and the service."

But returning to the important events in his career, early in November we find him on the eve of his trip to the Isthmus of Panama with President Roosevelt, availing himself of every source of information to refresh his acquaintance with the work, particularly that of the sanitary department under the direction of Colonel W. C. Gorgas, U. S. Army, which was going on in the Canal Zone, so that before starting he was conversant with important features of the great undertaking and thoroughly familiar with the details of the sanitary campaign. The trip was to be made on the *U.S.S. Louisiana,* in company with other ships of the Navy, and the President and his party left Washington November 8th on the *Dolphin* to join the *Louisiana* in waiting for him in Chesapeake Bay at the mouth of the Potomac.

ITINERARY OF THE PRESIDENT'S VISIT
TO THE ISTHMUS OF PANAMA AND PORTO RICO

November 8 to 27, 1906

U.S.S. Dolphin

Washington to Wolf Trap Light, Mouth of Rappahannock River-Chesapeake Bay; 134 miles—ten hours

Leave Washington Thursday evening, November 8th; Arrive Wolf Trap Light, Friday morning, November 9th.

U.S.S. Louisiana

Wolf Trap Light to Colon; 1788 miles—
138 hours—6 days

Leave Wolf Trap Light as soon as transfer can be made. Arrive Colon, Thursday morning, November 15th.

Colon to San Juan, Porto Rico: 1004 miles—
77 hours—3½ days

Leave Colon, Sunday evening, November 18th; Arrive San Juan, Thursday morning, November 22d.

San Juan to Wolf Trap Light: 1257 miles—
96 hours—4 days

Leave San Juan, Friday morning, November 23d; Arrive Wolf Trap Light, Tuesday morning, November 27th.

U.S.S. Dolphin

Wolf Trap Light to Washington: 134 miles—ten hours

Leave Wolf Trap Light as soon as transfer can be made; Arrive Washington, Tuesday evening, November 27th.

PROGRAM OF THE PRESIDENT'S VISIT TO THE ISTHMUS OF PANAMA

Thursday. Arrive Colon Thursday morning, November 15th; President and Mrs. Amador, Secretary Arias, Mr. and Mrs. Shonts, Chief Engineer and Mrs. Stevens to be received before leaving ship.

After landing at Colon, President and party will be taken directly to La Boca, train making slow run across Isthmus in order to give opportunity to see the towns, inhabitants, and parade of school children, and to make cursory examination of matters along the line.

At La Boca inspection to be made of the present terminals of the old French canal and the Panama Railroad, with indication of sites and explanation of the proposed dam, lock, lake, and other essential features of the plan of the canal and Pacific entrance thereto. A trip in the launch to the nearby islands, Perico, Naos, and Flamenco, showing the President the actual southern end of the canal in deep water, together with a view of the approaches thereto and of the harbors at La Boca and Panama, the city of Panama and surrounding country.

Return to Ancon for luncheon. After luncheon, trip around Ancon Hill and inspection of Ancon Hospital; balance of day and evening to be at the disposal of Panama Government. Details of their entertainment not yet determined, but will be about as follows:

The day will be made a "fiesta;" the town decorated and illuminated. At an hour in the afternoon to suit the

President's wishes, he and his party will be met at "El Tivoli" or other convenient point by the Panama officials and driven in carriages through the principal streets, accompanied by an escort of 100 young Panamanians on horseback, proceeding either to a special stand in one of the plazas or to the balcony of the hotel or Canal Administration Building, where an address of welcome will be delivered by President Amador and response made by President Roosevelt; after which, if time permits, the party will review a parade. President and Mrs. Amador desire President and Mrs. Roosevelt, Chairman and Mrs. Shontz and a few other members of the party, including Chief Engineer and Mrs. Stevens, to dine with them at the Presidencia. The party will be small, not to exceed twenty, including Secretary and Mrs. Arias and a few other prominent Panamanians. After the dinner President and Mrs. Roosevelt will go to the reception and ball for a few minutes, and then return to the hotel.

Friday. Leave Ancon in the morning by special train, going through and over Culebra Cut and to all points in that vicinity accessible by train, visiting quarters, hotels, shops, marine barracks, and other points of interest; luncheon at Culebra and spending the entire day in the Cut, returning to Ancon for the night.

Saturday. Leave Ancon early in the morning by special train and run without stop to Gatun; go over the site of the proposed dam and locks and other features of interest, and thence on to Cristobal, either by train, or, if the President desires, leaving the train at Gatun and going down the Chagres River, either in steam launch or native "casco," showing and explaining to him the situation of the lower Chagres, the old French canal, and possibly going to the old town at the mouth of the Chagres, being met there by tug and taken to Cristobal.

Luncheon at Cristobal. Afternoon to be devoted to inspection of Cristobal, the present and proposed terminals of the railroad and canal, the town of Colon, the hospitals at Colon, and other points of interest.

Saturday evening. Reception and ball on Pier No. 11 at Cristobal to the President and his party by the employees of the Commission. Practically every American on the Isthmus, as well as many Panamanians, will be present at this reception, and the President will probably make a short address.

Sunday. Sunday will be spent quietly at the hotel on the Isthmus, and during the evening the President and party will go aboard the *U. S. S. Louisiana* for their return trip.

PROGRAM OF THE PRESIDENT'S VISIT TO PORTO RICO

Thursday, November 22, 1906

Land early Thursday morning at Ponce; meet officials and leading citizens of that city; take automobiles across Island by military road, five hours trip, stopping at military barracks, Cayey for lunch; review Porto-Rican troops San Juan late afternoon if there is time; dinner and evening reception government house.

* * * * * * *

Nothing deserving of especial mention transpired en route to Panama, and the trip was pleasant and thoroughly enjoyed by all.

During the President's two weeks' absence from Washington on this occasion, Dr. Rixey was not called upon to attend him professionally but he acted to good purpose as the President's technical adviser on the same searching investigation of the sanitary affairs which he had given to the affairs of engineering and zone Government. The doctor, through his study of the methods and aims of the Chief Sanitary Officer, had equipped himself to be of the greatest possible service to the President, and by virtue of his professional affiliation and near relation to the President, he was also in a vantage position to infinitely further the cause of preventive medicine in that important region and to promote the interests of those charged with the responsibility of carrying on this work which he knew to be vital to the whole undertaking of canal construction. The four days sojourn on the Isthmus, it may be imagined, were busy in the extreme. In fact, so much was to be seen and accomplished that it seemed impossible that even the President with his wonderful physical vigor and quickness of intellect would be able to gratify his spirit of inquiry and obtain all the information desired—yet he left the Isthmus with a clear insight of every considerable problem, and what was most comforting of all to Colonel Gorgas and Dr. Rixey, he had come to realize, as perhaps never before, the full significance of the sanitary work as bearing upon the ultimate success of the canal project. This was the psychological moment, so to speak, to definitely strengthen the position of the Sanitary Department of the Canal Zone in a way which the medical profession of the country had been striving to effect for many months, and Dr. Rixey felt that the time had now come when an expression of opinion would be acceptable from him. He realized the necessity of giving the sanitary officer a free hand and unrestricted facilities, and he believed, moreover, it was due the dignity of his profession, with entire propriety and justice, and was demanded as a prerequisite to efficiency, that the Chief Sanitary Officer be made a member of the Canal Commission. In thus expressing himself to the President he took occasion to mention Col. Gorgas' dissatisfaction with his status and to laud the work being done by the Sanitary Department. The President had seen the highly complimentary letter which the doctor wrote to Colonel Gorgas after his return from the Isthmus and knew how deeply he had been impressed and, therefore, gave ear the more readily to Dr. Rixey in regard to the matter. What weight Dr. Rixey's opinion carried with the President in this instance may never be known, but it is of interest that a few months later the Isthmian Canal Commission was reorganized and that Col. Gorgas was appointed a member. Every one must feel constrained to admit that his influence counted for something in the President's decision to make the indicated change in the constitution of the Commission, and this represents but an example of the useful offices which Dr. Rixey exercised in many good causes outside of his more immediate concerns.

On the return trip from Panama, the question of accommodations for the sick and injured on board battleships was discussed. On the newest ships these accommodations were considered by line officers in general to be too spacious and those on the *Louisiana* took this opportunity of minimum illness on board to invite the attention of Dr. Rixey, in the presence of Mr. Roosevelt, to the size of the compartments assigned to medical department purposes. It is to be said, in this connection, that Dr. Rixey had revolutionized the equipment for the care of the sick and injured on board the ships of the Navy and he had contended for and secured adequate space, but on this occasion he was a little surprised at his own success and unhesitatingly admitted that on that ship under the existing circumstances the allowed spaces did seem over-generous, though he protested any desire, in respect to sick quarters, beyond what was necessary to efficiently care for the probable sick of the designated complement of a given ship or what was proper with due regard for the innumerable other legitimate claims upon space. He did not wish to even seem to be over-reaching his just claims upon the capacity of any ship for the uses of his department—indeed he saw a real danger to substantial progress in any such appearance; but at the same time he knew that in the absence of hospital ships frequent excessive demands would be made upon the sick-bay compartments and in his report for 1907, he addressed this word of caution to the Secretary of the Navy:

> THE PROVISIONS FOR THE CARE OF THE SICK AND INJURED on the ships of the Navy, though intended only for emergency purposes, are generous in point of space, and the equipment of these sick quarters is all that the most fastidious modern standard requires. In further reference to allowed space, however, it must be said that while it has been characterized as "generous," the Bureau is desirous of being understood to use the term only in recognition of the real end for which ships of war are built and of the innumerable other

Hon. Charles J. Bonaparte
Secretary of the Navy, 1905 to 1906

legitimate claims upon space. It was the pressure of these claims at a time of minimum illness which led the Bureau to consider whether the needs of the sick and injured could not be met by a smaller allotment of bunks, and although the possibility of this was conceded and several ships already built, and plans for future construction were altered accordingly, and although the Bureau does not desire more than its proper allowance of space as estimated upon the determined probable per cent of disabled in ordinary times, caution is to be observed that the accommodations for the most promising work of the Medical Department are not too scanty.

The first year of his incumbency as Surgeon General he took up the question of hospital ships and continued to urge their necessity in the Navy with increasing force, year after year. He had not now long to await the realization of his ambition for such an important addition to the resources of his department. It came in February 6, 1908, when the *U. S. S. Relief* was placed in service with a view to its meeting the North Atlantic Fleet on its cruise around the world upon its arrival at Magdalena Bay. The hospital ship was attained in physical being at this time and, what was quite as important, the principle of the right of a medical officer to command was conceded; but not without a bitter fight and unfortunately much feeling among those who had lost in the opposition to Surgeon General Rixey's aims. The events which marked the consideration of this subject and Dr. Rixey's final victory in his long contention were stirring in the extreme and deserve recounting.

It is an interesting fact that during the years which had elapsed since the war with Spain, the proposition for hospital ships never once elicited an expression of denial or even serious doubt as to the desirability and usefulness of such auxiliaries. The prolonged idleness of the hospital ship *Relief* which was equipped at great expense represented no active opposition to hospital ships *per se*, but hung on the point of command, and in spite of the decision which the Secretary of the Navy, Hon. Charles J. Bonaparte, on December 12, 1906, expressed in an endorsement on the Report of the Joint Board of Medical Officers—that "it is expedient to have one hospital ship in commission in time of peace" and that "the Department holds that such a ship, when in commission, should be treated as a floating hospital and, as such, placed under the command of a medical officer," the service continued to be deprived of this important provision.

In the fall of 1907, in anticipation of the Atlantic Fleet's cruise around the world, Surgeon General Rixey realizing that the time had arrived, precipitated the final struggle upon the question, which resulted, among other things, in the resignation of the Chief of the Bureau of Navigation and a long and misguided tirade in the public press upon the subject of hospital ships under the command of medical officers.

The cruise, as projected, represented a specific need for a hospital ship and created occasion for immediate action in the matter. On November 6, 1907, therefore, Surgeon General Rixey addressed the Department of the Navy in a letter which read as follows:

RMP. 113904

WCB-AM
November 6, 1907.

DEPARTMENT OF THE NAVY

BUREAU OF MEDICINE & SURGERY

Sir:

1. Referring to the Department's letter (No. 21095-2) of December 12, 1906, in which it is set forth that it is expedient to have a hospital ship in commission in time of peace, I have the honor to report that the hospital accommodations on the Pacific Coast, as at present constituted, barely suffice for the ordinary requirements of the sick on that station. In view, therefore, of a material increase in the personnel on that station, resulting from the presence of additional ships from the Atlantic Station, in the near future, the Bureau strongly urges that the Hospital Ship *Relief* be commissioned as soon as practicable, so that a floating hospital of 200 additional beds will be available by the time the Atlantic Fleet arrives on the Pacific Station, and thus furnish some relief to a situation which this Bureau views with deep concern. On the Pacific Coast there are only two hospitals, viz: that at Mare Island and that at

Puget Sound. As previously stated, these hospitals barely furnish the necessary accommodations for the sick of the present Pacific Fleet and Station, and for those patients invalided from the Philippines. The problem, therefore, of providing for a very material increase of accommodations for the sick, is urgent, and this Bureau can recommend no better solution of it than is afforded by the commissioning of the *Relief* as a hospital ship.

2. After mature deliberation and having in mind the best interests of the service, this Bureau concurs in the statement made in the Department's letter of December 12, 1906, "that such a ship, when in commission, should be treated as a floating hospital, and, as such, placed under the command of a medical officer, her navigation being controlled by a competent sailing master," and so recommends.

3. With respect to all matters not pertaining to the strictly hospital part of the ship, this Bureau is of the opinion that the status and maintenance of a hospital ship should be that of other naval auxiliaries, with a naval medical officer in general command, as the responsible individual. The maintenance of such a ship, when commissioned, will be the same as that now provided by law for naval auxiliaries. In the event of the *Relief* being placed in commission as a hospital ship, it is recommended that orders pertaining to this ship be issued by the Bureau of Navigation after reference to and on recommendation of the Bureau of Medicine and Surgery.

4. The Bureau is of the opinion that the presence of this ship in active commission will provide, not only additional hospital accommodations, which in view of the proposed cruise of the Atlantic Fleet, will be urgently needed on the Pacific Coast, but by accompanying the Fleet in all of its larger movements and relieving it of cases that at present have often to be kept on board, will conduce to the greater efficiency of the Fleet, and provide a means of transport of patients destined for shore hospitals, and often relieve the Commander-in-Chief of the necessity of diverting a regular man-of-war for the purpose. The functions of such a ship in time of war would, of course, be greatly enlarged.

5. In peace time a hospital ship accompanying the squadron would be available for the treatment of all the more serious cases of accident and disease occurring in such squadron; they would then receive better attention than is possible in a man-of-war; infectious cases would be isolated and lunatics would have the temporary accommodation suitable to their condition.

6. All the necessary arrangements for the commissioning of this ship have been considered by this Bureau in advance, and her stores are either on board or at the Navy Yard, Mare Island, in readiness to be placed on board at short notice.

7. As it is the Bureau's wish that the *Relief* be in full working order, and available for active work with the Fleet on its arrival on the Pacific Station, it is deemed advisable, on account of possible delay arising in connection with the necessary work under other Bureaus, to make timely recommendation to this end, and to respectfully urge that the Department's directions for placing her in commission be promptly given.

Very respectfully,

(Signed) P. M. Rixey,
Surgeon General, U. S. Navy.

To:
The Secretary of the Navy.

He was not content with this appeal, however, and, besides addressing the Department in several other strong letters, pushed the matter energetically in other directions, urging the employment of the *Relief* in accordance with the decision announced by Secretary Bonaparte and under the conditions which he laid down as appropriate. Surgeon General Rixey made no effort to have the point at issue brought before the President, feeling that it should properly be decided by the head of the Navy Department and would, if all arguments were duly considered, be decided in his favor; but at the same time it was his judgment, based upon the apparent rising tenor of the dispute, that it would ultimately reach the President and he, therefore, asked that, in that event, he be allowed a fair hearing.

Dr. Rixey had for a number of years been the dean of Bureau chiefs, and, according to military precedence and custom, it was his privilege, as such, to receive any one of the others, who sought a conference with him, in his own office. In this way, it happened that soon after Dr. Rixey had determinedly reopened the subject by letter, Rear Admiral Willard H. Brownson took occasion to call upon him in his office with a view to its amicable settlement by arrangement between the two bureaus and without controversy. He proposed Dr. Rixey's withdrawal from the contention for hospital ships under the conditions indicated. The doctor replied that he could not comply with the Admiral's request as he believed the best interest of the service demanded that his contention should be sustained by the Department. He regretted personally having to oppose Admiral Brownson whom he had always admired and looked upon as a very dear friend. However, the question of hospital ships was not a trifling idea with the doctor. From his point of view and according to his way of thinking, it represented a vital step in the evolution of resources for the care of sick and injured, in keeping with the scientific standard of the times, in recognition of the humane aims of the Geneva Convention and The Hague Conferences, and in obedience to the demands of a sovereign people for adequate government provision that those who are stricken in its service may be afforded the best care and the utmost assurance of recovery. He was always willing to compromise honorably—he was always willing to stop and wait when there was good reason to postpone a step in advance; but he was not willing to abandon the possibility of this splendid material provision, as he was asked to do. He could not have accepted the terms of Rear Admiral Brownson's proposition without breaking faith with his own honest conception of a real need or sacrificing a definite and tangible benefit to an uncertain future. The interview ended with these two officers having a mutual understanding that the issue would be fought unfalteringly and vigorously to a conclusion. In this way the active war between the line and the medical corps over hospital ships was instituted.

The Surgeon General made a detailed statement of his desires with regard to the manning and operation of the *Relief*, and the plans for carrying these into effect were pushed to the extent that Surgeon Charles F. Stokes was ordered north with a view to his taking comand of the ship. Against this course Admiral Brownson protested, on the ground that it was contrary to practice and illegal and would interfere seriously with discipline. Thus the battle raged back and forth up to the 23d of December when the climax was reached. The Secretary of the Navy had balked the decision of so important a matter, and it was laid before the President, who promptly directed Admiral Brownson and Surgeon General Rixey to appear before him simultaneously and present their respective sides of the case in person. For the information of those who are disposed to think that favoritism influenced Mr. Roosevelt to overrule Admiral Brownson, it should be said that this officer enjoyed possibly as close a friendship with Mr. Roosevelt as did Surgeon General Rixey. Admiral Brownson had been a house guest at Sagamore Hill and was frequently at the White House in a social and unofficial way, so that there is no ground for ascribing a bias on account of personal relation. Moreover, Mr. Roosevelt as Assistant Secretary of the Navy and as President, while eminently broadminded, had always, and perhaps naturally, showed, if partisan at all, a line leaning, and his decision in favor of hospital ships was, it is only fair to presume, therefore, based on the merits of the case as presented by the exponents of the two sides. Admiral Brownson, it is understood, offered no arguments that could carry any weight before a judge who exacted such sound reason, as Mr. Roosevelt might have been expected to do, whereas Surgeon General Rixey offered innumerable substantial arguments in support of his contention. The case was going against Admiral Brownson and in the hope of strengthening his contention he actually weakened it by interjecting the complaint, which the President knew to be unfounded, that Dr. Rixey was responsible for the diversion of some of the Ships of the Fleet, in its cruise to the South, for the purpose of landing a number of seriously sick men. Finally, Surgeon General Rixey cited various precedents, and among these pointed out that the Medical Department of the Army had for years enjoyed the advantage of provision for hospital ships under its direct control. He expressed his desire for similar provision in the Navy and the President, turning to Secretary Metcalf, directed that this be allowed. Thus the discussion ended, and it was following this action that Rear Admiral Brownson tendered his resignation of the office of Chief of the Bureau of Navigation, much to the regret of Admiral Rixey. There is no need to dwell upon the promptness with which this resignation was accepted. It is enough that Surgeon General Rixey had won the day in the interest of humanity and service efficiency as he saw it. For weeks the public press—both lay and medical—was full of serious and amusing comments on the subject. Cartoons appeared and illustrated jokes were published in the funny papers, with hospital ships commanded by Medical Officers as the theme. All sorts of opinions were expressed and results predicted, as much to the entertainment of Dr. Rixey as anybody else; but fortunately for the reputation of public intelligence, public utterance was not all on one side and such papers as "The Outlook" and "Collier's Weekly," together with medical journals, took a rational view of the innovation and printed editorials, applauding the persistence of Dr. Rixey in a good cause and commending the decision of Mr. Roosevelt.

Congress, as was to be expected, interested itself in the matter somewhat and made a feint at some action, but opinion was pretty much divided and it seemed only fair that the hospital ship should be given a trial, and the matter gradually faded from existence as a topic for discussion. Indeed, the successful operation of even such a makeshift as the *Relief* effectually silenced most opposition and even won advocates from members of the enemy's camp.

The hope was entertained in some circles and taken up feebly in the press that the new administration would reverse Mr. Roosevelt's decision, but contrary to such hopes and actual predictions, the Attorney General, on November, 1909, adjudged the legality of Mr. Roosevelt's decision, and Mr. Taft promptly thereafter affirmed Mr. Roosevelt's action by approving the detail of a medical officer to command another Hospital Ship, the *Solace*, for service with the Atlantic Fleet.

Another incident in the association of Dr. Rixey and the President, which occurred in the last year of Mr. Roosevelt's administration deserves to be recounted. It is the one-hundred-and-four-mile ride which they accomplished in a single day accompanied by Captain Archibald W. Butt, U. S. Army, and Dr. Cary T. Grayson, U. S. Navy, each having a relay of four horses to complete the trip.

President Roosevelt was contemplating an order similar to that affecting the Army, requiring all officers of the Navy to take an annual physical test by way of determining their physical efficiency. In the Army, officers of and above the rank of Major, except Major-Generals, were, in general, required to either walk 50 miles or ride 100 miles in three consecutive days once a year, and the question arose as to what should constitute a proper test for the Navy. There was a great deal of discussion over this point and a scheme was finally drafted in the Bureau of Navigation and submitted to the President. Its provisions, however, were not approved and the whole matter was referred to Surgeon General Rixey by Mr. Roosevelt, with directions to prepare a scheme. In connection with the study of the problem, it occurred to Dr. Rixey to try the Army test himself, but instead of covering the hundred miles in three days, to do it in one day. He announced his purpose to Mr. Roosevelt, who immediately determined to take the ride with him, much to the regret and anxiety of Dr. Rixey, for he feared that some accident might befall. The doctor made every effort to dissuade the President, even appealing to the influence of Mrs. Roosevelt; but in spite of all that was said or done, he remained firm in his determination. Maps were secured and arrangements for the relays were made, and, on January 13, 1909, at 3:40 a. m., the party rode away from The White House. The ride was to be to Warrenton, Va., and return, and after its completion out of kindly remembrance of his reception in Warrenton, President Roosevelt presented to the town a large and most excellent copy of a painting of himself by Melchor, in the same costume in which he made the ride. In transmitting this picture to the city of Warrenton, through Medical Director J. C. Wise, U. S. Navy, the president wrote in part: "We reached

Warrenton at 12 noon, took lunch, were most warmly and hospitably greeted by the people of Warrenton, and at 1:20 p. m. again mounted our horses and started back, reaching The White House at 8:40. The last thirty miles we rode with a driving storm in our faces."

The same picture was given to Dr. Rixey by the President as a souvenir of their ride together, and in the President's handwriting under the picture are the words:

> "To Surgeon General P. M. Rixey in memory of the 100 mile ride from his friend, Theodore Roosevelt, January 13, 1909. This was the costume I wore on the ride."

He also wrote kind letters to the other members of the party. To Captain Butt he wrote as follows:

THE WHITE HOUSE
WASHINGTON

January 15, 1909.

My dear Captain Butt:

I desire that this letter be filed with your record. On January 13th, you rode with me from The White House, Washington, to the inn at Warrenton, Virginia, and back, a distance which we have put at ninety-eight miles, but which I am informed was one hundred and four. We covered the distance between 3:40 in the morning and 8:40 in the evening, including an hour and a quarter at Warrenton and five or ten minutes at each of the places where we changed horses. We rode first to Fairfax Court-House, where we changed, getting on fresh horses; then to a farm-house near Bull Run, where we again changed; then to Buckland, where we changed again; and then to Warrenton, using the same horses back to Buckland. On the return trip we thus covered each stage with the horses we had used upon it going out. After the first stages the horses were ordinary cavalry horses, and two of yours were hard animals to ride, which materially added to the fatigue of the trip so far as you were concerned. The conditions of the weather and of the roads materially increased the difficulty of the ride, for from Centerville in, a blinding sleet storm drove in our faces, and from Fairfax Court-House in, we were in pitch darkness going over the frozen roads through the sleet storm.

You and Dr. Rixey alternately led the way and set the pace. You as well as the rest of the party returned in fine condition, convincing me of the fact that the test provided for the army and navy was not excessive.

Sincerely yours,

(Signed) THEODORE ROOSEVELT.

Captain Archibald W. Butt,
Aide-de-Camp to the President,
Washington, D. C.

A true Copy:
P. C. STEVENS,
Major, Paymaster, U. S. Army.

The writer has tried to outline some of the particular events in Dr. Rixey's career as Surgeon General of the U. S. Navy and in his relation to the occupants of The White House. It was impossible to go into more detail with the information at hand, though it is fully realized how much of interest has been omitted. At this time, though much was still to happen, he was approaching the end of his second term in office. The expiration of what Mr. Roosevelt chose to regard as his second term of office was also near at hand. In view of the warm friendship which existed between these two men and the simultaneousness of their work for betterment in their respective spheres of influence, it may not seem an effort to unduly exalt the services of Dr. Rixey by associating them in the remark that there was reason to look back upon the past seven and more years with entire satisfaction. Mr. Roosevelt was on his African hunting trip when Dr. Rixey was retired from active duty, and a letter telling him of it reached him on the Ibis on the Nile May 19, 1910, to which Mr. Roosevelt replied:

"I was very sorry that you were not continued but at any rate, dear doctor, you have rendered a very great service, and after all, next to one's domestic life, the thing best worth while having in life is the consciousness of having done one's full duty in an important position."

It is now timely to review the achievements of Dr. Rixey's administration as Surgeon General of the U. S. Navy. With a wise and comprehending mind, he conducted the affairs of the Medical Corps in a manner which has made its mark upon the history of the service. Think what it embraces! Any ignorance is inexcusable—not of the individual reforms accomplished, but of the real extent and meaning of the improvements he has effected. The keenness of our recollection of past conditions promptly fades and often leaves us without standards of comparison, so that those who are benefitting today by the work of Dr. Rixey little appreciate how much better is the present state of affairs than the old and how much better they are cared for in times of illness than their predecessors. A silent and perhaps unconscious appreciation of this would seem to be expressed in the fact that, instead of shunning naval hospitals when sick or in need of operation, officers now actually seek treatment in naval hospitals.

The keynote of Dr. Rixey's success was his ability to bring things to pass, not alone by his own energies necessarily but by surrounding himself with able assistants who would be enthusiastic and sympathetic in helping him to consummate the reforms and improvements which he had conceived. He often very modestly said that, if it had not been for the able support which he received from his immediate assistants, he would have been able to do very little, and, in the desire to thus fortify himself, he displayed excellent judgment and great discrimination. He was always most careful in his selection of those to be closely associated with him and thereafter was most cautious in his relations with them until their ability and loyalty had been tried. These once proven, however, his confidences were easily and liberally given, so that mutual understanding was quickly established and common effort exerted. He was fertile of ideas and was thorough in the sense that he made himself familiar with every detail of any kind of duty he undertook; but, in view of the many demands upon his time, he lacked opportunity, and to a certain extent, the taste and temperament to work out the prosaic details of the various administrative projects which he instituted. He showed a compensating genius, however, in his selection of assistants and always reviewed their work minutely and supplemented it by vitally important amendments borne of a quick perception of subtle defects, and an intuitive estimation of relative values, for he at once recognized and separated the salient and unimportant.

The columns of the Army & Navy Register for December 18, 1908, contain the following brief appraisal of Dr. Rixey's administration at the head of the medical department of the Navy, in connection with comments upon the merits of the last annual report of his second term:

> "The annual report of the Surgeon General of the Navy is a document which, as usual, possesses an interest beyond that of the average official expression. It shows commendable progress in the administration of Surgeon General Rixey since he has been chief of the Bureau of Medicine & Surgery. He has brought the naval medical corps to a high state of efficiency; he has placed the work of ship sanitation and hospital service on a basis which is, in all respects, an effectively modern system. The report shows certain needs of the medical branch, such as improved promotion for the commissioned officers, a more attractive situation for the acting assistant surgeons and the assistant surgeons, the provision of dentists, and the development of a medical reserve corps. The report is otherwise notable for the highly interesting discussion in narrative form of numerous details of surroundings, dress, food, and habits of those connected with the Naval service, the health of which has been amply protected. There is no getting away from the appreciable contribution to naval efficiency rendered by the naval medical corps on shore and at sea."

From the very beginning of his administration, he strove for the efficiency of the whole naval establishment, as far as was possible. He was on the alert to meet current needs and in undertaking reforms was guided by highest standards and a spirit of progress and foresight. He was always ready to consider suggestions and sought assistance in every promising direction. Besides employing every opportunity to make material improvements, effort was made to place individuals where best suited, and in general he tried to use the forces at his command to the utmost advantage. All the principal old hospitals of the service and their equipment were enlarged and modernized in every particular, including those at New York, Norfolk, Mare Island, and Philadelphia; new modern hospitals were built at Annapolis, Washington, Canacao, Yokohama, and near Chicago, on Lake Michigan, a splendid sanatorium for the care of the tubercular sick of the Navy was established and rapidly developed; new hospitals were planned and are in process of construction, at Portsmouth, N. H., Boston, Mass., and Newport, R. I.; plans were prepared for a new hospital in Hawaii and a sanatorium at Baguio, P. I. At many of the above, suitable living quarters for medical officers were provided, and in connection with all of them, plans were prepared for similar and other accessory buildings, such as nurses' quarters, the construction of some of which was under way before the end of Dr. Rixey's second term; provisions for the care of the sick and injured aboard ship, in point of space and equipment, were perfected in accordance with the scientific standard of the times; a naval medical school for the training of recent appointees and the instruction of older medical officers, subject to periods of isolation from professional opportunities, was established and developed in material provisions and curriculum; a training school for the instruction of hospital corps men in the duties of nursing to the end that they might become competent assistants in the care of the sick and injured, was established and developed to a high state of usefulness; the pay of the hospital corps was increased and, as a direct consequence, it was possible to increase the efficiency of that important Corps; a corps of women nurses was authorized and organized; the recognition of the need of hospital ships and their control by the medical department was secured; a quarterly medical bulletin, as a means of periodically communicating information of special value to the physical welfare of the Naval personnel, was created; two editions each of a book of detailed instruction to medical officers and a hospital corps drill manual, for the guidance of the members of the medical department in the performance of other important duties, were given to the service; a book on naval hygiene, which will be valuable to the service as the first complete guide for safeguarding the health of the sailor, was written and published under the direction of the Bureau; definite status with proper authority for the medical department and increased rank and numbers in the Medical Corps were attained; a liberal revision of the supply tables, with improvement and extention of supply depots was effected, a reorganization in the administration of hospitals, and the creation of the office of general inspector of hospitals were accomplished; plans for the further development of the medical department were clearly outlined and, at the time of his retirement from office, were ready to be carried into effect as rapidly as circumstances would permit or authority was granted.

Among the needed additional resources of the medical department which Surgeon General Rixey worked for are:

> "The reorganization of the Hospital Corps; a Corps of Dental Surgeons; a Medical Reserve Corps; two specially constructed hospital ships; and a modification of the laws relating to fleet surgeons."

As regards future construction, the plans which were prepared by him anticipate the needs of the service for many years to come.

With reference to the book on "Naval Hygiene," above mentioned, the New York Medical Journal said: "It is a real pleasure to review this book, not only because of its intrinsic merit, but of the evidence it furnishes of that general spirit of admirable professional zeal which animates the medical department of our Navy under its present efficient Surgeon General, Dr. Rixey."

An administration under which all these things were brought about was certainly a good one, to speak faint praise, and Dr. Rixey's record is eminently praiseworthy. Mistakes he unquestionably made, for he was humanly fallible; enemies he had, for no decided and strong characters are without them; but no candid review of his administration can deny it a prominent place in those pages of history which tell of the splendid evolution of the U. S. Navy. The victory in the long and persistent contention for hospital ships would alone make it memorable. The establishment and development of the U. S. Naval Medical School marks it hardly less strongly, though more quietly. But, perhaps, the amazing improvement in the professional standing of the medical department of the Navy is the most remarkable feature of it all. Individual professional attainment was encouraged and the highest degree of service was facilitated by every material provision, with results which justify the conviction that Dr. Rixey did not hope or plan in vain. Everything combines to make his administration at the head of the medical department of the Navy stand out distinctive from all previous ones, and the naval hospitals and other medical department institutions all over the country and at outlying stations are monuments to his energy, efficiency and large conception of the usefulness of his branch of the Navy. He was a master and warm adherent of proper economy and untarnished honor in his financial responsibilities, but a sworn enemy to red tape and niggardliness. He was liberal in outfitting medical officers for the work they might be called upon to do and held them responsible for the proper performance of their duties; but on the other hand he was quick to recognize merit and stood ready to give praise where praise was due. There are many lessons which Surgeon General Rixey's administration teaches and among these is the value of tenacity of purpose when the purpose is laudable.

This chapter of his career could not be better concluded than by quoting the words of appreciation published in the Army & Navy Journal for November 21, 1908:

> "Presley M. Rixey became Surgeon General of the Navy on February 10, 1902. At the time of his appointment to the head of the Medical Corps, he was a medical inspector, the second of that rank to be so honored, and he entered upon his duties with splendid ambitions for the medical department and a clearly-defined policy, which he has pursued with tenacity of purpose and consistency. From the first moment of his incumbency, he has manifested a determination to make his

department stand out as a vital example of a practical and productive organization in the Naval establishment and we are constrained to believe that he has succeeded with signal merit. So extensive have been the accomplishments and so noteworthy the progress in every important concern of the medical department of the Navy during his regime that it may well be said he stands pre-eminent among Surgeons-General of the Navy and that the development of the medical department under his leadership should be a gratifying, though silent, reward for the energy and enthusiasm with which he has striven for the best interests of all. It would seem impossible to ever entirely satisfy the ambition of a man such as he is, for the world does not stand still, but it is at least true that he has more than realized his early dreams and guided the medical branch of the service to a respected and proud position in the professional world."

CHAPTER VII

THE OFFICIAL AND THE MAN

THE composite of the official and the man is difficult to analyze, for it presents a complex personality, embodying almost irreconcilable elements. To those who had but a casual acquaintance with Dr. Rixey, therefore, either in his official capacity or out of office (and casual acquaintances usually saw but one side of his life), he must have been somewhat of an enigma, for his apparent characteristics under these different circumstances were as radically different as it is possible to conceive. In contemplating his career one such set of acquaintances must have been led to wonder that a man so reserved in manner, so firm in opinion, and so vigorous in the prosecution of his various concerns could have so many warm friends; and the other set must have equally been led to wonder that a man so simple, gentle, warm hearted, and, in many ways, diffident, could have accomplished so much at the head of a large department of the Navy, in the administration of which diplomacy, force, and executive ability were required. This very changefulness according to circumstances was itself a characteristic—albeit an acquired one, born of an introspective consciousness of his kindly impulsiveness, and nurtured as a protection and as an insurance to single-minded fidelity to service interests. It is this characteristic which dissolves the composite into its component parts and makes the task of his biographers comparatively simple, for his intimate acquaintances knew and comprehended each side of his make-up and to them the official and the man were entirely reconcilable. As his complex character was manifested in the manner and acts of his life under changing circumstances, so is it best to consider him in the pages of this sketch. Suffice it to say in general that his continuous official and intimate personal relations with the occupants of the White House during two administrations (covering a period of over ten years) and his lasting friendly associa-

Hon. Elihu Root

Secretary of War, 1899 to 1904 and Secretary of State, 1905 to 1908

tions with numerous distinguished men and women strongly attest the fact that he was an official and man of sterling worth. His good fortune in being so situated as to hear and witness the delivery of many of the magnificent utterances of two far-seeing Presidents and of the high-minded, patriotic men by whom they were surrounded, and to share the hospitality and some of the honors of which they were the recipients, while on their various tours and elsewhere—all contributed greatly toward the development and shaping of his character. Moreover, in his active career he knew every prominent man in official circles, and many members of Mr. McKinley's and Mr. Roosevelt's official families, and the diplomatic corps, including Mr. Hay, Mr. Root, Mr. Bonaparte, Mr. Knox, Mr. Whitelaw Reid, Mr. Metcalf, Mr. Shaw, Mr. Wilson, Mr. Cortelyou, Mr. Loeb, etc., are counted among the men with whom he enjoyed pleasant and beneficial intercourse. He also prized a cordial and extensive friendship among the leading men of his profession, but of all these the affiliation which has existed between Dr. Howard Kelly and Dr. Rixey is perhaps the strongest and warmest. He greatly admires Dr. Kelly for his personal qualities and ability and there is ample reason to believe that this feeling is fully reciprocated. Dr. and Mrs. Rixey revel in telling of numerous entertaining episodes which they have experienced and speak feelingly of the delightful intercourse which they enjoyed amidst this circle of cultured people, and the autograph likeness of their distinguished friends and souvenirs of important occasions, with which they are surrounded in their home, are proof against forgetfulness. Indeed, they are constant reminders of a very agreeable past and a promise that the future of their lives will be filled with the most pleasant recollections and wholesome companionship.

As a physician and an official, Dr. Rixey was widely known and appreciated. During his long service he has filled many positions with eminent fidelity and pronounced ability and was generally regarded as a most able and efficient officer. He was an active member of the Association of Military Surgeons and served successively through the various vice-presidential chairs prior to his election as President of that splendid organization at the Atlanta meeting in October of 1908. With reference to this event, "The Military Surgeon" of November, 1908, published an editorial congratulating the Association upon the fact that "The inevitable change consequent upon the progress of time has brought to the head of the Association one of its most distinguished and capable members in the person of Rear Admiral Presley Marion Rixey. * * * * * The accession of Admiral Rixey to the Presidency of the Association augurs good fortune for the organization, which is sure to be developed and advanced by the sagacity, tact, and ability which has characterized all the official acts of his successful career."

In accepting the office, Surgeon General Rixey said, in part:

> "I wish, as the representative of the Medical Corps of the Navy, to thank you for the honor conferred upon that branch of the service, and to express my appreciation of the personal compliment. * * *
>
> "I am deeply sensible of the responsibilities devolving upon the incumbent of this office, and in that consciousness I assure you that, so far as lies within my power, I shall, in the future as I have in the past, endeavor to do everything to promote the interests and welfare of this growing and important Association of Military Surgeons.
>
> "No one who has intelligently watched the trend of the times and given serious thought to the full meaning of medical advance—both within its own scientific sphere of activity and in relation to human enterprise the world over, particularly the development of the art of war on land and at sea and the growing complexity of life—can fail to realize the incalculable value of such an Association. The power for greatest benefit from the truths which medical science has given and is daily giving us rests upon the condition of cooperation in their application, and in no field of endeavor is this requirement more urgent than in the medico-military service, in which the first duty of those charged with the supervision of health conditions in the land and sea forces is that of the hygienist. Problems of preventive medicine, though the same in principle

everywhere, differ in many respects, as between civil and military life, in their practical applicability, and the dictates of sanitary science must be adapted to the varying conditions of special services. What more essential provision, therefore, than this annual gathering of representative medical men who have interests should in the very nature of things, be impossible, for no matter what the peculiar interests of the various factors of this organization may be, the very foundation upon which we have builded is community of interest and a greater or less inter-dependence, and we should be growing closer together as time passes. * * *

"Here (at these annual meetings), and through the agency of the Association journal, new ideas are presented and pertinent problems are discussed so that, besides the pleasure and refreshment of professional and social intercourse, there is the salient feature of individual intellectual profit by which each service and the government as a whole benefits immeasurably. The Association of Military Surgeons today wields a potent influence for the nation's welfare, and it is rapidly developing toward the realization of its destiny as a co-ordinating institution of all state and national medico-military organizations, and as a universal school of military medicine and hygiene. It has a splendid future if we will work together in unity of aim for its best possibility, and I entertain the ambition that, during my administration, progress will be no less marked than under the guidance of my esteemed predecessors."

As had been predicted by his friends, he worked untiringly for the welfare of the Association during the year he was at its head and numerous notable reforms were instituted, many of which were carried into effect. The distinctive features of his administration were economy, efficiency, and enthusiasm. Conscientious watchfulness over the finances was exercised and effort was made to order the business concerns of the organization on a sound basis; the increased efficiency and broader usefulness of the Association in fulfilling its purposes was given earnest consideration; and the stability of the Association was greatly fortified by stimulating an enthusiasm in the aims of the organization. The ambitious policy by which Dr. Rixey was animated in administering the affairs of the Association and the excellent results which attended his efforts culminated in the unprecedented success of the annual meeting in October of 1909 in Washington, D. C., at which he presided. The address which he delivered before the assembled delegates and general public in Continental Hall on the evening of October 5th was a notable one. It was referred to in terms of appreciation by both the lay and medical press and not only was it published in full in "The Military Surgeon" for November, 1909, but at the instance of Sir Alfred Keogh, Director General of the Medical Corps of the British Army, who was so impressed that he requested a copy to take back to England with him, and it was published almost simultaneously in the Journal of the Royal Army Medical Corps, Vol. XIII, No. 6, Dec., 1909, pages 695-701. The international trend of the Association was especially noticeable at this meeting to which were accredited an unusual number of foreign delegates, of whom the most distinguished ones, according to their own statements, were lead to attend by their acquaintance with the remarkable services of the President, The Surgeon General of the U. S. Navy, and their desire to meet him. Indeed, the Washington meeting was one of the crowning scenes of his active service in the Navy, and it is one to be remembered for the good it accomplished and because of the many tributes paid to Surgeon General Rixey by foreign delegates as evidencing the wide reputation which he enjoyed. In this connection the remarks of Sir Alfred Keogh on the night of October 5, 1909, in Continental Hall, deserve to be set down in full. He spoke extemporaneously, but at the request of the Assistant Secretary of the Association of Military Surgeons, he kindly wrote down the thoughts expressed that night and forwarded them with the following letter:

War Office,
Whitehall, S. West.
24 November, 1909.

Dear Dr. Bell:

It gives me the greatest possible pleasure to think that my few remarks which I made in the Hall of the Daughters of the Revolution are considered by you and Surgeon General Rixey's friends as worthy of reproduction. I think the enclosed represents exactly what I did say. I know that I have the same thoughts now that I had then.

Surgeon General Rixey's reputation in our Medical Service is great, and I only said what was absolutely correct when I gave expression to my feelings. I retain the pleasantest recollection of my visit to Washington.

Yours sincerely,

(Signed) ALFRED KEOGH.

The enclosure transmitted with this letter is as follows:

Ladies and Gentlemen:

I regard it as a great honor that I have been admitted a member of this Association tonight, for the Association is one of very considerable importance, the progress of which we in England have watched with very great interest. We recognized at the very outset the possibilities which a Society of this description opened up, and are fully aware of the role which the Association might be made to play in the future of Military Medicine. In previous years, it has been our custom to send Delegates to your meetings, and this is in itself a sufficient indication to you of how deep has been our interest in your organization. If this were the proper time and place, I should like to be able to suggest to you how wide a sphere is open for the movement which was initiated in America, when the idea of a meeting of those interested in Military Medicine and Military Surgery was first conceived. As an indication of my own personal recognition of the importance of the Association of Military Surgeons, I may mention the fact that I am here myself tonight, and that instead of delegating an officer of the Royal Army Medical Corps to attend your meeting, I myself have come on this occasion. I have come, and my colleague from the Admiralty has come, because we desire to render a tribute, however slight that tribute may be, to your great President, The Director General of the Medical Branch of the United States Navy. When we heard in England that he was to be the President this year, we felt that it was impossible for us to do anything less than to cross the Atlantic ourselves to support him in the honourable position which he holds. His reputation in Europe as an Administrator is great. We have watched his work with interest, and it only remained for us to make the personal acquaintance of one of whom you and we have every reason to be proud. It is a special occasion this—when we meet in your beautiful Capital under the leadership of one who has done so much for the cause of Military Medicine.

Dr. James Porter, Director General of the Royal Navy Medical Service, and Colonel G. C. Jones, Director General of the Canadian Medical Service—both strongly seconded all that Sir Alfred Keogh said, and the former assured the audience that "Surgeon General Rixey is an inspiration toward the attainment of all that is best among the members of the medical service of the Royal Navy." In a letter of courtesy to Mrs. Rixey, following his return to England, he expressed himself further as follows:

Admiralty, S. C.
November 16, 1909.

My dear Mrs. Rixey:

Please do me the honour to accept a trifling memento in the shape of a fan which I am sending you from the Army & Navy stores here—a very small mark of my appreciation of your unbounding kindness and hospitality during my recent visit to your beautiful Capital.

Your distinguished husband proved to be all my fancy had painted him, and much more besides. I am proud to have in him a personal friend for life.

I can never forget my splendid week in Washington, and the many warm hearted people it was my privilege to meet there.

We are now shivering over fires here.

Kindest regards to you and the Surgeon General, and believe me, always,

Yours very sincerely,
(Signed) J. PORTER.

Major General Cladio Sforza, Director-General of the Medical Service of the Italian Army, also addressed a letter of courtesy to Mrs. Rixey.

At the close of the exercises the following resolutions were passed:

RESOLVED: That the thanks of the Association are extended,

1. To Medical Director Boyd and the Committee of Arrangements for the judicious and ample preparations made for this meeting;

2. To General Harries and the officers of the National Guard of the District of Columbia for their interest and assistance in furthering the objects of the meeting;

3. To Mrs. Rixey and her charming associates of the Ladies' Committee for the delightful hospitalities extended by the ladies accompanying the members to the meeting;

4. To General and Mrs. George H. Torney for the enjoyable reception tendered by them; to Medical Director Boyd for the bountiful luncheon which he provided for us;

5. To Surgeon General and Mrs. Presley M. Rixey for the many courtesies and unbounded hospitalities evidenced all through the meeting, and in particular in connection with the reception of the foreign delegates at their town house and the delightful lawn party at their country seat;

6. To the commanding officer, troop and battery commanders at Fort Myer for the instructive and interesting exhibition drill;

7. To Surgeon General Wyman and the officers of the U. S. Revenue Cutter *Apache* for the courtesies of the trip down the Potomac;

8. To the retiring President, Surgeon General Presley M. Rixey, for the able manner in which he has conducted the affairs of the Association during the past year;

9. To the Washington Chamber of Commerce for their generous assistance;

10. To the manager of the New Willard Hotel for the many facilities generously extended us;

11. To the press of Washington for the interest displayed in advancing the objects of the Association;

12. To the many other public-spirited friends who have contributed so freely to the success of this meeting.

When Grant, in the earlier part of his military career, was assailed by captious and hostile criticism, Lincoln simply disposed of it all by saying: "I can't spare this man. He fights."

Thoughts of this character must have occurred to many, particularly in the Medical Corps of the Navy and throughout the Medical profession, when in the latter part of 1909, the question of a successor arose, and as they reflected upon the controversy over the hospital ship. An aggressive administration for the uplift of the medical department and the benefit of the whole service closed when he retired from the office of Surgeon General and it devolves upon his successor to carry on the good work which he planned and which he has expressed in the following terse paragraph: "My aim is not the aggrandizement of my Corps but its preparation to fully and creditably discharge the duties which may devolve upon it, no matter what the emergency. I do not desire to trespass beyond the bounds of propriety in strengthening the resources of the Medical Department and in furthering its usefulness in helping to advance the effectiveness of the Navy as an institution upon which the Government would inevitably place great dependence in the event of a national crisis. If the Medical Department is to be held accountable, as it should be, for the consequences of its work, adequate facilities must be provided, the special training of medical officers must be recognized and they must be given proper authority within their legitimate field of operation. We can afford no hesitancy in the contention for this principle."

This was the keynote of all his efforts in behalf of the branch of the service which he represented, and he made no compromise with what he believed to be right and reasonable. In pushing his plans to perfection he was always open to conviction, but he was not influenced by the interposition of mere traditions between himself and the goal toward which the actual needs of the times lead him, as a step in what he believed to be the necessary course of evolution. The essential characteristic of his administration is that it has been devoted to the welfare of the whole service and not the narrow benefit of his branch of the service, and though opinion may honestly differ as to ways and means, there can be no division of opinion about the ends achieved. His successor's task is made easier by what has gone before. "Mr. Roosevelt was an ardent believer in the necessity of a dominant sea power and in the maintenance of our military efficiency at its highest" and his clear view of what was being accomplished toward this desirable end in the medical department of the Navy during his administration undoubtedly lead him to reappoint Dr. Rixey to the office of Surgeon General. The friendship which existed between these two men may in part be accounted for by the fact that they were made of similar mettle. However that may be, it is because of such men as Dr. Rixey that our country's Navy has excited such wide and unfeigned admiration and respect.

His relations and well-wishers for whom this little sketch is written should be satisfied with the public opinion of his merit. We know men who do not like him who, nevertheless, cannot help admitting that he has done inestimable good for the service. His career was typically American. He had the usual hard wrought youth; he made his own way in the world; he prepared himself for a profession; he never compromised with his convictions for the sake of immediate profit; he believed in his capacity to accomplish things, and he pushed forward with determination. He made some mistakes, as any man of such impulse and energy as his is sure to make, but he had the strength of character and judgment to correct such mistakes by word of mouth or remedial action. He made sharp discrimination between official and social relations—a strict but usually kindly disciplinarian in office, with the good of the service as his incentive, and, though sometimes a little severe, perhaps, he held the devotion of those under him, for they knew that they could rely on his sympathy and support in the hour of their need; a genial gentleman, a warm-hearted friend, and a cordial host, true to the traditions of his native state, when out of harness. Those who knew him well and with whom he was associated in official and business relations, testify to his absolute integrity, and his unflinching courage in the face of difficulties, from which his life was far from being exempt. His personal attributes were of corresponding high character, and his genial and sunny disposition and broad charity endeared him to wide circles. A story of distress never failed to awaken his sympathy, but often in official life he was compelled to ignore his tenderest impulses and decide matters on their real merits in respect to public needs and exigencies. Yet, he was incessantly doing something to add to the comfort and happiness of those about him, particularly the less fortunate members of his family. His nature was so buoyant and virile that he was not easily depressed and to the very last he carried on his duties with the enthusiasm and energy characteristic of the well-established stage of his administration—there was no neglect of public affairs or slackening of interest and force and activity which is so often the case with others as the conclusions of their identification with certain duties approaches. Yet, through all, his happiness in his work was not unmixed with a quiet, deep sorrow, incident to the injustice and unkind judgment of some of those to whom he would naturally have looked for appreciation of his work. It was all so petty, however, that it did not weigh heavily or seriously upon him. He was usually able to throw its effect off by his philosophy and will-power, even in susceptible moods and at favorable hours for sombre reflections, and though he rode victorious over ill-founded and unreasonable opposition and criticism, it annoyed him.

Those who were privileged to know him amidst the closest intimacies of his life fully realized his freshness and charm. Dr. Rixey was, indeed, a man of unusually attractive personality. His firm step, erect carriage and commanding—yet, winning expression, and keen, alert, bright eyes were not easily forgotten, for they suggested the power of reserve strength and resourcefulness which were at his command in emergency. He was shrewd in observation, keen of penetration, fertile of original ideas and persistent when he believed himself to be on the right trail, and the long list of his achievements in behalf of progress should not be forgotten in the Navy or by the country. His penetration was sometimes a surprise to his friends and often a source of dissatisfaction to those who knew him less well and who were prepared for the long explanation they considered necessary to the understanding of some matter or device which was to be presented for his consideration. In his quickness of perception and penetration to the true inwardness of things, he liked directness and was impatient of superfluous details, so that when such an interview was suddenly brought to a close, the advocate usually left the doctor's presence with a feeling of having failed to complete his undertaking and unconvinced that the doctor had grasped the subject. As a matter of fact, it rarely happened that he did not fully understand every matter, abstract or material, brought to his attention, and because of this quickness of comprehension he was many times ignorantly and wrongfully accused of lack of interest and of being content with a superficial exposition of a matter. He was never trifling, but now and again some one would, for the above reason, gain the idea that he was, and it was hard to persuade him to the contrary.

His manner was simple and natural, without a suggestion of artificiality, save the caution and self-control with which his native reserve was noticeably heightened when in office. It was, however, difficult for him to entirely suppress his geniality and sense of humor. He was not himself productive of witticisms, but he was keenly appreciative of those emanating from others and always alive to the amusing side of a situation, so that even in his most serious moments a gentle smile would sometimes light his face and give evidence of the ever-present kindly humanity in his character.

Physically, he is tall, some six feet, and his frame large and rugged with the quality of great endurance. His presence—dignified and masterful—yet, combined with a certain blandness of manner, always inspired the respect of those who served him and his farm hands knew him to be kind to man and beast, though firm in his management. He liked to watch his farm hands at work, but frequently took a hand himself and set the pace, thus increasing the respect due him as a master by demonstrating his own capacity and ability to do the work required. He understood the nature of the negro thoroughly, and knew how to manage him, and the members of this race with whom he had to deal on his several farms in Virginia were well aware that he would brook no "nonsense." He was acquainted with the vices of the negro but at the same time was not unappreciative of his virtues, and he often spoke of the old colored mammy who had been his nurse when a child, in terms of the gentlest affection. No false prejudice ever influenced him in his relations to this race. He estimated each one at his true worth and treated him accordingly, but never used the misfortune of color as a basis for action—an attitude which was clearly expressed in his remarks, as President of the Association of Military Surgeons, when, during the Washington meeting, the question of admitting a negro to membership in the organization came up.

As stated elsewhere in this sketch, he disliked to speak in public, but when called upon to do so extemporaneously, his words were brief, well selected and to the point, spoken slowly and, if his interest had been aroused, with force. His voice tones were light, however, and, in delivering a written address—and he usually spoke from paper—his words would become muffled by his heavy mustache and be inaudible to all except those near him, unless he took especial care to speak slowly and distinctly. It was to improve his delivery in this direction that he often rehearsed his speeches aloud and read them over and over again until familiar with them beyond the possibility of nervousness or excitement. It was in the capacity of public speaker alone that he was somewhat ill at ease—yet, he accepted numerous invitations to take the rostrum from a sense of duty to the branch of the Navy which he represented. His handwriting was well formed and distinctive, but somewhat difficult to read. Indeed, he was himself often puzzled to read what he had written after a short lapse of time, but the substance was always worth the effort as his various official letters and published writings serve to indicate.

With the many widely placed interests which engaged his attention and the incessant demands upon his time—official, professional, and in a business way, his life was literally a mad rush. None but a man of good habits and a taste for healthful physical diversion, to balance his mental activity, could have survived the strain and retired from office with almost infinite powers for the future as he did. The foresight which he exhibited in administering an important branch of the Navy was equally remarkable with regard to the future value of real estate in and about Washington, and served him well in making investments. In other respects also his business judgment was good and he conducted his business affairs with an astuteness quite uncommon among professional men.

His first home in Washington was situated at 909 16th Street, N. W., quite as near the White House as it was possible to find a suitable residence, though before buying the small house that was standing on that site, he and Mrs. Rixey had lived, first, at the Hamilton Hotel, on the corner of 14th and K Streets, and, then, with Admiral English, Dr. Rixey's father-in-law, in the house which he built at 1518 K Street, Northwest. Later, when Dr. Rixey went to sea, he rented his house at 909 16th Street, and he and Mrs. Rixey occupied this old house again for a short while upon his return from sea duty, and then tore it down and built a new one. During its construction, he lived in Admiral McCalla's home at the corner of 20th Street and Massachusetts Avenue, Northwest. The new house was completed in 1889, when the Rixeys moved in, and here they resided continuously until 1906, except for the summer seasons spent at their country house in Virginia. At this time, November, 1906, they moved into the house Admiral English had built at 1518 K Street, N. W., which Dr. Rixey had bought from the heirs and remodeled. It is worthy of note that, in the remodeling, he turned the front rooms of the basement floor into an ideal physician's office suite, including reception hall, consulting chamber and operating room, all of which were fitted with the most modern conveniences and medical and surgical equipment. In this he exercised his characteristic foresight in anticipation of the time when he would be free to devote himself entirely to his private practice, and the character of this provision is symbolic of the high grade provisions with which he surrounded the medical officers of the Navy, while Surgeon General, and facilitated their professional work.

During the years of his duty in Washington, he acquired from time to time different farm properties. He now has in all four farms, which he has elected to characterize as "Farm No. 1—Netherfauld Farm," "Farm No. 2—Dairy Farm, near Falls Church," "Farm No. 3—Crystal Spring," "Shreve Farm—also near Falls Church," and "Ben Lomond Farm" of 2,000 acres on the banks of the celebrated "Bull Run." Farm No. 1 is the location of the country home, called "Netherfauld," which is in sight of Washington, overlooking the Potomac. It is a beautiful place and situated on a considerable elevation as it is, commands a magnificent view of the surrounding country. It is of this farm that President Roosevelt spoke, in his note to Mrs. Rixey, quoted elsewhere, and recently Dr. Rixey sold a part of it for the uses of the Washington Golf and Country Club. The doctor is particularly fond of this place where he keeps his fine horses and dogs and shooting traps, and, though he lives there only during the warm season, it is kept open throughout the year for his accommodation. He frequently spends the week-end there or uses it as his headquarters during the game season and, on holidays such as Thanksgiving and Christmas, Dr. and Mrs. Rixey liked to entertain friends or members of their family at luncheon there. It should be said, in passing, that, in true Southern fashion, their table was always most deliciously and beautifully set and that, in general, the hospitality extended was of an informal nature and cordial in the extreme. An invitation to be a guest on any of these occasions was always prized, but a warm welcome was never conditional upon an invitation and the "latch string" was always out. The present house is a neat, two story and basement building added to from time to time. The old house which was on the place when it was bought, was burned down several years ago. It is simple and unpretentious, but thoroughly comfortable. Every moment he spent there was refreshing and invigorating, and he was like a high-spirited colt turned loose in the paddock whenever he got out on his possessions in the country and donned his riding togs or shouldered a gun for a day's hunt or turned his hand to practical farming. Here he could lay aside the cares and annoyances of his work; here he could pursue one or another of the various lines of outdoor work or recreation which he needed and which his love of nature and physical energy suggested; and here he could enjoy the happiness of unrestrained and uninterrupted intercourse with his wife and the coterie of friends by which they delighted to surround themselves.

The doctor was not content that his farms should be merely the means of gratifying a hobby—he was too good a business man for that—and as rapidly as feasible after each separate property had been acquired, it was brought up to a state of productivity. His choice stock of Guernsey cattle was his especial sub-interest and he took great pride in furnishing certain milk dealers of Washington with a clean and wholesome dairy product.

He was not averse to playing his part in Washington society and he and Mrs. Rixey, who was one of the leaders in Washington's fashionable circles, discharged their formal social obligations with grace; but the doctor preferred the free and genial atmosphere of the country and it was there that he disposed of most of his leisure hours in those types of recreation and exercise toward which he inclined. His propensity and need at such times was physical rather than intellectual in order to offset the mental requirements incident to his office, his business ventures and his special professional activities, and he neglected no opportunity to take advantage of that relaxation which meant so much to him in the way of enjoyment and recuperation.

CHAPTER VIII

GENERAL CONSIDERATIONS

THE narration of the events and portrayal of the characteristics of the life contained in the preceding pages of this biographical sketch was undertaken humbly and with many misgivings as to our ability to get at that elusive essence of the individual—the true personality, and to do justice to his career—yet, it was undertaken in the firm belief that the subject was worth the effort—not only in the interest of those nearest and dearest to the doctor, who have great reason to be proud, as relatives, that he has made much of his life and who may well wish to pass the records of his achievements down to their descendants; but in the interest of his many close friends and the members of the service, whom he has so infinitely benefitted by his works and example, and who will ever cherish his memory.

It is believed that the tributes, which his biographers have themselves presumed to pay, are a faithful expression of the feelings entertained by those who know him best and were thus most qualified to speak, and by the subordinates of his department throughout the Navy. It will serve our purposes to here quote from the editorial published in "The Military Surgeon," of January, 1910, which expresses a graceful appreciation of Dr. Rixey's services in contrast with times before he took the reins of administrative responsibility:

> For all of us, particularly those discontented spirits who are prone to be hypercritical of present conditions, it serves a useful purpose to look back occasionally and contemplate the conditions and provisions under which our predecessors performed their duties. It is admitted as a truism that every age has its particular problems and annoyances. Nevertheless, a comparison of the conditions which prevailed in the United States Navy, with respect to the Medical Department during the early part of the nineteenth century and those which exist today, must bring to every thinking man a fair quota of com-

fort. He will find consolation in the fact that there are many things to be thankful for and a reassurance that we of today are performing our duties under conditions which are vastly more in accordance with the standard of the times than were the conditions under which our early predecessors labored.

To give tangibility to our thoughts, let us, for a moment, cogitate upon one or two word pictures, which have been handed down to us from the times which we may regard as almost ancient from the point of view of the very primitiveness of facilities. Dr. William P. C. Barton, United States Navy, in a treatise on "Marine Hospitals," published in 1814, after commenting upon the deplorable state of health upon the frigate "United States" in 1809, continues as follows:

"In this situation, on board of a ship just refitted, commissioned and equipped, I found myself, without half the comforts and necessaries for the sick that the hospital department should have been supplied with; yet this department had been reported as replenished with every requisite article for a cruise of two years, and together with the medicine-chest, had cost the Government fifteen hundred dollars. There were neither beds for the sick, sheets, pillows, pillow-cases, nor night caps—nor was there a sufficiency of wine, brandy, chocolate, or sugar; and that portion which the storeroom contained of these articles was neither pure nor fit for sick men. The medicine-chest was overloaded * * * and choked up with many useless and damaged articles. Such was the state of the medical department of this ship! Upon a representation of it, however, to her Commander—Comdr. Decatur—he generously allowed me all the necessaries I stood in need of, and thus enabled me to administer those comforts to my patients which they so much required. What would have been my situation had the ship immediately proceeded to sea for a cruise of eight or ten months upon my joining her and before I had an opportunity of examining into the condition of the medicine and store chests—which might have been the case, these having been reported as sufficiently furnished? What the consequence would have been must be obvious! The other ships were not better furnished than the one of which I am speaking—and I perpetually heard of complaints on this score.

"What was the cause of these abuses? The want of a regular board of medical commissioners, whose peculiar province it should be to order the proper proportions and quantities of medicine, comforts, and necessaries for the public ships, and who shall have no interest, directly or indirectly, individually or collectively, in the furnishing of articles thus ordered.

"As I was at that time a perfect novice in the routine of ship duty and having then but recently left the Pennsylvania Hospital, an institution in which order, system, and punctuality render the practice of medicine a pleasure, I was overwhelmed with the difficulties I had to encounter in the performance of professional duties, where every species of inconvenience and disadvantage that can be imagined was opposed to the exertions of the surgeon. My feelings revolted from the idea of continuing in such a perplexing and distressing situation, and I became disgusted with the unavailing toil attendant upon ship practice. I communicated my sentiments on this subject unreservedly to my lamented friend, the late Captain Wm. Henry Allen, then first lieutenant of the ship. I ventured, even at that early period of my naval service, to condemn the flagrant irregularities and abuses that I could not believe but existed to a ruinous extent. In my conversation with him I often declared that, if such was always the deplorable condition of sick men on shipboard, I wished no longer to be their medical attendant, for my feelings were every moment in the day subjected to harrassment and pain from contemplating afflictions I was unable to relieve for the mere want of comforts so easily procured on shore. He encouraged me, however, to persevere, and, at the same time that he lamented with me the want of a superintending medical board, he tendered an offer of his assistance in making any arrangements compatible with the internal economy of the ship that I might deem calculated to ameliorate the condition of the sick. I soon found that their situation was susceptible of much relief, even on shipboard—and I was not long concluding that, if proper steps were taken to furnish the ships with sick necessaries of a proper kind, the practice of medicine and surgery in the Navy could be rendered not only more beneficial to the sick, but less offensive to the human feelings of the medical officer. I never lost sight of the opinion I had conceived that the errors of the medical department of the Navy might be easily corrected and its abuses abolished.

"During the term of my sea duty I had many opportunities of seeing other irregularities in this department and the disastrous consequences attending them. These irregularities and abuses are those, the means of correcting and abolishing which I have endeavored to point out. If the propositions and suggestions exhibited in the few pages on these heads that follow the treatise on marine hospitals be thought worthy of adoption, and if, when executed, they shall be found calculated to achieve the object they have in view, I shall esteem the five years I have devoted to the naval service not passed in vain. Or, if the exposition that I have made of the abuses in the medical department shall elicit from an abler and more experienced hand and more feasible or efficient plan for accomplishing the reform and system I have had in view, my labors will be amply remunerated. I have been long enough in the Navy to have its interests much at heart, even if I did not believe (which I certainly do) that its existence is vitally important to our national prosperity and honor. Whatever, therefore, my humble endeavors shall effect towards reforming and systematizing that department, without the efficient and able administration of which the lives of thousands may be jeopardized or lost—whether this be by means that I have here proposed or by inviting the attention of others to the subject—will afford me the liveliest gratification. The labor is arduous, but it is not the toil of Sisyphus:

Dimidium facti, qui coepit habet."

This description should suffice to give the reader some idea of the conditions that obtained under *usual* circumstances—not so long ago but that they should have been immeasurably better. The preparations of the Medical Department for the serious moment of naval action was, if possible, even more crude and less likely to be attended with creditable consequences. Improvements did take place from this time up to the beginning of that last decade through the effort of a few optimistic and energetic spirits like Barton, but the reforms were all too slowly accomplished, and, when the present incumbent entered upon the duties of his office at the head of the Medical Department of the Navy, there was a vast amount of work to be done, if this branch of the service was to fill a respected position as a field of practice in the medical profession.

Let each one who is a part of the Medical Department of the Navy glance about and view the present state of affairs with a spirit of thankfulness that he is serving in this regime, and let the whole medical profession and the people of the country at large come to a full realization that in 1910, as never before, the medical branch of the service is in that state of preparedness which "is vitally important to the efficiency of the naval establishment and to our national prosperity and honor." In a word, the Medical Department of the Navy today conforms in every particular to the scientific standards of the age, in which fact it boasts a characteristic which distinguishes it from all preceding times. The spirit which has been inculcated during this period has been increasingly one of progress, and nothing that could be done to enhance the value of the Medical Department, to strengthen its resources and to advance the individual efficiency of its officers has been neglected.

* * * * * * *

The usefulness of a life thus far so honorably and purposefully and profitably spent is happily not yet done. Dr. Rixey would have appreciated a reappointment to office as a public recognition of his services and a further opportunity to carry out plans which had been projected, and in many cases matured, for future improvements in his department. It is doubtful, however, that in the very nature of such a personality, the hour would ever have been reached when interest and ambition would have lagged, so that from this point of view one time was as good as another in respect to his retirement from office and active service; but, from the point of view that he still represented a high potentiality of valuable service, his retirement was a great loss to the Navy, though we feel the utmost confidence in his assurance that he will always maintain an interest in the standing of the medical department and stand ready to contribute to its welfare by every means open to him. He made no effort whatever to be reappointed beyond making it known, in a letter to President Taft, that he wished to be regarded as a receptive candidate, feeling that anything like a canvass of his candidacy would be beneath the dignity of his office and an unjust interference from his position of vantage with those who aspired legitimately to the honor of appointment to the office which he had so long and ably filled and lifted to a status of importance never before realized. Moreover, he felt that his reappointment, if it was to come, should properly be based upon his record in office and be in the nature of an endorsement of his administration. He was retired from office February 5, 1910, and from active service on his voluntary application, February 4, 1910, but though 58 years of age, he is really in the prime of life as far as his physical and mental vigor is concerned. We feel sure that his energies will not lag but that they will be employed in some useful direction, and we wish him many years of health, happiness, and prosperity.

However he may elect to occupy himself and whatever he does, it may be confidently predicted that he will keep abreast of his profession, for he is a diligent reader of medical literature. He was never a prolific writer himself, though he well knew and often expressed the importance—indeed, the ethical obligation resting upon medical men—to contribute the fruit of their studies and their observation to the general fund of scientific information. He urged this conviction upon the medical officers of the Navy, through the medium of his annual reports, and he reiterated the idea in his address before the Association of Military Surgeons of the United States, on October 5, 1909, in these words:

> "There is a growing importance that each officer take part in the movement toward improvement in every direction where the slightest improvement is possible, and an exacting obligation rests upon all to communicate such observations, discoveries, inventions and ideas as are calculated to strengthen our hand and enlarge our resources in the discharge of that sacred responsibility reposed in us, especially in the crisis of war, when medical service is in greatest demand and its capabilities are put to the severest test. To have conceived an idea, to have profited by an experience, or to have conducted an investigation bearing upon the advance of medico-military science entails the ethical requirement that the knowledge gained be promptly communicated for the benefit of all who may be interested in or helped by the information." * * *

The establishment of the United States Naval Bulletin and its development to an exalted place among medical periodicals is a living evidence of his endeavors to encourage medical officers of the Navy to do their duty in this respect.

He was too busy with practical affairs to have had time for much writing outside of that required by his office—yet, his literary work comprises many speeches, reports and articles relating to strictly professional subjects, and these largely bearing upon one phase or another of the work or concerns of the medical branch of the Navy, in which he was deeply interested.

The more important of his writings are enumerated below:

Annual Reports of the Surgeon General of the Navy, Chief of the Bureau of Medicine & Surgery, to the Secretary of the Navy, for the fiscal years, 1902, 1903, 1904, 1905, 1906, 1907, 1908, and 1909, 8° Washington.

Medical and Surgical Report of the case of the late President of the United States (pamphlet), Washington, 1901.

The Relation of the Navy to the Study of Tropical Diseases" (read before the 6th International Dermatological Congress, New York Academy of Science, September 13, 1907), Abstracted Journal A. M. A., October 12, 1907.

"Naval Surgery," Keen's Surgery, Vol. IV, Chapter LXVII, pp. 1018-1074, Philadelphia and London, 1908.

"The Development of the Navy Medical Corps to Meet the Modern Requirements of Specialization in Medical Practice," (read by invitation before the Essex County Medical Society, Oct. 13, 1908), Journal of the Medical Society of N. J., Jan., 1909, pp. 1-22.

"The Medical Profession as Represented in the United States Navy," (read, by invitation, before the 39th Annual Session of the Medical Society of Virginia, held at Richmond, October 20-23, 1908), Virginia Medical Semi-monthly, Dec. 25, 1908, pp. 409-414.

On the occasion of the 6th International Dermatological Congress which met in the New York Academy of Medicine, Sept. 13 to 17, 1907, he was delegated to represent the President and delivered the address of welcome on behalf of Mr. Roosevelt at the opening session. His other addresses include those delivered before the graduating classes of the U. S. Naval Medical School for the past several years; one delivered to the nurses of the graduating class at Garfield Hospital, Washington, D. C., in 1907; two delivered before the Association of Military Surgeons—one in 1908, as President-elect of the organization, and another in 1909 as retiring President of the organization; and one (an address of greeting on behalf of the Medical Fraternity of the District of Columbia, the Army, the Navy, and the Public Health and Marine Hospital Service) delivered before the American Hospital Association which met in Washington, D. C., September 21, 1909.

What he said in the closing section of his paper, read before the 39th Annual Session of the Medical Society of Virginia, we believe may be applied to the doctor, himself a native Virginian and a graduate of the University of Virginia, as expressing in a reflective sense the character of his own services and the reason which Virginia has for counting him among her well-beloved and distinguished men. We quote from his concluding remarks as follows:

> "In addressing an Association of this State, I feel called upon to make some special reference to Virginians and graduates of Virginia institutions representing the medical profession in the Navy. * * Since the year 1870, a total of 105 Virginians or graduates of the University of Virginia have entered the Corps. This fact, in part, evidences a continuation of that large place which our citizens have always taken in honorable public life; and, in view of the proud history of Virginia through all the years from its Colonial inception, it would be strange, indeed, if its sons lost sight of the exemplar in their heritage and failed to conduct their careers, if need be, as the brave Ambler did, with a balance to the glory of the State and nation."

The patriotic and scientific societies with which he is identified include the National Geographic Society, the American Medical Association, the Association of Military Surgeons, The Washington Medical Society (by invitation), the Society of American Wars, and an associate member of the United Service Medical Society of the British Empire. He is a member of the Metropolitan Club of Washington, the Army and Navy Club, the Washington Golf & Country Club, and the Colonnade Club of the University of Virginia. In recognition of services rendered the officers and crew of the Spanish Caravel "Santa Maria," on the occasion of an explosion on that vessel, while in the harbor of New York in 1893, Alphonso VIII, King of Spain, conferred the Order of Naval Merit upon him. The insignia of this Order is to be seen upon his breast in the only portrait, a three-quarter length, life size, oil painting of Dr. Rixey. This portrait was painted by Miss Georgiana Campbell and hangs on the wall in the drawing room of his residence at Rixey, Arlington County, Virginia. It is considered an extremely good likeness.

Like the father, all the Rixeys were in the neighborhood of six feet in stature and inclined to angular proportions, and otherwise with a strong family resemblance. His younger brother, John Franklin Rixey, who was a lawyer of prominence and for many years in Congress on the democratic side of the House, representing the 8th district of Virginia, died in Washington at Dr. Rixey's home in 1908. His only sister, Lulu Henrie, died in Washington also at his house in 1909.

Numerous short biographical sketches of Dr. Rixey have been written and some of these may be found—one, in the Illustrated Congressional Directory; one, in the Military Surgeon Vol. XXIII, No. 5, Nov., 1908, pp. 406-408.

The restricted space allowed the authors of these precluded the possibility of a satisfactory review of a figure so prominent in professional and official circles.

Conclusion

His was an active life of service, which conformed, in a general and comprehensive survey, to the type of ministrations in the interest of his fellow-men and the common welfare, which President Elliott in a lecture delivered before the students of the "Eleventh Session of the Harvard Summer School of Theology" characterized as part and parcel of the religion of the future.

> "The spirit of saving and the spirit of destruction have grown up side by side in the hearts of men. Medicine and war are older than history, but history has taken but meagre cognizance of the heroes of medicine and has written large the names of the heroes of war, who have drenched the world with tears, manured it with blood, and the stories of whose lives have been handed down to us with precision and zeal proportionate to the mischief they have done."

If there is any joy which men should prize, it is the joy of relieving distress. There is but one greater, and that is the joy of preventing distress. Those who have done such things in the past, who are doing them now, and who will do them in the future of this world must be counted as apostles of the essence of religious principle and should be among the most blessed of men. Their reward will come, but if it comes slowly, we must be consoled by the conviction that it comes securely. It was Cato who observed that he would rather that posterity should inquire why no statues were erected to him than that it should inquire why they were.

PART II

Autobiography

INTRODUCTION

THE foregoing pages were written by William H. Bell, Captain, Medical Corps, U. S. Navy, during the latter part of my administration as Chief of the Bureau of Medicine and Surgery, and Surgeon General of the Navy. William C. Braisted, Rear Admiral, M. C., U. S. Navy, Assistant to the Bureau, came to me and asked me to write my biography, stating that official records were accessible at that time and much of interest would be lost if I delayed. My reply was that it was impossible. Besides the duties of the Chief of the Bureau I was White House physician, and accompanied President Roosevelt on most of his itineraries; also, I professionally cared for many cabinet officers and their families, Justices of the Supreme Court, Senators, Representatives, and others in official life, as well as a few of my friends in civil life who did not wish to give me up when I might be available. The importance of keeping these duties up as far as possible meant more than I can express towards what I had done in the past six years and to what I hoped to do towards putting the Medical Department of the Navy on an up-to-date war basis before the end of my administration. Dr. Braisted said to me that he knew that I did not have the time to devote to the work but that he and Dr. Bell would undertake it in order that the Medical Corps of the Navy might not lose the unprecedented records of the Bureau during my terms of office. I consented with one stipulation, that neither my nor their official duties should be interfered with. The preceding pages were written and handed to me at the expiration of my term of office in 1910. A careful reading of them I did not make until sometime after my retirement.

In May 1916, not feeling like undertaking an autobiography to complete the biography commenced by Dr. Bell and Dr. Braisted, I asked them if they could finish the biography with my help, and Dr. Braisted said that he could not but that he would write Dr. Bell.

DEPARTMENT OF THE NAVY
BUREAU OF MEDICINE & SURGERY
WASHINGTON

May 31, 1916.

My dear Doctor Rixey:

I enclose you a letter from Dr. Bell, received this morning in reply to one of mine asking him to consider taking up the work of writing your life history, as you suggested to me. I imagine he does not feel able to undertake it, from his letter, but thought you would like to see it.

With best wishes and kindest regards, believe me,

Sincerely yours,
(Signed) W. C. BRAISTED,
Surgeon General, U. S. Navy.

Surgeon General P. M. Rixey, U. S. N., Ret'd.,
1518 K Street, N. W.,
Washington, D. C.

U. S. S. Wyoming,
New York, N. Y.,
May 28, 1916.

Dear Dr. Braisted:

Your very kind letter of May 17th reached me in due time, but I have been too busy to give sufficient thought to the matter which you mentioned until today. I am fond of Dr. Rixey as you know, and very glad to have been able to put the facts of his interesting and distinguished service in some shape, but I would under no circumstances resume the work or attempt to extend it. That is a pleasant task for somebody else, Dr. Wise probably, but whoever it may be, is, as far as I am concerned, welcome to all I worked up without even a literary obligation to mention my name. It is sufficient to have felt and received the appreciation of Dr. and Mrs. Rixey for my efforts. The manuscript is absolutely and entirely theirs. Please make them feel this and that I think of them always with cordial remembrances, but the biography must be written by somebody else more in touch and more competent.

I have answered Dr. Wise's letter to this effect.

With warm regards and best wishes,

Always sincerely yours,
(Signed) WM. H. BELL.

After this the World War put all thoughts of my biography out of my mind until the ending of the war and I was free again. How near this biography came to never being completed is told in these pages, also how it was undertaken by me whose shortcomings I hope my readers may overlook, as I have no experience in such matters.

Early in 1922 I commenced assembling the data which had not been available for Dr. Bell and started writing up my life's work since I retired. A decision had to be made about the biography written up to my retirement from active duty in 1910 if it was to be completed. I naturally turned again to Admiral Braisted who had retired and Captain Bell who was at this Fleet Surgeon of the U. S. Battle Fleet. I wrote Admiral Braisted and asked if it were possible for Dr. Bell and himself to complete the biography with the data I had compiled and I invited him and his wife to make us a visit, hoping to interest him. His reply dated March 18 follows:

432 Montgomery Ave.,
Haverford, Pa.
March 18, 1922.

My dear Admiral Rixey:

I have just returned from a trip to Princeton and find the kind invitation from Mrs. Rixey and yourself to visit you at your beautiful home.

I appreciate the courtesy and the thought of and for us. I seldom get to Washington these days and just at present am in the midst of a campaign to raise money for a New College in Philadelphia.

We shall not forget your kindly invitation and if it should be possible will avail ourselves of it at some future time.

I should hesitate to review the biography which I take it will be largely reminiscent of your unusually eventful and active life. It is a difficult task and one which I should dread to undertake—as one must sponsor so much that relates not alone to themselves but to others.

With expressions of esteem and deep personal regards to you both, who have been much to me in my life, I remain,

Sincerely your friend,

(Signed) WILLIAM C. BRAISTED.

To this letter I replied urging him to come on for the visit and received the following letter:

432 Montgomery Ave.,
Haverford, Pa.
March 21, 1922.

My dear Admiral:

Your letter of the 20th has been received, and as I said before I will try to arrange to get out to your home the next time I visit Washington. Just when this will be I cannot say now—probably sometime in April or May. I want to take my car over to Washington for the spring overhaul and whenever I can get away for two or three days will do so.

I will let you know when I come over and we will drive out and spend some hours with you.

I have no special desire to be one of the "biographers." As far as I can remember, I wrote none of the material for the biography. If Dr. Bell did, he should receive the credit for it, and I should not want him to feel that I was in any way laying claim to his work.

I have a dread of touching anything in regard to Naval matters—however remote the touch may be. When I retired, I considered my naval career ended unless War should come, and I have tried my best to keep out of any further activities pertaining to the Navy in any way.

You and I probably view life from very different angles and while I always listen to advice, I find that I must consider my final action as my conscience and best judgment dictate. I treasure the memories of days gone, but as I said I hesitate—even dread—in any way to renew any association that may tend to break or mar what at present, for the most part, is pleasing and good.

I trust the Lord to lead me and do not place much reliance on my own wisdom.

Sincerely your friend,
(Signed) WILLIAM C. BRAISTED.

Nearly a month elapsed and not having heard from him I wrote a third time and his reply was:

432 Montgomery Ave.,
Haverford, Pa.
April 12, 1922.

My dear Admiral:

Your kind note of April 8th was received, and I appreciate it and your interest very much.

I shall not be able to take the time to get away this month and perhaps not next, but when I am in Washington next if I can get the time, will try to see you.

With best wishes to you both and very pleased to know you are happy and well, I remain,

Sincerely yours,

(Signed) WILLIAM C. BRAISTED.

Eight months have passed since the receipt of this letter and it seems that I will have no assistance from him. Dr. Bell has written that he will be unable to complete the work as his many duties, official and personal, will not permit of the time necessary. I am much pleased that Dr. Bell wrote the biography up to the time of my retirement and I appreciate his friendship as demonstrated. None but a true friend could write what he has written of me.

Much credit is due Dr. Bell for what goes before, as he had only records of the Department and newspaper clippings to refer to, besides what information my wife gave him. No change will be made in his work but I wish to add much that concerns my personal relations with President McKinley and President Roosevelt and their families, which was not accessible to him, especially the letters of President Roosevelt to me, and I will take up my life from 1910. The ties between the two Presidents and their families and myself were those of friends and family physicians.

I do not remember ever having received a letter from President McKinley, and the reason was that after the beginning of my service as White House physician up to the time of his death over a period of more than two years, I was always with him or where I could be called by phone in a few minutes. During the seven years I was with Mr. Roosevelt I was Surgeon General of the Navy, and the duties of that office required my absence when he could spare me. We corresponded regularly up to the time of his death and copies of his letters which I have held sacred and personal are among my most cherished possessions. Copies of these letters will be found in the following pages and show his and his family's appreciation of their old friend and physician, and I do not know of anything in my career that has given Mrs. Rixey and myself more pleasure. Some of these letters are typewritten but many are in the President's own handwriting.

As the time for my retirement approached a very serious question presented itself to me as to my future. I loved my profession and it and my duty as a naval officer had always been my first aim in life. I had fitted up my office at 1518 K Street and had taken care of patients in it for years whilst White House physician and Surgeon General of the Navy, usually in the early morning, at lunch time, or in the evening, and my patients were among the most prominent in official and private life. Although I had every inducement to devote myself to the practice of my profession, I viewed it as depriving me of much that I loved almost as well as my profession, and that was the outdoor life and farming on as large a scale as possible.

My financial interest in Virginia lands near Washington was considerable and just at this time a farm of nearly 2,000 acres of land near Manassas and lying on both sides of Bull Run in Fairfax and Prince William Counties, and owned by the family of my deceased brother, Congressman J. F. Rixey, was brought to my attention. This farm which my brother had bought as an investment was in poor condition, having been rented. I saw a wonderful opportunity to develop the property and I purchased it. My career as a practicing physician was for the greater part ended, and as a dirt farmer I went to work with the same zeal I had carried on my official duties on the active list of the Navy. I now had six homes to care for—town house, 1518 K Street, N. W.; "Rixey" (formerly called Netherfauld), about 40 acres; Crystal Spring Farm, 120 acres (the last two in Arlington County, Va.); Dairy Farm about 300 acres; Lilac Lodge, 200 acres, both in Fairfax County, Va., and adjoining each other; and my last purchase, Ben Lomond about 2,000 acres in Fairfax and Prince William Counties. All of these homes were mortgaged and the properties were in bad shape when purchased. I was successful in bringing them into a state of production by reversing the way they had been handled by preceding owners, that is, I put back on the land more than I got from it. Although tasking me financially to pay taxes, interest, and running expenses, the result in the end has been most satisfactory as the farms all lie in from 3 to 30 miles of the Capital of the United States. The only obligation devolving upon me in a professional sense was that I must use the knowledge obtained as a physician in family practice when requested by my old patients, and it would always be my pleasure to know of the efforts of my successors in keeping the Medical Department fit for any emergency which might confront our country and flag

CHAPTER I

ANCESTRY

MY ANCESTRY beyond my earliest recollections has never concerned me to any great degree, but now as this book goes on record it may be of interest to its readers, so I shall refer them to the ancestries of my family as written in a book recently written by the author, Mrs. Lucy Montgomery Smith Price, and published by the Shenandoah Publishing House, Inc., of Strasburg, Va., and then I shall give my own impressions as to my early ancestry, and add my own views as observed since my earliest recollections.

The book referred to above was the result of years of hard work, and gives in detail all the recorded facts attainable as well as the interpretation and personal views of the author.

My paternal grandfather, Captain Rixey, a fine type of the Virginia gentleman, over eighty years of age, tall, six feet, spare of build, very active and quick tempered, lived on his farm about three miles from Culpeper Court House, Va. He was a widower with four sons: my father, Presley Morehead Rixey, Franklin, John and Samuel. The latter, the youngest, lived with his father. The home was called "Hilly Farm," and the house of frame construction, colonial style and great columns, five feet in diameter across the front, and with the Lombardy Poplar Avenue leading to it gave the first impression as an ideal home. Here I first began the practice of medicine as a nurse when about ten years of age. My grandfather, now quite feeble, required someone sleeping in the same room at night, and Samuel being absent I was asked to take his place. Young as I was the old gentleman declared that I was the best nurse he had. My sense of responsibility made my sleep so light that his slightest movement brought me to my feet, and all through my long life I have found that my sleep was very light if I had much responsibility during my waking hours.

My grandfather on my mother's side died early, but my grandmother was a lovely woman and I loved to be with her and my mother's brothers. Her farm was about four miles from my father's farm where I was born and lived up to the beginning of the Civil War, when we moved to our beautiful home in Culpeper, where I lived up to 1872 when I left home for the University of Virginia.

On my mother's side my uncles were John Turner, Samuel, Powhatan, and Philip; my aunts were Matilda, wife of John Rixey, and Eppa, who later married George Poindexter of Richmond, Va.

So far, available records show the Rixey ancestry dates back to 1740 when one Richard Riccie makes a deed to his son Richard Rixey (note the change of name), and through all the following years to now the name seems to remain Rixey, owners of large tracts of lands, and always willing to add to their holdings when possible, and up to the beginning of my failing health it seemed my obsession, only I looked forward for the greater part of my reward in the fact that I purchased near a city certain to grow and create a demand for the land irrespective of crops.

The above is a very meagre description of my ancestry, and I leave to the younger generation to ferret out more detailed information.

It seems to me my branch of the Rixey family intermarried with the Moreheads more than any other of the allied families, and I remember a great aunt, Fannie Morehead, with much affection.

Note the name Presley Morehead Rixey, my father, and three generations of Presleys since my father's time. The Presley seems to date back to the intermarrying with William Presley's family of Northumberland County, Virginia.

The Morehead ancestry was originally of Scotch descent, dated back to 1454, and I have adopted the Morehead Coat of Arms as applicable to my branch of the family.

The Rixey of present day can claim Scotch and French Huguenots as the principal ancestors from which they sprung, but owing to intermarrying the ancestry is much mixed. However it may be, I, for one, am satisfied that we have an ancestry to be proud of.

CHAPTER II

EARLY SERVICE IN THE NAVY

AFTER receiving my commission as Assistant Surgeon, my first orders were as follows:

February 11, 1874.

Sir:

Proceed to Portsmouth, N. H., without delay, and report to Commodore J. C. Howell for duty on board the U. S. Receiving Ship *Sabine*.

By direction of the Secretary of the Navy.

DANIEL AMMEN,
Chief of the Bureau.

In obedience to these, my first orders, I reported to Commodore Howell without the prescribed uniform which I was informed an Assistant Surgeon required. Due to the few days that had elapsed since my commission had been received and the receipt of the above orders, my uniform was incomplete. The Commodore did his duty in no uncertain manner and I had my first and very impressive lesson as to reporting for duty in uniform. I tried to explain that I thought "without delay" in my orders meant that my services were badly needed and I should not wait for uniform as I could work just as well without it. The Commodore handed me my orders having endorsed on them to report to Commander John Irwin, Commanding the *Sabine*. I had never been on a ship and the *Sabine*, one of the old wooden sailing ships, was anchored about a hundred yards from the dock and communication with the shore was by a scow, a covered boat running on a rope and propelled by a windlass turned by a sailor. On board everything was new to me. My stateroom in the Ward Room on the berth deck was the smallest room I had ever occupied and between decks there was barely room for me to stand erect and I was constantly dodging great wooden knees, making it necessary for me to go in a stooping posture most of the time. The light in our staterooms was through a ten-inch porthole and a student's lamp. Fortunately we didn't have to remain on the berth deck. Surgeon Potter was not only the medical officer of the *Sabine* but of the Navy Yard also and had a medical dispensary in the Yard. He was an energetic, hard-working doctor, and when not engaged on official duties was called upon by the civil population of Kittery and Portsmouth, especially in surgical cases. He needed an assistant and I needed his experience so we were soon the best of friends, and he left most of the work of the *Sabine* and yard to me and frequently I assisted him in his operative work outside. After sick call on the *Sabine* every morning I went to the office of the Yard dispensary looking after any patients who came in and absorbing the medical literature in the library.

Thus engaged I was beginning to be acquainted with the officers and their families on this station as well as the jackies, marines, and civil employees of the yard, who needed medical or surgical care. A short time after my advent on the scene a dance was given on the *Sabine* and I met and fell in love with the young lady who was destined to be my future wife. Captain Earl English was Captain of the Yard, and his family consisted of his wife, a charming lady, his oldest daughter, Miss Mamie English, his second daughter, Miss Earlena Isabel English, about eighteen years of age, and his youngest daughter, Miss Frankie English, then about seven years old. The afternoon of the dance was a clear crisp one with snow on the ground and we officers of the ship as host were on deck watching the arrival of our guests in the scow which plied between the wharf and the ship. Among them I observed Miss Earlena and asked one of the officers of the ship who she was. From his description I knew she was a great favorite and an excellent dancer. If she had excited my admiration in her winter wraps and her fur turban cap, it was as nothing compared with what I felt after she had laid them aside and came out in a simple afternoon walking suit. I had met Mrs. McCook, who was chaperoning the English young ladies, and I begged an introduction and never enjoyed an afternoon more. Among the many attractive ladies was Miss Mariah Howell, the only daughter of the Commandant. As an officer of the ship I was introduced to Miss Howell, but I paid her very little attention as I was rather sore as to the Commodore's reception of me on my reporting for duty which had been augmented by his Secretary when dining in our mess a few days before when he had detailed how the Commodore had been amused at my first reporting for duty in the Navy. I was a young Virginian, proud of having gotten my M. D. and commission all within a year and a half. It hurt to be laughed at, especially by the Commandant of the station, and I decided that he had no interest in me, and I certainly did not feel a friendly interest in him. I therefore did not call upon him nor his family socially, but made myself as agreeable as possible to the rest of the ladies of the Yard, especially those of the English family. Miss Howell was an attractive and very accomplished young lady and had invited me to call on them and when I did not she was surprised and spoke to the English girls. They told her how hurt I felt at the Commandant's reception of me. She reported it to her father and told also of his Secretary's indiscretion. The Commodore was very angry with his Secretary and I don't believe that he afterwards ever again repeated anything he heard or observed in the Commandant's office without permission.

In a little while we were all friends and I loved Commodore Howell and learned to appreciate his worth as a naval officer, and when I was detached and went to say good-bye to him and his family, I found him out. Mrs. Howell informed me it was no use trying to find him as he disliked saying good-bye to anyone, and especially to those he was fond of. Years afterwards whilst one of the attending naval surgeons in Washington I was his family physician and took care of him in his last illness. At that time he was Chief of one of the Bureaus in the Navy Department.

My first experience in the Navy in reporting for duty was useful to me after I became Surgeon General and had established the Naval Medical School. I had a retired naval line officer, Lieutenant Downes Wilson, detailed as instructor on Naval Regulations, signals, drills, uniform side arms, and all the details which made the young civilian doctor at home with his brother officers of the line who had Naval Academy experience, and thus avoided in the future what I and others before me had experienced.

The six months at this station passed all too swiftly and a little incident here will show how intimate I had become with the English family. Captain English had given Miss Earlena a young heifer, and one morning the stable man came to the Dispensary office and told me that it had broken its hind leg just above the ankle and they wanted to know if I could do anything for her. Of course, I could and did rig up splints and saved the heifer's life, the bones having knit perfectly. I little knew that on my first duty in Washington this young heifer, grown to be a very fine cow, would belong to my wife.

The round of sleighing parties, dances, and social affairs of every kind was most pleasant, especially as I met my sweetheart at every one of them. Captain English in May was detached from the Navy Yard and ordered to command the *Congress* in European waters and his family were to follow him in June. The time had come for me to know my fate as regarded my sweetheart, and one afternoon on a drive behind a fine pair of horses I learned that there was no chance of her becoming my wife as she was engaged to the son of an old naval officer. My disappointment was greater than I can express, and I made application to the Secretary of the Navy to be ordered to the *Plymouth*, at that time fitting out for a cruise in the Pacific. No reply was made to my application and the English family had sailed for Europe. Much to my surprise a short time afterwards I received orders detaching me from the *Sabine* and ordering me to take passage on the White Star Steamer *Republic* leaving New York August 1st, for Liverpool, England, thence to London, and to report for duty on the *Congress*, the same ship that Captain English had been ordered to command. I received congratulations from all my friends on the prospect of a beautiful cruise. I was, however, much depressed and asked that I be given a few days leave to visit my father and mother before the sailing of the *Republic.* Bag and baggage I was on the *Republic* when she sailed feeling very lonely among so many, not one of whom I had ever known. However, looking over the passenger list I found Medical Director Richard Dean, wife, son, and daughter, also Passed Assistant Surgeon Corwin and wife, both officers ordered to the *Congress.* Evidently I had been looked out for by some one. Several years later I learned the secret. When my appointment as Assistant Surgeon went to the Senate for confirmation a cousin of my father, Hon. Eppa Hunton, of the 8th District of Virginia, noted it and wrote my father a very complimentary letter congratulating him upon having a son who, unaided, had gotten his commission. My mother replying told him of my struggles and asked him to keep an eye on me, and she hoped he might be of service. Surgeon General Beale's wife, was a cousin of General Hunton, and he frequently saw General Beale and evidently got him interested in my future, and when my application for duty on the *Plymouth* came to him he pigeon-holed it and had me ordered to the *Congress.*

I had never been on the ocean, indeed never aboard a ship until the *Sabine,* and the great passenger steamer was a revelation. However, I was not seasick and soon was well acquainted with Dr. Dean, Dr. Corwin, and their families. Arriving at Liverpool on August 10th, Dr. Dean wired B. F. Stevens to know where the *Congress* was and he was informed she was at sea, so we decided to visit places of interest before arriving in London. The first place was Chester, the old Cathedral City on the River Dee, then Eaton Hall, Leamington, Kenilworth, Warwick Castle, Stratford-on-Avon, Ann Hathaway's cottage, spring, etc., and Shakespeare's tomb in the old church on the Arno. Our next stop before reaching London, August 15th, was at

Oxford, visiting the college buildings and the museum. Many of these visits were made by coach.

My first visit in London was to Mr. B. F. Stevens, the U. S. Dispatch Agent. He could not tell us when the *Congress* would be in port but would keep us advised. On August 16th, Sunday, we visited Westminster Abbey, and remained to church; then took a stroll and met Messrs. Knight, Ryan, and other fellow passengers of the *Republic*. On August 17th, we visited the Zoological Gardens with my fellow passengers just mentioned. On the 18th went to London Tower and St. Paul's Cathedral. The 19th visited the Albert Memorial and the International Exhibition. On the 20th the Crystal Palace; the 21st, Windsor Castle and Hyde Park; 22nd, Parliamentary Building and Westminster Abbey. Left London the 23rd of August and arrived in Paris at 7 p. m. After dinner we visited Jardin des Ambassadeurs. On the 24th Drs. Lewis and Morrell called on me and we visited Notre Dame Cathedral, Sainte Chapelle, the Pantheon, Palais de Luxembourg, Hotel des Invalides, Champs Elysees, Bois de Boulogne, Arc de Triomphe, L'Etoile, and Zoological Gardens. After dinner Doctors Morrell and Green called and we went to the Alhambra, quite a novelty to me, also the way these young men learned French.

On the 25th, with Dr. and Mrs. Corwin visited the Louvre, Panorama of the siege of Paris, taking train at 8 p. m. for Genoa, having learned by wire that the *Congress* would be at Spezia, Italy, on the 28th. I was delayed by my baggage but arrived in time to catch the *Congress*, the Flagship *Franklin* also being in port. Reported on the Flagship and then on the *Congress*. Captain English and family were in Florence. The *Congress* went direct from Spezia to Nice where Medical Inspector Cleborne and Acting Assistant Surgeon Myers were detached and ordered home and Medical Inspector Dean and Passed Assistant Surgeon Corwin reported for duty. After a short stay at Nice we went to sea, our first port being Marseilles, then Barcelona, Port

Mahon, Messina, Zante, Piraeus, Athens, Smyrna, Syria, Milo, cruising in company with the Flagship, Suda Bay, Crete or Canida. During this cruise in which we were supposed to be looking for a port in which to establish a coaling station, typhoid fever developed among the crew, and I had my hands full. Every case was severe and the accommodations aboard ship for their treatment were poor and there was no chance to get the patients in a hospital ashore. The sick bay was in the eye of the ship and the anchor chains just above them made a tremendous racket either in dropping or hoisting anchor. At the request of the medical officers the Captain ordered a portion of the gun deck amidship screened off and the seriously ill patients were much more comfortable. I shall never forget the experience I had with the delirious patients before they were moved. I have had as many as four men holding a patient to keep him from throwing himself out of his cot. Imagine such a condition, a case of typhoid fever, abdominal symptoms prominent, struggling with four stout men. The result was that we lost several patients from hemorrhage before we reached port and could give the very ill patients the advantages of hospital treatment. The conditions for the care of the sick at sea are different today and I am deeply appreciative of the opportunity I had in after life to do so much towards this betterment. On that beautiful ship the quarters for officers and men were satisfactory, but those for the sick were on the berth deck forward, the noisiest and most uncomfortable section. Grateful I am that this does not exist today, and I hope and believe it never can again.

Our next stop was Messina, Palermo, where we visited the Cathedral, Vice Royal Palace, and Catacombs. We called on our Consul and his wife, Mr. and Mrs. Frazier of Warrenton, Va., who had been a former teacher of my sister, Henrie, and he said, "She had more natural grace than any young girl I ever knew."

Our next anchorage was in the beautiful bay of Naples, and much to my relief we could give our very ill patients

Captain Earl English, 1876
Commanding *U S S Congress*

the benefit of hospital treatment. After leaving Nice our Captain had his wife and oldest daughter with him, Miss Earlena and Frankie having been left at school in Paris. I am chronicling the principal ports and points of interest of a personal nature from my diary, as a full description is given of them in every tourist's guide book of today.

We arrived at Naples on October 29th and remained at anchor until November 18th, visiting the principal places of interest, Herculaneum, Pompeii, Capidimonte, Palezzo Riale, Grotto of Pausilipo, Virgil's tomb, half extinct volcanoes of Solfarena and Monte Nuovo, Lake Avenus, Lake Lucerne, and Vesuvius on horseback from Portici. We left Naples November 19th, for Genoa; head winds compelled us to put in to Porto Longone, Isle of Elba, and we arrived in Genoa November 22nd. We met our Consul, Mr. Spencer, his daughter and Miss Hiss, of Baltimore, Md. Here, as in Naples, we visited the most important objects of interest and enjoyed many social affairs, teas, dinners, and dances, meeting many interesting people. When I speak of visiting points of interest it must be understood that I was accompanied by one or more friends, officers of our own ship, or other ships in port, and occasionally I was a member of the Captain's party, with Mrs. and Miss English. Many of our officers had their families on the station and visiting them was always pleasant. We left Genoa at 5 p. m. on the 30th of December and arrived at Villefranche, France, at 9 a. m. on the 31st and tied up to No. 1 buoy. Here we remained until 28th of May, 1875, almost five months. The reason given was that it was to save coal. However that may be, it was most enjoyable meeting so many friends and making such delightful new ones. Of course, the families of the officers of the fleet came first. The memory of the charming friends, especially the ladies, whom I met there, is very dear to me as they were more than kind to the junior doctor of the *Congress*. (The baby pills, the smallest of all)—these two last designations were given me by my friend Assistant Surgeon George Harmon, who until my reporting on the *Congress* as the junior medical officer of the Fleet had held the distinguished position. The officers of the *Congress* at that time were Captain Earl English, Lt. Comdr. R. D. Evans and Horace Elmer, Lieutenants A. S. Snow, D. W. Davis, E. C. Pendleton, J. R. Selfridge, and C. A. Adams, Master A. P. Nazro, Midshipman W. C. Heacock, S. W. B. Diehl, J. P. Underwood, and F. A. Wilmer, Medical Inspector R. C. Dean, Passed Assistant Surgeon W. A. Corwin, Assistant Surgeon P. M. Rixey, Paymaster C. P. Thompson, Chief Engineer J. W. Whittaker, Passed Assistant Engineer C. R. Roelker, Assistant Engineer G. H. Kearney, Chaplain D. C. Tribou, Second Lieutenant of Marines J. T. Broadhead, Boatswain A. M. Pomeroy, Gunner E. J. Wough, Carpenter A. N. Whitehouse, Acting Sailmaker A. W. Stevens.

The wives and daughters of these officers at Nice were: Mrs. and Miss English until March 15th, where they were joined by Miss Earlena and Miss Frankie and Mrs. West, their grandmother, Mrs. Evans and daughter, Mrs. Elmer and daughter, Mrs. Pendleton, Mrs. Dean and daughter, Mrs. Corwin, Mrs. C. P. Thompson, and Mrs. Whittaker. Among the Americans established in Nice at this time were Mr. and Mrs. Willis, their three daughters, Mrs. Grubb, Mrs. Cerkez, General and Miss Keyes, Mr. and Mrs. Dawson, Mrs. and Miss Bull, Mr. and Mrs. Denazy, Dr. and Mrs. Draper, Mr. and Mrs. Howe of New York, and many others coming and going besides the permanent residents of Nice. I was entertained time and again by many of these friends and reciprocated by having them on the *Congress* to our dances, lunches, and dinners.

The beautiful rides and drives around Nice with every variety of entertainment in such charming company made time pass all too quickly. I had been attending typhoid cases on board about eight months when on March 16th I was stricken with a severe headache and fever and soon realized I was down with typhoid. The first week I suffered intensely, being ill in my little stateroom and growing worse each day, and finally I was invalided to the *Pension de la Metropole* in Nice by Drs. Dean and Corwin.

Assistant Engineer Kearney proved himself a friend indeed, he took me to the Pension and saw that I had everything that was needed. I was allowed my ward-room boy as nurse and a most faithful one he proved, for what he lacked in professional training he made up in devotion to me. Dr. Corwin had special charge of my case and as soon as I was placed in the large airy room of the Pension I felt that I would get well, and just so sure I felt that if I had been kept aboard ship I would have died. The fever ran its course in about three weeks, and then a slow convalescence which was made as pleasant as possible by so many dear friends, especially Mr. and Mrs. Willis and daughters, Mr. Campen, Mrs. Cox, and Mr. and Mrs. Bronson. Flowers and delicacies of all kinds were sent to me and no wonder I recuperated rapidly! On April 19th, I reported for duty and was given a week's leave, which I spent on shore with my friends, riding horseback and regaining my strength rapidly, and weighing almost as much as before I was taken sick. My shipmates were all considerate and sympathetic during my illness but those to whom I owe most were Mr. Kearney, Dr. Corwin, Paymaster Thompson, Chaplain Tribou and Dr. Dean. On January 18th, the *Franklin* had left Nice for Lisbon to change admirals, Admiral Case being relieved by Admiral Worden. The three days' carnival in Nice from February 7th to 9th, was thoroughly enjoyed. I should have mentioned that on March 15th, the day before I was taken ill, I went with Mrs. English to meet her mother, Mrs. West, Misses Earlena and Frankie. Miss Earlena had been ill in Paris and her grandmother who loved her dearly, had crossed the ocean to be with her.

On May 28th I went to Nice for the Bill of Health and to say goodbye to many dear friends. The ship was under way at 5 p. m. for Malaga, arriving 3rd of June. From there a party of us took train for Grenada, Spain, and we visited the Alhambra and other points of interest, joining the ship at Malaga on the 7th. Left for Gibraltar on the 9th, arriving the same day. Much visiting between

MRS. EARL ENGLISH, 1876

officers of the *Congress* and the Royal Engineers and Royal Artillery and we visited the galleries of the Rock, the Summit, and the Cave. Visited Algeria, had a boat race with the Englishmen, also a baseball game. On the 18th we had target practice and arrived at Algiers, Africa. 22nd, visited the Hospital du Dey, Military Hospital. Enjoyed a horseback ride and a visit by train to Blidah. 28th, our next port was Tunis where we arrived July 1st, and left on the 5th, having visited Carthage and other points of interest. We arrived at Malta on the 7th of July and anchored in the inner harbor. As in Gibraltar we were busy entertaining and being entertained by the Royal Army officers. Dr. Dean and I went through the Naval Hospital. Our next port was Tripoli, July 14th, and left 17th for Alexandria, Egypt, the Captain and officers having exchanged visits with the Bey of Tripoli. Arrived Alexandria 24th of July, visited principal points of interest in and around Alexandria, and on the 27th Captain English and the officers of the ship were given a special car to visit Cairo. Our first call was upon the Khedive in his new palace, after which we visited the principal objects of interest in and around Cairo. Ascended the great pyramid Cheops, 780 feet high, six and a half minutes to the top. A boat ride on the River Nile, and we returned aboard ship at 10:30 p. m. on the 29th. Up anchored on the 31st and arrived Corfu, August 5th. Here we enjoyed a week driving and horseback riding. Left on 12th for Malta, arrived 15th, where Captain received orders to proceed to Tripoli, and at 4 p. m. the same day we left Malta, arriving in Tripoli 17th. Lieutenant Arthur and myself went ashore to get pratique and call on our Consul. The native population was much worked up over something and a crowd followed us hissing and crying—"Cushma"—(meaning *Pigs*). Flagship came in on the 21st and the Consul's troubles with the Pasha were adjusted, and on the 23rd Lieutenant Arthur and myself accompanied by Lieutenant Commander Elmer and Lieutenant Gibson and two Marines were ordered to go ashore in full dress uniform, in order that Arthur and myself might receive an apology for our treatment on arriving. The Pasha apologized to the senior naval officer Captain Harmony for treatment of Consul and after usual visits of courtesy we left for Malta on the 28th, having on board our Consul and his family whom we left at Malta. We arrived at Corfu 31st. On August 2nd we left for Triest and arrived on the 6th, having had great gun target practice en route. Machinery needed repairs and we had to remain until 28th. Many of our officers visited Venice and on the 25th Mr. Kearney and I got a week's leave and went to Venice by passenger boat *Milano*, the next morning we were moored to buoy off St. Marco. We took a room at Hotel Bril on the Grand Canal and enjoyed Venice thoroughly. *Congress* having arrived I gave up a portion of my leave of absence so that Dr. Corwin could be with his family in the evenings. On October 2nd, we left Venice and touched at Messina, and then to Naples, arriving on the 7th, and on the following morning Lieutenant Pendleton and I, having obtained 16 days leave of absence, left for Rome, where we had a good guide and wore ourselves out with sightseeing. We left Rome on the 12th for Florence and stopped at Casa Grande. This visit to Florence was most enjoyable and restful. Since joining the *Congress* I had been going too hard; it was one round of duties and social events. It seemed to be an unwritten law of our Navy "that an officer must be agreeable to everyone, make friends especially on foreign stations, and keep them." As a matter of fact, the *Congress* was welcomed everywhere and our stay in port made as enjoyable as possible, and the officers expressed their appreciation by breakfasts, lunches, dinners, and dances on board. In Florence I met a number of members of my shipmates' families, and also Miss Alice Cady, Mrs. Rice, and many others in civil life. I spent much time sightseeing and enjoyed it all, especially the Uffizi and Pitti palaces. The horseback rides here were delightful. I went to Leghorn on the 25th and reported on the *Congress* on the 26th. November 10th, Mr. Kearney and I visited Piza, and it was good to be out of the ship whilst she was being caulked. *Congress* left for Genoa, arriving on the 19th. Orders were received to fill up with coal and proceed to Villefranche, where we arrived 22nd, and received orders to return to United States, leaving Villefranche November 29th. A week full of entertainments and good-byes to our dear friends of Nice and we hoisted our homeward bound pennant.

The Captain, having received permission of the Department, had his wife and three daughters on board for the trip home. The following day we encountered a heavy gale and many were seasick. Arrived Gibraltar December 4th and left for Madeira December 7th. Arrived Funchal, Madeira December 11th; left the 15th after stocking up with Navy Reserve Madeira and Old Malmsey. Our next port was St. Thomas, W. I. We left Madeira under sail so as to save coal. On Christmas day Captain English invited Dr. Dean, Paymaster Thompson, Mr. Whittaker, Lieutenant Pendleton and myself to dine in the cabin, and as Mrs. English and daughters were present it was very enjoyable. A more elaborate dinner could not have been served on shipboard. Sixteen bells at 12 o'clock the night of the 31st, and the New Year was with us. On the 3rd of January we anchored off St. Thomas, visited points of interest and left on the 9th for Port Royal, S. C., arrived on the 17th and found a number of our ships in port. Exchanged calls. About this time orders were received forbidding commanding officers from having their families live on board. About the first of March, I heard that the engagement of Miss Earlena had been broken off, and about the middle of the month I asked permission of Captain English to ask his daughter Earlena to be my wife, and at the first opportunity, which was in Beaufort, where the Captain's family were living, I proposed and was accepted. The wedding was to be immediately after my second examination which was due early in 1877. Mrs. English and Miss Earlena on the 27th started for Holly Springs, Miss., to join Mrs. West, Mrs. English's mother, and I went with them as far as Augusta, and on the following day we parted at the depot in Augusta, and I returned to Beaufort, arriving at 2 p. m., and took a room for the night. I returned to my duties aboard ship that following afternoon.

The *Congress* left Beaufort May 2nd, and after a pleasant run and a beautiful trip up the Delaware River, she anchored just outside the Receiving Ship at the Philadelphia Navy Yard. The *Congress* had been selected to represent the Navy at the opening of the Centennial, and the Captain and officers were to form a part of the escort of President Grant and Emperor Dom Pedro of Brazil who were to open the Centennial Exposition. 10th of May, 1876, ship dressed and 21 guns at sunrise and then one round of entertainments in which we were kept in special full dress uniform most of the time. The Captain and his staff, officers, Lieutenant Gibson of the Marine Corps, and myself were a special body-guard of the President and the Emperor, and were with them when the great Corliss engine was started and the exposition declared open. Here I met for the first time my dear friend, Dr. John C. Boyd of the

MEDICAL DIRECTOR JOHN C. BOYD
U. S. NAVY

Navy, and learned to appreciate his value as a friend. He had just finished his second examination for promotion and achieved an enviable record before the Board of Examiners. He gave me all the points he could as to the requirements of the board and how best to prepare myself for my examination, and before we parted I told him of my engagement to be married, and he promised to be my "best man." Early in July we proceeded to Portsmouth, N. H., and the *Congress* went out of commission on the 26th. Having been detached, ordered home, and placed on waiting orders, I spent a few days at home and received orders to proceed to Philadelphia and report to Captain Whiting for duty at the Naval Hospital, commanded by Medical Director Shippen. Dr. Tinkham was executive officer and Dr. Hawkes and I, assistants. Dr. Hawkes' wife and children had quarters in the hospital and I messed with them. My opportunity for study here was excellent and I commenced work in earnest, visiting the clinics and hospitals of the city, and there I reviewed my textbooks under Dr. Mears. My brother, John, made me a short visit and later Mrs. West and Miss Earlena stopped for a few days at the Exposition on their way from Holly Springs, Miss., to Portsmouth Navy Yard, which Commodore English had been ordered to command. My brother Jones came on to the Centennial and met Miss Earlena for the first time. My next distraction from my studies was on the occasion of the marriage of Miss Mamie English to Lieutenant Taunt, which was in the Commandant's house at the Navy Yard, Portsmouth, N. H. As best man I stood with Miss Earlena. It was a beautiful wedding and many of my friends whom I had known whilst attached to the Receiving Ship were present. I enjoyed a few days' good sleighing and returned to duty at the Hospital, Philadelphia.

I reported for examination April 2nd to Medical Director Wilson, President of Board of Examiners, for promotion. April 14th found qualified for promotion. Returned to Philadelphia and resumed duties at the Naval Hospital. April 18th, detached and placed on waiting orders. April 25th, Miss Earlena and I were married in the home of the Captain, Navy Yard, Portsmouth, N. H. Dr. Boyd was our best man, with a half dozen other groomsmen all in full dress uniform among whom was Dr. Ruth, and among the bridesmaids were Miss Josephine Bunting English, a cousin, now the widow of Henry Brown, Justice of the Supreme Court, and Miss Mamie Wise, now the wife of Admiral Benson.

The wedding was a beautiful affair and the house was packed with guests, Commodore English and his family having been for many years great favorites in Portsmouth, Kittery, and vicinity. We spent our honeymoon in Portland, Maine, and after a few days spent with my wife's parents we went to Culpeper, Va., my home, where we enjoyed ourselves for about three months, when I received orders to report to Admiral Creighton, commandant of the Norfolk, Va., naval station. I reported August 5th and was assigned duty at the Yard Dispensary under Medical

Director King. There being no quarters for me in the yard we lived at the old Atlantic Hotel during the whole of my duty on this station. The duty was pleasant, being from 9 a. m. to 5 p. m., and transportation between Norfolk and the yard by a comfortable tug. I was family physician to Mr. Dodson, proprietor of the Hotel, and frequently prescribed for his guests. We made many friends here and enjoyed Norfolk society. During our stay here my mother made us a visit and later on Commodore English came on to see his daughter, and I obtained a few weeks leave of absence and with my wife and the Commodore took steamer to Richmond on our way to Culpeper on a gunning trip. Going up the James River we heard the full cry of a pack of hounds on shore and in short time we saw a deer take to the water ahead of us evidently intending to swim the river. The Captain of the steamer lowered a boat and captured the deer. He was a beautiful buck. The event created quite an excitement on board and the Commodore remarked that it was a good start on our hunting trip. In Culpeper the Commodore met my family and we had good wing shooting, woodcock, quail, and partridges of which he was very fond and a good wing shot.

We accompanied the Commodore as far as Washington on our return to my station at Norfolk, and shortly after that he was ordered to Washington as Chief of the Bureau of Equipment. My tour of shore duty having about expired, I had a few days leave of absence and went up to Washington and saw the Assistant to the Bureau and told him that I would like duty on the *U.S.S. Tallapoosa*, as it would give me an opportunity to keep in touch with my profession. He assured me that there was no reason why I should not have the duty as Dr. Marstella's cruise would be up about the same time as my shore duty at Norfolk, which he said would be in about three months. Just before the time expired I heard that I was not to have duty on the *Tallapoosa* but that the Bureau had promised it to someone else. I immediately went to Washington, called on the Surgeon General, and asked him if I had been correctly informed. His reply was that he knew nothing about the detail of officers but left it entirely with his assistant to keep the roster. I then told him how his assistant had acted in my case. He did not seem inclined to interfere, however, and then I asked him if I could get the duty did I have his permission, and he replied, "Personally I would like to see you have it." I thanked him and went to see the Secretary of the Navy, Mr. Richard Thompson. I sent my name in and was admitted at once, and before I could say anything he said, "Are you any relation of Richard Rixey (Big Dick)?" I replied that he was my great uncle. He lay back in his chair laughing heartily and said, "Big Dick and I were great chums when we went to school together in Virginia and on one occasion the school master refused to allow us a holiday to which we older boys thought we were entitled. He saw we meant business so he made a break and ran to a farm house close by where we caught and threw him on the floor and put on a pile of sole leather, and commenced to get on the sole leather. Before we had all gotten on he gave us the holiday. Now what can I do for you?" I explained the situation to him and he said, "That's easy—the *Tallapoosa* is my ship, and I will have you on her." I at once returned to the Surgeon General's office and reported the result of my interview with the Secretary. My orders were issued at once and I relieved Dr. Marstella February 21, 1879, reporting to Captain David McRitchie and his Executive Officer, Lieutenant Jones—neither of them graduates of the Naval Academy but both good seamen, and they knew how to handle the *Tallapoosa*. The quarters for guests on this ship were nicely fitted up and we came in contact with many of those prominent in public life. Among those who took occasional trips on the *Tallapoosa* were the Secretary of the Navy and members of his family, and by the end of the cruise we were fast friends. This cruise proved to be all that I had hoped and enabled me to continue my studies and keep in touch with professional work in our large coast cities, especially Philadelphia, New York, and Boston. I visited the hospitals and attended clinics whenever possible, and when in Washington I was with my wife and her family. I enjoyed with them all that Washington society offered and kept in touch with Bureau work and also the work at the Dispensary. During the latter part of this cruise the *Tallapoosa* was commanded by Commander Kellogg. February 21, 1882, I was detached from the *Tallapoosa* and ordered to duty in attendance upon those of the Navy living or stationed in Washington, not otherwise provided with professional attendance. Medical Inspector Hoehling was in charge of the Naval Dispensary and I reported to him as his assistant as the relief of Passed Assistant Surgeon Streets, who informed me that the work consisted in writing the Medical Journal and sitting in the office from 9 a. m. until 4 p. m., except when Dr. Hoehling needed my services. I at once began plans for an office practice which developed much more rapidly than I expected, and Dr. Hoehling was sending me for office treatment many patients whom he had to visit. Medical Director Wales had been appointed Surgeon General before I was detached from the *Tallapoosa* and he had quite an extensive practice, not only among Naval officers and their families but also many patients from civil life. I had, before being ordered to the Dispensary, made myself useful to him as an Assistant and I felt sure I could have his approval and cooperation in making the office of the Dispensary of greater service. With Dr. Hoehling's approval I made out a very modest requisition for an office equipment for the treatment of eye, ear, nose, and throat infections, and Dr. Wales who had begun this work himself before being appointed Surgeon General approved the requisition and made several suggestions as to the development of the office work. Assistant Surgeon R. M. O'Reilly of the Army was assistant to Surgeon Norris on the same duty for the Army that I had at the Naval Dispensary, situated across the street, almost opposite each other. He was as progressive as I was and willing to work, and we soon became close friends and together we took up a special course in Dr. Swan M. Burnett's School of Ophthalmology with a clinical course under him at the Central Dispensary. I improvised a dark room out of a closet adjoining my dispensary office. The Surgeon General and Dr. Hoehling sent me many naval patients and the patients in turn made known my success in office treatment and after the first year I had all the patients I could care for during office hours. I was now studying medicine and practicing it in a most delightful manner. Surgeon General Wales and Surgeon Hoehling were both well equipped and successful practitioners of medicine and I was especially anxious to meet with their approval. Dr. O'Reilly and I continued our specialist's studies, each of us buying better equipment until we had about everything we required in the way of instruments and confidence in ourselves. In after years I was appointed Surgeon General of the Navy and about the same time he was made Surgeon General of the Army.

Our work was most attractive and many a night after dinner we worked together studying the technique and practice of surgery in all its branches. We bought pigs' eyes in the market and placed them in a face mask and performed every operation possible on them. Artificial light for examination and new instruments were tested. Occasionally patients for special interest would meet us at my office for a consultation. Thus engaged, the time passed swiftly.

Admiral English wished to fly his flag as Rear Admiral and asked to be relieved of duty as Chief of Bureau, and be ordered as Commander in Chief of a squadron. His orders were issued to take passage on the North German Lloyd Steamer *Fulda* sailing on September 10, 1884, for Southampton, to join his flagship the *Lancaster*. I was a great admirer of my wife's father as an officer and a man of sterling worth and as I had served under him as Captain of the *Congress* I wanted to be with him on this, his last cruise. My application for duty on the *Lancaster* was granted and I was detached from the Dispensary and orders issued to sail on the *Fulda*, September 10th for Southampton, to report for duty on the *Lancaster*. This order, much to my surprise, was revoked by the Secretary of the

Navy, Mr. Chandler. I immediately laid my case before the Secretary and told him I was especially anxious to make this cruise with Admiral English as it would probably be his last. My orders were renewed and I was on the *Fulda* in good time, having some good friends to see me off at New York, among them my dear friend, Dr. Boyd. On the *Fulda* going to the *Lancaster* for duty besides the Admiral and myself were: Paymaster C. P. Thompson, a shipmate on my first cruise, and Chief Engineer Johnson. We had a very pleasant passage and arrived at Southhampton September 18th. Lieutenant Paul from the *Lancaster* came alongside in steam launch and bag and baggage we were soon aboard the flagship. I reported to Captain E. E. Potter, the senior officer present, and met the officers of the ship. On the 20th the Admiral's flag was hoisted with the usual ceremonies. The medical officers of the flagship were Medical Inspector Henry M. Wells, Fleet Surgeon, Passed Assistant Surgeons P. M. Rixey and S. H. Griffith. Dr. Griffith and I alternated days duty, and every day that I was off I devoted to seeing the principal places of interest in and around Southhampton; one of special interest to me was the Royal Victoria Hospital and Netley Army and Navy Medical School at Netley. Called on Surgeon General Longmore and met Professor Aitkin. Heard General Longmore's opening address to a class of 37 candidates. He outlined the objects of the school and told the young men what was expected of them at the school and afterwards as Army and Navy surgeons. Met Surgeon General Murray in command of the hospital. Visited the *Hector*, a receiving hospital ship. I spent as much time at the school and hospitals as possible and was very much impressed with how much the English were ahead of the United States in the working out of medical problems, especially as to fitting the young surgeon of the Army and Navy for future service. A full description of the work done here before my time had been written by Medical Directors Dean and Shippen of our Navy, two of our ablest officers under both of whom I had served. On one occasion when I was deploring our want of facilities for the training of our young surgeons and telling him of my personal experience, I asked Dr. Dean what was the real cause of our being so far behind the English. His reply was that it was "the want of interest of those in authority. We have done our best to improve conditions, but our work has been in vain. As soon as we enter the Navy we are off to sea a good portion of our time and do not come in contact with the powers that be sufficiently to gain their interest."

Mr. B. F. Stevens, our dispatch agent, came down from London to consult me professionally. On October the 7th, we left for Lisbon, Portugal. Arrived on the 11th and were quarantined until 17th. One of the men fell from the main yard, struck on the rigging, and bounced into deep water, and was picked up considerably bruised and shaken up, but was soon well again. *Kersearge* in port, *Quinnebaug* came in on the 15th, and the Brazilian *Reacheulo* a new ironclad, and I was much interested in her arrangement for the medical department. The sick bay was amidship on the starboard side, the dispensary opening into it with every convenience up to date. The sick bay in time of action was fitted for torpedo appliances. No ship in our Navy at that time could compare with this ship in the care and comfort of those needing medical or surgical assistance. The following is a list of the *Lancaster* officers:

Commander in Chief—Rear Admiral Earl English.

Personal Staff—Chief of Staff, Captain Edward E. Potter; Aide, Lieutenant E. H. Taunt; Aide, Lieutenant Nathan Sargent; Aide, Paymaster Charles P. Thompson; Lieutenant Commander John Schonler; Lieutenants Henry N. Manney, Andrew Dunlap, Allen G. Paul, Duncan Kennedy, William P. Potter, and Korsuth Niles; Ensigns Joseph Beale and James S. Brown; 10 naval cadets; Medical Inspector H. M. Wells; Passed Assistant Surgeons P. M. Rixey and S. H. Griffith; Pay Inspector Edwin Steward; Chief Engineer George R. Johnson; Passed Asst. Engineers Charles W. Rae and A. B. Canaga; Assistant Engineers F. C. Bieg and A. O. Young; Chaplain David H. Tribou; Captain of Marines Alfred S. Taylor; Second Lieutenant of Marines Henry C. Haines.

In Lisbon I visited the principal places of interest and made many friends. Interested in Royal Hospital of St. Joseph for general diseases, capacity about 900 beds. Visited special hospital for cutaneous diseases.

Left Lisbon on October 29th and arrived Tangier, Morocco, on November 2nd. I was made caterer of the wardroom mess. Met Colonel Mathews and he promised the officers good hunting during their stay at Tangier. On the 4th we went wild boar hunting, a party of officers from the ship headed by the Admiral and Captain with Colonel Mathews and a party of ladies and gentlemen, all on horseback, fine horses and very pleasant, but more of a parade than hunt. There were about a hundred moor beaters but not much good. I did not get a boar. On the 6th, Mr. Manney and I went shooting and killed a number of red legged partridges. On the 7th I was consulted by the Minister of Foreign Affairs and found that he had cataract, both eyes. Dined with the Consul and daughter at a large dinner given in honor of the Admiral. On the 8th a boar hunt and I succeeded in spearing the first boar; we killed a number and brought two fine ones on board and we enjoyed eating them. Called on Mr. and Mrs. Perdicaris. Left Tangier 9th and arrived Gibraltar same day. Bought mess stores of Mr. Sacone. Left Gibraltar 14th. Since my visit to Gibraltar on the *Congress* in 1875 there had been few changes. Arrived at Port Mahon, Minorca, November 19th, and remained until the 26th. I enjoyed here two days' woodcock hunting in company with the Admiral and Mr. Manney as the guests of Mr. Bationi. Mr. Mer went with us with his two dogs and we bagged a number of birds. Arrived Villefranche November 29th. Just nine years since I left this port on the *Congress*, and on the *Lancaster* I had three of my best friends who were shipmates on the *Congress*, Admiral English, Paymaster Thompson, and Chaplain Tribou. Villefranche and Nice were much as when I last visited them but I missed very much the many friends who were there in 1874 and 1875. The Admiral rented the Villa des Orangers, No. 3, Avenue Verdi, Nice, for the winter for his family consisting of Mrs. English and Miss Frankie, Mrs. Taunt and baby Earlena Taunt, who lived with them. Miss Frankie was housekeeper, and a room was always ready for me when I was on shore. The family of the Admiral arrived early in December and took possession of the cottage. Andrew Erickson, seaman, died in the hospital ashore of pneumonia, December 13th. Quite busy looking after the sick, and getting our quarterly report ready, looking after mess affairs, and meeting social engagements. We gave two hops on board before Christmas and met many of the officers' wives, among them Mrs. Griffith, Mrs. Manney, Mrs. Schonler, Mrs. Vial, the Misses Baird, Dr. and Mrs. Wakefield and others. I took my Christmas dinner on board; as I could not be with my wife I wanted Dr. and Mrs. Griffith to be with Mrs. Griffith's father and mother, General and Mrs. Watmough, who had just arrived at Nice. On board, the men were all happy decorating and enjoying their Christmas dinner, as only sailors on sea duty know how. Orders had been received and after Christmas it became generally known that we were ordered to the mouth of the river Congo, West Coast of Africa, about February 1st. Much excitement was evident among the personnel of the ship as every one had hoped that the ship would return to the European squadron. A large percentage of the crew were foreigners, especially the bandsmen, and had enlisted with the expectation the Flagship would remain in or near the Mediterranean Sea where many of their families lived. The Fleet Surgeon, Dr. Wells, being away on leave, much work devolved on me to have the Medical Department ready for a long cruise. Medical stores must be bought, and a report for the fourth quarter, 1885, must be sent in with the yearly abstract of patients. Besides, I was still caterer of the wardroom mess and must see mess stores laid in ample for a long cruise, and social duties must be performed. I had hoped if the *Lancaster* remained in Europe to have Mrs. Rixey meet me in January at her father's cottage in Nice. She had remained behind, when her mother and sisters came over, to be with her grandmother, Mrs. West, who was in poor health. I was much disappointed and it was fortunate that I had my work cut out for me so that time passed quickly. We were the recipient of many hospitalities and any spare time I had was taken up with horseback riding, etc., a ride with Mr. Vial to Monaco, where we breakfasted, and afterwards rode over his country place. It was beautiful and he purposed to live there when he retired from business—this day I enjoyed more than any since I left my wife. A few other horseback rides and two hops on board in this month of January, besides breakfasts, dinners, and dances ashore, and on February 9th we left Nice and arrived Gibraltar on the 14th, and finished laying in our supply of stores. Here the officers of the ship paid the way home to the United States for a woman and little girl who needed assistance. We left Gibraltar February 19th and arrived Tangier, Morocco, same day, and left on the 21st. Arrived Santa Cruise, Tenerife, 26th. Under sail part of the time. Charles H. Francis died of pneumonia just as we dropped anchor; contracted the disease at Gibraltar; buried in the English cemetery. Left 8 p. m., 26th and arrived Sierra Leone, Africa, March 8th, anchored off Freetown. Lots of fruit, alligator pears, bananas, pineapples, oranges, beautiful pink apples, peanuts, and cocoanuts. Coaling ship. Steamer arrived with home mail on the 11th and we up anchored on the 12th for Geree Dakar, arrived March 15th. In our last mail the Admiral received orders after leaving the Congo to proceed to the South Atlantic Station. Much excitement at the news, and many of our men asked for their discharge, and our bandmaster assured me that he would die of yellow fever if he went to South America. Coaled ship on the 22nd and on the 24th we went on a picnic party over the new railroad and enjoyed the novelty and getting away from the ship awhile. The Admiral, Mr. Strickland, Lieutenant Sargent, Dr. Griffith and myself, with Harry, a wardroom boy carrying our lunch basket. We lunched near the terminus of the railroad. On our way back the engine and two coaches were derailed about sixteen miles from Dakar and already dark. Fortunately we were near the Ocean and a passing steamer from Sierra Leone took us aboard and we reached our ship quite satisfied with our experiences. I spent several days shooting here and bagged a number of partridges and other game. April 1st, we left for Libreville, Gaboon River, arriving on the 17th, and having taken in coal, left on the 23rd and at 8 p. m. we crossed the line and old Neptune came aboard and notified us that he would return the following day.

King Neptune's Visit to the Lancaster
April 24, 1885

"Ships our cradles, decks our pillows,
Lulled by winds and rocked by billows,
Gaily bound we o'er the tide,
Hope our anchor, and Heaven our guide."

Have you crossed the line? Did Neptune pay your ship a visit? and questions of similar import were the most momentous ones asked one of the other, and answered affirmatively or negatively by a number of our ship's company as we neared the Equator, on a passage from Europe to the Congo.

In the natural sequence of things earthly, these simple interrogatories fathered, and the precedent established in times past, by the ship's companies of nearly every vessel that had crossed the Equator, suggested to our old sea dogs that this would be a favorable opportunity of reviving the now nearly obsolete custom of shaving, which had for its object the twofold intent of affording amusement to relieve the monotony of the doldrums, as well as furnishing Neptune and his retinue with liberal quantities of stimulating beverages, which were paid as forfeit by officers and passengers, rather than be subjected to the rough handling incident to being shaved by Neptune's barber.

In a man-of-war, when the ship's company intend to have any amusement, that is, such as can be afforded by a boat race, athletic contests of any kind, or on occasions like the present, it is customary to interest one of the officers of the ship in the affair, in order to bring it to a successful issue. In the present case, Lieutenant A. G. Paul came to the assistance of the ship's company, and to his exertions and suggestions is partly due the success of the whole affair. The efforts of the humble "sea laborers" who took an active part must not be forgotten; they in their turn will be remembered when the duties for which they were detailed shall be narrated, or the performance of tasks self-imposed by a few of them shall be recorded.

Of the passage from Villefranche there is nothing of interest to write about until we dated ourselves the 23d of April, at Libreville, River Gaboon, West Coast of Africa, twenty-two miles north of the Equator. We called in here to coal ship; the coal all on board, we left our anchorage at 3:00 p. m. of the above date, bound south, and a few hours later we were in the domain of the "King of the Seas."

At 7:30 p. m., the startling cry of "ship ahoy!" was heard fore and aft; there's Neptune! there's Neptune! said all who heard the hail. "Halloo!" was answered from the bridge by the Officer of the Deck; and the questions of the interrogator, of what ship, where bound, etc., were answered by the Officer of the Deck. Who are you? in a commanding tone of voice came from the bridge of our ship. Neptune, King of the Seas, was answered, followed by a request to heave to, as he had a desire to come on board. In obedience to the request the Officer of the Deck rang two bells, at the same time informing the Admiral and Captain through their orderlies that his Majesty was alongside and desired to see them. Call all hands to muster, was now the order from the Officer of the Deck; the Boatswain's mates sounded their calls, and passed the order in a loud tone of voice, the ship's company immediately assembled on the port side, the Admiral, Captain, and officers at their customary stations on the starboard side of the quarter-deck. Neptune, accompanied by his wife, had by this time reached the quarter-deck; they boarded the ship over the starboard bow, instead of coming aboard by the more convenient way of the sea-ladder at the starboard gangway, which he was requested to use, if not for his own convenience, at least out of respect for his consort. Either the force of habit was too strong, or the rights of the fair sex are no more respected in the aqueous regions than they are among the inhabitants of terra-firma, and use the gangway he would not. Without any further preface than a nod of recognition, Neptune addressed the Admiral and Captain in the following words:

I make my respects, Admiral English, to thee;
You know Father Neptune, the King of the Sea.
I do you the honor to visit your ship;
So I wish you success, and a prosperous trip.
Likewise, Captain Potter, to see you I'm glad,
I remember I shaved you when you were a lad.
You command a fine ship, she carries big guns;
You do credit to Neptune as one of his sons.
You have a good crew, Sir, as I plainly can see,
But they'll be all the better when shaven by me.
This is my wife, Amphitrite, the Queen,
She has already detected how many are green;
And tomorrow I'll be ready with my razor and lotion,
To make them good sailors, and sons of the ocean.

My respects to you, Sirs, you know me of old;
I am proud of my sons who are valiant and bold.
You have long crossed my waters, my ocean so free,
And you know Father Neptune, the King of the sea.
Now lads, before long you will see me return,
Tho' the winds may blow strong you cannot leave me astern;
Tomorrow I know you'll be crossing my line,
So be ready for me at the hour of nine.
Good night to you all, and a blessing from me,
And now I and my wife will go back to the sea.

After finishing his address Neptune engaged the Admiral in conversation for a few moments, in which old times were referred to. Receiving his promise of returning on the following morning, he handed to the Admiral a package containing telegrams from the Equatorial Submarine Telegraph Company (Limited), and a mail bag containing letters for the officers and some of the crew, as well as certificates for all of the officers and crew whom he recognized as subjects; and similar ones, with the name and date blank, which were to be filled out and delivered to all who should on the following day undergo the process necessary to make them children of the sea.

Good night all hands! and he was gone. The order was now given by the Officer of the Deck to the Boatswain's mates to pipe down; a peculiar blast on their whistles which was well understood by the crew, and they slowly walked forward. In a few moments, and before an opportunity could be given to discuss the coming and going of Neptune, the Master-at-Arms was heard crying out on the spar deck, "Get your mail!" He was immediately surrounded by a number of the crew; he called out the names of, and delivered to, the persons to whom they were addressed the letters and certificates contained in the mail brought by Neptune from the line. Eight bells was now struck, the watch was relieved, and the customary silence of the night enjoined and enforced; the watch below in their hammocks dreaming of the morrow, and the watch on deck in subdued whispers relating their recollections of previous visits from Neptune, and the less favored or "Greenies" racking their brains as to the possible fate in store for them on the following morning.

At 9:00 a. m. on the morning of the 24th, everything was in readiness for the day's sport, all hands were called to muster, and as on the evening previous, the ship's company assembled on the quarter-deck to receive, as well as witness the reception of his Majesty by the Admiral, Captain and Officers. It was not the intention of his Majesty that anything should be omitted that would have a tendency to create the impression that he should receive, or was entitled to less consideration than is due to Earthly Sovereigns, and before presenting himself to the Admiral and Captain he ordered his police, headed by their chief, to form in two ranks in the starboard gangway. As soon as they were in marching order the band, which was stationed on the forecastle, struck up the Policeman's Song. They stepped out, marched down the starboard gangway to the mainmast, halted, faced to the front and sang:

When constabulary duties are to be done,
You will generally find us basking in the sun.
Taking one consideration with another,
Neptune's force is a bully one, bully one.
When we are sent for anyone,
You bet your life they come;
When we are sent for any one,
No matter who they are,
You can bet your bottom dollar,
They will come, they will come.

They emphasized the last word of each line by bringing down their clubs together on deck with a whang; when finished singing, they faced to the right, marched forward, and formed on both sides of Neptune's Chariot, he now being ready to be presented to the Admiral and Captain.

With his Majesty's kind permission we will take a look at him, his wife and retinue, as well as their make-up, before they move aft to the quarter-deck. The Chariot, on which he and his wife were seated, was made by lashing two halliard racks together; the motive power, eight of his followers, manned a drag rope secured to it; with his long grey beard of teazed manilla, tin crown on his head, and trident in right hand, he looked every inch a King. His better half, with long blonde hair of the same material as his whiskers, a richly colored calico dress, formerly the property of the ship's minstrel troupe, and stockingless and shoeless pedal extremities, she looked very little the Queen, which was attributed by his Highness to the fact that she had no desire to accompany him on this trip, and positively refused so to do; by the exercise of his power, however, backed by a material persuader in the shape of a big club, he induced her to consent to come at the last moment. The Doctor, evidently a renegade from this mundane sphere, under his Majesty's protection, was considerate enough to bring with him a grip sack well filled with all of the medicines that would be of any use to the seasick, or sick of the sea patients who might apply to him for treatment, or who should require something to strengthen their nervous system before undergoing the prescribed course at the hands of Neptune's tonsorial artist. That he gave satisfaction to all his patients is certain; their evidence, however, will not be recorded until after Gabriel has tooted his horn and they have returned from the "tongueless dust" to which his nostrums consigned them. The police, "rigged up" in what Neptune's better half had left of the minstrel's property, supplying deficiencies with gunny sacks, pieces of canvas, and the liberal use of paint, in everything but dress would have put to shame an equal number of the "Finest."

Neptune, being satisfied with the appearance of his retinue, concluded to move aft; the services of the band were brought into requisition, and to the enlivening strains of a march, the procession moved slowly aft. When the head of the line reached the mainmast, the Signal Quartermaster hoisted and broke at the main his Majesty's Royal Standard, which consisted of a white field sixteen feet by eight feet, bearing the inscription Neptunus Rex; in the center of the field was painted a large dolphin, and each of the four corners were ornamented with shell fish painted thereon. On the right of Neptune, manning a stout line secured to the neck of the stuffed effigy of a horse, stood twelve seamen bold, with countenances beaming with pleasure in consequence of the pleasant duty they were about to perform, which was nothing less than celebrating in manner following the death of poor old horse. As Neptune moved aft they at the same instant straightened out taut their line and commenced to drag the horse aft, each one in his turn singing a verse of a "shanty," to which all joined in chorus, the long strong pulls together being regulated by certain emphasized words in each line of song and chorus. Arriving abreast of the starboard gangway, they halted until Neptune's retinue had passed them, then picking up the old horse, they launched him with a shout into the big drink. This little side-show was intended to illustrate an event in the life of a sailor on a long voyage; that is, that he had been long enough on the voyage to work up his advance wages, or as he terms it, the "dead horse," and even in the pure atmosphere that he is accustomed to live carrion is objectionable as company, and so old horse must go not to the boneyard but overboard. Arriving on the quarter-deck, the policemen, bears, and other followers of Neptune halted and formed, faced to the front or inboard. Neptune and wife, followed by the Doctor and Barber on foot, continued on aft until within a few feet of the Admiral and Captain, when he and his wife alighted, bowed to the Admiral and Captain, and without further ado counter-marched forward to the bridge to commence the shaving. Neptune's wife on the arm of the Admiral, and Neptune himself escorted by the Captain. In their rear followed the Doctor, Barber, Clerk, and Officers of the Ship; the ship's company at the same time rushed forward to secure the best possible places to witness the shaving.

Amidship on the bridge were grouped, standing, the Admiral, Captain, and Officers. Neptune and wife were seated on the starboard side of the bridge. On the port side was a large tub containing the lather made of soap, molasses, and flour, over which the Barber and assistants kept a watchful eye. The Doctor stood hard by to render assistance whenever his professional services should be required. Neptune's Secretary, who was an important character, must not be forgotten; he also occupied a place on the bridge; his duties required him to call the names as they were arranged on lists in his possession of the individuals to be shaved. As the names were called, the victims either presented themselves voluntarily, or the ship was searched for them by the board side; arriving on the bridge, they received a nod of recognition from Neptune and were hurried across the bridge, turned over to the barber, received a good share of lather, applied with a white-wash brush, had it partly removed by a large wooden razor in the hands of the barber, and then they were carefully lifted from the bridge and dropped into an awning in the port gangway, so secured as to form a large tub, which was filled with water by a hose connected to the steam pumps. While in the awning, the individual shaved was attended to by the bears of Neptune, who were there to receive him; after undergoing a good ducking he was allowed to scramble out, and he was *henceforth* considered a bona fide son of the sea. As each new victim received his dose the cheers and laughter of the crew expressed their appreciation of the fun.

What means all this rushing and pushing? Have we not enough to engage our attention and amuse us? Who is it? What is it? asks one of another, as they climb on hatch combings and ship's rail to get a better view of the crowd who have collected in the vicinity of the starboard gangway. A deputation of mermaids, say some, to pay a visit to an American Admiral from the European Station, evidently a stranger to these waters, at least so it is recorded in the hotel registers of these parts. One of the Railroad Kings of Neptune's Domain trying the new rapid transit route to the water's surface, say others. The suspense, however, was not of long duration; the announcement that he was on board; that he was the late Honorable Secretary of the Navy, Mr. Chandler, accompanied by a travelling companion, one Mr. Sanford by name, was received with cheers, three cheers, three times three cheers; no following suit cheers, no affectation about these cheers, but three hearty cheers from everyone capable of voicing them, and from the bottom of their hearts; yes, and from still further down their anatomy. The medical records of this ship show that sixty-nine men and boys were under the Surgeon's care for fully three weeks, they having torn the toe nails from their toes by their efforts in the cheering line.

Escorted to the bridge, Neptune received them with a "heathen chinee" smile, paying marked attention to the individual with the lengthy prefix to his name. After passing the customary compliments, he interrogated them in a low tone of voice; the questions and answers thereto could not be heard; they were not for mortal ears to hear. Suddenly, Neptune arose from his seat, and with left arm raised and extended to full length on a line with the shoulder, the index finger pointing to the tub, he cried out, "bounce them!" Neptune's attendants immediately laid hold of them, and hurried them to the barber. After being lathered and shaved, the next dose was a ducking in the awning, but Neptune was on hand and forbade it. "Overboard!" he cried; "overboard with them!" and launched from the bridge they were, head foremost, to be domiciled in the bodies of whales until, Jonah-like, they should be cast out upon terra-firma.

The sport of the day was climaxed by the shaving of G. Savasta, Chief Musician, who had endeavored to escape shaving by securing a certicate under false pretenses; he was brought before Neptune and closely interrogated as to the name of the vessel, to what port bound, when he crossed the line, and a description of the port at which he arrived. His answers to all the questions, except the last one, could not be disputed; but failing to give satisfaction when asked for a description of Montevideo, his fate was sealed, and the order of Neptune to "bounce him" was received with a prolonged cheer from the crew. The barber's attendants gave him an extra lathering; the barber used both edge and back of the razor on him; and the bears paid extra attention to him when they received him in the awning.

It was now nearing the hour of twelve, and a longer continuance of the ceremony would render it dull and uninteresting, by reason of its sameness. Neptune declared himself satisfied with his reception; he ordered his clerk to proclaim the fact that all who had not been shaved would be granted certificates, and they could consider themselves as much his children as though they had been shaved; bidding the Admiral, Captain, Officers, and crew goodbye and a pleasant passage, he returned to the sea with his wife and gang, or more properly speaking, to the quiet recesses of the ship, to enjoy the beer received by the payment of the forfeits.

The day's amusement having been brought to a close, and the ship's people having dropped into their accustomed habits of every day ship's life, it will not be saying too much when it is asserted that the whole affair passed off pleasantly; the best of good humor prevailed, and those who were compelled to undergo the shaving process accepted the dose with all possible good grace, and entered as heartily into the sport as the old sea dogs who had crossed the line twenty or thirty years ago.

Old sailors are hard to please, and although they admitted that this visit of Neptune was on a grander scale than anything they had ever witnessed, yet they growled. What's the matter now? says a young Ordinary Seaman to an old Quarter-Gunner. He was answered with a disdainful look; the old Quarter-Gunner would not answer one so much his junior, but as he walked away he was heard muttering something about what a darned old fool Neptune was, to have his line in such a thundering hot country. All who witnessed, or those who took a more active part, either as Neptune, his wife, or gang, will remember with pleasure for a number of years to come the 24th day of April, 1885, in the good ship *Lancaster*.

My Diploma as a Son of the Sea

NEPTUNUS REX GREETING TO

ALL GOOD SAILORS AROUND THE WORLD—

Whereas, We have been pleased to take into Our Royal Consideration and give this as a Royal patent under Our sign manual to certify that P. A. SURGEON P. M. RIXEY has this day visited our Royal Domain in the *U. S. S. Lancaster* and gone through the requisite initiation and form to become one of us.

We, therefore, in case of losing his head and falling over board, recommend all Sharks, Dolphins, Whales, Crabs, Eels, and Pollywogs under our command to abstain from eating, playing with, or otherwise maltreating his person. We further direct all sailors, soldiers, marines, politicians, and land lubbers who have not crossed our Royal Domain, to treat him with that proper respect due to one who has visited us: Disobey under penalty of Our Royal Displeasure.

Given at Our Court on the Equator this 24th day of April, 1885, according to the computation of mundane generations.

A few words in reference to those who did their best to amuse the ship's company on this occasion: J. A. Fisher (Gunner's Mate), as Neptune, received the unanimous vote of the ship's company as the Perfection of a King, "he had been there before;" Henry Graham (Ordinary Seaman), as his wife, notwithstanding the little unpleasantness between herself and liege lord, acquitted herself in queenly fashion; Robert Lindsay (Quartermaster), as the doctor, received the credit of outdoing himself by his able representation of the quack; J. J. McDonough (Seaman), as Chief of Police, was declared to bear a marked resemblance to Captain Williams, although he lacked a little in physique the proportions of the celebrated New Yorker; while our funny man, George F. Bray (Seaman), as barber, enlivened the whole proceedings with his antics and clownish movements.

In the first half of the present century, through the agency of Fulton and others with their crude efforts in the application of the hidden powers of steam to mechanical contrivances of different kinds, and the intelligent labors of the engineer of the last two decades, a power has been produced for the propulsion of sea-going vessels that has almost entirely superseded sails, and in a few more years "the white winged messenger of peace" will be of the past, forgotten, save by song, romance and history. The old time sailors have, with a few exceptions, disappeared; nought remains of them but their disembodied spirits, hovering round either Cape in the Antipodes, as Albatross or Cape Pigeons; restless still as when in human form viewing with horror that new innovation of man, the *Ocean Express,* and giving vent to their pleasure with screams of delight at the laboring and vain efforts of the heavily ladened and poorly built *Ocean Tramp* to weather the boisterous gale.

The old time sailor no more, the sailing vessel almost gone, visits from Neptune in the future will be replaced by some more modern amusement.

Such amusements were of much use when sails represented engines and winds, steam or electricity. After the ships were out of sight of land for a month or more at a time, amusements of some kind relieved the homesickness and ennui of ship life.

We anchored off the mouth of the Congo River about dusk April 27th and next morning entered the river and anchored off Banana Point. Found the *Kearserge* in and got our mail. The Admiral had selected Lieutenant Taunt to go up the Congo and he went with the party of the Governor, a Colonel of the English Army. They started on May 2nd, Lieutenant Taunt having been detached from this ship. In the afternoon of the same day we up anchored and next stopped at St. Paul de Loando, arriving May 4th, coaled ship, and left 8th, arriving Jamestown, St. Helena, May 16th. We laid quite close in and found the English cruiser *Rapid* at anchor. I received thirty letters, most of them from my wife. From the *Lancaster*, St. Helena looked like an immense rock under the shadow of which we lay. We remained there nearly a month, giving the officers and men time to recuperate before going where we expected considerable exposure to epidemic diseases. I enjoyed St. Helena visiting every point of interest, horseback riding, and some good shooting. One shooting trip I enjoyed very much. Admiral English was staying at "Longwood" with Mr. Deison and I rode over to see how he was and took my gun, and we had a good quiet day's shooting, killing a number of the beautiful English pheasants and partridges. June 9th, we hoisted anchor and went to sea under steam but soon banked fires and relied on sails. Slow progress and on 26th we got up steam and arrived July 1st at Rio de Janeiro, Brazil, having been three weeks out of sight of land. On arriving there, orders were issued on medical officers' recommendation that no liberty would be given after sundown. However, as the band needed recruits the Flag Lieutenant gave permission to the Master of the Band, Sevasta and his first musician, Tremonti, so they could select recruits at the evening concerts. On the ninth day after our arrival in port, Sevasta was taken ill and reported at sick call. He informed me that he had been staying ashore, so suspecting yellow fever I had him isolated as much as possible and reported to Captain Potter. He said, "No sir, I never saw a case like Sevasta's. I would like to have the health officer of the port come off in consultation." He came and pronounced it a very bad case of bilious fever—gave me a permit to put him in Misericordia Hospital where I saw him again at 4 p. m., with black vomit before midnight, and he was dead the next morning—a typical case of yellow fever. Poor Sevasta's prediction that he would die of yellow fever had come true. Tremonti—who had assumed Sevasta's duties, was taken ill on the 22nd, had black vomit 24th, and died the 29th. All shore leave was stopped and there was no more yellow fever. At that time the mosquito theory of yellow fever had not been established and Dr. Sternberg of the Army was in Rio de Janeiro studying the disease. In view of what we know now these two men who were ashore in the evening had been bitten by infected mosquitos, with the result as stated. Lieut. Comdr. Schonler had been ill for a long while and was detached and ordered home. Pay Inspector Stewart was also ordered home. Paymaster Thompson took his place as Fleet Paymaster, Lieutenant Potter was detailed as Secretary to the Admiral. With several of the officers I visited Petropolis and most points of interest in and around Rio. Reported that the Admiral was to be ordered home. Visited Mr. Mackie professionally. On the 28th Dr. Griffith's wife arrived and he had leave of absence for a week. Dr. Wells was on leave at Tijuea. Called on Mrs. Jarvis professionally at the request of Governor Jarvis, our Minister to Brazil. Presented a fine pointer puppy by Mr. Ketelle, called him "Molique," and received permission to keep him on board.

September 29th left Rio for Montevideo, Uruguay. Arrived October 7th and anchored about three miles from the shore. Admiral and staff stopped at the Hotel Pyramid. Admiral English received orders by wire to proceed home. Steamer did not sail until 27th. We had the Admiral dine with us on 26th, Thanksgiving Day, and saw him off the next day. I felt deeply the position the dear Admiral was placed in. He was one of the most lovable men I have ever met, one of the most competent officers, and his whole life had been one of devotion to the welfare of the Navy—over 45 years of active service of which over 27 years had been spent at sea. This was my second cruise under him. On the *Congress* as commanding officer he was always on deck, night and day, when the ship was in peril; on the *Lancaster*, as Commander-in-Chief he was a model of efficiency where duty was concerned, and every ship in the squadron was kept fit for any emergency. Duty came first with him. Flag Lieutenant Sargent accompanied the Admiral home, also Lieutenant Fred Tyler, who was condemned by medical survey. I had treated the latter for yellow fever during the absence of Dr. Smith, his ship's surgeon. A number of officers from the flagship saw the Admiral on the steamer and said goodbye. Nothing would have suited me better than to have been of the party going home.

On the 28th, the Captain received orders directing the *Lancaster* to proceed to Madagascar and southeast coast of Africa. In Montevideo I had met Dr. Bourse, who was very fond of shooting and he told me of the great estencias, or farms in Uruguay, and proposed that we make a visit to one of them on a hunting trip. I was much pleased at the prospect and he made all the arrangements and on December 5th at daybreak Mr. Canega, Mr. Hewes, and myself left the ship at daybreak, met by Dr. Bourse at landing with a carriage, and took train from Central Station for Duranzo, passed through Santa Lucia, and stopped at Florida for breakfast, eight courses in 30 minutes. I had "Molique" with me and he behaved well for a ship dog. Arrived Duranzo about 3:30 p. m. and employed a diligence, a coach and five horses, a driver holding the reins over four white horses abreast, and an outsider with his lasso fastened to the end of the pole with which he, riding beside the coach horses guided the coach. We made a 4 a. m. start and crossed the

River Yi on a ferry propelled by a wire pulled by two oxen. Every eight miles horses were changed and at 11 a. m. we stopped at a cabin for breakfast which the lady of the cabin agreed to prepare for us, we furnishing meat, etc. On leaving we offered to pay but not a cent would she take, and the further we went into the interior the less we found the natives thought of money and the more of their mounts, bridles, and saddles, some of the latter real works of art mounted with silver plates, buckles, etc. We arrived at the Paraso Estencia of Don Carlos Reiley at about noon and killed a few birds and deer that afternoon. The estencia's casa (house) was quite picturesque and showed the owner was a man of tact and very great wealth. His immense estencia (farm) was about 500 miles square, and he had 100,000 head of cattle, 60,000 sheep, and any number of horses, ostriches, etc. The deer are wild, or supposed to be, and would run from a man on foot, but on horseback or in a carriage you could easily get within 100 or 300 yards of them. The first afternoon of our arrival after the rest of our party started off hunting I accompanied Dr. Bourse to see a patient of his on the estencia, and imagine my surprise when a beautiful landau, the special equipment of Don Carlos was driven up to take us in. This we used all the time we were at the estencia, shooting from it at deer and having it follow us when on foot. This immense body of land was devoid of trees, except where the eucalyptus trees had been planted; they are of very quick growth and already the casa had a fine grove of them alongside. From our arrival to our departure on the afternoon of the 8th we were shooting every hour of light and beautifully entertained when at the casa. We killed 25 deer and a number of birds and came into Duranzo with 15 deer on top of our coach, where we spent the night and next day arrived at Montevideo. Pampero blowing and we were unable to get off to our ship until next morning. December 10th—from now until we left we were busy getting in stores. On December 17th we pulled up anchor, swung ship, had target practice, and under sail alone we started our long voyage to Cape Town,

South Africa. Christmas 1885—since leaving port we had averaged about 100 miles; blowing, raining, and disagreeable on deck. We had Captain Potter and three steerage officers to dine with us in the wardroom. Christmas week was a very stormy one followed by an immense rainfall flooding the spar deck and running over the hatch combings, flooding the decks below, the wardroom getting its full share. On the 31st I resigned my position of caterer of wardroom mess, having held the position for fourteen months and received the thanks of the mess and was unanimously reelected; however, I declined to serve, and Chaplain Tribou was elected. January 1, 1886, I dined in the steerage. Caught an albatross and prepared the skin for mounting. With the New Year I commenced reviewing my French and German. Special full dress muster on the 3rd, the next four days were very uncomfortable, having three hard blows and driven below 40° and only made about 60 miles towards the Cape. About the 13th got a fair breeze and went due east for several days when we lost our wind and got up steam, after ten hours breeze freshened and we banked fires. On the 21st we got up steam and were in sight of land on January 23rd, just 37 days since we saw it last. As we came to anchor in Table Bay, Cape Town, saw fresh fruits and vegetables in abundance and what an appetite for them after so long a voyage. We had had no accidents and very little sickness since leaving Montevideo. This was Cape Town summer season, and we had strawberries, peaches, apples, nectarines, bananas, grapes, watermelons, cantaloupes, green figs and pineapples, all in season.

On the 25th, ship hauled in alongside the outer wharf and the gang plank was run out. One round of visits with the English officers and citizens of Cape Town. Horseback rides and visited Mr. Albrecht's farm, sampled his wines and enjoyed his and his wife's hospitality. A party of us dined with the Royal Scots on the 4th—good music, a brass band alternating with the Highland Pipers who marched around the table several times while playing. On the 6th we were still caulking ship. Paymaster Thompson, Mr. Manney, and Chief Engineer Johnson accepted Mr. Grady's invitation to visit Van Renan's place, High Costenzia. We had beautiful bays four in hand and made a day of it enjoying the scenery and refreshments of all kinds. On the 8th Dr. Wells and I called on Dr. Parson and were shown through the hospital. Mr. Day invited me to go shooting with him on the next Thursday and I invited him to dine with me the next day and talk it over. On the 18th the *Lancaster* went into dry-dock. I started on my hunt with Mr. Day and Mr. Lewis, a pair of horses, and two wheel carts well loaded up with hunting equipment. Good going and we stopped at Mr. Alexander's for a "pick-me-up" and "June" (a pointer). Arrived Olifants Kop owned by Mrs. Staffbury, where we spent five days and saw the home life of the Boers at close quarters. We got a number of small buck hares and birds and enjoyed Mrs. Staffbury's cooking. Poor "Molique" had convulsions and had to be shot. On the 23rd a cart with four horses came down for me and I got aboard at 10:00 p. m. Ship hauled out from wharf at daylight 24th and at 2:10 p. m. we were under way for Madagascar. Swung ship for compass deviation. Going south—clear and a beautiful cloth on Table Mountain. Arrived St. Augustine's Day 16th and Tullear Bay the 17th. It seemed we were here to demand an indemnity for the looting of one of our schooners by the natives when she was in these waters. Captain Potter busy with the Chiefs, his demand refused, and we went to Mozambique, arriving the 25th, and sent a cipher cablegram to the Department. Coaling ship. I went over the hospital. Sailed on the 27th for Zanzibar and arrived the 31st. Our consul Mr. Cheney and his wife were very nice to the officers—we had them to services on board Sunday 4th and breakfast in the wardroom. We found an American barque "Tekia Tapan" loaded with hides for Boston, Mass., and I sent home several boxes of curios collected since leaving home. Cadets detached and ordered home from here. On the 5th we were entertained at the Sultan's country palace and had a beautiful day—two elaborate meals served, and I ate my first salad made from the cabbage palm—a most delightful salad, and to obtain it they cut down a good size tree and take bud from its top to be served. New fruits, pomels, custard apple, mangoes, etc., were served. Left Zanzibar April 8th for Johanna, Comoro Island, on the 11th. Our visit here was due to the troubles of an American citizen, Dr. Wilson, with the Sultan, who was an old man and blind. I felt sorry for the old man who seemed nervous. However, the French having assumed a protectorate over the island I did not think the United States would be troubled as to its citizens being fairly treated. On the 20th went on shore to see patients, native princes and beggars—the sultan's brother one of them. On the 21st, saluted the French Governor and left for Nossi Bi. On the 22nd we had target practice, and the 23rd arrived at Nossi Bi and anchored off Hellville. On the 26th I visited Hellville and its small hospital of about 100 beds and went to Anibanaro in the Dinghy. Secured ebony for canes. The 28th at sea for St. Mary's, Madagascar, and anchored off Madame Island on the 3rd of April. Coaled ship and left the 7th for Tamatave, Madagascar, arrived on the 8th, and left the next morning at sunrise for Port Elizabeth, South Africa. Steamed and sailed until past most southern part of Madagascar, and then sailed alone until 16th when we got up steam and arrived May 21st. On the 13th while hauling the log we lost overboard Henry Knight O. Sea. Life buoy dropped and every effort was made to save him but the boat came back with only his cap. Port Elizabeth is a very interesting city and we enjoyed our stay of a few days and especially the large mail we received. Left May 25th for Cape Town and anchored in Table Bay 28th. Early next morning were alongside wharf and coaling ship. Mr. Day came off and we made up another hunting party for Olifants Kop, consisting of Mr. Manney, myself and Mr. Day. In a four horse carriage we started off, and enjoyed two days' shooting, bagging many stein bok, grey bok and birds. Met Mr. Uppington and family and enjoyed the walks and horseback rides around Cape Town until June 29th, when we left for St. Helena—arrived July

11th—a very good run for the *Lancaster*. We enjoyed the walks and rides, but there was no shooting as the season had closed. I secured a number of horns of African animals. Our Consul having heard of the loss of "Molique" on our last visit here presented me with an English retriever "Jack." Left Cape Town under sail July 26th and arrived Rio de Janeiro August 12th. Health of the port was better than this time last year. Captain Potter, Chief Engineer and Lieutenant Paul were detached and ordered home and I was quite homesick. Took up photography and took long walks on shore with my camera on my back. Mrs. Griffith was at Tijuea. Governor and Mrs. Jarvis were at their residence 1157 Laryngeris. Dr. McClurg gave ether and I operated on the Governor. September 15th Captain S. L. Breese took command of the *Lancaster* and he brought me a package from my wife. October 6th Rear Admiral Braine hoisted his flag on the *Lancaster*. Captain Breese, Chief of Staff; Lieutenant A. B. Wyckoff, Secretary; Lieut. Barroll, Flag Lieutenant; General Staff, Baker, Wells, Thompson and Taylor. Our stay in Rio for seven weeks had been spent when ashore in walks and rides, receiving many hospitalities, and making friends.

Left Rio November 6th and anchored off Montevideo November 13th. Found that cholera was epidemic at Buenos Aires and Roserio, and was spreading up the coast. First case of cholera reported on shore on 8th, and we left for Maldonado, Uruguay, on the 10th in company with the *Tallapoosa*. Here we remained at anchor until March 15th, three months and five days. On Christmas day we had a good dinner and some of the fruit cake my wife had sent me by Mr. Alexander, our new Pay Clerk. It was a beautiful cake and enough of it to go around, and I sent a piece of it to the Admiral and Captain—both of these officers were more than good to me, especially Captain Breese, who was fond of shooting and we spent many days at this sport. Shortly after anchoring here I had operated upon the Light House Keeper, Caledonio, after which he was my constant companion on shore furnishing me with his white horse "Arab" for my exclusive use. In January and February the plove and curlew were plentiful and so fat that when they fell to the ground after being shot they burst open. Ducks were plentiful and we shot many of them on a small lake where we took our skiff. In February the partridge season opened and "Jack" proved very useful in putting them up and retrieving. Shooting there was very pleasant, a good horse, good guide, and a good dog. Started early, lunched at one of the estencias, where we got all kinds of fresh fruits, occasionally spending the night or returning to the ship laden down with game. This, with the civil professional work that I was drawn into, made the time pass quickly. My first professional case on shore after that of Caledonio was Mrs. Potello, whose son ran a large estencia about fifteen miles from the coast. He came alongside early one morning and asked to see the Captain, asking that a medical officer visit his mother. Captain Breese sent for me and gave me permission to go with Potello. He had a four horse fix on the beach and we were soon at his casa; the mother had double pneumonia and was very ill. She had two beautiful daughters who acted as nurses. After 24 hours' work over the case I returned to the ship feeling that there was a good chance for the patient, the son promising to call for me the following day. Inside of a week my patient was out of danger. They were all very grateful and my reputation had spread rapidly and I was on the go visiting cases medical and surgical. March 15th we went up to Montevideo, only 60 miles. The cholera epidemic had been declared ended. The weather was delightful on shore but getting to and from the ship was rough, wet, and disagreeable. We anchored out three miles from shore. Dr. Griffith detached and ordered home. On the 23rd Mr. Canega and I got leave and went to Buenos Aires. Dr. Bourse went up with us. We visited La Plata, a city of 40,000 inhabitants and the capital of the Province of Buenos Aires, built in about five years. The inhabitants were hustlers and we enjoyed all points of interest. The 25th was the tenth anniversary of my wedding. Took passage on the *Minorca* for Montevideo—and we were aboard the *Lancaster* the following morning. On May 7th we left Montevideo for Ilha Grande, arrived May 14th, left the 15th and arrived Rio next morning. Got our mail and the *Lancaster* was to remain on the station and the *Trenton* to bring down relief for officers and crew. Governor and Mrs. Jarvis and other friends glad to see us again. August 9th, *Lancaster*, *Alliance* and *Tallapoosa* left Rio for Ilha Grande and arrived on the 10th. Smallpox epidemic at Rio. 17th, 18th and 19th, battalion drill on shore. 20th—one case of smallpox broke out on the *Alliance*; a case of verioloid on the *Lancaster*—both men sent to the hospital. We returned to Rio, looking anxiously for the arrival of the *Trenton*, which arrived the morning of September 10th.

Transfer commenced at once, breakfasted with Admiral Braine and dined with Governor and Mrs. Jarvis, meeting Captain Farquhar of the *Trenton* at both places. Mrs. Jarvis presented me with a beautiful diamond scarf pin. On the 23rd we dined with the Mendes at the Globe, having spent the afternoon with the Jarvises. On the 24th, the *Trenton* at 9 a. m. steamed out of the harbor of Rio flying the homeward bound pennant amid the cheers of the men of the ships at anchor, rigging manned, and music by the bands, "Home, Sweet Home." Arrived St. Thomas, West Indies, October 24th and left October 26th. Arrived New York November 3rd, but was unable to go ashore until the following day although I knew my wife was in New York City. The Senior Surgeon, an old bachelor, never thought of taking the duty and indeed during my whole service under him as Fleet Surgeon, I don't think he ever thought of his two Passed Assistant Surgeons, Griffith and myself, except how he could make the most use of us in order to gratify his own personal desires. I never wanted to meet him after this cruise and I never did. On November 4th about noon Dr. Wells came on board and I lost no time in getting ashore and finding Mrs. Rixey. Chaplain Tribou was most thoughtful to call on Mrs. Rixey to tell her that duty kept me on board. When I left home she weighed 140 pounds and now she barely weighed 109 pounds. She had never let me know that she had lost so much flesh and at first I was much alarmed. My detachment from the *Trenton* came the next day and we came to our home, 909-16th Street, N. W., where we found the Admiral and Mrs. English. The next day after my arrival in Washington I met Surgeon General Gunnell on the street, and having exchanged greetings he informed me that he wanted me to go on duty at the Naval Dispensary as Assistant to Surgeon Abel F. Price. I was very much surprised as I had noted that Dr. Arthur had only a short time before been ordered to that duty. The General explained that Dr. Arthur had been killed by a fall from a railroad train on his way south to be married. So November 7, 1887, I resumed the duty that I had left in September, 1884 much to the gratification of my friends as well as myself. After President Cleveland's election, Dr. O'Reilly had become White House physician but he still held the position of attending surgeon at the Army Dispensary. I had now not only the office work but had to do much of the visiting to the naval contingent too ill to come to the office. My work increased rapidly and although active practice pleased me I was pushed for all I was worth physically, especially from October to May each year. Although the Bureau furnished me a buggy and horse I soon found use for another team which I already owned. During the summer months I spent all my spare time on a farm I had purchased in 1888, about five miles from my office. I soon found it advisable to have a telephone to my country seat and had the poles cut out of my wood and wire strung connecting with the city system. The work was done under the supervision of a grateful patient in return for my relieving him of a painful malady, and cost me very little in actual cash. This was the first wire from my country home to Aqueduct Bridge, and it was a special service wire until I allowed Dr. J. Taber Johnson to come in on it a few years later, after he had bought a farm near mine. The horseback riding and farming during the months in which work was slack at my office put me in fine shape for the rush of work during the rest of the year. In 1888 I tore down the small brick building on 909-16th Street and built the comfortable new home now standing. An English basement with offices in the rear, a parlor, library, dining-room, and kitchen on the first floor. While the house was being built, I occupied Admiral McCalla's home on the corner of Massachusetts Avenue and 20th St., N. W. This charming home we enjoyed but I found it much more tasking on me in my professional work and was glad when I could get into my new home. In the fall of 1888 Mrs. Rixey and I left Washington for a coaching trip through the Shenandoah Valley to the Springs of Virginia, Natural Bridge, and through Rock Fish Gap to Charlottesville, Culpeper and Washington, D. C. This was a delightful trip. We started with a good pair of horses to a surrey with coachman in the rumble, and joined by Admiral English and his family in a four-in-hand coach at Harrisonburg, Va., after which Mrs. Rixey drove the surrey and I the four-in-hand most of the time.

My service at the dispensary from now on was one grind of medical and surgical work combining the work of the specialists with that of the general practitioner of medicine and surgery. My office in my new home helped me immensely, and I could not have accomplished all of the work I did without it. The death of Secretary Tracy's wife and young daughter by fire and my being called to care professionally for himself, his daughter, Mrs. Wilmerding, and her daughter who were suffering from injuries received and the nervous shock at the sudden death of Mrs. and Miss Tracy, has been described by my biographers, but this incident brought me in immediate contact with the Secretary and his family, and I remained the family physician as long as he was Secretary of the Navy. I had now reached the rank of Surgeon, and was in command of the Dispensary, with a Passed Assistant Surgeon as my assistant. I found that I was overworked, and knowing that I should have sea duty in 1892, while visiting the Secretary professionally I told him that I was overdue for sea duty and asked for that duty. He replied, "you can't leave Washington until I leave the Department, which will be in about a year, and then I will order you to any ship you wish." I thanked him and immediately got a few weeks' leave and went shooting in Virginia over my pet Irish setter, "Elcho." As much of the outdoor life as possible was essential if I was to keep in good physical condition. The year passed quickly and just before the change of administration, the Secretary sent for me and asked to what ship I wanted to be ordered. I selected the *Dolphin* as it would enable me to keep closer in touch with professional work than any other sea duty. I reported to Lieutenant Commander Buckingham, commanding the *Dolphin*, February 5, 1893. Lieutenant C. J. Badger was the Executive Officer. This ship, although performing the same functions as the *Tallapoosa*, except carrying freight, was entirely different, and I found the routine duties and discipline were as thorough as on the larger cruisers. And this pleased me very much as I believed that a happy ship was one upon which every man not only knew his duties but was required to perform them. The *Dolphin* was handsomely fitted up for the accommodation of passengers and everything about the ship was kept in beautiful order. Officers attached to the ship were Lieutenant Urshur, Lieutenant Horrigan, Lieutenant Phelps, Chief Engineer Baird, and Paymaster Hunt, all of whom proved good shipmates.

The new administration had been inaugurated and our Secretary was Mr. Hileary Herbert, who had two charming daughters and a son. The oldest daughter married Mr. Benjamin Macon, who was in the Secretary's office. On our first visit to Washington, I, with my wife, called upon the Secretary and family and we were soon good friends. Mr. Herbert was a veteran of the Civil War and had rendered distinguished service to the Confederacy. The Secretary and family were frequently on board the *Dolphin*, and shortly after I met them he consulted me professionally as he thought he had serious heart trouble; I disagreed with him in this and found some difficulty in convincing him that I was right and that if he would carry out the course of treatment I prescribed he would have no more trouble. He was not convinced that I was right and fortunately he was now going on the *Dolphin* to make an inspection of some of the Navy Yards and his itinerary took us to Newport, R. I. This was in the summer, and I knew that Dr. William Pepper of Philadelphia would probably be in Newport. I got the Secretary to consent to a consultation with Dr. Pepper. His diagnosis and prognosis were the same as mine. I was, from that time, the Secretary's family physician when they were aboard the *Dolphin*, or when the *Dolphin* was at the Washington Navy Yard.

Captain Buckingham was an ideal Captain for this ship, had a fine personality, and was especially equipped for this duty, having been naval aide to our Ambassador at Paris and a favorite in society. He seemed to have no difficulty in making friends with everyone who came aboard. In fact, the officers of the *Dolphin* seemed to vie with each other in attention to the ship's guests, so Captain Buckingham was ably seconded, especially by his first lieutenant, Charles J. Badger, and Chief Engineer George W. Baird. The Captain always, when not on deck, messed with guests in the main saloon, and frequently he invited some of the wardroom officers to join them at luncheon or dinner. Our Captain was an ideal type of Naval officer, a handsome man, and his dress, whether uniform or civilian, always seemed just right. However, there was one subject we did not agree upon, that was the relative standing of line and staff officers. This did not prevent us from being the best of friends and we were destined to have this relationship cemented by new ties, that of physician and patient, than which there are few dearer. About this time he was taken ill, an obscure slow fever, which I soon diagnosed as due to sepsis, evidently an abscess. Hospital treatment became necessary and he consented to be sent to the old Washington Naval Hospital, and I promised to see him every day and follow up his case. The Commanding Officer of the Hospital was a man whom the Captain disliked exceedingly, and instead of improving I found him quite nervous, and he asked me if I could not find some place near my country home where he could be taken. I told him not to worry and we would fix it up for him, and I went to the Secretary and told him that the Captain felt that he would never get well where he was and explained his serious condition. Mr. Herbert was very fond of Captain Buckingham, and asked what I could do for him. I replied that I knew Mrs. Rixey would be glad to do anything for the Captain and that Mr. Badger could be left in command of the ship and a medical officer detailed to take my place aboard until our patient had much improved. My biographer has told how this was carried out. For many weeks Captain Buckingham was in our home with a faithful nurse and his sister with him. I gave up my whole time to him and it was most gratifying to see his confidence and appreciation. As soon as he was well enough to travel I took him to Poland Springs and there he improved rapidly and reported for duty about a month afterwards. I had left him at the Springs and resumed my duties aboard ship. When he came aboard he was wonderfully better and I now had the key to his disease, and he improved steadily and soon was himself. Sometime after he assumed command after his illness, he invited me to luncheon in the cabin to meet some ladies, and introduced me to Miss Margaret C. Freeman, and others; later on he told me that he was engaged to marry Miss Freeman. My congratulations were most cordial, as I hoped he would retire after this cruise. On several occasions after this I met Miss Minnie and her sister, Miss Isabel Freeman, on the *Dolphin*, and soon Mrs. Rixey and her mother were good friends and I saw much of the young ladies. Mrs. Rixey and I attended the beautiful wedding at 1525 H Street and Captain Buckingham dined with us in the evening before to meet his sister, Mrs. Colt, who was staying with us and who had been with us in our country home when the Captain was so ill.

CHAPTER III

SERVICE LEADING UP TO APPOINTMENT AS PHYSICIAN TO THE PRESIDENT OF THE UNITED STATES

WHEN MY tour of duty on the *Dolphin* expired, I was detached, and on December 10, 1895, was ordered to duty at the Naval Dispensary, Washington, D. C. for the third time. This was due, for the most part, to Secretary Herbert, whose family physician I was at this time. After this tour of duty on shore I expected to make one more cruise, probably as Fleet Surgeon. Medical Inspector Dixon was in command of the Dispensary, and at first I was his assistant, and we had all the work we could do. Later on Dr. Dixon was detached and Surgeon Eugene Stone was ordered as my assistant. The Cleveland administration had now come to an end and the McKinley administration, with Governor John D. Long as Secretary of the Navy, was inaugurated. In my position as the attending physician I was called in to attend Governor Long and his family as a part of the Naval contingent and we were soon fast friends, and no friendship could be more delightful. Mr. Long, as Governor of Massachusetts and in public life, had already made an enviable reputation for himself. He was a good speaker, his speeches scintillating with good humor and amusement. He was a great favorite with all who had the pleasure of knowing him, and I loved him for his considerate treatment of his young surgeon. In the fall of 1908, I very unexpectedly received an order to be a member in a professional capacity of the President's party to Atlanta, Georgia, and other points, a description of which, leading up to my appointment as White House physician, has been written by my biographer. An after dinner speech of Mr. Long's on this Southern trip of the President is worthy to be repeated here. In response to the toast *to the Navy*, he said in part:

"As to the Navy, ladies and gentlemen, what can I say that is not already in all your hearts? Everybody knows about the Navy, knows about its achievements which occurred, so brilliant, so effective, that it seems preposterous in me to refer to them as though I could suggest anything to you that is not already in your hearts. The American Navy is the pride of the American Republic. The trophies of Miltiades would not let Themostocles sleep, and the trophies of Sampson and Dewey and Hobson will not allow the youth of America to sleep. What more can be said than that the Navy maintained the high reputation which it won in the war of the Revolution under Paul Jones, in the war of 1812, under Hull and Decatur and Bainbridge, in the war for the Union there were men on both sides, who showed their great abilities and who, joined together as they are now joined, God let us trust, forever, will make the Navy our pride, will make the Navy irresistible.

"The victories of Manila and Santiago are unparalleled in history. All this work has been accomplished, too, practically without loss of life or almost without loss of limb to any appreciable extent. Through this war ran—it never was forgotten—utter lack of animosity towards the foe as a matter of personal consideration. No war was ever fought—thank the President for giving us the lead—where from beginning to end so little personal animosity towards the foe existed.

"It was a most interesting fact which Captain 'Fighting Bob' Evans told me, that at the Battle of Santiago, his men, while the fight was going on, were like demons and fiends; they swore, they raved, they cried, 'Remember the Maine,' there seemed to be no limit to their expression of wrath and of anger; but the moment the battle was over, in his own exquisite words, they became as gentle as women, and great stout sailors sprang into the water to rescue drowning Spaniards, and when they lifted some of them, wounded and bleeding, expressed in the kindest and gentlest terms their hope to raise the poor fellow and to save him from any pain. That is the spirit of the American Navy from top to bottom, efficiency and generosity. The professional standard of the Navy is of the very highest and very best.

"But let me also say that I do not forget that the Navy is only one arm of the means of force and defense in the hands of the Commander-in-Chief. The Navy cannot be separated from the Army; the two are together, the right and left hand —nay, they are each the right hand of the Commander-in-Chief. They work together, they are coordinated together. The Secretary of War has uttered words with regard to the Navy for which I thank him, because they are generous, and they are just. I might say to him that the preparation of the Navy was not so entirely complete as he may think. It was thoroughly prepared for any exigency that might arise at once; but additional preparation was necessary. Some twenty millions of dollars were spent for new ships; scores of new ships were bought, chartered, and fitted out. A hospital ship—an innovation in modern warfare—was prepared and built; a great blacksmith shop in the form of the cruiser Vulcan was made, by which all repairs were done; three great refrigerator ships carried out supplies to the east and the west that would last the Navy for months together. Distilling ships; and not only this, but the fighting power had to be prepared, and was prepared so delicately, so quietly, so thoroughly, and with so little question, that perhaps the country at large does not recognize fully the work of preparation that was done by the Navy as well as the work of achievement which it accomplished. But it was a matter of cooperation between the Army and the Navy. The Navy could aid the Army by lending its transports to carry troops; they landed the troops in its launches and its boats; but the Navy would have been powerless to main itself either at Santiago or at Manila, unless reinforced by the splendid power and intelligence and force of the Army under its accomplished commander. It is the two together that have done this work. And what that power of the Army is, you had some indication of today in the review. You saw them march in seried column; you saw their bayonets glistening in the sun; you thought that if that was 10,000 men, what would 275,000 be; what would have been the million men that would spring, as armed men sprang from dragon's teeth in the classic days of old, in case there should be need of their services! I cannot help thinking of that little story of John L. Sullivan. You have heard it a thousand times; how a little spitfire in a Chicago hotel ordered him to apologize in three minutes for jostling him as he went by, and the great giant looked down with a kindly smile and said, 'I won't put you to that trouble, I will apologize now.' And somebody told the little fellow afterwards that was John L. Sullivan, and asked him what he would have done if Sullivan had not apologized within three minutes; he said, 'I think I should have given him time.' If Spain had realized what a giant she was about to meet she would have extended the time."

Major General Wheeler responding to a toast to "Women" said:

"I ask my friends could a man be more utterly stricken dumb than to be requested to reply to a toast to woman? A subject so vast in its grandeur, so illimitable in its sweetness and infinite tenderness. I can only bow my head in reverence before that which is not possible for any poor words of mine to express. To these uncrowned angels we owe the best that life affords. As mothers, daughters, sisters, or as wives, they bring to us the sweetest music of our lives. In all the eighteen hundred years since she stood last at the Savior's cross and earliest at His Grave, she has reigned a saintly queen over all nations, and in all these years no great achievements or histories have ever been accomplished by warriors or statesmen, and no great battles won which have not been inspired by that white gentle hand that can reach up nearer heaven than any other earthly power to bring blessings upon mankind. Where can a man be found, no matter how happy and successful has been his life, who does not on many a weary night say in his heart: 'Rock me to sleep, mother, rock me to sleep.' They talk about a 'Woman's Sphere' as if it had a limit—

'There's not a place in earth or heaven,
There's not a task to mankind given,
There's not a blessing or a woe,
There's not a whispered yes or no,
There's not a life, or death, or birth,
That has a feather's weight of worth
Without a woman in it.

'The bravest battles that ever were fought,
Shall I tell you where or when?
On the map of the world you will find it not,
'Twas fought by the mothers of men.'

"She is always first in love and tenderness;. first in sympathy for the sorrows of others; first in healing the sick; first in all that is human; Lo! first where the Nazarine trod! Oh! Woman—Oh! Beautiful Woman! Be thou first in the Kingdom of God."

CHAPTER IV

THE MCKINLEY ADMINISTRATION

RETURNING to Washington after this memorable southern trip of the President I resumed my duties as attending Naval surgeon and a short time afterwards was directed by the President to take up the duties of physician to the Executive Mansion. This duty was (in addition to my already large practice) quite a task and comprised all that related to the health of the inmates of the Executive Mansion, in addition to my duties as Surgeon in charge of the Naval Dispensary. My special care was the President and Mrs. McKinley. By direction of the President I made at least two visits every day, the first at 10:00 a. m., and the second at 10:00 p. m., and as many more as were required. The evening call was always in evening dress, as I would find the other guests so attired. At the appointed time I always found my distinguished patients ready to receive me no matter who might be present, and I was expected to remain until Mrs. McKinley had retired with her maid, and enjoyed frequent conversation with the President until his bedtime. I never allowed anything of personal interest to annoy the President during these visits. To show how he appreciated this, after I had been White House Physician for over a year, one morning just as I was leaving after my 10:00 a. m. visit he called me into his office and, with the kindly smile for which he was noted, said, "Do you know that you have been taking care of us for over a year and you have not asked me to do anything for you? Isn't there something that you want that I can do for you?" I answered, "Mr. President, when I came on duty here I made up my mind not to add to your cares but to do all in my power to make them as light as possible." He said, "I am sure that there is something I can do for you and it will do me good to do it." After a little hesitation I said, "I have a nephew named after me. He served in the Spanish American War as a cadet on one of our ships and was honorably discharged after the war was over. I want him to study medicine but he likes the line work and will never make a good doctor. I have tried to get him the opportunity of taking the examinations for the Marine Corps but thus far have failed." The President said not a word, but took up his card and wrote, "The Secretary of the Navy will appoint Presley M. Rixey, Jr., to fill the first vacancy in the United States Marine Corps, subject to examination"—and signed it. I took the card to the Secretary of the Navy the same day. Mr. Long looked up at me in his quizzical way and said, "And so you have been after the President?" I replied, "No, Mr. Secretary, he has been after me." The boy passed the examination successfully and is now a Lieutenant Colonel in the Marine Corps, with a wife and four children.

Shortly after the above incident, I found that I was much overdue for sea duty and did not think it fair to my distinguished patient for him not to know it, as I knew that so long as my present relations existed at the White House the Navy Department would not give me other orders unless directed to do so by the President. I informed him of my status in regard to sea duty, at the same time telling him how much I was interested in my present duty, the greatest honor I had ever received. He looked grave but remained silent. At my evening visit he and Mrs. McKinley were alone, and Mrs. McKinley complained to her husband that the medicine I was giving her was abominable, and that she would not take any more of it. The President said, "My dear, I am glad you bring this up now, as Dr. Rixey has informed me that he is due for sea duty, and if you don't want him we will let him go." Mrs. McKinley was silent for a few moments and then said, "We will not let him go until I say so." She was a much better patient after this, and my relations were those of a trusted friend as well as family physician.

Time passed quickly and my interest in my patients had increased and the responsibility was correspondingly heavy. The President consulted me as to the advisability of a tour to the Pacific coast which he was anxious to make provided it would do Mrs. McKinley no harm. She was anxious to make the tour and I knew from my short experience with her that she was a good traveler as long as she was with her husband. All arrangements were made and on April 29, 1901, the beautiful special train pulled out of Union Station with the President and Mrs. McKinley and most of the Cabinet officers and their wives; Secretary Cortelyou and his wife, Dr. and Mrs. Rixey, Mr. Henry T. Scott, Mr. Lawrence I. Scott, Mr. Charles A. Moon and wife, Mr. M. A. Digman, with an officer of the Southern and Southern Pacific Railroad, three stenographers, nine representatives of the press, one photographer, and a representative of the Western Union Telegraph Company and Postal Telegraph Cable Co. Accommodations were spacious and everything the best the Pullman company could furnish. My duty was clear cut, that is, attending physician and surgeon to the whole party, and I was prepared accordingly. Again I must refer my readers to my biographer's description in the first part of this book and confine myself to a report of my care of the party professionally. We had very little sickness until just before arrival at Los Angeles, California, Mrs. McKinley developed an abscess (bone felon) on her thumb which was relieved quickly by an operation, and she improved for a few days when other serious symptoms developed, and I advised the President that she must have complete rest. At once he decided that he, Mrs. McKinley, and myself, would go direct to Mr. Henry T. Scott's residence in San Francisco, while the rest of the party carried out the program as far as San Francisco. Mrs. McKinley grew steadily weaker and I called in consultation first Dr. Hirschfelder, a little later Dr. Gibbons, and still later Dr. Cushing, all prominent physicians of San Francisco. We had every convenience in Mr. Scott's beautiful home with excellent nurses, and every comfort and attention from everyone, especially the President, whose devotion to his wife was perfect. It seemed almost impossible that she would live to return to the White House. In a remarkable way she regained her strength and made the home trip without a set back. The Pullman Company and Railroad had made every provision and I had two trained nurses and medical preparation, even to a tank of oxygen. The special train was ordered to obey any orders I might deem necessary for the patient. In Washington I had Surgeon General Sternberg, Dr. Wm. Johnson, and Major Walter Reed, on duty at the Army Medical Museum, in consultation, and Dr. Reed made the necessary examinations of the blood, excretions, etc. Mrs. McKinley continued to gain in strength and in August was able to accompany the President to his home in Canton. Here the comparatively quiet home life with its drives among home scenes was ideal, and she gained several pounds before starting on the trip to Buffalo about September 1st. Francis B. Gessner writing at this time said:

> "Dr. P. M. Rixey, who was with the President at Canton all summer, is a surgeon in the Navy, detailed on special duty. He is a young man, a Virginian, and very advanced in his profession.
>
> "Dr. Rixey has done Mrs. McKinley so much good that both the President and Mrs. McKinley insist on his remaining in Washington.
>
> "Years ago, when a youth, Dr. Rixey became intimately acquainted with another great man who became President, U. S. Grant. Their introduction was rather abrupt. General Grant decided to use the Rixey mansion in Virginia as Headquarters, and the famous Rixey hospitality was demanded.
>
> "Even so, the household, although opposed to Grant and fond of Lee, learned to like the calm, self-reliant General. A few years later Grant, as President, appointed Rixey to the Navy, and signed his first commission.
>
> "It is hoped that society will see more of Mrs. McKinley than usual in the White House festivities this winter. Her health improved wonderfully during the stay in Canton, and she gained ten pounds, which, in view of her long invalidism, was little short of marvelous."

Mrs. McKinley regained her strength after the serious illness in California slowly, until the summer of 1901 which I spent in their home in Canton, Ohio. By the last of August she was better than she had been since I had known her.

Among those who would join the McKinleys in the evening besides their relatives were the Honorable Charles G. Dawes and Mrs. Dawes, Captain Stephen B. Rand and Mrs. Rand. A game of cards was usually in progress when I arrived and I was frequently called to take part in the game.

My biographer has given in detail the account of Mrs. McKinley's illness in California, as also of the last illness and death of President McKinley, embodying my official report. To adequately express my personal feelings at the loss of these dear friends is an impossibility. Up to the seventh day of the President's illness, I and all the consultants were most sanguine of his recovery, but about midnight of that day I noted for the first time a restlessness, tossing of the head from side to side, and sighing, although apparently asleep. This seemed to increase towards morning so much that I called Dr. McBirney who had a room occupied by one of the consultants every night. As soon as Dr. McBirney came into the room the patient opened his eyes and said he was feeling fine. They chatted for a few moments and I went back to Dr. McBirney's room with him. The doctor thought my nerves were giving way and advised that I get out of the sick room occasionally. I explained that the restlessness only showed itself when he was apparently asleep. Going back to the patient's bedside I noted the same condition existing under the same circumstances, and called Dr. McBirney a second time with the same result. He believed at that time that our patient would get well, and to relieve my mind said he would return to New York early that morning. By 8:00 a. m., just before his train left the depot, a hurry call was sent out for all the consultants. Dr. Janeway, Dr. Johnston, and Dr. Stockton also were called and Dr. McBirney was requested to return. The patient's strength, which had kept up wonderfully, gave way slowly but surely until 2:15 a. m., of the ninth day, when he breathed his last. The universal gloom and grief at the departure of this noble spirit from earth was international, and was a fitting tribute to so splendid an example of Americanism. With so much to live for, his last thought was for that dear wife whom he was leaving. He made not a complaint, but an all pervading solicitude for her. "What will become of her? It's God's will, His will be done."

The trip from Buffalo to Washington and the official tribute at the National Capital and his last journey to Canton, Ohio, and his obsequies there were like a nightmare to me, and I felt like a wooden man. I believe that what kept me up and doing was Mrs. McKinley, and our duty to take his place as far as possible. His faithful secretary, George B. Cortelyou, was all that could be asked, and performed the duties required in a business sense with the same faithful devotion as when the President lived, relieving me of everything except the professional care of Mrs. McKinley.

From now on I seemed to walk in a dream, benumbed by my great sorrow, but not for a moment forgetting the bereaved wife. This duty called for all the gentleness and professional knowledge possible to keep her up to undergo the trails before her, the funeral services in Buffalo, the funeral train to Washington, the public services in Washington, the last trip to Canton, Ohio, and his resting place. Mrs. McKinley under strong medication bore up far better than I expected and now in her Canton home I remained with her and her trained nurses. At first she took little interest in anything. Something was needed to get her on her feet and in her carriage. I asked if she did not wish to visit her husband's last resting place—it aroused her at once and arrangements could not be made too soon. At the tomb the soldiers on guard were always most considerate and no curious onlookers were allowed near whilst she was there with her beloved dead, and it was almost a struggle at first to get her to leave the abiding place of her dearest. After leaving the cemetery I made the coachman drive about until she showed signs of fatigue. Arriving home I arranged for her to rest in bed. This was repeated day after day as long as the weather was good and nearly every day was fine in Canton in September. Soon she was able to see her many friends from far and near and her outdoor driving in her carriage was increased as much as possible. I remained with Mrs. McKinley at her home in Canton, Ohio, until she was out of immediate danger of a collapse, and then returned to my duty in Washington, visiting her occasionally by the order of President Roosevelt.

My duty now called me back to Washington, having promised to return to see the dear patient as often as possible and to bring Mrs. Rixey with me. Arriving in Washington I reported at the White House and the President, Mr. Roosevelt, informed me that I was to continue my duties as White House physician in addition to my duties at the Naval Dispensary with the additional duty of visiting Mrs. McKinley as often as my services were required. These visits to Canton were continued up to her last illness, during which I was with her and saw her wish fulfilled—that she might be with her "dearest." So often she had said so pathetically, "I want to be with my dearest," and when she felt she was going to join her noble husband seemed happier than at any time since his death.

From the time of the death of her husband up to the time of her own death, nearly seven years, I was constantly in communication with her family physicians in Canton, Ohio, Dr. Phillips and Dr. Portman, and with her nurses, Miss A. Moses and Miss Maud Healy, all of whom I found most sympathetic, competent and attentive. My visits soon became less frequent and only when Mrs. McKinley called for me or the physicians sent for me did I go to Canton. The many friends of President McKinley and his wife were all helpful in making this dear lady's last years as happy as possible, and among those I must mention Mrs. Hobart, the wife of Vice President Hobart, and Mrs. Herrick, the wife of our ambassador to France, Mr. Myron T. Herrick. It seemed that everyone wished to do something for her.

CHAPTER V

THE ROOSEVELT ADMINISTRATION

MY SERVICE of more than ten years as White House Physician, in addition to my other duties, stands out before me today as the most arduous as well as the most delightful of my life—to serve as family physician and friend under two such men whose love and devotion to their country in the loftiest position obtainable, falls to the lot of few men—especially when the relations were such as existed between them and their families and Mrs. Rixey and myself. Both Presidents were imbued with the spirit of Americanism in its loftiest aspect, love of Flag and Country, of family and friends, and were determined to accomplish all that in them lay for the good of their fellow-men and their country.

Yet physically so different from Mr. Roosevelt, Mr. McKinley appeared in good health when I became his family physician, his mentality perfect but his muscles were not exercised, and the consequences were a lowered vitality and little resistance to disease or injury. The man was not the cause of this, but an invalid wife whose whole life without children was tied up in her husband, and in his absence she was never really happy. He, recognizing this, reduced his absence from her side to a minimum and even then she was constantly on his mind. His outdoor exercise was a short walk or a ride beside his wife, usually in a closed carriage. Mrs. McKinley did not wish any change, and would have soon dispensed with my services if she thought I was urging any. However, I tried to have him drive himself in an open trap with a good pair of horses, his wife beside him and a footman in the rumble. After a short while Mrs. McKinley put it aside. Then I tried short horseback rides. This took him too much from her presence. When the emergency came, his enfeebled constitution could not stand the shock and gangrene around the wounds caused death.

—Courtesy of Pach Bros., N. Y.

President and Mrs. Roosevelt seated in chairs. At the President's right, Quentin, Ethel next, Kermit in center, Theodore, Jr. and Archie on the arm of Mrs. Roosevelt's chair. "There are many kinds of success in life worth having. It is exceedingly interesting and attractive to be a successful business man, a railroad man, or farmer or a successful lawyer or doctor or a writer, or a President, or a ranchman, or a colonel of a fighting regiment or to kill grizzly bears and lion But for unflagging interest and enjoyment, a household of children, if things go reasonably well, certainly makes all other forms of success and achievement lose their importance by comparison."

Roosevelt in his Autobiography

On the other hand, Mr. Roosevelt, imbued with every attribute that goes to make good government, was an athlete, his vitality enormous, his charming wife and children equally devoted to the outdoor life. What a contrast for the family physician, for instead of building up methods I must endeavor to systematize and often reduce, as there was a disposition to take on too much flesh on account of the indoor work which took so much of the President's time. I had fortunately always taken a great interest in the outdoor life and was a good horseman, drove my pair of horses or tandem of four-in-hand as occasion permitted. I was also very fond of shooting on the wing and loved my dogs and gun, but like most Virginians preferred to follow the dogs on horseback and even to shoot from the saddle. But I had all I could do to keep up with Mr. Roosevelt on his walks and horseback rides and hunting trips. Mrs. Roosevelt enjoyed the outdoor life equally with her husband, and often accompanied him on his walks and rides and the children from Miss Alice (now Mrs. Nicholas Longworth) to baby Quentin were always ready for anything. The playfellows they loved to be with more than all were their father and mother. A happier, more beautiful life, than the one led by this family I do not think could be found. Mrs. Rixey and I, not having children of our own, were most fortunate to have them to come into our lives and we loved everyone of them from the beginning, we love them now, and always will love them and the memory of those departed. The children seemed, when alone with us, to look upon us as a second father and mother, and for nearly eight years that we were so closely associated I cannot remember a cross word or a disagreeable incident. Mrs. Rixey and I have always loved children, and it was with the greatest delight we entered into their lives as much as possible.

The President, although he frequently rode horseback with Mrs. Roosevelt, would take long rides and rode hard, and on these occasions I was usually with him. When we came in, the horses had enough for one day, even though

Dr. Rixey, in addition to everything else, has been a most efficient and helpful military aid on these trips; he has done me great service,

The above lines were written by President Roosevelt to his wife just after we had made a seventy-five mile ride from Laramie to Cheyenne, Wyoming. It was really a race, changing horses frequently and before entering Cheyenne the President inspected the Army Camp at that place and as I was the only one of the President's immediate party with him, I acted as his aide for the day.

we had been in the saddle only a few hours. On one of these rides to Great Falls on the Potomac River, the President had Mr. Garfield, Mr. Pinchot, and myself with him, and about three miles from the city Mr. Garfield and Mr. Pinchot got to skylarking on horseback, each trying to unhorse the other. It ended in Mr. Garfield getting a cut on one of his eyebrows about an inch long, and deep enough to let the lower flap fall over the eye. We all dismounted. I always carried an emergency outfit when with the President and it became necessary to take several stitches to hold the lips of the wound together. The President assisted, and after a first aid dressing we were off again. At a cabin at Great Falls hot water sterilized by boiling was used freely, and the wound redressed. The next morning Mr. Garfield came to my office in Washington and the wound healed by first intention. This little incident is mentioned to show the necessity of a surgeon with the President being always prepared for any emergency. My pockets were always filled with artery forceps and first aid equipment.

My rides with Mrs. Roosevelt on "Ygenka" and the children on their ponies over the Virginia hills and my farms are full of pleasant reminiscences. Often the trap would be brought along and the White House luncheon basket enjoyed in the shade by a running brook. After luncheon the dear mother would read and the children would probably build a dam or wade in the brook, whilst I overlooked farm operations and enjoyed my cigar. Mrs. Roosevelt, accompanied by some friends, occasionally would walk out to "Netherfauld," our summer home, and back to the White House. Mrs. Rixey would have tea for them on the lawn. Later on in the administration, Mrs. Roosevelt bought a few acres of land in Albemarle County, Virginia, where she built a comfortable little cottage as a camping-out place near the Wilmers, and called it "Pine Knot." Here I spent many a happy outing with the family, hunting, riding, etc. In the hunting season we would take up my beagles and setters. Quail, rabbits, squirrels, pheasants, and wild turkeys could be found and there the President shot his first wild

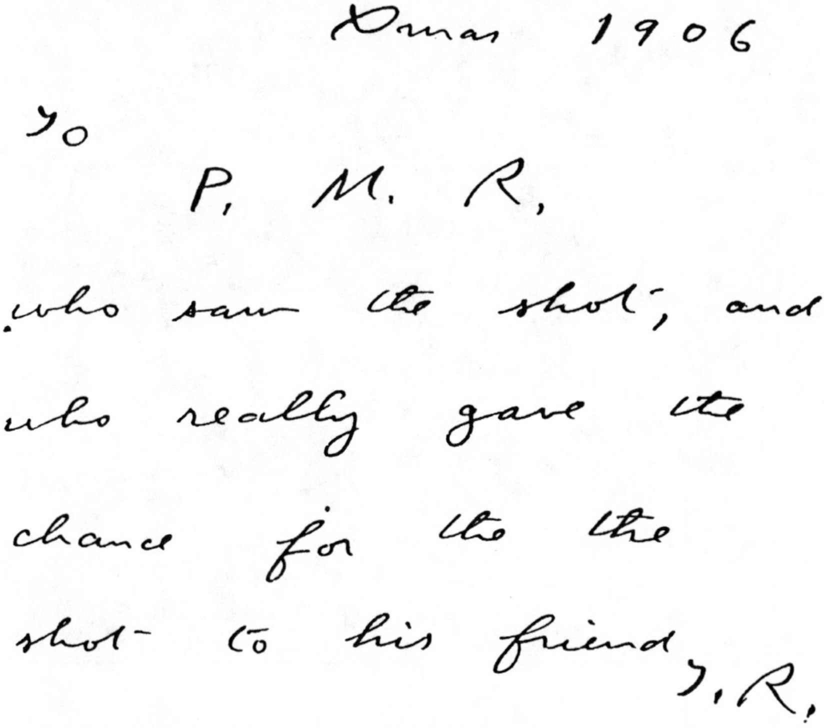

Xmas 1906

To

P. M. R.

who saw the shot; and who really gave the chance for the the shot to his friend,

T. R.

President Roosevelt shot his first Wild Turkey on the wing near Mrs. Roosevelt's Outing Camp, "Pine Knot," in Albemarle County, Virginia. The above note accompanied the wings of the Turkey, mounted and bearing a silver plate with the date on it.

turkey. So many reminiscences of the children crowd themselves in my memory that I scarce know where to stop. The girls thought they must do everything that their father and the boys did, walking, climbing, horseback riding, and jumping. I must not forget "Dutchess Betsy," as the President called the black pony of thoroughbred Virginia stock which I owned and kept at my home during the winter months. Every summer she went with the children to Oyster Bay. She was fleet of foot and a good jumper, and the young people enjoyed her immensely. She was about fourteen hands high, and when they could do Betsy they were ready for any mount.

The children were seldom sick. Ted had a serious attack of pleuro-pneumonia at Groton School, and Mr. Roosevelt sent me up in a special car to bring Mrs. Roosevelt and the boy to the White House. My instructions were that no risk was to be taken in moving him. At another time, Archie had a serious attack of diphtheria. These two cases gave me much concern, but most of the children's troubles were cuts and bruises—and many stitches I had to take to make them comfortable. The children in the White House would have pillow fights and rough and tumble times in which their father would often join. They would walk on stilts several feet high, and on one occasion Kermit, wishing to reach some article in the clothes closet placed the upper end of the stilt in his mouth; it slipped off his teeth and tore the mucuous membrane from the hard palate back to the soft palate. This curtain fell down in his throat and with the blood almost strangled the boy. On my arrival he was sitting in a chair leaning forward, and I saw at once that the membrane must be stitched back in place—although he thought if I would let him have my scissors he could cut it off and be all right. He did not murmur at the discomfort I had to put him through in the operation.

So it was with Archie when I had to sew up a wound, the whole family was present, and he submitted with the same stoicism as Kermit. The President patted Archie on the back and said, "My brave boy." Quentin, then a small boy, looked up at his father with the worship that they all had for him, and said, "Father, I notice you do not say anything about me." Young as he was he would have undergone anything to have the approval of his father.

Every American should be more than proud of such a family, and no wonder when the father was denied the privilege of going on the fighting line in the World War all of his children volunteered and acquitted themselves with credit, and dear baby Quentin, grown to manhood, was killed in action.

The above are only a few of the many incidents as seen by the White House physician in the Roosevelt administration, and I hope will give some idea of this devoted family, devoted alike to country, home, and friends.

CHAPTER VI

LETTERS OF THEODORE ROOSEVELT AND OTHERS

IN FEBRUARY, 1902, Mrs. Roosevelt was called to Groton, Mass., by the illness of Theodore Roosevelt, Jr., who was a pupil at that school. On the 18th of February the President had his secretary send me the following note:

WHITE HOUSE
WASHINGTON

February 18, 1902.

Dear Dr. Rixey:

The President would like to have you go to Groton, Mass., leaving here tomorrow (Wednesday) afternoon at 4:50 o'clock. Arrangements will be made to have a private car there by Thursday noon, subject to Mrs. Roosevelt's orders, for the purpose of bringing Master Theodore Roosevelt, Jr., back to Washington, the departure from Groton of course to depend upon his condition. If it is found inadvisable to move him Thursday, the car will be held at Groton until he is sufficiently improved to be moved with absolute safety; and it is the President's wish that you remain there to accompany the young man when he returns.

Arrangements will be made for your transportation and I will communicate with you a little later about this.

Very sincerely yours,
(Signed) GEORGE B. CORTELYOU,
Secretary to the President.

The President's verbal instructions were to bring Ted and his mother home as soon as Ted's condition would permit, but to run no risk. I found Ted with pleuro-pneumonia, with acute symptoms subsiding. I felt that he would regain his health more rapidly in the White House and his mother would be with her husband and little ones, so in spite of several feet of snow and after consultation with the school physician and Mrs. Roosevelt I decided to take him to his father. A heated closed carriage on runners took us to the special car waiting for us, on which there was a trained nurse and a bed warmed for the patient. The trip was successfully made and he was placed in bed at the White House in good condition, much to the gratification of his mother and father. His convalescence was slow, and the President's New York family physician, Dr. Lambert, was called in consultation.

In May 1902, the question of the appointment of a postmaster at Culpeper, Va., was before the President, and he, knowing that Culpeper was my home prior to entering the Navy, sent me the following note, enclosing a letter from Judge Lewis:

WHITE HOUSE
WASHINGTON

May 10, 1902.

Dear Dr. Rixey:

I have great regard for Judge Lewis. Will you give me some comment on his letter?

Faithfully yours,
(Signed) T. ROOSEVELT.

Judge Lewis' letter was a strong recommendation of a Republican for the position and stated his opponent for the position was a Democrat. I certainly could not recommend Judge Lewis' candidate, as I knew both men and stated my reasons to the President, stating that politics had nothing to do with my advice, but I would like to see the people of Culpeper satisfied. The President turned to some friends and said, "Here it is, Judge Lewis against Dr. Rixey, each believing that he is right. What am I to do?" I replied, "May I suggest that I believe you can have us both on the same side? I know Judge Lewis and I am satisfied that if he knows as much of the two men as he should, he would agree with me. If you will send a letter to the Judge, telling him to go to Culpeper personally, and inform himself of the standing of the applicants, you will give the position to the man he selects." Judge Lewis was a staunch Republican, but he replied to the President endorsing the Democrat.

On September 23, 1902, I was much shocked by the receipt of the following telegram:

Indianapolis, Ind., Sept. 23, 1902.

For Surgeon General P. M. Rixey,

Through Secretary of the Navy, Washington, D. C.

President has developed small abscess on left shin result of trolley accident at Pittsfield. Condition requires minor operation and rest for a few days. Rest of itinerary abandoned. Party will return to Washington after speech.

G. A. Lung,
Surgeon, U. S. N.

Richmond, Indiana
September 23, 1902.

Dr. P. M. Rixey,
Surgeon General, U. S. Navy,
Washington, D. C.

This gives you the entire situation. Dr. Lung asks me to request that you have an ambulance meet us upon our arrival at Washington six-thirty tomorrow, Wednesday evening, Pennsylvania Station. Also, will you be good enough to go over to 22 Jackson Place, temporary White House, and see that Pinckney, the Steward, has everything in readiness for the President's arrival.

As a result of the trolley accident at Pittsfield, Mass., the President received several serious bruises. One of these on the left leg between the knee and the ankle has developed into a small abscess. The President is entirely well otherwise, and has continued to meet the several engagements of his itinerary, but in view of the continuance of the abscess and out of an abundance of caution, Drs. Oliver and Cook of Indianapolis, Dr. Richardson of Washington, D. C., being also one of the number. In the opinion of the doctors the trouble necessitates an operation which they think should be performed at once at St. Vincent's Hospital in this city. As after the operation the President will require entire rest probably for at least ten days or two weeks, it has been necessary to cancel all the remaining engagements of his trip and he will go directly from Indianapolis to Washington this evening. The physicians say that the case is not in any way serious and that there is no danger whatever. This statement is made so that no false rumors may disturb the people and that they may be authoritatively advised of the exact nature of the case.

George B. Cortelyou,
Secretary to the President.

(At 3 p. m.)

At 3:15 p. m., the President went from the Columbia Club to St. Vincent's Hospital in his own carriage and shortly after he was in the hospital the operation required was performed by Dr. George H. Oliver, of Indianapolis in consultation with the President's physician, Dr. George A. Lung and Dr. Geo. J. Cook, Dr. Henry Jameson, and Dr. J. J. Richardson. At the conclusion of the operation the physicians authorized the following statement:

As a result of the traumatism (Bruise) received in the trolley accident at Pittsfield, Mass., there was found to be a circumscribed collection of perfectly pure serum in the middle third of the left anterior tibial region, the sac containing about two ounces which was removed. The indications are that the President should make speedy recovery. It is absolutely imperative, however, that he should remain quiet and refrain from using the leg. The trouble is not serious but temporarily disabling.

(Signed) GEORGE B. CORTELYOU,
(5 p. m.) Secretary to the President.

The White House was being renovated at the time and the temporary White House was 22 Jackson Place. I met the President with the ambulance at 6:30 p. m. of the 24th of September. As soon as I saw the bruise on the left leg about midway of the tibia, I felt sure the bone was injured and I asked the President for a consultation and he directed Dr. Newton M. Shaffer of New York to be called. Dr. Shaffer arrived the following morning and a consultation was held with him, Dr. Lung, and other officers of the Navy. It was decided that the bone was injured and an operation demanded at once. I had everything ready and under a local anaesthetic an incision was made, the periosteum laid back, the bone cureted and an antiseptic dressing applied. The wound healed quickly and the President was soon on his feet. The anxiety in regard to this incident by the general public was very great and the reporters would have given me much trouble if I had not adhered to my decision not to give anything out except through the Secretary to the President. The reporters, however, were after Dr. Shaffer and tried to get a statement, and to show how careful the White House physicians should be, I publish Dr. Shaffer's letter to me of October 1st in reply to my note informing him of the splendid progress of the patient.

NEW YORK STATE HOSPITAL
FOR THE CARE OF
CRIPPLED AND DEFORMED CHILDREN

October 1, 1902.

Dear Dr. Rixey:

I thank you for your kind note of yesterday which came this morning. I sincerely hope your illustrious patient will continue to improve.

I made up my mind, while I was on my way home on Monday night that I would have nothing further to do with the reporters. I was, however, going to bed on the evening of my return when a "Herald" reporter appeared with a recent telephone message from their representative in Washington, saying that the President was much worse—He had had a bad chill; temperature was very high, etc. Of course, I duly corrected this.

Yesterday a "World" reporter called with much the same story. Again in the interests of the truth, I made a statement. Of course, I was not correctly reported, but I at least disproved the statement that the President was doing badly.

It is my distinct impression that on both of these occasions, there was an attempt to influence the stock market, especially so the night I reached home.

If the President says anything about these interviews, please tell him the circumstances.

Do you think it worth while to use the X-Ray? You may remember that I suggested it. At the time, however, it did not seem to be indicated, or even worth while. But if matters do not progress satisfactorily, please consider it. We might find something—a splinter, for instance.

I shall esteem it a great favor if you will kindly send me word daily as to your patient's progress.

With high regard,

Sincerely yours,

(Signed) NEWTON M. SHAFFER.

To: P. M. Rixey, M. D.,
Surgeon General of the Navy.

I made my report of the President's condition twice a day to Mr. Cortelyou, and he usually gave out my report word for word.

The danger to the President on horseback from the crowds who would frequently join the party and almost ride over him caused me to write out the following:

RULES OF THE ROAD FOR THOSE INVITED TO ACCOMPANY THE PRESIDENT ON HORSEBACK RIDES

1st. The President will notify whom he wishes to ide with him. The one so notified will take a position on the left of the President, and keep his right stirrup back of the President's left stirrup. When the President is accompanied by Mrs. Roosevelt no one else will ride with him unless requested.

2nd. Those following will keep not less than ten yards in the rear of the President.

3rd. When the President asks anyone in the party to ride with him the one at his side should at once retire to the rear. Salutes should be returned only by the President, except by those in the rear. Anyone unable to control his horse should withdraw to the rear.

(Signed) WM. LOEB, JR.
Secretary to the President.

Approved: May 11, 1903.

Mr. Loeb at once had a large number of copies made and a supply always ready for distribution. Mr. Roosevelt was a hard rider and the above rules, which were enforced, added much to the President's comfort and to my peace of mind.

The President frequently consulted me concerning the health of Cabinet Officers and others, as well as about the appointment of medical men to important positions. (See page 308—selection of Dr. White for Superintendency of St. Elizabeth's Hospital for Insane). On July 14, 1903, I wrote the following letter to Col. Roosevelt.

NAVY DEPARTMENT
BUREAU OF MEDICINE AND SURGERY
WASHINGTON

Dear Mr. President:

Shortly before you left Washington you spoke to me in regard to health of the Postmaster General. Since then I have followed his case very closely and I find that there has been a decided increase in his indisposition. The attacks, or seizures, are much more frequent, occurring principally at night after any unusual excitement or worry. Last night was quite an uncomfortable one for him and Dr. Magruder spent a good portion of the night with him. This attack was directly caused by some unusual worry at the Department.

I am detailing, by direction of the Secretary, one of my Assistants, to accompany him on a trip of from ten days to two weeks on one of the Revenue Cutters, who will make a concise report to me at the expiration of the trip of the Postmaster General's physical condition during the cruise. I write you this, as I feel that you should be thoroughly acquainted with the conditions.

From the papers, I think you must be enjoying your summer in spite of the work and annoyances that come to the Chief Executive. I hope to write Mrs. Roosevelt today. Please remember me to the children and tell them how much we miss them, and believe me,

Very respectfully,
(Signed) P. M. Rixey.

In July 1903, I wrote to the President at Oyster Bay and spoke of how much I was discouraged in my efforts to secure a proper recognition of my Bureau and work in harmony with the Bureau of Navigation. In conclusion of this letter I wrote that I was so much disappointed that I felt like asking to be relieved of my duty as Surgeon General. He replied by next mail as follows:

Oyster Bay, N. Y.,
July 18, 1903.

My dear Dr. Rixey:

I have written to Secretary Moody. Of course, you can not leave your present position and I know you do not seriously mean to.

Always yours,
(Signed) Theodore Roosevelt.

to which I replied as follows:

Department of The Navy
Bureau of Medicine and Surgery
Washington, D. C.

July 22, 1903.

My dear Mr. President:

In reply to your letter of the 18th instant, I have to state that I have not the least idea of resigning my position here, and in time of peace if I should resign it would be to go into the active practice of my profession. If war should come you will find me ready for the duty in which you think I could best serve my country. Again I wish to thank you for all your kindness to me.

We are enjoying our evenings and mornings in the country, and work in my office is fairly comfortable. I am arranging for walks, drives, and horseback rides over the farms, and I hope that you, Mrs. Roosevelt and the children will enjoy them this fall. I am planning several long horseback rides for you on your return to the city.

A letter just received from Dr. Taylor, whom I sent with Mr. Payne, tells me that the Postmaster General was improving. Mr. Moody leaves here Friday morning.

I hope that Mrs. Roosevelt is enjoying Wyoming, and that you are all very well.

Yours very respectfully,

(Signed) P. M. Rixey.

Early in June, 1907, I received a letter from Dr. John A. Fordyce of New York in which he asked me how best to approach the President in regard to an address by him at the opening exercises of the International Dermatological Congress from the 9th to the 14th of September. I replied as follows:

Department of the Navy
Bureau of Medicine and Surgery
Washington

June 22, 1907.

My dear Doctor:

Yours of the 21st received. The only way in which I would advise approaching the President of the United States in regard to the opening exercises of the Sixth International Dermatological Congress would be that you write to him stating what you wish. His interest in the medical profession has been manifested in many ways and I am sure that he will do anything that is possible to make the Congress a success.

I make it a rule not to bring questions of any kind to him which may add to the great burden which he has to bear. As you know, the President of the United States is approached on every side and at all times, and as his physician, I have endeavored to shield him as much as possible from over work. I do not, however, see any objection to your writing a letter as suggested above. You will be sure to receive a courteous reply which could be read at the meeting of the Congress.

With best wishes, believe me,

Very sincerely,

(Signed) P. M. RIXEY.

This letter was addressed to Dr. John Fordyce, 80 West 40th Street, New York City. In July, I received the following letter from Col. Roosevelt:

THE WHITE HOUSE
WASHINGTON

July 11, 1907.

Sir:

I shall be glad if you will attend the meeting of the Sixth International Dermatological Congress to be held in New York City, September 9th to 14th, 1907, and convey to it my appreciation of its invitation to be present and my regrets at not being able to accept. Please greet in my name the Congress, especially the foreign delegates, and wish them a most prosperous meeting.

Sincerely yours,

(Signed) THEODORE ROOSEVELT.

Surgeon General P. M. Rixey,
Navy Department,
Washington, D. C.

I attended this Congress in New York, read the letter, and in a short address said:

"Mr. President and Gentlemen of the Congress: I greet you in the name of the President of the United States, especially the delegates from foreign countries who have honored us by their presence, and I trust the occasion will be the means of forming many ties that may be mutually beneficial.

"We hope to learn much from you as representatives of other nations and trust that you may return feeling repaid for the long journey that you have undertaken. The interest that our President takes in all matters pertaining to the welfare of the people is well known, but it may never be known how much he has done for the medical profession on many occasions. I wish to take this opportunity, however, of saying that we as a profession have much to thank him for and can always rest assured of his hearty cooperation in any effort of ours for the general well-being.

"He takes a deep interest in all that concerns the medical profession, and realizing our need for help and assistance, never loses an opportunity to strengthen and support us in the many progressive steps we have taken. So you may feel assured that he will take a special interest in the proceedings of this Congress, and join with us in the hope that from its deliberations much good may be derived.

"During the past twenty years, the subject of skin diseases, which we have met here to consider, has received, with all other medical subjects, a great impetus. The introduction of laboratory methods has opened up a world of useful information, and especially to those of us in the Government services the period has been one of constant advance and discovery brought about particularly by our advent into tropical and heretofore little known countries. So important has the subject become that we are now bending our efforts to perfect the members of the medical corps of the services in a knowledge of this specialty and to equip them for research and practical work in all parts of the world. I have been more than pleased at the active steps taken by this Congress to demand from educational institutions more careful consideration of the study of diseases of the skin, to require more study and a deeper insight into this very important branch of medical science.

"Following out this idea, we of the Navy, at our Medical School in Washington are giving more and more attention to skin troubles, both in our didactic teaching and in the laboratory, and many of our most interesting reports today are on this subject, especially in connection with tropical medicine.

"Once more I give you all a most hearty welcome from our Chief Magistrate, and hope that this the Sixth Meeting of this International Congress may be one long to be remembered for the good it has accomplished."

My duties in Washington deprived me of the pleasure of attending all of the sessions of the Congress and I left to the Bureau's delegate, Dr. Harmon, to deliver before the Congress my paper on the relation of the Public Services to Dermatological Research. In my letter to the President of June 15th, I mentioned that Mr. Taft was under treatment and I was somewhat anxious about him. He replied as follows:

Oyster Bay, N. Y.,
June 17, 1907.

My dear Dr. Rixey:

Many thanks for your letter of the 15th instant. I, too, am concerned about Taft. I have regarded his strength and power to stand work as greater than mine. I shall see him soon.

I do hope that dear Mrs. Rixey and you will have a lovely time this summer.

Ever yours,
(Signed) THEODORE ROOSEVELT.

P. S. Duchess Betsy is in fine shape.

On a bear hunt with the President in the Louisiana cane brakes I wrote to my wife, and quote from that letter as follows:

"Here we are in camp about fifteen miles from the railway station, and in order to describe the camp I send you a pencil sketch. No. 1 is the President's tent in which I am quartered and it is very comfortable. No. 2 is occupied by our hosts, Mr. McIlhenny and Mr. Parker. No. 3, Dr. Lambert and Ben Lilly, an old bear hunter. No. 4, mess tent. No. 5, large tent for horses. Nos. 7 and 9 are for the negro attendants, etc. No. 8 is a store tent. The clearing for the camp is made in the midst of a great forest on a bayou. There are a number of dogs already in with the promise of 50 or 60 more to be divided into packs to run on alternate days. No. 10 are camp fires.

"Arrived in Camp Saturday evening the 7th and next day being Sunday the President enjoyed in a quiet way, after our lively experience with the crowds since leaving Washington. Monday, an all day hunt showed that the making of the camp had frightened away all bear and other game in this locality, and the President requested a move to some point where there was game and no preparation made for a President. It was decided to start the following morning for a small hut on a lake about 20 miles from the present camp. We hunted the whole distance and killed deer and bobcat but no bear. In our new camp we were not so comfortable but the President was after bear, and he was always ready for a start. He soon had killed his bear, a large one, weighing about 250 pounds. When the dogs were in full cry we often had to ride hard and over fallen trees—some of them very large. I was riding a stout bear pony and the larger horses could not leave him behind. Coming to one of the fallen trees he would jump on top of it and then clear it as a goat would have done. I shall always remember this cane brake hunt in Louisiana, and the warm hospitality of our southern friends."

We met a number of Gentlemen, old hunters in that section among them Messrs. Harley and Clive Metcalf, and when parting I invited them to visit me in Washington, as had the President. They came on in December and stayed a few days with me, and the President gave them and other members of the bear hunt party a lunch on December 2, 1907.

THE WHITE HOUSE
WASHINGTON

December 2, 1907.

My dear Dr. Rixey:

The President requests me to ask if you will not bring Messrs. Clive and Harley Metcalf to lunch at The White House on Thursday next, at 1:30 o'clock. Please advise if you accept.

Very truly yours,
(Signed) WM. LOEB, JR.
Secretary to President.

And he also had them for dinner on December 6th.

My dear Dr. Rixey:

The President requests me to say that he would be glad to have you dine informally at The White House on Friday,

December 6, at 8:00 o'clock. Dress clothes will not be worn on this occasion.

Please advise if you accept.

Very truly yours,

(Signed) WM. LOEB, JR.
Secretary to President.

The following letter was written in the President's own hand on the occasion of the death of my brother, Congressman John F. Rixey:

THE WHITE HOUSE
WASHINGTON

My very dear friend:

Our hearts have gone out to you in this time of your sore trial. No people have ever had a truer friend than you have been to us; we love you dearly, all of us, the children too; anything that concerns Mrs. Rixey or you concerns us. In this great grief of yours we only wish we could be of service. May the Unseen Power be gentle with you.

Your devoted friend,

(Signed) THEODORE ROOSEVELT.

There were always invitations coming to the White House for the President to go hunting for all kinds of game from jack rabbits to elephants. The following is one addressed to me and I was glad to have him decline as it was a fox hunt at Warrenton, Virginia.

Oyster Bay, N. Y.,
July 13, 1908.

My dear Doctor:

I have your letter of the 11th and return the enclosure herewith. It would not be possible for us to take that ride, attractive though I am sure it would be. It is always a pleasure to hear from you.

Give our love to Mrs. Rixey. We are all well here.

Faithfully yours,

(Signed) THEODORE ROOSEVELT.

Colonel Roosevelt continued in excellent health up to the time of leaving the Presidential chair and I had no fear of his standing the African trip and would have chosen to go

WHITE HOUSE
WASHINGTON

March 2d 1909

My beloved friend,

We sorrow with you in your loss; whatever affects you affects us also. I wish we could be of any comfort to you.

No words could express in adequate fashion what you and dear Mrs. Risley have been to us throughout our stay in the White House. No people ever had more loyal, devoted and self sacrificing friends that we have had in you and her,

You have taken a personal care of and interest in me which I can never forget; and the relationship has been as close socially as professionally; it has been been the relation of devoted personal friendship between us.

May all good fortune ever attend you and yours,

Faithfully your friend

Theodore Roosevelt

THE DEATH OF ADMIRAL RIXEY'S ONLY SISTER (See p. 167) WAS THE OCCASION OF THIS LETTER

with him if he wished it but he said: "No, you have nearly two years as Chief of the Bureau and are needed where you are."

While on his way home he received a letter from me telling of my retirement from active duty, and of my intention to develop my farms, and he wrote me as follows:

Aboard the *Ibis* on the Nile,
May 19, 1910.

My dear Dr. Rixey:

It was delightful to get your letter. I don't think I have ever been in better health than during my African trip; and you would have enjoyed the whole experience to the full. You would have found me distinctly a slowpoke in the field, but I verily believe that even your long legs would have had all the employment they wished in keeping up with Kermit. I could not pretend to do more than half what Kermit did. He was willing to ride at full speed after anything over any type of ground and to walk or run throughout the entire day or the entire night if there were any object in the way of game ahead. He is not a good shot, indeed not quite so good a shot as I am—and Heaven knows that leaves much to be desired—but he is as keen as mustard, entirely indifferent to fatigue and hardship, possessed of great endurance, with excellent eyes, and absolutely cool in danger. A charging lion or elephant has no more effect upon his nerves than a gazelle running in the opposite direction. Indeed, at first he almost reduced me to a jibbering insanity of wrath by the way he would plunge after dangerous game into situations where the odds were all in favor of the hunted beast. The only way I produced any improvement was by gradually making his fear of me surpass even his lack of fear of the lion or leopard. Seriously, he grew to have much more wisdom towards the end, and he is the staunchest and pleasantest companion that any human being could wish on such a hunting trip as we have had. He is just a trump.

How is dear Mrs. Rixey? Give her my love. Of course, I was very sorry that you were not continued, but at any rate, dear doctor, you have rendered a very great service, and after all, next to one's domestic life, the thing best worth having in life is the consciousness of having done one's full duty in an important position.

Ever faithfully yours,

(Signed) THEODORE ROOSEVELT.

To: Dr. Presley M. Rixey, U. S. Navy, Washington, D. C.

Sometime later I wrote inviting Col. and Mrs. Roosevelt to visit us, to which he replied as follows:

New York, N. Y.,
November 22, 1910.

Dear Dr. Rixey:

On my return home I found your attractive invitation. I was so sorry to miss you when in Washington, but it was a joy to catch even a glimpse of dear Mrs. Rixey. That is a most delightful invitation of yours, but experience has taught Mrs. Roosevelt and me that the one way we can get a real rest is by staying at home. It is hard enough to do it even here and impossible elsewhere. I wish I could have seen you.

What a trump you are!

Ever yours,

(Signed) THEODORE ROOSEVELT.

Dr. P. M. Rixey,
"Ben Lomond,"
Manassas, Va.

and in February he wrote as follows:

New York, N. Y.,
February 7, 1911.

Dear Doctor:

This is just to remind you how much we wish to see you. Whenever you and dear Mrs. Rixey are to be in New York be sure and let us know in advance for we so wish to have both of you come out and spend a night with us at Oyster Bay.

Ever yours,

(Signed) THEODORE ROOSEVELT.

Mrs. Rixey and I accepted this invitation and spent the week-end with the family at Oyster Bay which we thoroughly enjoyed. Col. Roosevelt was not as good physically as when he left the White House and I urged him to follow a course of treatment which I had found of service in his case. About October 1, Mrs. Roosevelt was taken ill and I spent several days at Oyster Bay in consultation with Dr. Lambert, their New York family physician for many years. Her convalescence was slow and the whole family was much worried. Col. Roosevelt's next letter was to Mrs. Rixey:

New York, N. Y.,
December 26, 1911.

Dear Mrs. Rixey:

I think it was just dear of you and the Doctor to remember me and to remember all of us, but then you two dear friends always do remember us. Many, many happy New Years to you and yours.

Sincerely yours,
(Signed) THEODORE ROOSEVELT.

P. S. I am adding a P. S. of special thanks for the pretty and useful pincushion which I did not speak of in my letter.

(Signed) EDITH K. ROOSEVELT.

Mrs. Presley M. Rixey,
Washington, D. C.

Colonel Roosevelt was much annoyed at having to bring the libel suit against the Marquette Editor, and wrote me as follows:

New York, N. Y.,
December 17, 1912.

Dear Dr. Rixey:

Mr. Pound, my lawyer in the libel suit, would like from you a statement as to your knowledge of my sobriety and temperance from your personal experience. He wants to know just what he has to rely upon in the case. I have sent him the statement of Jacob Riis already. Can you give him such a statement?

Always yours,
(Signed) THEODORE ROOSEVELT.

I forwarded my statement and the following May received this letter from his Secretary, Mr. Frank Harper:

New York, N. Y.,
May 21, 1913.

Dear Dr. Rixey:

Mr. Roosevelt has asked me to thank you for your letter and to say how much pleased he is that you are able to come to Marquette. He would not have troubled you, but he feels that your testimony is of such great importance and it will have so much more weight if delivered in person that he decided to ask you to spare time enough off to come on. Herewith is an identification card. I will hand you on the train a ticket and reservation for you from Grand Central Station to Marquette.

The train will leave Grand Central Station May 24th at 5:30 p. m. It is the Lake Shore Limited and Mr. Roosevelt will be glad if you will go straight to the train. This is what he will do when he comes from Oyster Bay.

Sincerely yours,

(Signed) FRANK HARPER,
Secretary.

At the trial before Col. Roosevelt's witnesses had all been heard the Editor came forward and acknowledged that his paper had printed the libelous articles on "hear-say evidence" and not one of his witnesses could testify that he ever saw Col. Roosevelt under the influence of alcoholic liquors. The following from the New York Tribune is worth reproducing:

THE ROOSEVELT TIPPLE

THE COLONEL A STALWART EXAMPLE OF MILK AND SPRING WATER

If Colonel Roosevelt's reputation as the most remarkable of Americans was in any danger of impairment, that danger is likely to be removed by the libel trial in Michigan. Not a teetotaller, wearing an ostentatious blue ribbon and a sour expression, he has yet been able to go through life where alcoholic opportunities were plentiful without touching cocktails, highballs, whisky, except as medicine; beer, or a red wine. It is an extraordinary record.

And yet, what is the use of all the witnesses in corroboration? The Marquette jury has seen the Colonel on the witness stand, and he himself is the best evidence of the alibi of John Barleycorn. What is the need of piling the Abbotts on the Riises, the Garfields on the Pinchots, the O'Laughlins on the Loebs and the Rixeys, and producing the evidence of physicians attending him at the time of his shooting to disprove the silly libel of the Marquette editor?

But just as Lincoln wished he knew what brand of whisky Grant drank, so that he might send a barrel of it to each of the other Union generals, the public will seek to learn just what dairy it is from which the Colonel buys his milk.

I did all in my power to prevent the South American trip of Col. Roosevelt, but under full pressure he must work at something and fully realizing the necessity of an outdoor life for him as much as possible I had written him on November 2, 1914, begging him and Mrs. Roosevelt to make us a visit. I was anxious to study his physical condition and try to persuade him to adopt a less strenuous life as from what I had seen of him since the South American trip it was absolutely necessary if he were to have, as I hoped, a ripe old age. He was seven years younger than I and I had already realized that I could not keep up the pressure of work which had been mine for over forty years.

Mr. Taft's decision not to appoint me for a third term as Surgeon General was most fortunate although I was willing to undertake it as there was still much that I would have liked to have done for the increase of efficiency of the Navy. The sense of relief from the responsibility of official life was very great and I decided to give up all professional work while enjoying my great interest in it and lead the outdoor life of a Virginia farmer with hunting and golf as recreation. What I hoped for Col. Roosevelt at this time was that he would curtail his activities along the same lines, while his interest in all that pertains to our country and his writings would occupy his mind. My mode of life as outlined for myself was most pleasant and I was on the go from sunrise to sunset, having several thousand acres of land to farm within a radius of thirty miles.

Colonel Roosevelt in reply to my letter outlining for him what I have written was answered as follows:

Oyster Bay, Long Island, N. Y.
February 1, 1915.

My dear Doctor:

Your letter touches me so much that I must send you this line of thanks from both Mrs. Roosevelt and myself.

In a few weeks a book of mine will be sent you and I think you will agree with the Americanism it teaches.

Faithfully yours,
(Signed) THEODORE ROOSEVELT.

He was evidently feeling well when he wrote this letter and did not mention my advice. His next letter however made me unhappy.

30 East 42nd Street,
New York, N. Y.
February 22, 1915.

My dear Dr. Rixey:

There is no letter that could have touched and pleased me more than yours. Only the other day Mrs. Roosevelt and I were saying that no other man whose friendship we had won in later life had ever been as much of a friend to us and had meant so much to us as you. We talk of you all the time and the children talk of you all the time. Just the other day Archie, who is now a sophomore in Harvard and a fine fellow, was describing his experience as a very small boy when you took him out to hunt. I regard you and dear Mrs. Rixey as having been among the best influences for my children. I feel that they and we owe both of you very much. That was a fine tribute that Dr. Braisted paid you and that Admiral Dewey paid you; and both were absolutely deserved.

As for me, my dear doctor, I am practically through. I am not a man like you who keeps his youth almost to the end; and I am now pretty nearly done out. I would not say this except to my old friend, who was also my old physical adviser, because it is rather poor business to speak about one's personal ailments; but the trouble is that I have rheumatism or gout and things of that kind to a degree that makes it impossible for me to take very much exercise; and then in turn the fact that I cannot take exercise prevents my keeping in good condition. I am more pleased than I can say that I was able to take the South American trip. I knew it would be my last thing of the kind.

I was pleased but amused, my dear fellow, at your saying that I had work to do in the future. I have none. The kaleidoscope has been shaken. All the combinations are new and I am out of sympathy with what seems to be the predominant political thought in this country.

With warmest love to dear Mrs. Rixey,

Faithfully yours,

(Signed) THEODORE ROOSEVELT.

This letter made clear to me his state of mind so I wrote him as cheerfully as possible and received the following letter:

Sagamore Hill,
December 23, 1915.

Dear Doctor:

Mrs. Roosevelt and I have read and re-read your letter; and we do not believe any people ever had a stauncher and more devoted friend than you have been to us—and dear Mrs. Rixey has been just as staunch and true and devoted.

You two made a very great part of our happiness, and the happiness of the children, when we were in the White House. Good for Betsy and her colt! Indeed, I do hope that the grandchildren may ride them. As for the turkey and the pig, we shall *all* of us stuff ourselves on them! The children and grandchildren arrive today, all of them, except of course Kermit and Belle who are on the opposite side of the world; I know you will be glad to hear that the stork is to visit them in February.

Well, old friend, you and I did our work faithfully, and I think I may say with reasonable efficiency, in the Navy, did we not? I, of course, feel very badly about the course our country has followed in international affairs for the last five years. What we have submitted to from Germany and Mexico has been a cause of sore national humiliation; and it seems almost unbelievable that we should not have begun one particle of preparation during the year and a half since the European war wrote before our eyes in letters of fire and blood the warning of what may happen to the foolish who are not ready to defend themselves.

A merry Christmas to you both, with dearest love from all of us.

Ever yours,
(Signed) THEODORE ROOSEVELT.

One year later I received the following letter:

432 Fourth Avenue,
New York, N. Y.
December 27, 1916.

My dear Dr. Rixey:

It's fine to hear from you! Indeed you don't have to tell us ever that you and Mrs. Rixey think of us, for we have never had two stauncher, or more loyal friends. I am awfully pleased at what you tell me about your farming and what you are now doing.

We have had a delightful Christmas; all of our children were here and all of the grandchildren but one. Mrs. Roosevelt seems really well.

With heartiest good wishes, old friend,

Always yours,
(Signed) THEODORE ROOSEVELT.

P. S. The roasting pig has just come; I am looking forward most eagerly to eating it.

Christmas of the year 1916 was the last one on which the whole family would ever be together again on earth. The World War was on and all four of Col. Roosevelt's sons were at the front or on their way after intensive training at home. I wrote him and Mrs. Roosevelt telling them how pleased I was at the fine Americanism of our boys and offering them Duchess Betsy's beautiful colt now being broken for use of the grandchildren. His reply was:

432 Fourth Avenue,
New York, N. Y.,
July 23, 1917.

My dear Doctor:

Mrs. Roosevelt and I were delighted to get your letter. It is most characteristic of you. We have just been down to see Quentin off. All four of our boys are now on the ocean, or on the other side. They have done their duty, and I would not have them do anything else, but of course it is very hard for their mother, and for their gallant little wives.

We were greatly interested about Betsy and her colt. Indeed, if we had stable facilities, we would accept the colt at once, my dear Doctor, but I hardly venture to do so under existing conditions, for none of the six grandchildren are yet old enough to ride it.

I am very glad to hear about your two nephews, the sons of Congressman Rixey, and about Ellis Jones. Give our warmest love to dear Mrs. Rixey. You knew, did you not, that Ethel has a little daughter who is five weeks old?

Faithfully yours,
(Signed) THEODORE ROOSEVELT.

The following October, I received a letter from Col. Roosevelt from New York as follows:

October 25, 1917.

Dear Dr. Rixey:

That's awfully good of you to have sent me that review. I am so pleased to know you are at work. I wish I were at work. The boys are doing well, I believe.

Faithfully yours,
(Signed) THEODORE ROOSEVELT.

To: Dr. P. M. Rixey,
Navy Department,
Washington, D. C.

The next year, 1918, he wrote me the following letter:

432 Fourth Ave., New York.
March 18, 1918.

My dear Dr. Rixey:

Your letter pleased us both very much. Indeed, my dear fellow, if I had half of your vitality I should be more than content.

At the moment we are both very proud and not a little anxious about Archie. His most serious wound is in his left knee, but he has another wound on the body and his arm is broken. But our information is that he will surely recover.

With love to Mrs. Rixey.

Faithfully yours,

(Signed) THEODORE ROOSEVELT.

A few days later he wrote me again:

March 27, 1918.

Dear Dr. Rixey:

That's fine. I am so pleased to have you speak as you do about Archie; though, in a sense, it was needless, as I knew how Mrs. Rixey and you would feel.

Faithfully yours,

(Signed) THEODORE ROOSEVELT.

Immediately upon hearing of the death of Quentin, who had been killed in action on July 14, 1918, in France, I wrote to Col. and Mrs. Roosevelt, expressing our deepest sympathy, and received a reply as follows:

Oyster Bay,
Long Island, N. Y.,
July 27, 1918.

My dear Dr. Rixey:

Mrs. Roosevelt and I were greatly touched by your letter. I know how you and Mrs. Rixey loved all the boys, and we are absolutely sure of your sympathy. The four little fellows you used to take around have done pretty well, haven't they?

Faithfully yours,

(Signed) THEODORE ROOSEVELT.

In November of 1918 I was in communication with Col. Roosevelt and his reply to my letter was as follows:

New York, N. Y.,
November 11, 1918.

Dear Doctor:

It is fine to hear from you. Your plans for your future life seem most attractive. At the moment I am laid up in bed and can only send you this line of thanks and acknowledgment. Love to dear Mrs. Rixey.

Faithfully yours,
(Signed) THEODORE ROOSEVELT.

On hearing of his bad health, I immediately replied, expressing my anxiety, and a week later I received the following answer:

November 21, 1918.

My dear Dr. Rixey:

My indisposition is of no consequence. It is only bothersome and soon I will be as fit as ever.

With love to you, and dear Mrs. Rixey,

Faithfully yours,
(Signed) THEODORE ROOSEVELT.

This letter reassured me, at least for the time. It was the last letter I received from him. He died January 6, 1919.

The death of Quentin was a terrible blow to both Colonel and Mrs. Roosevelt and that, with his inability to take an active part in the war, no doubt shortened his life.

My illness in August of 1918, due to hemorrhage, after which I had a slow convalescence, prevented my seeing Colonel Roosevelt again.

CHAPTER VII

FOUR ADDRESSES OF PRESIDENT ROOSEVELT

THE following four addresses of President Roosevelt will give to the Medical Profession some idea of his appreciation of themselves and their calling:

ADDRESS OF PRESIDENT ROOSEVELT AT THE OPENING SESSION OF THE MILITARY SURGEONS' ASSOCIATION, WASHINGTON, D. C., JUNE 5, 1902

Mr. President, Ladies and Gentlemen:

I am glad to have the opportunity to bid welcome to the members of this Association and their friends today. The men of your Association combine two professions each of which is rightfully held in high honor by all capable of appreciating the real work of men—the profession of the soldier and the profession of the doctor. Conditions in modern civilization tend more and more to make the average life of the community one of great ease, compared to what has been the case in the past. Together with what advantages have come from this softening of life and rendering it more easy there are certain attendant disadvantages. It is a very necessary thing that there should be some professions, some trades, where the same demands are made now as ever in the past upon the heroic qualities. Those demands are made alike upon the soldier and upon the doctor; and more upon those who are both soldiers and doctors, upon the men who have continually to face all the responsibility, all the risk, faced by their brothers in the civilian branch of the profession, and who also, in time of war, must face much the same risks, often exactly the same risks, that are faced by their brothers in arms whose trade is to kill and not to cure. It has been my good fortune, gentlemen, to see some of your body at work in the field, to see them carrying the wounded and the dying from the firing line, themselves as much exposed to danger as those they were rescuing, and to see them working day and night in the field hospital afterward when even the intensity of the strain could hardly keep them awake, so fagged out were they by having each to do the work of ten.

I welcome you here, and I am glad to have the chance of seeing you, and I wish to say a word of congratulation to you upon this Association. In all our modern life we have found it absolutely indispensable to supplement the work of the individual by the work of the individuals gathered into an association. Without this work of the association you cannot give the highest expression to individual endeavor, and it would be a great misfortune if the military members of the surgical and medical profession did not take every advantage of their opportunities in the same way that is taken by the members of the medical and the surgical profession who are not in the Army or the Navy or the Marine hospital service—who are in civilian life outside. I am glad to see you gathered in this association. Just one word of warning; pay all possible heed to the scientific side of your work; perfect yourselves as scientific men able to work with the best and most delicate apparatus; and never for one moment forget—especially the higher officers among you—that in time of need you will have to do your work with the scantiest possible apparatus, and that then your usefulness will be conditioned not upon the adequacy of the complaint that you did not have apparatus enough, but upon what you have done with the insufficient apparatus you had. Remember that and remember also—and this especially applies to the higher officers—that you must supplement in your calling the work of the surgeon with the work of the administrator. You must be doctors and military men and able administrators.

REMARKS OF PRESIDENT ROOSEVELT AT THE UNVEILING OF THE STATUE IN FRONT OF THE U. S. NAVAL HOSPITAL, WASHINGTON, D. C., OF BENJAMIN RUSH

June 11, 1904.

Mr. Chairman, Ladies and Gentlemen:

I accept on behalf of the nation the gift so fittingly bestowed by one of the great professions—this statue of a man who was eminent not only in that profession, but eminent in his service to the nation as a whole. We have listened to the interesting study of the life of Benjamin Rush, and it must surely have been brought home to each of us here that his career derives its peculiar significance in part from the greatness of his pioneer work as a physician on this continent, in part from the way in which he combined with arduous and incessant labor in his profession the greatest devotion even outside of that profession to the welfare of his fellow-countrymen. Here at the national capital it is earnestly to be hoped that we shall finally see commemorated as the services of Rush are henceforth to be commemorated by this statue, all the great Americans who, working in widely different lines, by the aggregate of their work make the sum of achievement of America in the world. I thank and congratulate you of the medical profession today upon what you have done, not merely in commemorating the foremost pioneer in your own profession, but in adding at the National capital a figure to the gallery of great Americans who should be here commemorated.

As you said, Dr. Wilson, Benjamin Rush was not a specialist in the modern sense. He could not be. There were not any specialists in the modern sense, as you pointed out. There was no possibility of there being such. But I would like, in this age of specialization, to say one word in the way of a short sermon to eminent specialists. Today, no specialist in a democratic country like ours can afford to be so exclusively a specialist as to forget that one part of his duty is his duty to the general public and to the state. Where Government is the duty of all, it of course means that it is the duty of each, and the minute that the average man gets to thinking that Government is the duty of somebody else, that minute the republic will begin to go down. It is a fortunate thing for our country that we should have before us the lives of men like Rush, who could take a part in our public life as distinguished as is implied by having been a signer of the Declaration of Independence, and yet do it without a particle of neglect of the man's own proper duties.

I would earnestly plead in addressing this audience, and especially the members of the high and honorable profession which has given this gift to the nation, that you never for one moment permit yourselves to forget the fact that the well-being of the republic ultimately depends upon the way in which as a rule and habitually the best citizen of the republic does his duty to the state; and that we have a right not merely to expect but to demand from our hardest worked men, from the leaders of the great professions, the full performance of that public service which consists in a zealous, intelligent, and fearless performance of the ordinary duties of public life by the ordinary private citizen.

I thank you for having presented to the national capital, to the people of the United States, the statue of a man who was foremost as a leader and a pioneer in his profession, who was a great physician and a great American.

ADDRESS OF PRESIDENT ROOSEVELT TO THE GRADUATES OF THE U. S. NAVAL MEDICAL SCHOOL, WASHINGTON

March 25, 1905.

Ladies and Gentlemen, and Especially the Members of the Graduating Class:

I am glad to have the chance of saying a word of greeting to you this morning. You represent two professions, for you are members of the great medical body and you are also officers of the Navy of the United States, and therefore, you have a double standard of honor up to which to live. I think that all of us laymen, men and women, have peculiar appreciation of what a doctor means; for I do not suppose there is one of us who does not feel that the family doctor stands in a position of close intimacy with each of us, in a position of obligation to him under which one is happy to rest to an extent hardly possible with anyone else; and those of us, I think most of us, who are fortunate enough to have a family doctor who is a beloved and intimate friend, realize that there can be few closer ties of intimacy and affection in the world. And while, of course, even the greatest and best doctors can not assume that very intimate relation with more than a certain number of people (though it is to be said that more than any other man, the doctor does commonly assume such a relation to many people)—while it is impossible this relation in its closest form shall obtain between a doctor and more than a certain number of people, still with every patient with whom the doctor is thrown at all intimately he has this peculiar relation to a greater or less extent. The effect that the doctor has upon the body of the patient is in very many cases no greater than the effect that he has upon the patient's mind. Each one of you here has resting upon him not only a great responsibility for the care of the body of the officer or enlisted man who will be under his supervision, but a care—which ought not to be too consciously shown, but which should be unconsciously felt—for the man's spirit. The morale of the entire ship's company, of the entire body of men with which you are to be thrown, will be sensibly affected by the way in which each of you does his duty.

Just as the great doctor, the man who stands high in his profession in any city, counts as one of the most valuable assets in that city's civic work, so in the Navy or the Army the effect of having thoroughly well-trained men with a high and sensitive standard of professional honor and professional duty is well nigh incalculable upon the service itself. I want you now, as you graduate, to feel that on your shoulders rests a great weight of responsibility; that your position is one of high honor, and that it is impossible to hold a position of high honor and not hold it under penalty of incurring the severest reprobation if you fail to live up to its requirements.

I am not competent to speak save in the most general terms of your professional duties. I do want, however, to call your attention to one or two features connected with them. In the first place: In connection with the work you do for the service you have certain peculiar advantages in doing work that will be felt for the whole profession. For instance, it will fall to your lot to deal with certain types of tropical diseases. You will have to deal with them as no ordinary American doctor, no matter how great his experience, will have to deal with them, and you should fit yourselves by most careful study and preparation, so that you shall not only be able to grapple with the cases as they come up, but in grappling with them to make and record observations upon them that will be of permanent value to your fellows in civil life. You can there do what no civilian doctor can possibly do. There probably is not a branch of the profession into which, during your career, you will not have to go; no type of disease that you will not have to treat. But there are certain diseases you will have to treat that the ordinary man who stays at home, of course, does not; and it is of consequence to the entire medical profession that you should so fit yourself by study, by preparation, that you shall not only be able to deal with those cases, but to deal with them in a way that will be of advantage to your stay-at-home brethren.

There is one other point. Every effort should, of course, be made to provide you with ample means to do your work. Every effort ought to be made to persuade the national legislature to take that view of the situation; to remember that in case of war it is out of the question to improvise a great medical service for the Army and the Navy. The need of the increase would be more keenly felt in the Army than in the Navy because it is always the Army that undergoes the greatest expansion in time of war. But it is felt in both services. And when, as is perfectly certain to be the case if ever a war comes, and if we have made no greater preparation than at present; there is fever in the camps, there is sickness among the volunteer forces, it will be more dishonest folly for the public men, and especially for the public press, to shriek against the people who happen to be in power at that time. Let them, if ever such occasion arises, solemnly think over and repent of the fact that they have not made their representatives provide adequately in advance for the medical system in its personnel and its material, for the organization, and for the physical instruments necessary to make that organization effective. Only adequate preparation in advance will obviate the trouble which otherwise is certain to come if we have a war. Let critics remember not to blame the people in power when such a breakdown comes, but to blame themselves, the people of the United States, because they have not had the forethought to take the steps in advance which would prevent such breakdown from occurring.

Means ought to be provided in advance. That is part of our duty. If we fail in it then it is our responsibility, not yours. But now for your duty. I want to impress, with all the strength that in me lies, upon every medical man in either the Army or the Navy, to remember always that in any time of crisis the chances are that you will have to work with imperfect implements. And your conduct will then afford a pretty good test of your worth. If you sit down and do nothing but say you could have done excellently if only you had had the right implements to work with, you will show your unfitness for your position. Your business will be to do the very best you can do, if you have nothing in the world but a jack-knife to do it with. Keep before your minds all the time that when the crisis occurs it is almost sure to be the case that you will have to do no small part of your work with make-shifts; to do it, as I myself saw at Santiago, the Army physicians do their work, roughly and hastily, when worn out with fatigue and having but one-fourth or one fifth of the appliances that they would expect normally to have. Make up your mind that while you will do all you can to get the best material together in advance, you will not put forward the lack of that material as an excuse for not doing the best work possible with imperfect tools. Make it a matter of pride to do your utmost, without regard to the inadequacy of your instruments.

I am sure that all of us outsiders here realize the weight of responsibility resting upon those who now join the great and honorable body of men who in the Navy and in the Army have by their actions upheld not only the standard of honor of the medical profession, but the standard of honor of the officers of the Army and the Navy of the United States.

I greet you on your entrance into the service. I welcome you as servants of the nation, and I wish you every success in the great and honorable calling which you have chosen as yours.

REMARKS OF PRESIDENT ROOSEVELT TO THE LONG ISLAND MEDICAL SOCIETY AT OYSTER BAY, N. Y.

July 12, 1905.

Mr. President, Members of the Association, Friends and Neighbors:

I needed no invitation to come before you today. All I needed was permission. As soon as I learned that this association was to meet in our village I felt that I must take advantage of the opportunity to say a word of greeting to you in person.

Of course, it is almost needless to say that there is not and cannot be any other lay profession, the members of which occupy such a dual position, each side of which is of such importance—for the doctor has on the one hand to be the most thoroughly educated man in applied science that there is in the country, and on the other hand as every layman knows, and as doubtless many a layman in the circle of acquaintance of each of you would gladly testify, the doctor gradually becomes the closest friend to more people than would be possible in any other profession. The feelings that a man has toward the one human being to whom he turns, either in time of sickness for himself, or, what is far more important, in the time of sickness of those closest and dearest to him, cannot but be of a peculiar kind. He cannot but have a feeling for him, such as he has for no other man. The doctor must, therefore, to the greatest degree develop his nature along the two sides of his duties, although in the case of any other man you would call him a mighty good citizen if he developed only on one side. The scientific man who is really a first class scientific man has a claim upon the gratitude of all the country; and the man who is a first class neighbor, and is always called in in time of trouble by his neighbors, has an equal claim upon society at large. But the doctor has both claims. Yet, in addition to filling both of these functions he may fill many other functions. He may have served in the Civil War; he may have rendered the greatest possible service to the community along any one of a dozen different lines.

Take for instance just what is being done in one of the great works of this country at the present time—the digging of the Panama Canal. That is a work that only a big nation could undertake or that a big nation could do, and it is a work for all mankind. The condition precedent upon success in that work is having the proper type of medical work as a preliminary, as a basis. That is the first condition upon the meeting of which must depend our success in solving the engineering and administrative problems of the work itself. I am happy to say that the work is being admirably done, and I am particularly glad to have this chance of saying it. Now and then some alarmist report will come from Panama. Just a couple of weeks ago there seemed to be a succession of people coming up from Panama, each one of whom had some tale of terror to tell. You will always find in any battle, even if it is a victorious battle, that in the rear you will meet a number of gentlemen who are glad that they are not at the front; who, if they have unfortunately gotten at the front have come away, and who justify their absence from the front by telling tales of how everything has gone wrong there. Now the people that flee from Panama will carry up here just such stories as the people that flee from the forefront of a battle carry to the rear with them. The people to whom this country owes and will owe much are those who stay down there and do not talk, but do their work, and do it well. Of course, in doing a great work like that in the tropics, in a region which until this Government took hold of it was accounted to be a region exceptionally unhealthy, we are going to have trouble, have some yellow fever, have a good deal of malarial fever, and suffer more from the latter than from the yellow fever although we will hear nothing like the talk about it. We will have every now and then trouble as regards hygiene, just as we will have trouble in the engineering problems, just as occasionally we will have troubles in the administrative work. Whenever any of those troubles come there will be a large number of excellent but timid men who will at once say what an awful calamity it is, and express the deepest sorrow and concern, and be rather inclined to the belief that the whole thing is a failure. It will not be a failure. It will be a success; and it will be a success because we shall treat every little check, not as a reason for abandoning the work, but as a reason for altering and bettering our plans so as to make it impossible that that particular check shall happen again.

What is being done in Panama is but a sample of the things that this country has done during the last few years, of the things in which your profession has borne so prominent a part. Take what we did in Cuba, where we tried the experiment which had not been tried for four hundred years—of cleaning the cities. One of the most important items of the work done by our Government in Cuba was the work of hygiene, the work of cleaning and disinfecting the cities so as to minimize the chance for yellow fever, so as to do away with as many as possible of the conditions that told for disease. This country has never had done for it better work, that is, work that reflected more honor upon the country, or for humanity at large, than the work done for it in Cuba. And the man who above all others was responsible for doing that work so well was a member of your profession who when the call to arms came himself went as a soldier to the field—the present Major General Leonard Wood. Leonard Wood did in Cuba just the kind of work that, for instance, Lord Cromer has done in Egypt. We have not been able to reward Wood in anything like the proportion in which services such as his would have been rewarded in any other country of the first rank; and there have been no meaner and more unpleasant manifestations in all our public history than the feelings of envy and jealousy manifested toward Wood. And the foul assaults and attacks made upon him, gentlemen, were largely because they grudged the fact that this admirable military officer should have been a doctor.

CHAPTER VIII

APPOINTMENT TO AND TERM IN OFFICE AS SURGEON GENERAL

AFTER Mr. McKinley's death my time was taken up with the routine duties at the Naval Dispensary in addition to those of White House physician and visits to Canton, Ohio, to see Mrs. McKinley. My relations with Mr. Roosevelt were such that I was enabled to make a close study of his physical condition and of those around him. Detached from the Naval Dispensary February 10, 1902, commissioned Surgeon General of the Navy and Chief of the Bureau of Medicine and Surgery, I began my administration by a study of the conditions existing in the Bureau. At the first opportunity after expressing my appreciation of Mr. Roosevelt's action in appointing me to be Chief of the Bureau of Medicine and Surgery I asked him if he had any special instructions to give me as to the conduct of the Bureau. He replied, "The Navy is our first line of defense and must be prepared to fight at the drop of a hat. Your most important duty will be to see that its personnel is physically fit and kept fit for any emergency." The following ten problems seemed the most important to commence with.

I. Personnel. Only half the number of officers needed to perform the duties required of them. 150 Assistant Surgeons to be asked for at once. No provisions for keeping those in the service up to modern standards in medical and surgical science, or for preparing the Assistant Surgeon for the special requirements of the Naval Service. This last provision must be solved by the solution of Problem II.

II. Establish a Naval Post-graduate medical school, with modern bacteriological and chemical laboratories.

III. Remodel old hospitals and build new ones where required.

IV. Modern improvements for the care of sick and wounded aboard ship until in reach of a shore hospital or a hospital ship.

V. Sanitation of Navy Yards, Training Stations, and other Naval Stations.

VI. Train nurses, men for ships and women for hospitals.

VII. Establish a dental Corps.

VIII. Develop specialists.

IX. Make clear the Regulations of the Navy as to the duties of the Medical Department.

X. Build a sanitarium for the treatment of Tubercular sick.

Considering these and many other difficulties which confronted me, I was much discouraged, and my only hope was that my personal relations with those to whom I must apply for assistance were such as to give results; among whom were Mr. Roosevelt, the Secretary of the Navy, Mr. Long (my patient and friend, than whom there was never an abler or more loyal one), the Cabinet officials, many members of the Senate Naval Committee, especially Mr. Eugene Hale, the Speaker of the House, Chairman and members of the House Naval Committee, and other Congressmen. And, last, but not least, I relied upon my brother, a member of the Naval Committee of the House, and the reputation that I had achieved in my professional work at the Naval Dispensary and at sea.

I had three tours of duty at the Naval Dispensary, fourteen years altogether. During this period besides the active practice of my profession I took up a special course on the eye, ear, nose, and throat, recognizing at that time the coming in the near future of specialists in almost every branch of Medicine and Surgery—also bearing in mind the absolute necessity of the naval medical officer's ability to care for the personnel of the Navy aboard ship for any disease or injury until facilities were available for hospital treatment. To prepare myself for this had been my first object in life, and was what I hoped each medical officer in the Navy would be qualified to perform. My three immediate predecessors as Surgeon General were Tryon, Bates, and Van Reypen. In regard to each, it is of interest to go into the history of their appointment to the highest office in our Corps. Dr. Tryon in his four years in the Bureau did much to place the Corps on a more efficient basis. He started a medical school in New York and his energy and progressive ideas were felt throughout the service. If he had been continued another term we would, I do not doubt, have had many reforms and better working conditions. Perhaps the school started by him would not have been discontinued. He was anxious to succeed himself and made every effort to do so even after the rest of us knew and he should have known it was not to be. President McKinley had a family physician and friend in Medical Director Bates and determined that he should be our next Surgeon General, and he was appointed. He died a short time afterwards. A few days after his death the Secretary of the Navy came into my home office one morning as he frequently did, being a patient, and informed me that the President had told him to appoint a Surgeon General, and he (the Secretary) wished me to advise him as to the best man. I replied at once, "Appoint Dr. Tryon" and gave my reasons. He said, "That is impossible; he is the one man Mr. McKinley has decided shall not have the office." I feel certain Dr. Tryon would have had the office for a second term if he had not tried to force Mr. McKinley to do something that he had made up his mind that he would not do. So politicians had no influence in this case except to annoy the Chief Executive. Mr. Long asked me who was the next best man for the position, and stated that he wanted a man of business capacity and one who would attend especially to the handling of the finances of the Bureau successfully. He referred to an unfortunate occurrence in the Bureau under the administration of Surgeon General Wales when he had signed duplicate vouchers without reading them, due to a dishonest clerk. I took down the Naval register and commenced at the top of the list of medical officers, describing each of them to him as I knew them, until I came down to Dr. Van Reypen. I explained to him that he would have no trouble so far as Dr. Van Reypen's business ability was concerned; that economy in Government expenditures was a virtue with him; but I did not think that the Medical

Corps would make much progress under him professionally. After further conversation he rose to go, and placing his hand on my shoulder said, "I had rather have you than anyone else." After expressing my appreciation of his confidence in me I said that would not be practicable as I was only a surgeon and I was better off where I was, and besides it would bring criticism upon him and the President for going over the heads of so many good men. Little did I see what was to come to me in the next few years—White House physician, the promise, without solitication, of Mr. McKinley to make me Surgeon General of the Navy when a vacancy should occur, his death, and the appointment of Surgeon General by Mr. Roosevelt, and the friendship of two such men, their families, and all that went with it. In the last analysis there is no relation dearer than true friendship, especially when combined with the relations of the family physician, who goes into the most intimate phases of his patient's life, physically, mentally, and spiritually.

I notified Dr. Van Reypen and advised that he see the Secretary at once. He was appointed and his four years of administration are part of the history of the Medical Department of the Navy.

I hope that my readers may excuse this digression from the subject of this autobiography, but my object in citing it is to have the future Surgeons General beware of opposing the "powers-that-be" too far. Opposition will make powerful enemies—a cheerful compliance will make friends.

Now, referring to my administration of the Bureau I take up—

Problem 1. Personnel.

Having placed on active duty every man on the retired list who was physically fit for duty, and getting the Secretary and President to allow me to take in 25 acting Assistant Surgeons allowed by law for an emergency, which I proved to them existed, I next got the Secretary of the Navy to approve a bill to Congress for 150 Assistant

Surgeons, 25 each year for six years. I knew that 25 selected medical men each year would, in all probability, be all that we could get, and the school which I proposed to start could accommodate. In the House of Representatives I felt sure that this bill would be passed, but in the Senate, although Mr. Eugene Hale was a friend and often a patient, I knew he was opposed to any increase in Personnel. The members of the Senate Naval Committee, most of them friends of mine, I interviewed, except Mr. Hale, and they agreed that we needed the increase, but all stated they could do nothing unless Mr. Hale thought favorably of the bill, as he ran the affairs of the Navy so far as the Naval Committee was concerned, he having a better knowledge of Naval affairs. About this time I was invited to a banquet given by General Draper at the corner of K Street and Connecticut Avenue. While taking off my wraps in the cloak room, Mr. Hale came in, and as soon as he saw me said, "Dr. Rixey, do you know what you are trying to do, double your Corps?" I replied, "Yes, Mr. Senator, and I am asking you to help me. I can show you exactly why the need exists." "No, sir," he said, and turned away. After the beautiful dinner and in the smoking room I quietly asked the Senator if I could see him the following morning before he went to the Capitol. He gruffly said, "Yes, come to my house at nine o'clock." I worked that night after reaching home arranging papers, showing where every man was on duty and where vacancies existed, and pointed out that if we had the whole 150 assistant surgeons asked for we could put everyone on duty immediately. In addition to this, I made a concise statement of the saving to the Government in many ways if the enlistments and other duties then performed by civilian physicians were performed by trained medical men of the Navy. I was promptly at his beautiful residence at 9:00 a. m. The Senator entered and asked what I had to say about the bill. I explained the papers I had brought with me and he considered for a few minutes and said, "Give me those papers. Good morning, sir!" The bill passed and became a law.

It is to be remembered that this bill, although doubling the Corps, made no provision for increase in numbers or promotion for those who were in the service. I knew that such a provision at that time would kill the bill, but it made it hard to get men to come into a service where promotion was so slow.

PROBLEM II. The Naval Medical School.

The Naval Hospital at that time was near the Navy Yard, and was entirely inadequate—really a disgrace to the service, and I contemplated building a new one on the grounds of the old Naval Observatory at the foot of 24th Street, N. W., a beautiful site, and having on it the old observatory building, well built and substantial. This I proposed to make into a naval medical school with a bacteriological and chemical laboratory, operating rooms for operating upon the cadaver, classrooms, library, etc. To do this it was necessary to build an extra story on the east and west wings of the old building and remodel the whole building.

The observatory building after it had been turned over to the Medical Department was being utilized as a museum to show defective plumbing, etc. Mr. Long, then Secretary of the Navy, always a true friend of the Medical Corps, informed me about this time that if we wished to hold the old observatory and this beautiful site for the Navy we must make a better use of them as the greatest pressure was being brought to bear on the Department to have them transferred to the George Washington University. The same pressure had been brought to bear on me to have me approve this plan. I at once placed before Mr. Long my plan for the school and new hospital; this he approved and entered most heartily into the plan. To him and Mr. Roosevelt is due the fact that my plans were carried out and we have this site occupied by our school and hospital today. It is to be regretted that my immediate predecessor as Surgeon General had consented to part with a portion of the ground which is now occupied by the Public Health Service. My inability to regain this ground made it necessary to make plans for the new hospital as they exist today.

The next point in the solution of this problem was the selection of the medical men in the service for professors; one of the most important of which was to select a surgeon as head of the bacteriological, chemical, and tropical disease departments. Looking over the records of every officer in the service, I decided upon Dr. Edward R. Stitt, now Surgeon General of the Navy, although I did not know him personally. He was promptly ordered to report to me and I outlined my plan, explaining to him the necessity of economy in the start but not at the expense of efficiency. The outlining of the course under him and the selecting of the equipment for the laboratories were left to him, subject to my approval. The selection of Dr. Stitt for this work was most fortunate as few mistakes were made, and from the beginning his energy and his equipment for the work he entered upon relieved me of an immense amount of embarrassment. I had orders issued to Dr. Stitt to visit the Hoagland laboratory and such points as this duty required. While he was thus engaged, I had the extra story put on the wings of the old observatory building. Within a year the first class was assembled and the school started. It would be difficult to estimate the value of this school towards bringing the personnel of the Corps up to modern requirements. The work done by the faculty was most gratifying and the influence of the school was felt through the whole Corps, and the Assistant Surgeon, after graduating from the school, knew what would be expected of him in his future life of sea or shore duty. This school has had an uninterrupted prosperous course until it is capable today, under the leadership of Admiral Stitt, as Surgeon General, of solving any problem relating to the health of the Navy and secures its personnel the best that modern medical methods can give for the prevention and cure of disease. Specialists have been developed as competent as can be found in civil life. The study of tropical disease and bacteriology is up to date and carried on by those who have had the benefit of Dr. Stitt's teaching and example.

At my request, Surgeon General Stitt recently sent me the following letter:

Department of The Navy
Bureau of Medicine & Surgery
Washington, D. C.

27 December 1923.

My dear Admiral Rixey:

In connection with our recent conversation relative to the establishing of the Naval Medical School, I shall endeavor in this letter to make notes of some of the incidents attending the development of this most important adjunct to the efficiency of the Medical Corps of the Navy. Of course, in writing this letter I can only bring to your attention those matters connected with the laboratory activities of the school, and the professional subjects assigned to me in the School work.

Following my nomination to this duty in July 1902, I told you of my desire to have an opportunity to get in touch with recent advances in bacteriology and pathology, as I had not worked along such lines since 1899. You kindly gave me the opportunity to work at the Hoagland Laboratory in Brooklyn, N. Y., and following this, to visit the leading chemical and bacteriological laboratories of several of our Eastern universities, and to observe their methods in teaching the practical application of bacteriology, pathology, and chemistry.

Upon my return to Washington following this period of study, it became necessary for me to arrange for the equipment of the laboratories of chemistry and bacteriology in order that the School might be in readiness for the young officers you had detailed for this post-graduate course.

I have been much impressed by the plan you adopted in adapting the buildings of the old Naval Observatory to the purposes of the Naval Medical School. In adding a second story to the passageways, connecting the different buildings of the Observatory, you provided laboratories, which from the standpoint of lighting and desk accessibility, left little to be desired. In fact, even at this day, I am always impressed with the appearance of these laboratories whenever I visit them. Anyone with an appreciation of the difficulties I had to encounter in conducting these laboratory courses, which took up one-half of each day, besides the time necessary for preparation of material and carrying on the routine clinical and laboratory work sent in by the Naval Dispensary, together with lectures every other day, would agree that I had more to do than could rightly be expected of anyone. Unfortunately, my rank at that time was that of Lieutenant, while the other members of the Faculty were taken from the senior grades of the Medical Corps, and with the accepted Naval practice of giving the young man plenty to do, I was required to conduct the course in connection with drills and setting-up exercises, as well as serving as recorder and member of the Examining Board. This experience has influenced me since becoming one of the senior members of our Corps, always to endeavor to see that I did my part of the work, and that the junior medical officer was not called upon to do more than might be his share of the duty.

As to your attitude towards the equipment of the laboratories and giving your support to any measure to advance the scope of the School, I heartily express my appreciation. So far as I can remember, I do not know of any instance where you refused to allow the money necessary for the school work. Since becoming Surgeon General of the Navy, and realizing the pressure that must have been exerted to have you discontinue the School in order that the great shortage of medical officers which then existed might be relieved, I can more than ever appreciate what the School owes to you.

At the present time, it is difficult for the young man just entering to understand the need the School met at that time, but this can be best be emphasized by relating a conversation I had with the late Medical Director Harmon relative to the School. In speaking of the value of the School work, Dr. Harmon said that if it had accomplished nothing else, it had made it impossible for young men who had had some little experience in laboratory technique to assert their superiority over their less fortunate brothers. In those days the man who could make a differential count, or even a white count, was an exception, so that a course such as was conducted at the Naval Medical School, where the students obtained a training not only in blood work, but in bacteriology and volumetric chemical analysis, as well, tended to establish professional standards in our hospitals which were of great value to the Service.

Referring again to your utilization of the spaces in the old Naval Observatory, I was particularly impressed with your converting the old boiler room under the Library into an amphitheatre for surgery on the cadaver. As you will remember, this met with extreme opposition from the Commanding Officer of the School and some of his associates, but upon the completion of this large circular room, with its adjoining cold-storage rooms, as well as lavatories, incinerators, etc., it made an ideal adjunct to the school. In fact, I have heard a number of our leading surgical teachers remark on the exceptional features of this operating room.

Along with the development of the practical courses in the School, the Service has to thank you for providing the necessary equipment in our hospitals and on our ships to carry on the work begun in the School. It was indeed an advance in our equipment when you put a microscopic outfit on board every ship to which a medical officer was attached.

At the commencement of the second year of the school work, we were fortunate in having Doctor Charles Wardwell Stiles associated with us as professor of medical zoology. The enthusiasm and genius for teaching of this well-known zoologist served as a stimulus for those of us who were his colleagues in conducting the laboratory courses. In recent years, I have had many opportunities to observe laboratory courses, but I have never met one who was his equal in arousing the interest and industry of laboratory students.

Another very valuable course which was added about this time to the earlier departments of naval hygiene, military surgery, administrative duties and tropical medicine, in addition to the laboratory courses before mentioned, was that in psychiatry conducted at St. Elizabeth's Hospital. In this course we had a combination of lectures and the practical demonstration of mental cases, which at that time, 20 years ago, compared favorably with the modern methods of teaching. Psychiatry is recognized as a peculiarly difficult subject for a lecture course from the standpoint of holding the attention of the senior student or general practitioner. During many years I attended these lectures, and have yet to hear anyone of the officers in these several classes express other than the greatest enthusiasm for Dr. White's lectures. These two men in zoology and psychiatry added great strength to the school. I may here state that in recent years we have felt that psychiatry was of such importance for our medical officers that we have devoted one day each week to work in St. Elizabeth's Hospital. This day is divided between gross pathology, neurology, and psychiatry.

You may remember your conversation with Dr. Welch of Johns Hopkins University, at the time he delivered the address at the closing exercises of the Class of 1905. In this conversation he advised you to adopt similar methods of teaching tropical medicine as held in the London School of Tropical Medicine under Sir Patrick Manson. In answer to your query as to the type of man who should conduct such a course, he advised you to send someone who was familiar with bacteriology, medical zoology and pathology, to take the course under Dr. Manson, and subsequently engage in practical work in the Philippines. I was so fortunate as to have been selected by you for this undertaking, and about two years later, when I returned to the United States, I put into operation a course in tropical medicine, including lectures and laboratory work, based on the methods obtaining at the London School of Tropical Medicine. Our great obstacle in conducting this course was in the difficulty of getting cases of so-called tropical diseases in the hospital attached to the school.

At this point, I wish to emphasize the value to the School of the Naval Medical School Hospital which you constructed about this time. Without the wards of a hospital to demonstrate clinical cases and to obtain clinical material for study in the laboratory there is much that is lacking in a post-graduate medical school.

I have not referred to the courses given in the school other than those with which I was immediately connected, as it would seem better for any statement as to the initiation and development of such courses to come from those teaching such subjects. We were all much indebted to the first president of the school, Medical Director Marmion, for his hearty support and interest in our work. He was a representative of the type of highly cultured medical man marking the officers of his period. In addition to being president of the school, he was also president of the Medical Examining Board, and gave the lectures in naval hygiene.

Another course which brought about the preparation of the Manual of the Medical Department was that conducted by Medical Director J. C. Boyd on the duties of medical officers. The lectures this officer prepared in giving this course were amplified and concisely systematized by him to make a most valuable book of instructions for the Naval Medical Officer. This original edition has been followed by subsequent editions but the plan of the book, and the method of presentation of the material, have been adhered to.

Another book, originating from the School, was that of "Naval Hygiene" by Captain J. D. Gatewood. This treatise on the various problems of Naval Hygiene served as a textbook at the school, and book of reference on our ships for many years, and still holds its place, although published in 1909. This book represented the best thought of a scholarly man with exceptional mathematical ability.

In concluding this letter I feel that I can unqualifiedly state that you have done the Naval Medical Corps a greater service by the establishment and support of the Naval Medical School

> than by any of the other measures instituted by you for the improvement of the Medical Department of the Navy. I make this statement with full recognition of your achievements in hospital construction and rehabilitation, because without adequate opportunities for post-graduate instruction for the medical officers of the Navy, hospital facilities cannot be fully utilized.

In connection with the school I wish to add a few words as to how I succeeded in getting an appropriation for the new hospital on the Observatory Ground which, with the school and its laboratories, would make a complete establishment for the care of the health of the station.

Early in my first tour of duty in the Bureau in my hearings before the Naval Committee of the House of Representatives, I condemned the old Naval Hospital and asked for an appropriation to build a new one. Finally I asked the Chairman of the Committee to appoint a committee to visit the old hospital as I knew they would condemn it as they would be ashamed of it, as I was. A committee was appointed and I took them to the hospital at the appointed time. Their report was what I expected and thus we got the appropriation for the new hospital. My brother, John F. Rixey, was at this time on the Naval Committee and did much to assist me.

Problem III. Remodel old hospitals and build new ones where required.

I have just shown how I solved this problem as regard to legislation, giving us the new Naval Hospital at Washington, D. C. My first inspection of naval hospitals after assuming the duties of Surgeon General took in the near by hospitals—New York, Philadelphia, Boston, Newport, and Norfolk. All were out of date and most unsatisfactory in the view of modern requirements. The New York hospital was probably in the best condition, Philadelphia next; the Boston hospital a dungeon, dark and dismal; Newport a frame building and a fire trap; Norfolk a fine old building badly arranged and inadequate for this station and filled with vermin. The morning after my return from this inspection I was in my office feeling immensely discouraged. If these hospitals visited were so bad what must be the condition of those further away. Fortunately for me one of the men I most wanted to see came in—Mr. Flagg, an architect of distinction, who, as architect, had charge of building the Naval Academy and also the new Washington hospital. I explained to him the conditions that I had found in the different hospitals and told him that I wished I could send him over the route that I had been and have his views as to what was best to be done, but the Bureau had no funds for this service. What I needed was an expert's opinion to back up my own views and the approximate cost of reconstruction, etc., where required. To my surprise he offered to go over the route and make me a full report without cost to the Government, provided he would have an opportunity of bidding on the work decided upon by Congress. I accepted his offer with one proviso; that the Bureau of Medicine and Surgery would not be considered under any obligation to advise the acceptance of his bid. His report was most satisfactory and served me well in my hearings before Congress and in my annual report. Although I was neither an architect, nor a builder, I could bring out in this way the work that was absolutely necessary and its probable cost. In the preceding pages my biographers have shown what was done and I have cited the above as some of the trials and tribulations at the beginning of my administration. Each year as results began to take form I gained more confidence as to ultimate results. As hospital construction and reconstruction went on I worked out the problem of sick officers' quarters, quarters for women nurses, quarters for the hospital corps and officers on duty at the hospitals. At the beginning there were no homes, as the Army had, for officers on duty other than for the senior medical officers in command. Special sick officers' quarters and those for women nurses and the hospital corps were built as fast as I could get the necessary money appropriated.

PROBLEM IV. Modern conditions for the care of the sick and wounded aboard ship until shore hospitals or a hospital ship was available.

The Secretary of the Navy, Mr. Long, when I was speaking of the antiquated conditions on our battleships and cruisers for the care of our sick and wounded cautioned me as to expenditure of Government money. I needed an object lesson for Mr. Long, and about this time I heard of the Russian ship *Retzvegan* being built at Cramp's Yard and I knew that the new *Maine* was being built at the same yard. Practical inquiries developed that the *Retzvegan* was modern in every respect, especially as to the requirements for the care of the sick and wounded; whereas the *Maine* had its sick quarters in the eye of the ship, practically what they were on our ships when I entered the Navy in 1874. At my first opportunity I went to Cramp's Yard and close together lay the two ships, and I noticed such a contrast! The Russian ship was so far ahead of the *Maine* that I was ashamed. My first step was to secure plans of both ships which I took to Mr. Long, expressing my chagrin at what I had found. He looked them over carefully and then said, "What can I do about it?" I replied, "If you will issue an order to the Bureau of Construction as follows:

> "In the future the Chief Constructor will see that such space as may be allowed for the sick on our ships will be referred to the Bureau of Medicine and Surgery for approval, and when decided upon will be fitted up as directed by that Bureau."

He gave the order and the conditions that existed during my administration of the Bureau were most satisfactory. In most instances the space allotted has been ample and in some cases more than needed. The cooperation between the Bureau of Medicine and Surgery and the Bureau of Construction and Repair was perfect.

PROBLEM V. Improve sanitary conditions of Navy yards and all naval stations. Improved and better equipped dispensaries.

This problem was solved as fast as the money therefor was obtainable.

PROBLEM VI. A well trained nurse and hospital corps must be provided. This problem was solved as fast as the hospital and nurse corps were authorized.

PROBLEM VII. The establishing of a dental corps was desirable but was delayed by the dentists in civil life who asked too much as to rank and emoluments in the beginning. I could not approve their bill before Congress without modification.

PROBLEM VIII. Specialists in every branch of medicine and surgery had reached the stage where the Navy must have them also, and the wishes of the officers in this direction was encouraged. The result has been the development of specialists in the service second to none as shown by many of them resigning from the Navy and entering successfully into private practice.

PROBLEM IX. Recognition by the line of the medical officer's standing in the Navy had been taken up by some of our most prominent colleges, notably Harvard University where President Elliott was directing attention to the loss of prestige if his men should enter the Navy as medical officers, and he advised them not to go into the Navy. We were anxious to have our share of the Harvard graduates to fill the vacancies in the Medical Corps. My attention was called to this in 1903 by a letter from the senior medical officer at the Norfolk Hospital writing me that an official communication signed by him as in command of the hospital had been returned to him by the Commanding Officer of the Receiving Ship *Franklin* directing him, the Commanding Officer of the Hospital, to eliminate the word "command" and to sign himself as "in charge." Personally I had never thought of having our Corps deprived of the use of any words in the English language which signified control, and the word "command" was the most useful one in a Naval sense, and so understood by the enlisted personnel better than any other word.

I was absent from the Bureau with the President when the Bureau of Navigation took the matter up to Secretary Moody and had him sign an approval of the Receiving Ship's action. In plain words we could not use the word "command" officially. I was satisfied that Mr. Moody had signed his approval of this matter without understanding its far reaching effect upon the personnel of my Corps. President Roosevelt frequently consulted me in regard to appointments and on July 11, 1903, I wrote to him as follows:

NAVY DEPARTMENT
BUREAU OF MEDICINE & SURGERY
WASHINGTON, D. C.

My dear Mr. President:

I have carefully gone over the enclosed papers of Dr. William A. White, and judging from them alone I should say that he was well qualified for the position of Superintendent of St. Elizabeth's. I do not know him personally, and as I suppose you want the best man obtainable for the Superintendency of the poor unfortunates at St. Elizabeth's I would advise that the papers of all the applicants be referred to the Medical Board of Visitors for an expression of opinion as to the best qualified man for the position. The medical members of the Board are: Medical Director F. M. Gunnell, U. S. N., Retired (Formerly Surgeon General, U. S. Navy,) Walter Wyman, M. D., Surgeon General of the Public Health, and Marine Hospital Service; and G. L. Magruder, M. D.

The weather in Washington has been quite warm the last few weeks, but we find the nights comfortable at the farm. I sincerely hope that you are getting some rest and that Mrs. Roosevelt and the children continue well.

With kindest remembrances to all,

Sincerely yours,

(Signed) P. M. RIXEY.

and in letter of July 16, 1903, as follows:

Dear Mr. President:

Your letter notifying me that you thought you would appoint Dr. White Superintendent of St. Elizabeth's, with the excellent reasons mentioned, was received by me yesterday. I do not know of a better man for the place but, as I wrote you before, I am not personally acquainted with him, and therefore, only gather my information of him from his writings and what has been written about him.

I hope sincerely you are enjoying your summer at Oyster Bay, and that you are all keeping well. I miss you and every member of your family more than I can tell you—you especially, as everything seems to go smoothly when you are in Washington.

Just now I am being annoyed, in addition to lots of work preparing for the care of the sick of the Navy, by a matter of form, of which I spoke to you on the western trip. You remember my mentioning to you that I had been taken up by some of the line officers on my using the word "command" in regard to the Hospitals under our control. The Secretary has turned me down, and says we cannot use the word "command." I have gotten him to take up the question again and have written a strong protest against the Naval Surgeon being the only military surgeon in the world denied the use of a word which means more than any other where control of men is concerned. You will pardon my mentioning this to you, but I feel every humiliation put upon the hundreds of young officers—professional men of high standing, many of whom I have urged to enter the service. When considering this question I feel much like resigning my position of Surgeon General.

With best wishes and kindest regards to all your family, believe me, always,

Yours very respectfully,

(Signed) P. M. RIXEY.

The President,
Oyster Bay, L. I.

At the first opportunity I spoke to President Roosevelt and explained the importance of a proper recognition of my Corps by the line officers and informed him that Congress had given us the additional number of officers required, and this matter, if allowed to stand, would turn away many good young men from the Navy who were considering their future. Then, I told him of President Elliott's action and how few men we were getting from Harvard, his and Mr. Moody's alma mater. The President replied at once, "The Secretary did not understand this matter as you have explained it to me, and he will reopen the question." At the first opportunity I took this matter up with Mr. Moody and he reversed his decision and on June 25, 1904, ordered the following:

Memorandum for the Bureau of Navigation:

The Bureau of Navigation will make such changes in the Navy Regulations and submit them to the Secretary of the Navy for approval, as shall permit the use of the words "in command" for all departments of Naval Stations under the Commandant of the Station, and the Bureau will cause the regulations to be changed to accomplish this end.

(Signed) W. H. Moody,
Secretary of the Navy.

Up to August 16th, almost two months after the above memorandum of Mr. Moody had been given, the Bureau of Navigation had not carried it out. In the meantime, Mr. Moody had resigned as Secretary of the Navy and Mr. Morton had succeeded him. Making my morning visit to the White House on August 16th, the President asked me if the question of "command" had been satisfactorily arranged. I informed him that Navigation had apparently done nothing to put the Secretary's order into effect. By the time I reached my office, the copy of the following memorandum which had been sent Mr. Morton was handed to me by a messenger:

August 16, 1904.

Memorandum for the Secretary of the Navy:

The Secretary of the Navy will publish the order of Secretary Moody, dated June 25, 1904 (a copy of which is appended), so far as it relates to the Medical Corps of the Navy.

(Signed) Theodore Roosevelt.

The Secretary of the Navy was absent on an inspection trip when this order of the President reached the Navy Department. I thought surely the matter was closed now and a general order would be issued at once, so paid no further attention to the matter until August 22nd. Visiting the President's office to say good-bye on the eve of his departure for Oyster Bay for the summer, Mr. Roosevelt asked if his order of August 16th had been carried out. I told him that I had not heard of it but I thought of course his orders had been carried out. The following letter addressed to the President on August 22nd explains the situation:

NAVY DEPARTMENT
BUREAU OF MEDICINE & SURGERY
WASHINGTON, D. C.

August 22, 1904.

Dear Mr. President:

On the occasion of my visit to the White House to say good-bye to you this morning, you asked if the memorandum which you had sent to the Secretary on August 16th had been carried out. I had no idea at that time that there could be any misunderstanding of your intention in regard to it. Imagine my surprise and chagrin when upon inquiring of the Judge Advocate General if the order had been promulgated and being referred to the Bureau of Navigation, I was informed by Admiral Converse that it would not be acted on until Mr. Morton's return. That means it was just in the state it was before you signed the memorandum to the Secretary. I told Admiral Converse that in referring the matter to you I was trying to save Mr. Morton a long siege of petty annoyance over a matter in which he was not experienced and in which you were, having had personal experience in the Navy Department. He therefore, although, my junior, started to take me to task for going over the Secretary's head. I quickly stopped him and informed him that I had the permission of the Acting Secretary, Mr. Darling, to do as you had directed before I had gone to you, and the reason that I had gone to you was that the difficulty seemed to be with the Bureau of Navigation.

Mr. President, in as concise terms as possible, the whole matter is this: The regulations say we shall not exercise military command except in our own Corps. Inferentially that means that we can exercise it in our own Corps. That is all that this order contemplates. Nevertheless, medical officers have, on more than one occasion, been in active military command over others in emergencies.

Mr. Moody's order during your western trip deprived us of the use of the words "in command." He reopened the case for us at my earnest request to be heard in regard to it. Before he went out of the Department he gave the memorandum, marked No. 1, a copy of which is herewith enclosed, to the Bureau of Navigation.

After nearly two months, and not having heard from it, and satisfying myself that the Bureau of Navigation intended to have Secretary Morton go over the whole matter again, with all the annoyance to himself and the Bureau of Medicine & Surgery which we have already gone through, I was impelled to go to you. Your decision was immediate. Your memorandum to the Secretary of the Navy, marked No. 2, a copy of which I enclose, says: "The Secretary of the Navy will publish the order of Secretary Moody, dated June 25, 1904, (a copy of which is appended), so far as it relates to the Medical Corps of the Navy."

This memorandum, according to Admiral Converse, is interpreted that it shall await Secretary Morton's return. If that is so, it is exactly in the state as when I took the matter to you.

If you can sign the enclosed memorandum, marked No. 3, and send to the Acting Secretary of the Navy, there will be no further difficulty in the matter.

I sincerely regret to annoy you again about this matter and I know that you understand my position and will sympathize with me in having to annoy the President of the United States by referring a matter of this character to him.

I was sorry to see that you did not make as quick a trip home as usual, but am very glad to hear of your safe arrival with your family.

With warmest regards for all of them, and with deep appreciation of all your goodness to me, I am,

Very respectfully,

(Signed) P. M. RIXEY.

On the same day I wrote to Mr. Loeb, the President's Secretary:

August 22, 1904.

My dear Loeb:

I am writing the President by this mail, which with enclosures explain what I wish. I do not see how the Department could hold up an order of the President's as plain as that memorandum of August 16th signed by the President. It says explicitly: "The Secretary of the Navy will publish the order of Secretary Moody, dated June 25, 1904, so far as it relates to the Medical Corps of the Navy." Of course, it might be published a hundred years from now, but in my opinion, the President's order meant that it should be published at once, and it seems to me that it should have been acted on within twenty-four hours.

If the President will sign the memorandum marked No. 3, which I enclose, I think it will be satisfactory, and the matter, I hope, will be closed.

I was sorry to see that you had some delay in reaching Oyster Bay, and I was a little alarmed from the newspaper reports of someone trying to reach the President.

I am sure you will understand my wishes in this matter and my anxiety not to have a long delay over a matter which I had considered closed. By helping me in this, you will greatly oblige,

Yours very sincerely,

(Signed) P. M. RIXEY.

To William Loeb, Jr.
Secretary to the President.

I also wrote the Secretary of the Navy, Mr. Morton, as follows:

NAVY DEPARTMENT
BUREAU OF MEDICINE & SURGERY
WASHINGTON, D. C.

August 22, 1904.

Dear Mr. Secretary:

I did not think that I should have to bother you during your tour of inspection, but a matter has come up which has given me considerable worry and which I had considered as settled by your predecessor, Mr. Moody. While with the President on his western trip, the question was brought up by a line officer of how medical officers in control of hospitals should be addressed. Mr. Moody decided that they should not be addressed as "in command." When Mr. Moody joined the President later, I called to his attention certain points in connection with this order which did injustice to my Corps, and asked if he would reopen the question on returning to Washington. This he kindly consented to do, and after being posted as to our contentions he decided by memorandum (copy of which I enclose you herewith, marked No. 1.) that the Regulations should be changed so as to permit the use of the words "in command." This was manifestly just, as the Regulations state already that officers of the staff corps shall not exercise military command except in their own Corps. Inferentially this would mean that they could in their own corps exercise military command. That is all we have claimed. Admiral Taylor went into this matter with the Secretary and asked only that other staff corps should have the same privilege, and as you see by the memorandum they are included in it. After nearly two months, and the order not having been promulgated, I asked the Acting Secretary of the Navy if I could use certain blanks which we had ready to send out for the use of hospitals, to be signed as "in command;" he said, "Certainly." When about to do this, I found that the question had been brought to you for further discussion, and as it has been under discussion for a year or more you very properly put it aside for the time being. When I found out the condition of affairs naturally I was extremely annoyed at being checkmated by Navigation. It meant that this matter would be held up until matters of greater importance had been gone into by you, and with your inexperience in naval affairs, would have taken a long while to decide. I therefore saw the President and explained the case to him. He at once said that he would arrange it and issued the order marked No. 2, copy of which I enclose.

My object in going to the President was two-fold. First, to save you and the Bureau of Medicine & Surgery from a long siege of petty annoyances concerning the matter which should have been closed, and I hope that the President's action will close this matter so that you will not be annoyed by it in the future. I write this to you as I wish you to know exactly what I am doing in this case.

I hope you are having a pleasant trip and have had a little time to devote to the hospitals en route.

Yours very sincerely,

(Signed) P. M. RIXEY.

I wished Mr. Morton to hear of what had been done up to the present time from me before Navigation made its statement as to this case. Under date of August 24th Mr. Loeb wrote to me as follows:

WHITE HOUSE
WASHINGTON

(Written at Oyster Bay, N. Y.)

My dear Dr. Rixey:

I am directed by the President to send you for your information the enclosed telegram. Please return it to me for our files after you have read it.

Sincerely yours,

(Signed) W. M. LOEB, JR.
Secretary to the President.

enclosing copy of memorandum for the Navy Department signed by the President.

WHITE HOUSE
WASHINGTON

Memorandum for the Navy Department:

Referring to my memorandum of August 16, 1904, it is so far modified that you will cause to be changed immediately the regulations of the Navy so as to permit the use of the words "in command" by the Medical officers of the Navy and have it clear that they have military command in their own corps.

(Signed) THEODORE ROOSEVELT.

This not having been acted upon and being informed by Admiral Converse, Chief of the Bureau of Navigation that he did not propose to comply with the President's order until Mr. Morton's return, I notified the President and on the following day received from Mr. Loeb the following letter:

Oyster Bay, N. Y.,
August 23, 1904.

My dear Dr. Rixey:

Referring to your communication of the 22nd instant, the enclosed copy of telegram explains itself. Of course, keep it confidential.

All are well here.

Sincerely yours,
(Signed) W. M. LOEB, JR.,
Secretary of the President.

and the enclosed official order of the President to the Acting Secretary of the Navy explains itself:

OFFICIAL TELEGRAM

Oyster Bay, N. Y.,
August 23, 1904.

To: The Acting Secretary of the Navy.
Washington, D. C.

Promulgate today the order relating to the medical corps of the Navy in exact compliance with my memorandum of August sixteenth. Explain in full why it was not promulgated immediately upon my sending it to the Navy Department.

THEODORE ROOSEVELT.

As does the reply of the Acting Secretary of the Navy to the President's last order:

OFFICIAL TELEGRAM

Navy Department, Washington, D. C.
August 23, 1904.

The President,
Oyster Bay, N. Y.

Replying your telegram today understood I was carrying out your orders in full. Showed your order 16th to Navigation on receipt. Confirmed same directions in writing to Navigation 19th as follows: "The President directs that the Secretary of the Navy will publish the order of Secretary Moody, dated June 25, 1904, so far as it relates to the Medical Corps of the Navy," and the Bureau, therefore "will make such changes in the Navy Regulations and submit them to the Secretary of the Navy for his approval in pursuance of this order." Understand Navigation since engaged in preparing amendments to regulations, but in view of your telegram today have ordered as follows: "Medical officers in charge of naval hospitals or other medical department of a medical station, under the Commandant of the station, are hereby authorized to use the term "in command of" instead of "in charge of" to designate their respective official positions."

Charles Darling,
Acting Secretary.

This matter of staff officers' command in their own Corps, so small in itself, should have been settled by the Bureaus concerned and not compelled me to bother the head of the Navy Department and the President in regard to it. The whole trouble was with the Bureau of Navigation which considered itself the Navy without considering those important bureaus which made the Navy as a whole the best first line of defense in the world.

The above episode I hoped would for all time settle the standing of the staff corps with the line. This, however, was not to be and I now have to bring up another unfortunate contention between my bureau and Navigation. I refer to the command of hospital ships. Admiral Brownson, a personal friend of mine for many years, had been made Chief of the Bureau of Navigation. I had great admiration for Admiral Brownson and hoped and believed that our Bureaus would work smoothly for the best interest of the Navy. While he was Superintendent of the Naval Academy we had worked together to select a site and build a new hospital for the Academy, and his helpfulness as Commandant of the Naval Academy was all that I could ask. I publish here a letter from the Admiral dated October 20, 1903:

U. S. NAVAL ACADEMY
ANNAPOLIS, MARYLAND

Dear Rixey:

The question of the location of the new hospital will soon have to be decided on definitely, and preferably before the specifications are entirely printed.

While, as I told you before, I am anxious that you should decide this matter yourself, don't you think it would be well if someone is called in to help us both in the matter? I myself, personally, certainly should not decide the question. In the end, it is like the question of the new experimental engineering building; I asked that a Board might be ordered to determine the location of it, as it is too important a matter for me to decide myself, I might make an error which could never be corrected.

I am still strongly of the opinion that the site that you thought very favorably of, where the old Marine camp stood, would be preferable to overlooking the Marine Barracks on top of the hill. However, it may be that an investigation would show that you were entirely right in the location that you decided on after a casual inspection of the place. Think the matter over; or better still, come down and bring Mrs. Rixey with you, and look over the ground again.

Very sincerely yours,
(Signed) WILLIAM H. BROWNSON.

I replied to this letter on October 21, 1903.

NAVY DEPARTMENT
BUREAU OF MEDICINE & SURGERY
WASHINGTON, D. C.

Dear Captain Brownson:

Yours of October 20th just to hand. I have gone over the grounds for the new hospital on three separate occasions and I am satisfied that the site selected is the one that should be occupied by the Hospital. It is the most elevated, has the best shade, and in every way, in my opinion, is the site for the hospital. I shall not make any change so far as I am concerned, and I hope that Mr. Flagg has not been kept back with any idea that there would be a change. I have impressed upon him from the start that I would not change my selection of the site. You informed me that you would not oppose any site that I selected, and I hope you will allow the work to go on as it has been agreed upon and hurry Mr. Flagg up all you can. You know how I view the situation in regard to the care of the sick of the Academy. The accommodations are not in any way satisfactory to the Bureau, and under no conditions will I keep back or prevent the earliest possible consummation of a suitable hospital. This hospital was recommended by my predecessor and I have been in the Bureau almost two years, working hard all the time to get a hospital started, and even now it looks as if it would be the end of my four years before I could see the hospital completed.

Anyone looking over the records of this office will see that it is certainly not my fault.

Mrs. Rixey would enjoy very much a visit to you and Mrs. Brownson, and we remember our visit with the greatest of pleasure. We should love to have you both make us a visit as soon as we are settled for the winter. I want to drive you both into the country and show you how much Washington is improving.

Remember me very kindly to Commander Badger and any friends, and believe me,

Yours very sincerely,

(Signed) P. M. Rixey.

Captain W. H. Brownson, U. S. N.,
Superintendent, U. S. Naval Academy,
Annapolis, Md.

which shows that before he came to be Chief of the Bureau of Navigation we worked together successfully for the best interest of the Navy.

In my letter addressed to the Navy Department under date of November 6, 1907, appears this paragraph, marked No. 2:

"After mature deliberation and having in mind the best interests of the service, this Bureau concurs in the Department's letter of December 12, 1906, that such a ship when placed in commission should be treated as a floating hospital and, as such, placed under the command of a medical officer, her navigation being controlled by a competent sailing master, and so recommends, etc."

Much to my regret Admiral Brownson was opposed to a medical officer having command of a floating hospital. This whole question as it worked out and was settled has been fully described by my biographer. I merely mention it here to show that I was compelled to oppose the contentions of the Bureau of Navigation on account of my duty to care for the patients of this floating hospital in war as well as in peace. On January 30, 1908, when I requested Navigation to order a Paymaster to the Hospital Ship *Relief*, the Chief of the Bureau of Navigation informed me that "to order a Paymaster to the Hospital Ship *Relief* would be illegal"—and I immediately took to the Secretary the following memorandum:

January 30, 1908.

Memorandum for the Secretary of the Navy:

I beg permission to call your attention to the statement of the Bureau of Navigation that "to order a Paymaster to the Hospital Ship *Relief* would be illegal."

The hospital ship being a floating hospital with a Medical officer in command is just as much a part of the Medical Department as is a shore hospital, to which pay officers have been ordered for years and at two of which they are serving at present. It is therefore submitted that a pay officer ordered to this ship becomes a part of the Medical Department for the time being from the time he reports to the Medical Officer in command of said ship. Such evidently was the intention of Ex-Secretary Bonaparte in his special order regarding hospital ships when he states "A hospital ship should be provided with a chaplain," who is a commissioned officer in the same status as a pay officer.

This hospital ship when in commission in the Army had a Quartermaster always on board, and this Bureau hopes that the Department will see that this ship has the same facilities for a successful administration under medical officers of the Navy as it had under medical officers of the Army.

(Signed) P. M. RIXEY,
Surgeon General, U. S. Navy.

The hospital ship had its Paymaster and the pátients received their pay just the same as any other ship of our Navy.

This matter of command would seem small if it were not that the proper recognition of medical officers as officers the equal of any, whether line or staff, in their respective duties had been assailed by the line, and they wished to deny the medical officer of the Navy that which had long been enjoyed by the medical officers of our Army. No wonder our professional brethren in civil life advised the young medical men not to enter the Navy. My principal object was to place the Corps on the same footing as that of the Army in order that I could compete with them in getting the best equipped young men for the Navy.

President Roosevelt's interest in all that concerned my efforts to bring the medical department of the U. S. Navy up to the highest point of efficiency was manifested by questions, and I talked freely with him and drew a parallel between the Army and Navy Medical Corps, and called the President's attention to the Revised Regulations for the Government of the Navy which were promulgated by Secretary Morton June 30, 1905, just before he was relieved by Mr. Bonaparte, and they were never passed upon by me and were very unsatisfactory so far as my Corps was concerned. The result was a call for the Surgeon General of the Army and myself, to meet the President at the Executive Office January 15, 1906. The following memorandum of this meeting between the Chief Executive and the Surgeons General of the Army and Navy was given the Secretary of the Navy and I was furnished a copy.

Memorandum for the Secretary of the Navy:

Subject: Conversation between Surgeons General of the Army and Navy with the President.

The President of the United States sent for the Surgeons General of the Army and Navy and discussed with them the efficiency of the Medical Corps of the Army and Navy to meet present conditions and emergencies, and asked for a comparison with the Japanese medical corps during the late war.

During the conversation, the question was asked the Surgeon General of the Army what the conditions were in the Army. His answer was that they were satisfactory as to facilities for teaching, control of the hospital corps, etc., and deficient as to the number of medical officers, having only about 40% of those necessary for the present army in case they were called into the field. A bill now before Congress it was hoped would soon become a law and remedy this deficiency.

The Surgeon General of the Navy being asked the same question, stated that conditions in the Medical Corps of the Navy were the reverse of those in the Army, in plain terms they were unsatisfactory as to a clear definition of the duties of the medical department and of the officers on shore stations as to epidemic disease; also as to the technical schools for the education of the officers of the medical and hospital corps; also as to transfers to and from the hospital corps, promotions, and details for duty, which should be made on the recommendation of the Bureau of Medicine and Surgery; as to records of enlistment in the hospital corps, and other papers relating to the technical education of members of the Corps.

He stated that there are no provisions in the Navy Regulations which give a clear statement of the general duty of the Medical Department and insure uniformity of practice necessary to efficiency in these matters. Asked what suggestions he would make, he stated that he would submit to the Secretary of the Navy on his return from Charleston a memorandum of a proposed General Order to be issued now and embodied in the Navy Regulations hereafter, as follows:

> 1. The medical department is charged with the duty of supervising the sanitary condition of the Navy and making recommendations in reference thereto; of advising with reference to the sanitary features of ships under construction and in commission, regarding berthing, ventilation, location of quarters for the care and treatment of the sick and injured; of the provisions for the care of wounded in battle; and in the case of short stations, in advising in regard to health conditions depending on location, the hygienic construction and care of public buildings, especially of barracks and other permanent habitations, such as camps, etc. It shall have supervisory control of water supplies used for drinking, cooking, and bathing purposes, and drainage and the disposal of waste. It shall provide for the care of the sick and wounded, the physical examination of officers and enlisted men, the management and control of naval hospitals, the recruiting,

instruction, and control of the hospital corps, and the furnishing of all medical and hospital supplies. It shall advise in matters pertaining to clothing, food, etc.

2. The senior medical officer of shore stations, under the direction of the commanding officer, will supervise the hygiene of the station and recommend such measures as he may deem necessary to prevent or diminish disease. He will examine monthly and note in the medical journal the sanitary condition of all public buildings, the drainage, the sewerage, the amount and quality of the water supply, the clothing and habits of the men, the character and cooking of food, and report in writing the conditions to the Commandant of the station, together with such recommendations as he may deem proper.

The Commanding Officer will endorse his views and action thereon, and if he deem the action recommended undesirable, will state fully his objections. He shall then return the report with endorsements to the Surgeon for his information and immediate action, if necessary. The Surgeon will enter the endorsements in the medical journal and forward the report to the Chief of the Bureau of Medicine and Surgery, through official channels, for the information of the Bureau.

A special sanitary report shall be made at any time when an emergency arises, and at once be forwarded to the Bureau of Medicine and Surgery.

3. Technical schools for the education of medical officers and the hospital corps shall be under the supervision and control of the Bureau of Medicine and Surgery.

4. In the hospital corps all enlistments and promotions, transfers to, and discharges from, the service, except upon expiration of term of enlistment, or by sentence of court martial, and all details for duty, shall be made by the Bureau of Navigation on the recommendation of the Bureau of Medicine and Surgery.

5. Records of enlistments in the hospital corps, and all other papers relating thereto, will be referred by the Bureau of Navigation to the Bureau of Medicine and Surgery for information and recommendation; and on examination, report on a form issued by the Bureau of Medicine and Surgery will be forwarded in every case of enlistment or promotion.

The above leaves all orders to the Bureau of Navigation on the recommendation of the Bureau of Medicine and Surgery, and provides a uniformity of procedure in those matters, which is a necessity if the most efficient service is to be maintained.

In regard to the number of medical officers, the number allowed by law will be sufficient for a number of years, provided the vacancies can be filled, but in all probability to cause properly qualified medical men to enter the Navy and to retain them afterward it will be necessary that they be given additional inducements to those now provided—certainly to make it equal to those offered by the medical corps of the Army, viz:

(a) The Army Surgeon gets 15% more pay than the Naval surgeon on shore.

(b) The Army Surgeon can retire after 30 years service; the Naval Surgeon must serve 40 years or retire for age.

(c) The Naval Surgeon must serve at sea two or three years at a time and only while at sea receives the same compensation as the Army Surgeon who lives ashore.

(d) Promotion is slow, there being but one retirement for age in 1905, one in 1906, none in 1907, and one in 1908. To remedy this no increase in the total number of officers is asked for; but a reapportionment is needed to give officers of proper rank for new ships under construction and projected, to officer new stations beyond seas, to provide experienced men for important naval hospitals and shore stations. There are seven fleet divisions under flag command, requiring the inspector grade.

The senior officers in the grade of surgeon are between 50 and 60 years of age, approaching retirement, and have only the grade of lieutenant commander.

No change has been made in the number of directors and inspectors since 1871, when the grades were first established, although the personnel has increased from 16,000 to 44,000.

A reapportionment increasing the directors by five, the inspectors by ten, and surgeons by fifteen, with the increase already provided by law (25 assistant surgeons each year until 1910) will meet every present need. So far it has been found impossible under existing conditions, to fill the vacancies provided for by law—55 vacancies remaining to date.

This memorandum going to Secretary Bonaparte from the President was most opportune and a few days afterwards he sent me the proposed General Order for comment:

GENERAL ORDER

It is hereby ordered, in accordance with the provisions of Section 1547, United States Revised Statutes, that the following alterations be adopted in the Regulations for the Government of the Navy, promulgated on June 30, 1905, namely:

Article II, paragraphs (1) and (2) are amended so as to read as follows:

(1) The Bureau of Medicine and Surgery shall have control of all hospitals and of the force employed there; it shall have advisory power with respect to all questions connected with hygiene and sanitation affecting the service and to this end, opportunity for unobstructed inspection; it shall provide for all physical examinations; it shall pass upon the competency, from a professional standpoint, of all men in the Hospital Corps for enlistment and promotion by means of examinations conducted under its supervision; and it shall have information as to the assignment and duties of all enlisted men of the hospital corps, with opportunity to call the attention of the Department to any changes which may seem to be desirable.

(2) The duties of the Bureau of Medicine and Surgery shall comprise all that relates to medical supply depots, medical laboratories, naval hospitals, dispensaries and technical schools for the medical and hospital corps. It shall require for all supplies, medicines, and instruments used in the Medical Department of the Navy.

The following five Articles are adopted and promulgated to follow Article 1168 and form a part of Chapter XXIV, entitled "Medical Instructions," Section 3, entitled "General Instructions:"

1168 *a.* The medical department is charged with the duty of supervising the sanitary condition of the Navy and making recommendations in reference thereto; of advising with the Department and other Bureaus in reference to the sanitary features of ships under construction and in commission, regarding berthing, ventilation, location of quarters for the care and treatment of the sick and injured; of the provisions for the care of wounded in battle; and in the case of shore stations, in advising in regard to health conditions depending on location, the hygienic construction and care of public buildings, especially of barracks and other permanent habitations, such as camps. So far as practicable it shall have supervisory control of water supplies used for drinking, cooking, and bathing purposes, and drainage and the disposal of waste. It shall provide for the care of the sick and wounded, the physical examination of officers and enlisted men, the management and control of naval hospitals, the instruction of the hospital corps, and the furnishing of all medical and hospital supplies. It shall advise in matters pertaining to clothing and food, so far as these affect the health of the Navy.

1168 *b*. The senior medical officer of shore stations, under the direction of the commanding officer, will supervise the hygiene of the station and recommend such measures as he may deem necessary to prevent or diminish disease. He will examine monthly and note in the medical journal the sanitary condition of all public buildings, the drainage, the sewerage, the amount and quality of the water supply, the clothing and habits of the men, the character and cooking of food, and report in writing the conditions of the Commandant of the station, together with such recommendations as he may deem proper. The commanding officer will endorse his views and action thereon, and, if he deem the action recommended undesirable, will fully state his objections. He shall then return the report with endorsements to the Surgeon for his information and immediate action, if necessary. The Surgeon will enter the endorsements in the medical journal and forward the report to the Chief of the Bureau of Medicine and Surgery, through official channels, for the information of the Bureau. A special sanitary report shall be made at any time when an emergency arises, and at once be forwarded, through official channels, to the Bureau of Medicine and Surgery.

1168 *c*. Any technical schools which are, or may be, established for the education of medical officers and the hospital corps shall be under the supervision and control of the Bureau of Medicine and Surgery.

1168 *d*. In the hospital corps all first enlistments, including transfers to the service, shall be made upon the recommendation of the Bureau of Medicine and Surgery, and all discharges from the Corps, except upon expiration of enlistment or by sentence of court martial, and all details for duty, shall be made by the Bureau of Navigation on the recommendation of the Bureau of Medicine and Surgery.

1168 *e*. Records of enlistments in the hospital corps, and all other papers relating thereto, will be referred by the Bureau of Navigation to the Bureau of Medicine and Surgery for information, and to afford an opportunity for recommendation; and an examination report on a form prepared by the Bureau of Medicine and Surgery and approved by the Bureau of Navigation will be recorded in each Bureau in every case of enlistment or promotion.

A few days later, under date of January 29, 1906, I wrote the Secretary the following letter, returning the copy of proposed General Order:

Dear Mr. Secretary:

I think you have pretty thoroughly covered the ground necessary to place the medical department of the Navy in a position to carry on its work to the best interests of the service. I would, however, suggest the following changes:

Article II, paragraph (1), 6th line. After the word "Inspection," insert "it shall provide for all physical examinations."

Article II, paragraph (2), 2nd line. After "relates to," insert "medical supply depots, medical" —, and by leaving out the word "and" before "dispensaries" in the 3rd line and after the word "dispensaries" in the 3rd line add the words "and technical schools for the medical and hospital corps," making the Article read as follows:

> "The duties of the Bureau of Medicine and Surgery shall comprise all that relates to medical supply depots, medical laboratories, naval hospitals, dispensaries, and technical schools for the medical and hospital corps. It shall require for all supplies, medicines, and instruments used in the medical department of the Navy."

Article 1168 *c*, 1st line. Insert "are or," making the line read: "Any technical schools which are or may be established."

Article 1168 *d*, 7th line. After "Navigation" substitute "on recommendation of the Bureau of Medicine and Surgery" for the words "After considering any comments thereon by the Bureau of Medicine and Surgery;" or, if you prefer, substitute, "After reference to the Bureau of Medicine and Surgery for comment or recommendation."

I am satisfied that the provisions of this General Order are such that they should supersede all those in existing regulations where they conflict.

I agree with you that the Bureau of Navigation should be given the opportunity of commenting upon this proposed order, and also that the Judge Advocate General should be directed to prepare the General Order in proper form for publication.

I return herewith the form of General Order submitted by you, and also enclose a form embodying the slight modifications which I suggest.

(Signed) P. M. Rixey.

The General Order was issued as above and was most satisfactory to my bureau. The following letter explains itself and shows how I endeavored to make clear the duties of medical officers so as to avoid as far as possible any cause for disputes with the line:

DEPARTMENT OF THE NAVY
BUREAU OF MEDICINE AND SURGERY
WASHINGTON

April 22, 1908.

Sir:

The Bureau takes the view that when enlisted or other personnel of the Navy are under the charge of, or acting on duty as a part, of the Medical Department, such personnel becomes to all intents and purposes, for the time being, a part of the Medical Department and as such that the right to command all such personnel is vested in the Senior Medical Officer.

With this view in mind, the Bureau requests that the Judge Advocate General be directed to formulate for the information of this Bureau an interpretation of the law, based on existing Naval Regulations, of the right of medical officers to command, in order that, if necessary, the present laws may be so amended as to give proper and due authority to Medical Officers to perform such duties as may be assigned them and to properly maintain discipline.

The points occurring to the Bureau at the present time involve:

1. Naval Hospitals.
2. The right to act as President on Boards.
3. The right to administer oaths.
4. The right, when in command of stations, to order Summary Courts-Martial.
5. Under what other circumstances, if any, to exercise command of the enlisted and other personnel.
6. Under what circumstances, and what punishments may be administered by a Medical Officer.
7. The right to issue orders.

Very respectfully,

(Signed) P. M. RIXEY.
Surgeon General, U. S. N.

To: The Secretary of the Navy.

I do not remember receiving an answer to this letter and it was not of enough importance to follow up, especially as a change of administration was taking place about this time.

PROBLEM X. Funds for building hospitals and a sanatarium for the treatment of tubercular sick.

Early in 1908, I was much disturbed in regard to the hospital fund of the Navy which I was relying upon to complete our hospitals when sums appropriated by Congress were not adequate, and although the fund was being used in the maintenance of hospitals when required, I was in doubt as to spending large sums for finishing hospitals where Congress had authorized a specified sum. Moreover, the Judge Advocate General was urging the Secretary to give him a portion of it for prisons. I called on my friend, the Hon. Charles J. Bonaparte, our Attorney General, and asked him if he could give an unofficial opinion. He kindly consented and I received the following letter:

DEPARTMENT OF JUSTICE
OFFICE OF THE ATTORNEY GENERAL
WASHINGTON, D. C.

June 19, 1908.

Personal and Unofficial

Rear Admiral Presley M. Rixey, U. S. N.,
Surgeon General of the Navy,
Washington, D. C.

My dear Dr. Rixey:

I send you herewith a memorandum which has been prepared with regard to the method of defraying the expenses of the new naval hospital buildings. I have made a pencil notation thereon to which I would call your attention. Of course, it is understood that this is purely a personal and unofficial reply to your personal inquiry, and is not in any sense an opinion of the Attorney General, although, of course, it might be regarded as in a sense indicative of the view the Attorney General might take of such a question as is herein suggested if it should be formally presented to him.

Trusting that you may find the memorandum of some interest to you and with best wishes, I remain, as ever,

Yours most truly,

(Signed) CHARLES J. BONAPARTE.

and the following is a copy of the memorandum which he enclosed:

SUBJECT: Where Congress has made appropriation for a naval hospital building naming a fixed amount found not to be adequate, to what extent may the naval hospital fund be used in completion or enlargement of such building while under construction, and for such items as the heating, furnishing, and equipment thereof?

After the building thus appropriated for by Congress shall have been completed, is there any legal restriction upon the use of the Naval hospital fund for the purpose of making additions thereof?

By F. E. HUTCHINS.

Sections 3732 and 3733 of the Revised Statutes provide:

No contract or purchase on behalf of the United States shall be made unless the same is authorized by law or is under an appropriation adequate to its fulfillment, except in the War and Navy Departments, for clothing, subsistence, forage, fuel, quarters, or transportation, which, however, shall not exceed the necessities of the current year.

No contract shall be entered into for the erection, repair, or furnishing of any public building, or for any public improvement which shall bind the Government to pay a larger sum of money than the amount in the Treasury appropriated for the specific purpose.

And it is a very general rule that when Congress appropriates a specific sum for a particular purpose, this is intended as the limit of its cost. And, but for the other acts referred to, I would have very little doubt that this would be the rule in the present case.

But these acts leave little ground for the supposition that the hospital buildings referred to were to be erected and maintained only as and when Congress should appropriate sufficient money therefor. On the contrary, a naval hospital fund is created for the benefit of officers, seamen, and Marines of the Navy, and the commissioners of this fund. Afterwards, the Secretary of the Navy was directed to procure, "proper sites for naval hospitals, and if the necessary buildings are not procured with the sites, to cause such to be erected, having due regard to economy, and giving preference to such plans as, with most convenience and least cost, will permit of subsequent additions as the fund will permit and circumstances require."

This, of itself, makes it certain that neither the procurement of the sites, the erection of the buildings, nor the maintenance of the hospitals were to depend upon appropriations made by Congress. It shows, also, as does the whole tenor of the legislation upon the subject, that this hospital fund is to be used for those purposes. And with this imperative direction to procure sites and these buildings and maintain these hospitals and with no other adequate means provided therefor, it is quite obvious that this not only warrants but requires the use of this hospital fund for these purposes.

Then, if Congress makes a specific appropriation for either of these purposes, the whole legislation, being *in pari materia*, will be read together, and the appropriation, unless otherwise expressed, be treated as an addition to this fund for the purpose specified and not as abrogating or restricting the requirement of the former act to procure the sites and erect the buildings and maintain the hospitals. Indeed, it would require plain and express legislation in the appropriation act to abrogate either the right or the obligations thus imposed to erect and maintain these hospitals, or to use the hospital fund for those purposes when necessary.

The legislation which is believed to justify these conclusions will be found as stated below:

By the act of July 10, 1798, Congress provided for the relief of sick and disabled seamen of the Merchant Marine. (1 Stat., Sec. 2, Page 729.)

By the act of March 2, 1799, the Secretary of the Navy was directed to deduct twenty cents per month from the pay of officers and enlisted men of the Navy, and the money so collected to be applied to the same purpose as the money collected under authority of the act of July 16, 1798. (1 Stat., P. 605.) By this act the officers and enlisted men of the Navy and Marine Corps were enabled to receive the same benefits as disabled seamen of the Merchant Marine, and from the same fund.

AN ACT

Establishing Naval Hospitals

Approved February 26, 1811

(Altered and amended by Act approved July 10, 1832)

Section 1. *Be it enacted*, etc., That the money hereafter collected by virtue of the act, entitled "An act in addition to

An Act for the relief of sick and disabled seamen," shall be paid to the Secretary of the Navy, the Secretary of the Treasury and the Secretary of War, for the time being, who are hereby appointed a board of commissioners, by the name and style of Commissioners of Navy Hospitals, which, together with the sum of of $50,000 hereby appropriated out of the unexpended balance of the Marine hospital fund, to be paid to the commissioners aforesaid, shall constitute a fund for Navy hospitals.

Section 2. *And be it further enacted,* That all fines imposed on navy officers, seamen and Marines, shall be paid to the commissioners of Navy hospitals.

Section 3. *And be it further enacted,* That the commissioners of Navy hospitals be and they are hereby authorized and required to procure at a suitable place or places proper sites for navy hospitals, and if the necessary buildings are not procured with the site, to cause such to be erected, having due regard to economy, and giving preference to such plans as with most convenience and least cost will admit of subsequent additions, as the funds will permit and circumstances require; and the commissioners are required at one of the establishments, to provide a permanent asylum for disabled and decrepit navy officers, seamen and Marines.

Section 4. *And be it further enacted,* That the Secretary of the Navy be authorized and required to prepare the necessary rules and regulations for the Government of the institution, and report the same to the next session of Congress.

Section 5. *And be it further enacted,* That when any Navy officer, seamen, or Marine shall be admitted into a Navy hospital, that the institution shall be allowed one ration per day during his continuance therein, to be deducted from the account of the United States with such officer, seamen, or Marine; and in like manner, when any officer, seamen, or Marine entitled to a pension shall be admitted into a Navy hospital such pension during his continuance therein shall be paid to the commissioners of the Navy hospital and deducted from the account of such pensioner. (2 Stat., 650.)

By the act of July 10, 1832 (4 Stat., 572), the powers conferred upon the "Commissioners of Naval Hospitals" were transferred to the Secretary of the Navy, who was made the sole trustee of the Naval Hospital Fund. The sources of revenue of said hospital fund, in addition to specific appropriations, are provided in the following acts:

The act of March 2, 1799 (1 Stat., Sec. 2, P. 729);
The act of February 26, 1811 (2 Stat., 650);
The act of July 10, 1832 (4 Stat., 572);

The act of March 3, 1855
The act of July 2, 1890 (26 Stat., Sec. 5, 213);
The act of March 3, 1899 (30 Stat., 1027);
The act of June 7, 1900 (31 Stat., 697).

And throughout these acts, it is apparent that the fund thus provided is for the purpose of these hospitals, the procurement of sites and buildings for, and the furnishing, equipping, and maintenance of these hospitals; and except where specific appropriations are for specified purposes, the fund is as available and appropriate for any one of these purposes as for any other, due regard being had for the relative needs of each. But while a specific appropriation for a specified purpose must be used for that purpose, yet it does not follow here—as it would in ordinary cases—that this is all that can be used for that purpose.

The same considerations are pertinent in cases also of additions to or enlargement of buildings already erected, and this is made still more apparent—and also as showing that these buildings or additions thereto were not intended to depend upon appropriations by Congress—by reference to section 3, above quoted, of the act of February 26, 1811, which shows that such additions were not to be made from appropriations, but "as the fund will permit and circumstances require."

As the balance of this fund is now over $800,000, it is evident that a needed new building or additions to an existing one need not wait or depend upon Congressional appropriations.

Nor would the use of this fund for procuring a site for, or the erection of a hospital building, or additions to or repair of one already erected, be within section 3732 of the Revised Statutes above quoted; nor would the use of this sum therefor "bind the Government to pay a larger sum of money than the amount in the Treasury appropriated for the specific purpose," as prohibited by section 3733.

The case is entirely different from one where a public improvement is to be made from moneys in the Treasury, to be appropriated by Congress, and where the previous appropriation is intended to limit the cost.

On the contrary, it would seem that these specified appropriations were not made with reference to the cost only, but in view also of the state of the fund applicable to the same purposes, and as additions thereto. Indeed, it is impossible to suppose that these appropriations were to cover this cost, leaving the hospital fund to accumulate.

In view of the acts referred to, the purpose and object of this naval hospital fund and the requirement that sites and

buildings shall be procured and hospitals furnished, supplied and maintained, I have no doubt that unless an appropriation act expresses a different intention, this naval hospital fund may be used when necessary for the purposes named in either of the two questions submitted, notwithstanding that specific appropriations have been made therefor.
June 15, 1908.

(On this memo. Mr. Bonaparte made a notation which reads: "This is O. K. *so far as it goes*, but in any particular case the language of the appropriation act must determine whether Congress meant the amounts appropriated to cover the entire expenditure.")

The Attorney General had placed my mind at rest as to how far I could legally go in the handling of the fund. The next point was to stop the Judge Advocate General of the Navy from influencing Mr. Newbury to take a portion of the fund from us. I explained the whole matter to my friend, Hon. Elihu Root. Mr. Root, who was well versed in such matters, having been Secretary of War, said, "What an absurdity to take from your Bureau what is needed for prisons, and thus both of you have to go to Congress, who, when its attention is called to this fund, might turn it over to the Treasury, and both of you lose. Let the Judge Advocate General ask Congress for what he needs for prisons." He probably spoke to the President about it and he asked me what the trouble was. I explained the situation and told him that with a portion of the fund I proposed to build a hospital at Portsmouth, N. H., where there was none, and further explained that the medical department took care of sick prisoners as well as all others in the Navy, and the prisoners cost more per capita than other patients as special provision had to be made to prevent their escape from the hospital. A few days after this conversation I received this letter:

THE WHITE HOUSE
WASHINGTON

December 14, 1908.

My dear Dr. Rixey:

By direction of the President I beg to send to you, for your information, the enclosed letter from the Secretary of the Navy regarding the Naval Hospital Fund.

Very truly yours,

(Signed) WM. LOEB, JR.,
Secretary to the President.

Surgeon General P. M. Rixey,
Navy Department.

and the following is a copy of the enclosure:

NAVY DEPARTMENT
WASHINGTON

December 12, 1908.

My dear Mr. President:

I have the honor to acknowledge the receipt of your letter of the 11th instant referring to the Naval Hospital Fund and expressing your wishes that its present status should not be in any way changed. I am very glad to be able to tell you that this is exactly my own view of the matter and, as I verbally informed you, I have expressed this view to the Judge Advocate General, who, in showing a very proper zeal for the care of prisoners, suggested legislation by which their sanitary condition could be improved out of the fines which they, themselves, now contribute to the Hospital Fund. This plan is reasonable and might well be recommended when the Hospital Fund becomes larger than the needs of the service require. This, however, is not the condition at present, nor will it be for several years, and no recommendation will go from the Navy Department, or from any officer connected therewith, this year, which would either attract the attention of Congress to the Fund or suggest any change therein.

I have the honor to be,

Very sincerely yours,

(Signed) TRUMAN H. NEWBURY.

The above made it possible for the Bureau of Medicine and Surgery to proceed in its plans for three hospitals, one at Newport, R. I., one at Boston, Mass., and one at Portsmouth, N. H., and made possible their being built. The Attorney General's unofficial opinion made me satisfied that I was justified in asking the President's assistance in holding this fund for hospitals which were so much needed. His action decided where the fund should remain and during my administration of the Bureau after this date there was no question as to how this fund would be used.

My second tour of duty as Surgeon General was drawing to an end and I was a receptive candidate as I thought it would be for the best interests of the Navy. I was fifty-seven years of age, and felt able to accomplish as much work as at any period of my life. A new administration had come in since my last appointment and I knew that our new Secretary, Mr. Myer, would be much influenced by the line with many of whom I was *persona non grata* on account of my determined stand for the proper and necessary recognition of the medical corps of the Navy as to its standing with the line officers. There were many applicants for the position and I asked my Assistant in the Bureau, Medical Inspector, William C. Braisted, to put in an application for the position. This he told me he would not do; that he wanted me to continue in office, and as my assistant he could not try for the position. I told him that I did not believe I would be appointed for a third term in the Bureau. He declined to make a move for himself as my assistant, and I determined that his position in the Bureau should not jeopardize his chances for appointment. I had him detached and Surgeon Pleadwell ordered as Assistant to the Bureau, explaining to Dr. Braisted my reasons for so doing. I was making my arrangements for retiring from office, especially as regarded three new hospitals, one at Newport, one at Boston, and one at Portsmouth, N. H. The sites had been selected, the plans and specifications drawn, and the lowest bid accepted, only waiting for the Secretary's signature before commencing the work. In the year and a half I had been under Mr. Myer I had found him most helpful and considerate of me personally, but I was afraid that if as I expected he did not intend to reappoint me, he would hold up the contracts for the approval of my successor. I knew that the Navy needed these hospitals and I had spent a lot of work to get and hold the money for their construction, a good portion of which was to be from the hospital fund. So I took the contracts to Mr. Myer and asked him to sign them. After my explanation of the need of these hospitals, he signed the contracts. This was the end of big business during eight years service as chief of Bureau. I did not wish to embarrass Mr. Myer by a direct question as to his intentions in regard to the appointment of the next surgeon general, so I called upon the Hon. Elihu Root, whom as a friend and occasional patient, I had known since the McKinley administration. I asked him if he could find out whether or not I was to be reappointed and told him my position in the matter. He kindly consented and informed me after seeing President Taft that I was not. In the President's office I had many friends and one of them told me that Mr. Root had asked the President who was to be the next Surgeon General of the Navy and he said it had not been decided. Mr. Root then asked, "why not reappoint Dr. Rixey?" The President then sent a message to the Secretary repeating Mr. Root's inquiry and Mr. Myer replied that he did not think it advisable. I called on Mr. Myer and told him that I wished to be retired from the Bureau under the thirty year retirement law, having at that time thirty-six years of service to my credit. He approved it and asked some question as to my successor, mentioning a number of applicants among them, Doctors Stokes and Braisted. I saw that he rather favored Dr. Stokes, and as the doctor had been of professional service to the Secretary and family I thought they would be good friends and the new Surgeon General would have no difficulty in keeping up the good work of the Bureau of Medicine and Surgery, which I had inaugurated.

CHAPTER IX

AN UNPRECEDENTED INSPECTION BY A SURGEON GENERAL OF THE U. S. NAVY

MY BIOGRAPHER has written of my reasons for visiting the Philippines in 1906, and of my inspection of medical activities of every description, foreign as well as our own. My decision to return home by way of Europe was made to enable me to compare the European hospitals and schools with our own and especially the Naval Medical School at Hasler which had been established since my visit to Netley on my third cruise. Netley was at that time a combined Army & Navy School and was now devoted to the Army alone and Hasler was the Naval School. After this inspection I was satisfied with the work we had accomplished since I became Chief of the Bureau and I observed much which was to be of use in my second term of office as Surgeon General. Mrs. Rixey and Mrs. James were given to understand that they must not interfere with my official duties and at any time if they were late they would be left or if sick I could not be detained. They were good travelers and gave me no trouble. My orders read:

NAVY DEPARTMENT
WASHINGTON

May 3, 1906.

Sir:

Proceed to San Francisco, Calif., and take passage in the Steamer *Manchuria* of the Pacific Mail Steamship Line, sailing from that port, on or about Friday May 25, 1906, via Honolulu and Yokohama for Cavite, P. I., for special temporary duty.

Upon your arrival at Cavite, P. I., you are authorized to perform such travel as may be necessary in the proper performance of this special temporary duty.

The Officer in Charge of the Navy Pay Office, San Francisco, Calif., has been directed to secure your passage in the steamer of the Pacific Mail Steamship Line, sailing for Cavite, P. I., on or about Friday, May 25, 1906.

Upon the completion of this duty, return to Washington, D. C., via Europe, if deemed advisable in the interests of the service, and resume your present duties.

This is in addition to your present duties.

Respectfully,

(Signed) TRUMAN H. NEWBERRY,
Acting Secretary of the Navy.

Surgeon General Presley M. Rixey,
Chief of the Bureau of Medicine and Surgery,
Washington, D. C.

My aide going out was Assistant Surgeon H. H. Old, who rendered me valuable service in making notes for future use. I left him on duty in the Philippines and on my trip from Manila home, I had Dr. Freeman ordered but he missed the steamer that I came home on and I did not see much of him. I wrote President Roosevelt from San Francisco and at Yokohama I received the following letter from him:

THE WHITE HOUSE
WASHINGTON

June 11, 1906.

Dear Doctor:

It was delightful to hear from you, and Mrs. Roosevelt will be as pleased with your letter as I am. What you say about California was just exactly what I wanted to hear and considerably relieves my mind.

Dr. Braisted and Dr. Pryor are taking splendid care of us. I like them both, particularly Dr. Pryor, who is such a nice little fellow. Dr. Braisted was awfully nice to Quentin. He took him out to your place on Sunday and had him spend the night, Quentin enjoying himself to the full, as he usually does.

All three children have now gone to Oyster Bay and Mrs. Roosevelt will follow them in a fortnight. When Congress will end I do not know.

Ethel has had great fun with the Mayflower. There is such a nice set of young officers there. Some of them are playing tennis with Belle Hagner now, just outside of the window as I am writing.

With warm love to Mrs. Rixey, and best wishes for both of you, believe me,

Ever yours,
(Signed) THEODORE ROOSEVELT.

To: Surgeon General P. M. Rixey,
Care of U. S. Naval Hospital,
Yokohama, Japan.

At almost every port visited we were entertained and our sojourn made as pleasant as possible. I kept in touch with the work of my Bureau by letters from the Assistant to the Bureau or by cable as required, and heard from other officers, especially Dr. Braisted and Dr. Pryor whom I had charged to look out for the President and family. Before leaving I had given Dr. Braisted and his wife permission to occupy my summer home during my absence. This unprecedented inspection of a Surgeon General of the Navy was well thought out before asking for the orders and proved of incalculable service to me in my second tour of duty as Chief of the Bureau. I now considered myself competent to judge of the needs of our possessions over the seas and felt capable of passing upon the location and kind of hospitals needed in the tropics as well as all other sanitary and medical activities which would be brought to me for action. For the study of tropical diseases I had ordered Dr. Stitt to Manila before I started and on the ground I had his views and explanation after a careful study of the situation. Dr. Stitt was the best equipped man in the Navy for this work and by his writings and work was making a reputation second to none, and at this writing he is Surgeon General of the Navy, as a reward of merit. On leaving Manila I had orders issued for him to visit Guam and other points of interest and to return home and report to me at the Bureau. The new hospital which I had authorized built was doing excellent work under Medical Director F. S. Nash, its commanding officer. There were still considerable improvements to be made, which I authorized to be done as soon as possible.

At Olongapo I found the need of additional sick quarters and at Cavite a deplorable state of affairs. My orders required me to make an inspection of any naval ship that came under my observation and I was glad of the opportunity to see how well the medical activities were carried on at sea, especially as regarding sanitation, accommodations, and care of the sick.

An incident on the inspection of the *U. S. S. Cincinnati*, commanded by Captain Sharp, will show that I demanded the honors of my rank shown me in foreign as well as home waters. The Flagship gave me a boat to make the inspection of the *Cincinnati*. On coming to the quarterdeck of the ship I was surprised to find that no preparation had been made to receive me as my rank required. I informed the Captain that if every facility for my inspection and every honor due my rank was not paid me I would report him to the Navy Department. I had no further cause of complaint. The Marines were on deck, the side boys at the gangway when I left the ship, and a proper salute was fired. This really was the only disagreeable incident of the whole trip and was due to Captain Sharp's teachings in the Bureau of Navigation prior to his going to sea.

En route to join the *Manchuria*, the ship which took us from San Francisco to Hong Kong, I stopped to see Mrs. McKinley at Canton, Ohio, and at San Francisco I inspected the Naval and training stations. The first stop of the *Manchuria* was at Honolulu where I inspected the proposed site of the Naval Station and the location of a proposed hospital; our next stop was at Yokohama, Japan. I was much interested in the Japanese naval medical activities which they had developed prior to and during the Russo-Japanese war. During this war I had succeeded in having two medical officers, Dr. Braisted in Japan and Dr. Speer in Russia, as observers of medical activities and their reports were most flattering as to the Japanese Medical Department, showing that the Japanese, although in small numbers compared to the Russians, made up the difference by intensive medical work in the direction of prevention and cure of disease. The comparison of this war with the Spanish-American war was a lesson we ought never to forget. Disease during the war instead of far outnumbering the killed and wounded barely equalled them, and in General Oku's army, out of 24,642 on the sick list only 40 died; and bear in mind that most of those sick were back on the firing line in a short while. Comparing this record with our Army of the Spanish-American war, 274,717 men were raised of whom only 60,000 saw service in the field. Of the latter 290 officers and men were killed, 65 were wounded and 2,565 died of disease. This was bad enough but the home camps were ravaged by disease and 2,305 more of our soldiers were sacrificed to typhoid fever and other preventable diseases, besides adding many thousands of names to the pension rolls at a cost to the Government of many millions of dollars. This shameful state of affairs was due to a false sense of economy where men are brought together in large numbers without a previous training of the medical personnel and supply department in time of peace. The lesson has been learned at a great cost and it is hoped it will never be forgotten.

At Yokohama, Kobe, and Nagasaki, Japan, the *Manchuria* remained about five days and we left her at Yokohama and joined her by rail at Kobe, having visited Tokyo and Kyoto. My inspection of our naval hospital at Yokohama was very satisfactory and the commanding officer, Dr. Percy, was given authority for some necessary improvements. The *Manchuria's* next stop was Shanghai, China, then Hong Kong and on June 23rd we took passage on the small steamer *Rubi* for Manila, arriving on June 26th. From this date to July 7th, I made an intensive study of medical conditions making notes for future reference and authorizing what I considered was urgent. Every consideration was shown me by my old friend, Major General L. Wood, and officers of the Army, as well as by the Commandants of Naval Stations and other officers generally. I was also the recipient of many courtesies from Governor General Ide, Mr. Forbes, and many others.

The 4th of July was observed by an immense parade and we were invited on the reviewing stand. I was unable to be present but Mrs. Rixey and Mrs. James enjoyed it very much. Early on July 7th we left Manila on the small steamer *Zapiro* for Hong Kong arriving on the 9th. The first steamer sailing was the N. German Lloyd *Roon* on July 11th. While waiting I made a visit to the English Hospital and took a trip to Canton. The first stop of the *Roon* was at Singapore, then Renang, Columbo, and from there we visited Kandy; thence to Aden, Suez, Naples, and Genoa, where we left her and went by rail to Paris, London, and Southampton, leaving August 22nd on the *Kronprinz Wilhelm.* We arrived in New York the 28th of August and Washington the same day, making a total of 103 days absence from my office, having visited hospitals and schools in Europe, which I was anxious to inspect.

I found much on my desk waiting my return and I was anxious to have it as clear as possible before the return of the President and family from Oyster Bay. A visit to Oyster Bay and also to Canton, Ohio, to see Mrs. McKinley was made.

CHAPTER X

MY ATTITUDE TOWARDS A THIRD TERM AS CHIEF OF BUREAU

AS THE expiration of my second tour of duty as Chief of the Bureau was drawing near and I did not wish to continue in office if I had to trouble my friends to work for reappointment, I wrote President Taft as follows:

Bureau of Medicine & Surgery
Navy Department
Washington

December 13, 1909.

Sir:

Wishing to clearly define my position as an applicant for reappointment as Chief of the Bureau of Medicine & Surgery, I desire to state that I should consider such reappointment one of the greatest honors that could come to me and would stamp the approval of a third President upon my work in the service. Mr. McKinley, without solicitation on my part, promised to appoint me Chief of the Bureau of Medicine & Surgery when a vacancy should occur. After his death Mr. Roosevelt carried out his expressed wishes, and, after four years in the Bureau, he reappointed me. This second appointment expires February 6, 1910. I do not retire on account of age until July 14, 1914, and therefore, if not reappointed, I shall be reduced to the rank of Captain with corresponding loss of pay and have to serve under one who has been under me for eight years or, with your consent, to retire under the thirty-year retirement law, holding the same rank I now have and three-fourths pay.

I entered the Navy January 31, 1874; have had 11½ years sea duty, 24½ years shore and other duty, 10 months unemployed. In addition to other duties during ten years of this time, I was physician to the White House.

Under my administration of the Bureau much has been accomplished; and I may mention, first, the establishment of modern operating rooms and equipment on every battleship and cruiser in the Navy; second, the establishment of a post-graduate medical school in Washington for young men entering the service and to keep those in the service up to modern methods for the care of the sick and injured; third, the building of eight new hospitals and remodeling of practically every old hospital where they have not been replaced by new ones, with corresponding work on the grounds and additional buildings necessary for these hospitals.

The Bureau has been fortunate, with the approval of the Department, in obtaining a certain recognition for the Hospital Corps, women nurses have been provided for shore work and the instruction of our hospital apprentices for sea duty.

There still remains before Congress a bill to reorganize the Hospital Corps, to establish a dental corps and a medical reserve corps. The need of these I have explained to the Naval Committee of the House in my hearing on Friday last.

I had hoped, during my active work, to have completed the hospitals now being built and the new hospitals laid down, and to round out 40 years service in the Navy by retiring from the Bureau. In making this statement, I do not wish to minimize the services of any medical officer in the Navy who is an applicant for the position of Chief of Bureau, but I wish to say that, during my administration of the Bureau, I could not wish for a body of men to show greater zeal in their work. They are a live, wide-awake working body of men second to none, and I believe, if properly handled and given the necessary assistance asked for, they will meet any demand the naval service may require of them.

Forwarding this application through the Secretary of the Navy, I am,

Very respectfully,

(Signed) P. M. Rixey,
Surgeon General, U. S. Navy.

The President,
The White House.

and not having heard from him I wrote:

Department of The Navy
Bureau of Medicine & Surgery
Washington

17 January, 1910.

Sir:

In forwarding these letters and testimonials of Secretaries of the Navy, under whom I have served, through the present head of the Department, I wish to say that it is for the purpose of informing you of the value they placed upon my services as Chief of Bureau. I wish to further state that the Admiral of the Navy and many of the higher officers of both line and staff have expressed themselves, either verbally or in writing, most favorably as to my work as Chief of Bureau. These statements can all be substantiated if you wish them, and I can assure you that there is no disposition on my part to influence you in your decision—except by seeing that you have as accurate a record of my services as possible; and moreover, I have requested all of my friends not to make solicitations in my behalf, except so far as their interest in the service may demand.

I am sorry, Mr. President, to have to trouble you with these papers, but I feel that it is my duty to you, as well as to myself, to give you every information in my power before you come to a final decision. No matter what your decision may be, you will always find me most loyal to my Commander-in-Chief.

Respectfully,

The President, (Signed) P. M. Rixey.
The White House.

and enclosed copies of letters of the Secretaries of the Navy under whom I had served.

Hingham, Mass.
January 14, 1910.

Dear Dr. Rixey:

I am very happy to bear witness to your valuable work during my secretaryship as Surgeon General of the Navy. You have brought the medical and surgical service to a high standard of efficiency and usefulness. I have with interest and pleasure noted its growth under your direction, the new and most instructive school at Washington, the improved equipment of the hospital and the infusion into all branches of an increased spirit of the best practical and scientific advance. In my opinion you have made for yourself and for the Navy a most deserving and creditable record.

Very truly yours,

(Signed) J. D. Long,
Ex-Secretary of the Navy.

Surgeon General Rixey,
Navy Department.

Charles J. Bonaparte
Attorney-at-Law
216 St. Paul Street,
Baltimore, Md.

January 12, 1910.

My dear Doctor Rixey:

I recollect with much pleasure how valuable was your advice and cooperation to me while I was Secretary of the Navy, and how satisfactory to the Department, during my incumbency, was your administration of your own Bureau. I hope the country may continue to have the benefit of your services in a position which you then filled so well.

Yours most truly,

(Signed) CHARLES J. BONAPARTE,
Ex-Secretary of the Navy.

THE COREY HILL HOSPITAL
BROOKLINE, MASS.

January 30, 1910.

My dear Admiral:

I received your letter some days ago, should have replied to it earlier, but the conditions of illness will not admit of punctuality in correspondence.

You would like my estimate of your services as Chief of the Bureau of Medicine and Surgery during the time I was Secretary. I will very gladly give it. I found nothing to criticise and much to commend. You were active, zealous in the performance of your duty, and always working for the interests of the service as you saw them. The period of my holding office was one of great activity and marked the beginning of the development of a larger Navy. There was growth on every side, and you saw to it that the Medical Corps did not lag behind. I think you did an enormous amount to uplift the standard of your Corps. The severest test to which the Navy was put in my time was the sudden orders to fit out and dispatch the expedition to Panama.

It is enough to say that there was no lack whatever in your Bureau or any other for that matter.

The health of the landing force was phenomenally good, and that certainly was attributable to the efficiency of your Bureau.

I need say no more, for the foregoing marks clearly my estimate of your services.

With best regards, I am,

Sincerely yours,

(Signed) W. H. MOODY,
Ex-Secretary of the Navy.

THE EQUITABLE LIFE ASSURANCE SOCIETY
120 Broadway, New York, N. Y.

January 12, 1910.

My dear Admiral:

I am reminded that next month your commission as Chief of the Bureau of Medicine and Surgery will expire. Inasmuch as you are in good health, and fully capable of giving the same efficient service to the Government that you have given during the past eight years, I hope that you may be reappointed so that the Government may continue to receive the benefit of your good work.

With best wishes, believe me,

Very truly yours,

(Signed) PAUL MORTON,
Ex-Secretary of the Navy.

VICTOR H. METCALF
Law Offices
Oakland, California

January 20, 1910.

My dear Dr. Rixey:

I had intended writing to you before leaving Washington for the purpose of expressing to you my deep appreciation of your services as Chief of the Bureau of Medicine and Surgery under my administration.

I know of no public official who has been more faithful or more conscientious in the discharge of his duties than you. I was in close touch with the work of your bureau for two years and had an opportunity of judging of the nature and character of your work. It was in the highest degree satisfactory and I sincerely hope that for the good of the service you will be continued as Chief of the Bureau of Medicine and Surgery.

I should like to write the President in your behalf, but, of course, would not think of doing so without your consent.

With kindest regards both to yourself and Mrs. Rixey, and with best wishes for your future, believe me, as ever,

Sincerely your friend,

(Signed) V. H. METCALF,
Ex-Secretary of the Navy.

All of these letters to the President were forwarded to Mr. Taft through Secretary of the Navy, Mr. Myer.

On these gentlemen and all my friends, I tried to impress my desire that if appointed for a third term it must be on my record. Among the great number of letters was one from Secretary of Agriculture:

DEPARTMENT OF AGRICULTURE
WASHINGTON, D. C.

December 21, 1909.

My dear Sir:

Saw Secretary—your matter is open—undecided—recognition of great services prominent.

Sincerely,

(Signed) JAMES WILSON.

Admiral Rixey,
Navy Department.

One letter I received was from the Chairman of the Naval Committee of the House of Representatives:

January 25, 1910.

My dear Dr. Rixey:

You certainly have made a splendid record and are entitled to the fullest consideration.

With kind regards and best wishes, I am,

Very truly yours,

(Signed) GEORGE E. FOSS.

DEPARTMENT OF THE NAVY
BUREAU OF MEDICINE & SURGERY
WASHINGTON

November 6, 1908.

Dear Doctor Rixey:

We have the honor to inform you that Admiral Dewey called at the Dispensary this morning and requested us to tell you that he had occasion, recently, to visit the U. S. Naval Medical School Hospital, this city, with his wife, for professional purposes, and that they found the attendants presenting a very clean, neat, and efficient appearance, particularly the female nurse present, and that the Hospital was deserving of the very highest commendation.

He especially requested us to inform you that you are not only the best Surgeon General the Navy has ever had, but you have done more for the Medical Department, and its developments, than all of them.

He was very emphatic in his praise of you and the most excellent work accomplished by you as Surgeon General of the Navy.

It is practically impossible for us to convey his message to you in the same forcible manner in which he expressed himself to us.

We are,

Very respectfully,

(Signed) R. M. KENNEDY,
Surgeon, U. S. Navy.

(Signed) CARY T. GRAYSON,
P. A. Surgeon, U. S. N.

U. S. NAVY YARD
NORFOLK, VA.

November 6, 1909.

My dear Doctor:

Should you not be reappointed as Surgeon General for another term, I would like to do my little towards favoring as your successor, Du Bose.

I know that you are favorably inclined to him. I do not know what the probabilities of your reappointment are, but should you not expect reappointment, which I am sure your services to the Department fully warrant, I am inclined to write an official letter as Commandant, Du Bose being on this station now, to invite the attention of the Secretary to his merits and record in the consideration of your successor.

In view of my inexperience in such matters, I thought I would ask for an expression of opinion from you.

I retire and leave this station on the 20th of November, and will take no step in this direction unless it meets with your approval.

I am doing this without consulting and without the knowledge of Du Bose.

Hoping sincerely, should you desire to succeed yourself, that you may be reappointed, I am,

Very sincerely,

(Signed) E. D. TAUSSIG,
Rear Admiral, U. S. Navy,
Commandant.

1418 Eutaw Place,
Baltimore, Maryland

26 December 1909.

Dear Dr. Rixey:

A very Happy Christmas to you and your dear wife. I am off to Mexico tonight.

I am told as to reappointment that you do not seek it and that you do not in any way object to Dr. Stokes' pursuing an active candidacy. If this is true I believe in common with many of your friends that in Stokes you will find an excellent interpreter of your plans and ideas. I do not wish to take one step of which you do not cordially approve and so write to ask if I am at liberty to help Dr. Stokes.

With sincere affection,

(Signed) Howard A. Kelly.

Among many other letters that I appreciated very much were:

1810 South Rittenhouse Square
Philadelphia

January 12, 1910.

Dear Dr. Rixey:

I have been intending for sometime to ask your position in regard to the question of reappointment. I have been asked to write notes in favor of certain gentlemen who seemed to me to be very good men, but have declined because I understand that you were eligible, and because I had no knowledge that you did not desire the reappointment.

If you are at liberty to tell me how you feel, and what you wish, it would be a help to me at this juncture. I have no idea that I can be of *very* great use to anyone, but I might help, and anything I could do would first of all be at your disposal. If you do not desire reappointment, or if you think there is no possibility of it, I should be glad to have any confidential criticism you may feel disposed to make upon the candidates that have appeared.

Please believe me, with warm regards,

Yours faithfully,

(Signed) J. William White.

J. H. Musser, M. D.,
1927 Chestnut St.,
Philadelphia, Pa.

January 17, 1910.

My dear Admiral Rixey:

I have been told that it is your purpose to retire from the Navy at an early date. I have also been asked to urge the claims of one or more aspirants for the position. I should like to know your feelings in this matter so that I may be guided properly.

Thanking you for many courtesies, I am, with kind regards,

Very truly,

(Signed) J. H. Musser.

On the eve of taking my official leave of the Department I called to say goodbye to Secretary Myer, and found him not in his office. A few days later I received the following letter:

THE SECRETARY OF THE NAVY
WASHINGTON

February 7, 1910.

My dear Doctor Rixey:

I am sorry that I was not in my office on Friday afternoon when you called to make your official farewell.

During your term of office as Surgeon General of the Navy you accomplished much and brought about many improvements in the service, especially, the establishment of modern operating rooms and equipment on battleships and cruisers in the Navy; the establishment of a post-graduate medical school in Washington for young men entering the service; and the building of eight new hospitals and the remodeling of many of the old ones. I desire to take this opportunity to congratulate you upon the result of your labors and the interest that you have always shown in your duties.

Permit me to assure you that I look back with pleasure upon our relations during the past year, and accept my best wishes for the future.

Believe me,

Very truly yours,

(Signed) G. W. MYER,
Secretary of the Navy.

Dr. P. M. Rixey,
Surgeon General of the Navy (Retired)
1518 K Street, N. W.,
Washington, D. C.

DEPARTMENT OF THE NAVY
BUREAU OF CONSTRUCTION & REPAIR
WASHINGTON, D. C.

February 5, 1910.

My dear Rixey:

My note of yesterday was apparently written after you had been retired, at your own request, although, of course, I was totally unaware of that fact.

In all sincerity I desire to congratulate you upon your retirement from active duty, with its attendant worries and turmoil.

All those who are in any wise acquainted with the splendid

work you did while Surgeon-General of the Navy cannot help appreciating the unusually good results attained by you in the development of your branch of the Navy during the eight years that you have served at the head of your Corps. That good work remains as a monument to your ability, zeal, and devotion to duty.

Your private interests and love of outdoor life will leave you no lack of opportunity for useful and pleasurable occupation, and I feel quite sure that retirement at this time will add many years to your life.

With best possible wishes, always, for you and Mrs. Rixey, believe me, most sincerely your friend,

(Signed) W. C. Capps,
Rear Admiral U. S. Navy.

To: Surgeon General P. M. Rixey, U. S. N.,
Navy Department,
Washington, D. C.

1413 Fillent St.,
Philadelphia, Pa.
February 7, 1910.

My dear Doctor:

The official mail of this morning brings the information that you have voluntarily retired. This to me is a cause of mingled feelings of pleasure and pain. I am sure that you will enjoy the brilliant career which your past life forces me to believe awaits you in civil life, and you are freed from the petty annoyances which would have harrassed you in having to perform various disagreeable duties in the service, which under any conditions must happen to us all, and as there still remains to you, in the ordinary course of such things, some 15 or 20 years active, useful years for splendid work for which your magnificent past has eminently fitted you. Your friends and admirers who remain in the active list of the Corps will regret your retirement greatly from selfish as well as from patriotic motives.

You have done so much for the service and have increased the efficiency of the medical corps and of the service so much that while I think it is a good principle not to appoint any one man to more than two terms as Surgeon General, except in most unusual circumstances, I had most earnestly hoped that in your case, for many evident reasons, an exception would have been made. We beg that you will not forget us in your retirement, but will still help to make it possible for us to do good and even better work in the future, and free us from a miserable conservatism that I believe has its birth in selfishness, ignorance and prejudice.

With sentiments of the highest regards and best wishes, I am,

Affectionately yours,

(Signed) F. S. NASH,
Medical Director, U. S. Navy.

DR. REGINALD KNIGHT SMITH
2600 Jackson Street
San Francisco, California

February 5, 1910.

Dear Doctor Rixey:

The morning papers print a dispatch that you are retiring from the Navy under the thirty year clause and I wish to express to you again my appreciation for the many acts of kindness and consideration shown me when I was in the service.

Truly, during your administration of the Bureau of Medicine and Surgery there have been wonderful improvements in the appliances for the treatment of the sick and wounded on board ship, and it is too bad that the Navy is to lose your services while you are just in the prime of life.

Trusting that your health is all that you could wish it to be and that you will some day visit the coast and allow us the pleasure of seeing you at our own home, I am,

Very sincerely,

(Signed) R. K. SMITH.

WM. S. DONNALLY, D. D. S.,
1018 Fourteenth St., N. W.,
Washington, D. C.

February 6, 1910.

My dear Dr. Rixey:

I was unable to carry out my purpose of calling on you yesterday, so I am resorting to this means of assuring you of my appreciation of the exceedingly valuable and highly important service you, as the well-equipped Chief of the Bureau of Medicine and Surgery, have rendered the Government.

You have worthily represented and honored your profession. You have been increasingly active in wise and well-directed effort to enlarge and extend the beneficent function of the medical department for the benefit of the whole Navy personnel, and you have been signally successful in meeting the delicate duties and diverse responsibilities of the office of Surgeon General. Your achievements will be increasingly appreciated as the passing of time enlarges perception and discloses results. Besides what you have fully accomplished you have paved the way for the attainment of other aims of the Bureau. The one thing in which I have been especially interested—legislative authority for a Navy dental service—will soon show the results of your efforts and I regret exceedingly the especial effort to accomplish results before your retirement was not altogether successful. It may be some satisfaction to know that some of the members of the Naval Committee earnestly worked with this object in view, feeling that you would want to see the end which seems so near. I shall always remember with satisfaction the courtesy with which you have treated me personally and as the representative of my profession, and the kindly way in which you accepted my cooperation. I acknowledge gratefully the concessions you have made at my solicitation in behalf of a more liberal recognition of my profession. If I have appeared too persistent in urging the recognition implied by regular rank, I trust you will not attribute it to a failure to sympathize with your views but, rather, to a proper zeal and loyalty to dentistry and its fifty odd educational institutions.

Knowing your policy contemplated a recognition fully satisfying in its extent, as soon as certain opposition in Congress could be overcome, I am impressed with the debt of gratitude my profession owes to you for conceding so much while that opposition was still active. (Happily our chief, if not only, opponent in Congress has been shorn of his power to defeat our aim.)

With best wishes for your welfare and a long extension of your useful life, I remain,

Sincerely yours,

(Signed) WM. S. DONNALLY.

In acknowledgment of an invitation to the dinner which I gave Surgeon General Stokes on the occasion of his appointment as Chief of the Bureau of Medicine & Surgery, Dr. Howard A. Kelly wrote me the following letter:

1418 Eutaw Place,
Baltimore, Maryland

February 12, 1910.

Dear Dr. Rixey:

What a beautiful, generous thing for you to do. I see you keep the same old spirit you have always had ever since I have known you.

While I am a great admirer of Stokes, when I found that you were willing to remain at your post I was, of course, utterly unwilling to take the slightest step to promote any other interest.

I am sorry I cannot be with you at the dinner as I have an address to deliver in Chicago at the opening of a new society there on that very date.

Give my affectionate regards to Mrs. Rixey,

Faithfully and affectionately yours,

(Signed) H. A. Kelly.

Dr. Stokes accepted the invitation, disappointed my guests, as well as myself, by not being present. The guests having assembled I phoned to his home and the reply came back that he was ill. He made no excuse afterwards. Such was the man who was to be Surgeon General of the Navy for four years.

CHAPTER XI

FARMING AND THE PLEASURES OF A COUNTRY LIFE

RELIEVED of the cares of official life, I at first thought that I would devote my energies to the practice of my profession, but after mature deliberation I decided to live the outdoor life as much as possible. My principal business was to be farming.

From 1910 to the beginning of the World War, (1917), I was a farmer in real earnest, having many interests on each of these farms. The first farm was purchased in 1888 and added to from time to time; a good portion of this farm was wooded and the remainder had been worked too much and was overgrown with bushes, briars, etc. The time I spent on it had been one of continued improvement of the soil, and in a short time after purchase I had built a barn and established a dairy, commencing with a few cows but before long had forty head. During my active work, I could give little time to the farm operations but I had a good honest farmer and under my direction the farm improved rapidly, until in 1908, a number of gentlemen conceived the idea of a golf club, and purchased seventy odd acres of this farm, and the club was organized under the title of the Washington Golf and Country Club, Incorporated. I was the principal creditor, a member of the Board of Directors, and Chairman of the Greens' Committee. I knew very little of golf at this time but I realized that most of the work required of the Greens' Committee for the first year was such that the knowledge of farming would be very valuable. The experts planned out the work and it was carried out under my direction. The only time I could give to this work was from sunrise to 8 a. m., and after 4 p. m. each day. Land having now (1901) increased in value so that a dairy farm, to be productive, must have larger and better facilities, I purchased my first 150 acres near Falls Church and started a dairy there, moving my equipment from "Netherfauld" the name of the first tract of land purchased nearer Washington. The Falls Church farm was increased rapidly by purchase until I owned over 500 acres and it was developed into a paying investment. In 1909 and 1910, seeing my retirement drawing near and having always hoped that I would own and farm a large estate, I purchased Ben Lomond, a tract of nearly 2,000 acres of land. Immediately upon my retirement, I took up the Ben Lomond proposition and soon had it improved so as to make it profitable. First, I tried buying young steers and fattening them for beef, and many a carload of these steers I shipped to Baltimore and New York. About the time of my leaving office, I had a misfortune with my dairy cows on the Falls Church farm in the shape of bovine tuberculosis and had to get rid of most of my herd, and was so disgusted at the loss of my beautiful Guernseys that I gave up the dairy business and used the dairy farm and barns for finishing off my fattening steers from Ben Lomond. I drove them over the road from Ben Lomond (about 25 miles) and shipped them when in proper condition, from Alexandria. There was not much money in this and I decided to buy heifers instead of steers and raise calves for the market and cows to sell to the dairies. Much cultivation had to be done and in addition to mules and horses I put on a tractor and other mechanical appliances. My great interest and pleasure in these pursuits made the time pass swiftly until the World War was in sight, and I knew I must again go on active duty. Realizing that I could not afford to run the farms if I was to be away, I sold the Ben Lomond farm, January 1917, got out my uniform, and was ready for duty when war was declared.

This farming experience was a most interesting one; it enabled me to enjoy many pleasures that had been denied by reason of the demands of duty. In going over the farms I was principally on horseback, having good horses at each farm and an automobile for the long runs between farms. On a well trained horse with gun and dogs I would be in the saddle most of the time, and there was good shooting,

MEDICAL INSPECTOR PRESLEY MARION RIXEY, U. S. NAVY 1901
Inspecting work on his farms

especially on the Ben Lomond farm. I posted the farms and thus preserved the sport for myself and friends. Soon after buying this farm and posting it, I and my foreman had our hands full in trying to enforce the law in regard to trespass. The pot hunters and indeed everyone who wished to shoot, overran the place, cut my wire fences, and went so far as to kill some of my young stock. Coming from Washington one morning in my little Ford runabout, and coming in on the Fairfax side, I crossed the meadows on either side of Bull Run. I found two of my beautiful heifers on the ground with their limbs broken by a heavy cudgel of some kind. I had to kill them and was more determined than ever to forbid trespassing on the farm. Gradually I got control and kept it as long as I was the owner of the farm. However, I lost at least a half dozen head of stock and I was notified by one of my "supposed-to-be" friends that I should be more careful as he had heard a party say that he wished he had shot my eyes out the day before when I had come near catching him and that next time he would be sure of me. I could not get the name of the party but I requested my so-called friend to notify the party if possible that he had better be sure and put out both eyes. Such happenings only added to my enjoyment. I was a great lover of good horses and I had them from my hunting pony to best Virginia riding horses, tandem and four-in-hand. My dogs were wonderful companions and as a memorial to them I will go back to my boyhood days towards the end of the Civil War and describe my first pet "Ponto," a Scotch terrier. He was a wee puppy and I gave a pet hog for him. "Ponto" soon was the pet of the family and he and I were inseparable friends. He was useful in many ways, especially to my father who was blind. Also, in our ball games he never allowed a ball to be lost.

"Elcho" and "Molique"—Favorite Hunting Dogs

My next dog was "Elcho," a beautiful Irish setter, who was one of the best bird dogs possible, beautifully trained but would not hunt for anyone but me. When I left home for my third cruise, that on the *Lancaster*, I left him with my wife and he was her inseparable companion, whether she was visiting or at home; and after more than three years, he knew me and worked in the field as if I had been shooting over him every season, this too when I had been told that he was no good, simply because he would not pay attention to anyone but my wife and myself. My next two pets were "Puff" and "Rex," presented to me as puppies when I was with Mr. McKinley at Canton, Ohio. They were English setters, "Puff" almost pure white and "Rex" black and white. I sent them to a trainer, a Mr. Davies, an Englishman, to bring up and train. There never was a better trained pair and good as long as they had a tooth in their heads. I must not forget "Daisy," a pointer, over whom Colonel Theodore Roosevelt, Jr., as a boy shot his first quail. I have mentioned these faithful canine friends whose memories are dear to me, but they are only a few. I owned and kept on my farms a pack of beagles, a St. Bernard, Great Danes, and shepherd dogs, and the last two, "Puff" a black and white shepherd and "Tobias" a Gordan setter. My uncle Philip Jones of Culpeper, during my hunting days, always had a pack of fox hounds and many a run I have had behind them. When I could get off for a week or so from duty, my greatest pleasure was to be with this uncle, for he was always ready to go with me whether it was for fox, opossum, coon, rabbit, squirrel, wild turkey, quail, snipe, plover, woodcock, or pheasant.

After the World War when my health was impaired, I tried renting the Falls Church Farm and soon found that without my personal attention there was no profit in holding it. My uncle's son, Lieutenant M. E. Jones, had just been relieved from duty in the Army and informed me that he preferred farming to any other pursuit except the Army and that he saw no opportunity in that direction. Young Jones had lived with me as a boy and knew my way of doing business, and I made him a proposition which would give my wife and self the advantages of this young and active officer in the managing and working of our lands. We were very fond of Ellis, as we had always been of his father and mother, and I personally was greatly relieved. I had gone to considerable expense and was satisfied as prospects were bright as to its being a good investment under his management. One morning he came in with a paper from the War Department offering him a permanent appointment in the regular army as Lieutenant. He said that he did not propose to leave us but he had not foreseen this offer and he would not accept it without my consent. I at once released him of his agreement with me and took over his work. The impossibility of my carrying it on successfully was soon demonstrated and I had the most of the farm sold at an auction sale at a loss which would have made Ellis well off in worldly goods if he had remained with me. However his success in the Army for which he is well qualified, has been most gratifying.

CHAPTER XII

THE WORLD WAR

IN the fall of 1916, seeing that war was inevitable, I practically stopped work on the farms and by January, 1917, had sold the Ben Lomond Farm and was ready for active duty. To an inquiry from the Navy Department as to what duty I could perform, I answered, "Any duty that I have performed in the Navy," and to the inquiry when I would be ready, I answered, Immediately."

NAVY DEPARTMENT
WASHINGTON

April 16, 1917.

To Surgeon General P. M. Rixey, U. S. N., Retired,
1518 K Street, N. W.,
Washington, D. C.

SUBJECT: To duty Bureau of Medicine & Surgery, Navy Department.

1. Report to the Chief of the Bureau of Medicine and Surgery, Navy Department, for such duty as may be assigned you in that bureau.

2. This employment on shore duty is required by the public interests.

(Signed) JOSEPHUS DANIELS.

NAVY DEPARTMENT
BUREAU OF MEDICINE & SURGERY

April 18, 1917.

1. Reported.

(Signed) W. C. BRAISTED,
Surgeon General, U. S. Navy.

Some time before this, Colonel Roosevelt was trying to get permission to raise a division for the front and I wrote him that if he raised a division I would like to be with him, and he replied:

New York, N. Y.,
March 23, 1917.

Dear Dr. Rixey:

Indeed, if I am allowed to raise a division, I should

particularly like to have you with us.

Sincerely yours,

(Signed) THEODORE ROOSEVELT.

In addition to duties in the Bureau, I was directed by the Surgeon General to report for duty on the Council of National Defense.

April 16, 1917.

To: Surgeon General Presley M. Rixey, U. S. N., Retired.

1. Report to Doctor Franklin A. Martin, Council of National Defense, Munsey Building, for duty in connection with the Navy Medical Department where needed with the Medical Sector of the Council, and to represent the Surgeon General at meetings when he may not be able to attend.

(Signed) W. C. BRAISTED,
Surgeon General, U. S. Navy.

This duty was not satisfactory to me and I asked the Bureau to assign me to more active work, and I was ordered as General Inspector of medical activities in the United States, in addition to duty in the Bureau of Medicine and Surgery, Washington. The first order was as senior member of a board to investigate and report upon the training station and hospital at Great Lakes, Illinois.

NAVY DEPARTMENT
BUREAU OF NAVIGATION

August 3, 1917.

To: Surgeon General Presley M. Rixey, U. S. N., Retired,
Bureau of Medicine & Surgery, Navy Department.

SUBJECT: Temporary duty at Great Lakes, Ill.

1. When directed by the Surgeon General of the Navy, you will proceed to Great Lakes, Ill., and report to the Commandant of the 9th, 10th, and 11th Naval Districts, for special duty as senior member of a Board to investigate and report upon all matters of sanitation and medical administration at the Training Station and the Naval Hospital.

2. Upon the completion of this duty you will return to Washington, D. C., and make report with recommendations to the Surgeon General of the Navy, and resume present duties.

3. This is in addition to your present duties.

(Signed) JOSEPHUS DANIELS.

The Assistant to the Bureau, Surgeon R. C. Holcomb, was a member of this board and a most efficient officer. This training station at Great Lakes, was one of the largest in the Navy, having over 25,000 men under training at a time, all coming in green from private life, and as they were trained were graded up to men ready for foreign service. It was most important that no contagious diseases should get into the camps and that the health of these boys must be kept up to the highest standard while going through intensive training. The importance of the duties assigned this Board was recognized by the Commandant of the station, Rear Admiral W. A. Moffet, and every assistance was given us. I reported my return to Washington, D. C. on August 10, 1917.

After I had been on inspection duty for a short time, Admiral Braisted, having been my assistant in the Bureau prior to my retirement in 1910, feeling that I would be of more service to the Bureau in Europe than anyone else, informed me that he wanted to have me ordered on Admiral Sim's staff as an observer of the medical activities of the Allies as well as of our own Corps and to keep the Bureau informed as to the Navy's needs in Europe. I was more than pleased and informed him that I could start at once. He went at once to Mr. Daniels, the Secretary of the Navy, to have my orders issued. The Secretary refused on the ground that I had been on the retired list for a number of years and was too old. My disappointment was great and I appealed to the Secretary personally, stating my experience as Chief of the Bureau as well as my relations with many of the medical officers of our Allies. Mr. Daniels was always very nice to me but my persistence did not change his decision and he added that it would not be justice to me to send me overseas. Personally I was willing to serve my country where I could be of most service, and if I had to die during the war I wanted to be as near the front as possible. Writing Mr. Roosevelt of my disappointment he replied as follows:

THE ROOSEVELT BOYS IN SERVICE IN THE WORLD WAR

432 Fourth Avenue,
New York, N. Y.,
October 4, 1917.

Dear Dr. Rixey:

It is fine to hear from you. I am so driven to death that I have not time to do more than to send you a few lines. Of course, I am very sorry you were not allowed to go abroad. Physically, and every other way, you could have done that job in fine shape.

Mrs. Roosevelt is well but not strong. She is easily tired. Kermit by now must be in Mesopotamia. Quentin is flying with the French. Ted and Archie are under Pershing as Major and Lieutenant in the 26th Infantry. Dick Derby will go abroad in two or three weeks. Ethel and her two babies are in the house with us. I am bitterly disappointed that I am not allowed to do something useful, and I am almost driven to death by unimportant things.

Faithfully yours,
(Signed) THEODORE ROOSEVELT.

This letter made me feel better as I knew that Mr. Roosevelt not only knew me better than Mr. Daniels, but also knew the Navy's requirements.

My next orders were as follows:

NAVY DEPARTMENT
WASHINGTON

September 24, 1917.

To: Surgeon General Presley M. Rixey, U. S. N., Retired,
Bureau of Medicine and Surgery,
Navy Department,
Washington, D. C.

SUBJECT: Temporary additional duty.

1. When directed by the Chief of the Bureau of Medicine & Surgery, you will proceed to Fort Lyon, Colo.; thence to San Diego, Calif.; thence to San Pedro, Calif.; thence to San Francisco, Calif.; thence to Mare Island, Calif.; thence to Puget Sound, Washington; thence to Great Lakes, Ill.; reporting to the Medical Officer in Command, Commanding Officer, or to the Commandant, as the case may be, connection inspection Naval Hospitals, Navy Yards, Medical Departments, and Medical Department construction.

2. While carrying out these orders, you will look into any questions pertaining to medical and sanitary features of the

various stations that may need attention, particularly in connection with new construction for housing the increased personnel, taking up the question of supplies at the Naval Medical Supply Depot, Mare Island, Calif., the sanitary and medical features of the Naval Training Stations, of prisons or prison ships, and the Hospital Corps Training School at San Francisco, Calif.

3. This is in addition to your present duties and upon the completion thereof you will return to Washington, D. C., and submit your report to the Chief of the Bureau of Medicine and Surgery.

(Signed) JOSEPHUS DANIELS.

This duty kept me constantly on the go for a full month and was tasking in the extreme, often instructing and inspecting medical activities day after day, and traveling most uncomfortably as a rule. It was gratifying to me to receive everywhere the cooperation of all officers of the service, both line and staff. Everyone seemed to take their duties seriously and one of my principal duties was to coordinate their work so as to produce best results and to make such recommendations to the Bureau of Medicine and Surgery as would be most helpful. Urgent recommendations I made from each station, as time was a great element in preparing men for the front. This duty was completed October 24th and after my verbal report to the Surgeon General it took some time to have my written report put in shape. My next orders were as follows:

NAVY DEPARTMENT
BUREAU OF NAVIGATION

November 8, 1917.

To: Surgeon General Presley M. Rixey, U. S. N., Retired,
Bureau of Medicine & Surgery,
Navy Department, Washington, D. C.

SUBJECT: Temporary additional duty.

1. Upon receipt of this order you will proceed to the place (or places—in the order given) indicated below, for temporary duty. This is in addition to your present duties, and upon the completion thereof you will return to your station:

To: Annapolis, Md., proceeding when directed by the Chief of the Bureau of Medicine & Surgery, for duty in connection with the Medical Department matters and general sanitary situation at the Naval Academy, Ships, Rifle Range, Dairy Farm, Experimental Station, and Naval Hospital. You will report to the Superintendent of the Naval Academy for this duty.

(Signed) L. C. PALMER,
Rear Admiral, U. S. Navy.

I had taken great interest in the medical activities at the Naval Academy before my retirement in 1910, especially as to sanitation and prevention of disease in the student body, and the new hospital had been built under my administration of the Bureau of Medicine & Surgery; and so I found this very pleasant duty and I was extremely interested in the farm work, especially the Academy dairy which supplied milk.

On my return to Washington I made my written report to the Surgeon General and resumed duties in the Bureau—that is, the study of best methods for the medical corps to carry on for the best interests of the Navy. This was most interesting for an old surgeon general who had planned and worked for so many years for such an emergency as now confronted us, the winning of this great war. Going from one unit to another, consulting with those in charge of those units, making notes of where my attention, as inspecting officer, was most needed when making my inspections and getting the views of these splendid young officers after their study of problems confronting us, was a great help to me in my work and such splendid work the Bureau was doing, well organized, and everyone alert to the demands of the needs of the Navy that we have the best material that our country could produce in personnel and material and keep it at the highest standards of efficiency. As an example of one of these units I may mention that of the prevention of disease which was conducted by officers of the Public Health Service, who, during the period of the World War, were assigned duty under the Bureau of Medicine and Surgery of the Navy. Dr. Cumming, now Surgeon General of the Public Health Service, was immediately in charge of this unit and was ably assisted by Dr. Fox of the same service. In addition, this unit was in communication with every District and in every one of these was stationed a public health officer who made a study of the prevailing health conditions. In the main office of this unit was a great map which showed, from day to day, the presence of communicable diseases in every place where our men might be exposed. In my inspections, I had Dr. Fox with me often, and he was most helpful, but he was needed at the Bureau so I usually made use of the Public Health Officer of the District I was inspecting. I found everyone of them keenly alive to the importance of their duty and of great assistance in my work. I have always had a high opinion of this service, but after my association with its officers in the World War there is a very close tie added—that of comrades in an emergency. The next orders issued to me:

NAVY DEPARTMENT
WASHINGTON

December 18, 1917.

To: Surgeon General P. M. Rixey, U. S. N., Retired,
Bureau of Medicine and Surgery, Navy Department.

SUBJECT: President, Board of Medical Examiners and Naval Examining Board.

1. You are hereby appointed President of a Board of Medical Examiners and President of a Naval Examining Board to convene at the Bureau of Medicine and Surgery, Navy Department, Washington, D. C., as soon as practicable, for the examination of Medical Director Edward R. Stitt and Medical Director George H. Barber, preliminary to promotion to the grade of Medical Director with the rank of Rear Admiral.

2. Surgeon General William C. Braisted and Medical Director Cary T. Grayson are hereby appointed as the other members of the board, and the latter will act recorder.

3. This is in addition to your present duties.

(Signed) L. C. PALMER,
Acting.

This was an anomalous order recognizing me as the senior of Surgeon General Braisted at the same time I was serving under his Bureau; that is, my duties placed me under my old assistant but now temporarily he was placed under me. I made no comment but performed the duty and both

Dr. Stitt and Dr. Barber were promoted to the rank of Rear Admiral. The only question raised in my mind was as to the physical condition of Dr. Stitt, who had been operated upon for a serious condition and from which he had not completely recovered. He was on duty, and was performing a most important duty, and the service could ill afford to lose his valuable services, so we decided to state the facts and recommend him for promotion. His work up to the present time, when he is the Chief of the Medical Corps of the Navy, has amply justified our recommendation.

NAVY DEPARTMENT
BUREAU OF NAVIGATION
WASHINGTON

November 27, 1917.

To: Surgeon General Presley M. Rixey, U. S. N., Retired,
Bureau of Medicine & Surgery,

SUBJECT: Temporary additional duty.

1. Upon receipt of this order you will proceed to the place indicated below, for temporary duty. This is in addition to your present duties, and upon the completion thereof you will return to your station:

Norfolk, Virginia, thence to Hampton Roads, Va., for observations in connection with the care of the sick and the possible necessity for additional accommodations.

(Signed) Acting Chief of Bureau.

This was important, as it was foreseen that this hospital would have to be much enlarged almost immediately. This duty was completed December 15th, and my next orders were as follows:

NAVY DEPARTMENT
BUREAU OF NAVIGATION
WASHINGTON

February 13, 1918.

To: Surgeon General Presley M. Rixey, U. S. N., Retired,
Bureau of Medicine & Surgery, Navy Department.

SUBJECT: Temporary additional duty, Navy Yard, Washington, D. C.

1. Report to the Commandant, Navy Yard, Washington, D. C., for temporary duty in connection with the inspection of the Naval Hospital, Washington, D. C.

2. This is in addition to your present duties.

(Signed)

Acting Chief of Bureau.

This hospital, under the command of Medical Director Kennedy, was a pleasure to inspect, and compared most favorably with others I had inspected. My next orders were:

NAVY DEPARTMENT
BUREAU OF NAVIGATION
WASHINGTON

March 27, 1918.

To: Surgeon General Presley M. Rixey, U. S. N., Retired, Bureau of Medicine & Surgery, Navy Department.

SUBJECT: Temporary additional duty.

1. Proceed to the place indicated below, for temporary duty. This is in addition to your present duties, and upon the completion thereof you will return to your station:

To: Fort Lyon, Colorado, in connection with the inspection of the hospital and increased hospital accommodations at that place.

(Signed) THOS. J. SENN,
Captain, U. S. N.,
Acting Chief of Bureau.

This long trip was necessitated by the failure of the Commanding Officer at Fort Lyon, Colorado, to carry out the views of the Bureau as I had explained them to him on my previous inspection in October, 1917. The result was that complaints came to the Department from patients and their friends complaining of the want of proper care and treatment. As soon as I was made acquainted with their complaints I told the Surgeon General that the whole trouble was that the Commanding Officer was more interested in his dairy, irrigation plans, and the raising of crops than he was in sanitarium work, and I had warned him on my previous visit. I was fond of this officer, whose promotion to Rear Admiral I had just passed upon, and he was most considerate of me personally, putting me up in his own home while I was on the station. So it hurt me to have to injure him, but my duty had to be performed and I read him my report which I should make to the Surgeon General. He said, "You don't think it is as bad as that?" I replied that it was the report I must make. My next temporary duty was:

NAVY DEPARTMENT
BUREAU OF NAVIGATION
WASHINGTON

April 16, 1918.

To: Surgeon General Presley M. Rixey, U. S. N., Retired,
Bureau of Medicine and Surgery.

SUBJECT: Temporary additional duty.

1. Proceed to the place indicated below, for temporary duty. This is in addition to your present duties, and upon the completion thereof you will return to your station:

TO SUCH Places within the 1st, 2nd, 3rd, 4th, 5th, 6th, 7th, and 8th Naval Districts as may be directed by the Chief of the Bureau of Medicine and Surgery, as representative of the Surgeon General, U. S. Navy, to look into all medical department activities within the above mentioned districts.

(Signed) THOS. J. SENN,
Captain, U. S. Navy,
Acting Chief of Bureau.

These orders took me to Quantico, Va., Boston, Mass., Portsmouth, N. H., New London, Conn., Newport, R. I., New York, N. Y., Philadelphia, Pa., Cape May, N. J., New Orleans, La., Gulfport, Miss., Pensacola, Fla., Jacksonville, Fla., Key West, Fla., Port Royal, S. C., Charleston, S. C., Norfolk, Va. From these places I visited by automobile or otherwise, all points where my services as inspecting officer might be required, and the Public Health Officer of each district would show me his copies of reports made to the Bureau since I started on this round of inspections, those made previously I had seen. The officer for each district accompanied me and pointed out any difficulty he had found in complying with the Bureau's circulars as to health conditions. The Commandants of stations, most of them old friends, gave me every facility at their command for carrying out my orders from the Department.

NAVY DEPARTMENT
BUREAU OF NAVIGATION
WASHINGTON

July 2, 1918.

To: Surgeon General Presley M. Rixey, U. S. N., Retired, Bureau of Medicine & Surgery, Navy Department.

SUBJECT: Temporary additional duty.

1. Proceed to the place indicated below, for temporary duty. This is in addition to your present duties, and upon the completion thereof you will return to your station;

To: Annapolis, Md., in connection with inspection of Medical Department affairs.

(Signed) THOS. J. SENN,
Acting Chief of Bureau.

The above orders had been complied with on July 6th, and my physical examination recorded on July 15, 1918, showed physical defects—NONE; B. P. 120; "Fit for the duties of his grade and for the proposed physical exercise." I was on my regular duty in the Bureau, when about the latter part of the same month I was taken seriously ill. The active life I had been leading as an inspecting officer had tasked my physical endurance to the utmost and I was trying to build up on my country place, and at the same time was making arrangements to move my family to it as a permanent residence summer and winter. Our town residence at 1518 K St., N. W., I had rented unfurnished, and I was making arrangements for moving our furniture to the country when this illness came. It commenced as a slow hemorrhage and I kept on my feet and went home early from the Bureau. Finding that my wife had gone to Union Station to meet her niece who was not strong, I ran my sedan down to bring them home. Before I got back I found that I had miscalculated my strength and as I stopped the machine at our door I collapsed and was put to bed, and the surgeon took me at once to the Naval Hospital. In my condition, operation was out of the question, transfusion only temporary if any good—the hemorrhage continuing, and now I vomited a wash-basin full of pure blood and was completely exhausted. I called my friend, Hon. John S.

Barbour, and made some changes in my will, and became unconscious—never expecting to open my eyes again on earth; nor did my family, physicians or nurses. They expected that each breath would be my last. I evidently held on longer than expected and Dr. O'Malley suggested one more transfusion and Dr. Strine, who had everything ready, at once operated. To the surprise of everyone, the heart's fluttering improved and then came the building-up process and a most delicate one it was, and made possible by the devotion of my physicians and nurses. It was slow but sure and my strength came back with a wonderful appetite, especially for baked Irish potatoes. I believe that after all the blood was out of my body, the lips of the ulcer came in contact and glued together, or possibly a clot of blood filled the opening with sufficient strength to resist the feeble blood pressure which the transfusion gave, but the new blood kept the heart going sufficiently to sustain life until proper nourishment could be supplied otherwise. I cannot be too grateful for the affectionate care of all who were with me at this trying time, especially Dr. Howard C. Strine, Dr. O'Malley, Dr. Kennedy, Dr. Grayson, Dr. Stitt, and the nurses, Miss Walton, my day nurse, and Mrs. Monday, my night nurse. My faithful friend, Charles Brown, was always there, when possible. When I was unconscious and everyone thought I was dying, Dr. Grayson, whom I had known from his boyhood, was asked by one of my friends if he thought there was any chance for me, and he replied: "If it was anyone else but Dr. Rixey I would say,'*No,*'—but you never know what he is going to do." My convalescence in the Naval Hospital was really delightful; flowers and dainties of all kinds came to me, and the dearest friends that man ever had, visited me. The end of the war was in sight. In six weeks I was at my home in the country—reported for duty and was informed by the Surgeon General that there would be no orders for travel at present, and that I could come to the Bureau when I felt able.

This record of my illness would not be complete without showing the devotion of my wife. When I was taken to the hospital her niece about the same time was taken from our home to Columbia Hospital, and, as already stated, I had rented our K Street home and all the furniture, etc., had to be moved to our country place. The only thing I could find out from her as I got better was that "everything was all right." Her heart and hands were more than full.

Immediately after the signing of the Armistice I asked the Surgeon General to have the Department relieve me from duty, and received the following:

NAVY DEPARTMENT
WASHINGTON

November 16, 1918.

To: Rear Admiral Presley M. Rixey,
Medical Corps, U. S. N., Retired,
Bureau of Medicine & Surgery.

SUBJECT: Detached duty Bureau Medicine & Surgery; to home.

1. You will regard yourself detached from all duty in the Bureau of Medicine and Surgery; will proceed home.

2. Immediately upon your arrival home you will report your local address in full, and the date of your arrival to the Bureau of Navigation. See Article 705, Instructions to Navy Regulations, 1913.

(Signed) FRANKLIN D. ROOSEVELT,
Acting.

NAVY DEPARTMENT
BUREAU OF NAVIGATION
WASHINGTON

November 23, 1920.

From: The Bureau of Navigation.

To: Rear Admiral (MC), Presley M. Rixey, U. S. N., Retired,
Rosslyn, Va., R. F. D. No. 1.

SUBJECT: Transmittal of special letter of commendation.
ENCLOSURE: Letter of commendation and Silver Star.

1. The Bureau takes pleasure in forwarding herewith a special Letter of Commendation awarded to you by the Navy Department for services rendered during the World War.

2. A copy of the Letter of Commendation will be made a part of your official record.

3. Please acknowledge receipt of this communication.

4. The receipt of this letter entitles you to wear a Silver Star upon the Service Ribbon when that ribbon is worn in lieu of the Victory Medal.

(Signed) D. B. BEARY,
By direction.

THE UNITED STATES OF AMERICA
NAVY DEPARTMENT

THE NAVY DEPARTMENT HAVING CAREFULLY CONSIDERED ALL REPORTED INSTANCES OF MERITORIOUS CONDUCT BY OFFICERS AND ENLISTED MEN OF THE NAVY DURING THE WORLD WAR, TAKES PLEASURE IN COMMENDING

REAR ADM. PRESLEY M. RIXEY (MC), U. S. N. (RET.)

FOR THE FOLLOWING SERVICE WHICH IS RECOGNIZED AS ACCORDING WITH THE BEST TRADITIONS OF THE NAVAL SERVICE:

HE PERFORMED EXCEPTIONALLY MERITORIOUS SERVICE IN A DUTY OF GREAT RESPONSIBILITY AS A MEMBER OF THE COUNCIL OF NATIONAL DEFENCE AND LATER AS INSPECTOR OF HOSPITALS AND GENERAL MEDICAL ACTIVITIES.

NOVEMBER 11, 1920

Seal of the
Navy
Department

(Signed) JOSEPHUS DANIELS,
Secretary of the Navy.

At my country home I gained my strength rapidly and soon was busy making my summer cottage comfortable for the winter of 1918. During this winter and the following spring I revised plans for my new home on the site where my old home, "Netherfauld," stood. This home had been destroyed by fire many years before and I had delayed building as I was so much interested in other pursuits. I realized that building operations at this time would be very uncertain and expensive, but my late experiences had warned me to proceed at once if we were ever to enjoy living in the new home we had planned for so many years. Before my illness, Mr. Percy C. Adams, an architect, had made a sketch

"Netherfauld," Rear Admiral Rixey's First Home At Rixey, Va
Destroyed By Fire

Cottage Saved From the Fire and Added to and Lived in as a Summer House Until 1921 The Dear Little Home Had Hospitality Written on Every Inch of It

plan with the understanding that the finished and working plans and specifications could not be considered until the war was over, and his associate, Mr. Frank Upman (an architect and a friend of long standing) had returned from overseas where he was on duty. Mr. Adams was busy doing war work at home. In the spring of 1919, Captain Upman having returned, working plans and specifications were soon ready and contract let to Messrs. Arthur L. Smith & Co., a well known building firm. Ground was broken August 11, 1919, and we moved into the new home on Thanksgiving Day 1920, but the building was not finished until the end of the year and the last payment made March 15, 1921. From the beginning to the end of building operations, it was a constant struggle—material and labor, both skilled and unskilled, almost impossible to obtain, even at enormous cost. Living in my cottage alongside, I was the first one on the job in the morning, stayed with the workmen all day, and after they left my rule was to go over their work before going in for the night. I was anxious to have this home as perfect as possible and the results, after living in it three years, have been all that we could ask. In our beautiful home we are as comfortable in winter as we could be anywhere, and in summer it is just as comfortable. In our declining years there could be no home nor place more satisfactory, and I view with pleasure the work of my three score and ten years—50 years a doctor of medicine, 50 years in the Navy, of which eight years I was Surgeon General of the Navy, and over 10 years White House physician under Presidents McKinley and Roosevelt. The review of the work accomplished during my term of Surgeon General, I had observed under war conditions while I was serving in the Bureau of Medicine and Surgery as inspecting officer.

My official duties over, I had time to think over my work done during the war, and reading over Surgeon General Braisted's annual reports for 1917, I noted he had not mentioned my name although all officers on special detail were recorded. I thought this might have been an oversight

The Rixey Country Home at Rixey, Va.

so I took up his report for 1918, during which year I had been on duty in the Bureau ten months and eighteen days; to my surprise he had not mentioned my name although credit was given to many younger officers for special duties performed. Shortly afterwards in the Surgeon General's office, I told him of his omission and asked him to give me a letter stating that I had served in the Bureau during the war.

DEPARTMENT OF THE NAVY
BUREAU OF MEDICINE AND SURGERY
WASHINGTON

January 16, 1919.

My dear Admiral:

It gave me great pleasure to see you yesterday restored to apparent health and vigor after your very serious and nearly fatal illness. All your friends rejoice that you have been spared and trust that many years of happy life may be before you.

I wish to take this opportunity to tell you how pleased I was to be able to gratify your great desire to serve your country in the war now just closing.

Your service dating from April 16, 1917, to November 18, 1918, covered a part of our greatest activities and as Inspector, acting for the Surgeon General, I was enabled to give you the opportunity to see at first hand a large field of our activities at home. The splendid organization and enormous expansion marked the proudest and highest state of efficiency the Medical Department of the Navy ever reached, and coming from some years of retirement must have filled your heart with a justifiable pride in the work of your successors. I recommended you for the same duty abroad in order that you might see the splendid work of the Medical Department in the fleet, the unusual and splendid achievements in overseas transportation and the hospitals and overseas work of Medical Department abroad.

It would have been a great pleasure for me to have had you review this most important part of our work under actual war conditions, but the Secretary of the Navy wisely considered that so hazardous a duty would be too much to impose upon you at your time of life, and your later physical condition showed his good judgment.

It has pleased me to meet you after your return from the tour of observation of our important stations in the United States and to hear from your lips the warm expressions of appreciation of our work, and I have no doubt your presence at the various stations was a source of encouragement to the many officers who had known you and worked under you during your previous active service.

Let me take this opportunity of thanking you for your sympathetic interest in all that pertains to the service in which you have spent the best years of your life and trust that your remaining years will see still greater accomplishments in what I believe is at present one of the finest organizations of its kind in the world.

With esteem and personal regard, I am,

Very sincerely yours,

(Signed) W. C. Braisted,
Surgeon General, U. S. N.

Rear Admiral P. M. Rixey, M.C., U. S. N., Ret'd.,
R. F. D. No. 1, Rosslyn, Va.

This letter was most unsatisfactory and there was nothing in it to assure me that I had done my full duty in his estimation. In the first place he places himself in the position of granting me a favor as to being ordered on duty. My orders to duty were signed by the Secretary of the Navy and to duty in the Bureau to which I had been assigned on the roster in case of war since my retirement in 1910. As to Dr. Braisted sending me on sight-seeing trips and the proposed sight-seeing trip overseas, I have to say that the duty which I performed was in doing my share in the making of the "proudest and highest state of efficiency the Medical Department of the Navy ever reached." He says nothing of the Bureau's foresight eight years prior to my retirement in preparing for war. As to a justifiable pride in the work of my successors, I considered that the four years of Surgeon General Stokes were not creditable but that Surgeon General Braisted's preparation for the war and his war work were most creditable, and I was proud of my old assistant. In the fifth paragraph he says nothing of my written reports and recommendations. In other words I had no work to do but he was sending me on sight-seeing trips. As a matter of fact, my orders were signed by the Secretary of the Navy or his representatives, and the special points to be reported upon were outlined by the Bureau.

I took this letter to Dr. Braisted and told him that I did not want it but a simple statement of my service. This he refused to give me. I went to the Bureau of Navigation and secured a copy of my last fitness report, from March 31, 1918 to November 18, 1918, and this showed conclusively that my work had been most satisfactory to the Surgeon General. He had given me 4, the highest mark obtainable in everything whether professional or administrative, my professional ability—"above the average; temperamental qualities, calm, even, forceful, active, painstaking." Under the head of "Remarks" he had written:

> This officer was detached from all duty and ordered home at his own request on November 18, 1918, coincident with the signing of the Armistice. During the period covered by this report, and due in part at least to his unusual activities and while preparing for further inspection work, this officer was taken severely ill with profuse and frequent hemorrhages which threatened his life and from which he ultimately recovered.
>
> The long experience of this officer in the Medical Corps of the Navy, and for years as Chief of Bureau, made his services of special value for general inspection work, in administrative and executive work, as well as on many Boards and Committees, such as the Council of National Defense. He was also of great service in connection with special duties and problems that were constantly arising in connection with the war.
>
> The Surgeon General considers that he was particularly fortunate during the great war, in having the valuable services of this experienced and able officer. Surgeon General Rixey's loyalty to the service and devotion to duty was particularly commendable. His deep interest in all that pertained to the work of the Navy in which he had been engaged so prominently so many years of his life has endeared him to me, and to all the members of his Corps, and his expressed

desire to continue in active work, notwithstanding his serious illness, shows a spirit of devotion to his duty and his country that was most commendable.

On April 2, 1914, in an address at the closing exercises of the Naval Medical School, Dr. Braisted said:

> "We are fortunate to have with us today some of the greatest men the medical department has ever known, men who have given their lives and earnest effort to make possible this great and beneficent arm of the Naval service. Foremost among them is our beloved and respected Surgeon General Rixey, than whom no one individual has ever accomplished more, or perhaps ever will, for the medical service of the country."

Again in June 1920, writing for the "Military Surgeons," he said:

> "It is safe to say that when war became imminent the United States had the most magnificent system of naval base hospitals in the world on a peace-time basis, and to meet war conditions it was only necessary to complete the emergency construction already planned."

Early in 1918, a careful investigation of the conduct of the Navy in war was made by sub-committee of the House Committee on Naval Affairs. Referring to the statement of that committee: "The first battle of the war, that against disease, was won by the Medical Department"—he should have added—and the preparation for it was begun in 1902 under Surgeon General Rixey by order of President Roosevelt—under whose administration I was enabled to build, on an average, one new hospital every year at the same time bringing the old ones up to modern requirements; the personnel of the Medical Corps almost doubled and the Medical School established, hospital corps, nurse corps, and all brought up to modern requirements.

The report of the committee reads in part as follows:

The first battle of the war, that against disease, was fought and won by the Medical Department of the Navy. After diplomatic relations with Germany were broken in February, 1917, we find recruits streaming into the service in increasing numbers, and in April there was grave danger that the overwhelming influx of volunteers would overtax all training stations and receiving ship facilities and bring disaster to the Navy at the very beginning of the war by the introduction and spread of epidemic diseases which unfortunately were widely prevalent throughout the country at that time. In spite of all the difficulties in the way of rapid expansion and the sudden necessity for the training of new medical personnel and hospital corpsmen, the health of the Navy has been even better than in peace times.

The Medical Department facilities have undergone tremendous development everywhere. The excellent and finely equipped base hospitals which were built before the war, have been greatly expanded with a speed which could not have been attained if the organization of the Medical Department as a whole had not been carefully thought out long before war came and plans perfected for the immediate enlargement of base hospitals and the construction of emergency hospitals of the finest type wherever necessary. The total bed capacity of naval hospitals was thus increased in a period of a few months from 3,800 to more than 15,000 beds. The mothers of the country can rest assured that in these hospitals their sons will receive excellent care and nursing and the most skilled treatment that modern medical and surgical knowledge permits. The Navy Nurse Corps, comprising women of the highest type in the nursing profession, has been increased to more than 700.

On board ship and at naval stations the health of the men is protected by all the safeguards known to preventive medicine. The Hospital Corps, upon which falls exclusively the nursing of the sick and wounded outside of hospitals, has been increased from 1,500 to nearly 9,000. Hospital Corps training schools have been established in connection with the training stations at San Francisco, Great Lakes, Newport, R. I., and Hampton Roads. In these schools young men of good character and aptitude are intensively trained for their duties at sea.

Foreseeing that the hospital ship now under construction would not be completed in time to meet the war needs of the service, two large liners were secured and converted into hospital ships to supplement the work of the Hospital Ship *Solace*.

Admiral Braisted arranged that the transports operated by the Navy should have ample medical department facilities and necessary equipment, and so far as naval facilities exist, has assumed responsibility for the medical and surgical care of all Army sick and wounded who may be transported home on naval vessels from Europe.

For the care of our naval forces in England, France and European waters, three base hospitals are already in operation abroad.

In expanding the Medical Department to meet the present and future needs of the Navy, we were glad to find that the needs of the increasing numbers of industrial workers and other civil employes in the large manufacturing plants and Navy Yards had not been overlooked. The peace-time humanitarian work is also being continued in connection with Haiti, Santo Domingo, Virgin Islands, Samoa and Guam, involving a population of over 2,000,000 people.

The report concludes with the statement: "It may well be said that the reason for this successful record is to be found in the Bureau's preparedness due to foresight and cooperation."

In the early months of the war, when the medical members of the Council of National Defense were studying our organization and work, they repeatedly expressed admiration of the smoothness of operation and the celerity with which large undertakings were accomplished. In fact they and others competent to judge, were of opinion that there was no finer medico-military organization in the world at the outbreak of war than that of the United States Navy.

For a true perspective of medical department preparedness it is necessary to go back several years. It is our business at all times to prepare for war. Long before events suggested the probability of war among European nations, preparations for war—any war—were going on steadily.

President Roosevelt, as early as 1902, had directed me to be ready for any emergency and the "excellent and finely equipped (permanent) base hospitals" were built or remodeled during my administration of the Bureau and with the idea of ready expansion.

I do not know of another permanent new naval hospital that has been built since I got Secretary Myer to sign the contracts for one at Newport, one at Boston, and one at Portsmouth, N. H., just before I was retired. Even with this start Surgeon General Braisted's administration just before and during the war is deserving of the highest commendation and much he owes me for sending him as an observer of the Russo-Japanese War and afterwards as my Assistant in the Bureau. For eight years I worked to make the medical department of the Navy ready for war. Seeing the importance of having observers of the medical activities of the Russo-Japanese War, I had surgeons Braisted and Speer ordered as observers and their reports are a matter of record. This unprecedented duty was made possible by President Roosevelt at my earnest request. Secretary Josephus Daniels at the closing exercises of the Naval Medical School, April 12, 1916, said:

> "Three of the greatest contributions that have been made in recent years to the literature of your profes-

sion were made by Naval officers. During the Russo-Japanese War your distinguished surgeon general, Dr. Braisted, was sent to study conditions in the Japanese fleet and Dr. Speer in that of the Russians. They wrote reports which you should read and which have helped doctors in all the countries engaged in the European struggles, and only this year, Dr. Fauntleroy made a study of conditions in Europe that is illuminating and invaluable.

"I am glad to see Dr. Rixey here, under whose administration the Medical Corps of the Navy made giant strides. * * * "

This shows conclusively what our World War Secretary of the Navy thought of my foresight.

Writing the Secretary of the Navy in 1918, I congratulated him upon his determination to reappoint Dr. Braisted as Surgeon General, and he replied:

THE SECRETARY OF THE NAVY
WASHINGTON

February 12, 1918.

My dear Dr. Rixey:

I am very glad you wrote me your warm commendation of my determination to reappoint Dr. Braisted. I recall when I was trying to decide who should be named four years ago you commended Dr. Braisted and I was largely influenced by your commendation, and I am now happy to thank you for it. He has lived up to all the good things you said about him.

With warm personal regards and highest esteem, I am,

Sincerely yours,

(Signed) JOSEPHUS DANIELS.

Rear Admiral Presley M. Rixey,
Surgeon General, U. S. N., Retired.

I was sorry to see Dr. Braisted give up the Bureau before his second tour of four years was completed as there was so much that he was best qualified to deal with and I felt that any new man would not be able to deal with as well, especially as Dr. Braisted's administration of the Bureau during the war had met with the Department's approval.

The work of bringing medical activities from a war to a peace-time basis was almost as great as preparing for the war. Fortunately Admiral Stitt was selected as his successor and I wrote my congratulations to the Secretary on his selection:

THE SECRETARY OF THE NAVY
WASHINGTON

December 2, 1920.

My dear Admiral:

I was very glad to get your note of congratulation upon the appointment of Admiral Stitt as Surgeon General of the Navy. I appreciate your approval very much because you know the character of man necessary to hold that important position.

With every good wish, I am,

Sincerely yours,

(Signed) JOSEPHUS DANIELS.

A few days afterwards I invited Mr. Daniels to dinner to meet Admiral Stitt and received the following reply:

THE SECRETARY OF THE NAVY
WASHINGTON

December 7, 1920.

My dear Admiral:

I thank you sincerely for your invitation to dine with you on December 11, at seven o'clock to meet our mutual friend, Rear Admiral Stitt, Surgeon General of the Navy. It has been with genuine regret that I find myself unable to accept, having previously accepted an invitation to attend the dinner of the Grid Iron Club at which I am to speak that evening at 7:30. I should greatly enjoy being with you and your guests, and am sorry I am unable to do so because of the conflict in dates.

My wife joins me in warm regards to you and Mrs. Rixey.

Sincerely yours,

(Signed) JOSEPHUS DANIELS.

* * * * *

In 1916, I was ordered as president of a board of examiners with Medical Directors Boyd and Lowndes as members to examine Medical Inspector Braisted for promotion to Medical Director, and while the board was in session I received an order from Secretary Daniels to examine Passed Assistant Surgeon Cary T. Grayson for promotion to the rank of Medical Director.

NAVY DEPARTMENT
WASHINGTON

January 17, 1917.

To: Surgeon General Presley M. Rixey, U. S. N., Retired,
President, Board Medical Examiners and
Naval Examining Board,
Bureau Medicine and Surgery, Navy Department.

SUBJECT: Examination of Passed Assistant Surgeon C. T. Grayson.

1. As the examining boards for the examination of Surgeon General Braisted are now in session, you will also conduct the examination of Passed Assistant Surgeon C. T. Grayson, who is recommended for the grade of Medical Director.

The Board gave Dr. Grayson practically the same examination we had given Dr. Braisted, only a somewhat more searching one as we recognized he was skipping the grades of Surgeon and Medical Inspector. The Board found both of these officers qualified for promotion to the grade of Medical Director and so reported.

This rapid promotion of Dr. Grayson from Passed Assistant Surgeon with the rank of Lieutenant to Medical Director with the rank of Rear Admiral was unprecedented and was due to his position as White House Physician. As such he had won the confidence and esteem of President Wilson, the Commander in Chief of the Army and Navy. Dr. Grayson had made himself personally and professionally almost indispensable to the President and he wished his physician to have the rank which this position justified. His promotion over the heads of so many officers of the Medical Corps was productive of much adverse criticism, not only by those officers, but by the rest of the officers of the Navy and especially by the Line, and there was a decided disposition to make him uncomfortable except by those of his friends who knew him best. There should have been no criticism of this young surgeon because he had made good in the difficult position assigned him. His record in the service was good and during my administration of the Bureau he was a general favorite personally, and his professional work most satisfactory whether ashore or afloat.

The feeling against him, however, on account of the President's order was so great that it was claimed that the board that examined him was packed and I, the President of the board, was his uncle. As a matter of fact, he had been ordered to appear before a board which had been convened to examine Dr. Braisted, and as to my being his uncle, I was no relation of Dr. Grayson and was only a connection by marriage, his half sister having married my youngest brother.

Having served as White House Physician myself for over ten years and having had the confidence, appreciation, and love of two great Presidents, I can thoroughly understand how Mr. Wilson felt towards his physician and his desire to do everything possible for him.

Dr. Grayson in accepting the extraordinary honor conferred upon him by his patient did only what any other man would have done, and moreover by being White House Physician he was in a position to do more for the upbuilding of his department than any other officer in the service—this I know from actual experience.

I had known Dr. Grayson for many years prior to his entry into the Navy and advised him how to proceed with his medical education so as to become a naval surgeon, and in the service he made good in every assignment I gave him. He was my aide on the "100 mile ride in a day" with President Roosevelt, and he was a friend of the Roosevelt family.

While Dr. Grayson was in Paris with President Wilson he sent me the following letter which gives some idea of his service overseas.

OFFICE OF THE PRESIDENT OF THE
UNITED STATES

Paris, 23 April, 1919.

Dear Doctor:

I was terribly disappointed to miss seeing you and Mrs. Rixey during my brief visit home the latter part of February, but I had lots of things to attend to, and while Gertrude and I fully intended running out to see you both, things developed at the White House so that I could not get away. Doctor Dennis at the Dispensary told me that he had seen you and that he never saw you looking better—which news pleased me very much. I hope everything continues to go well with you. I can imagine at this season of the year you are very busy with your farms and enjoying the out-door life.

I am having a wonderful experience in every way over here, but am kept very closely confined. In addition to my professional duties, the President gives me a lot of things of a personal nature to attend to, and as a personal aide I have to be on hand all the time. It is a great experience to meet the various foreign representatives and to know them, and it is a great privilege to see what is going on in the world's affairs behind the scenes here. I appreciate the great honor of being associated with the President and of having his confidence, especially during this grave period in the world's history. It is hard to realize on your side of the water the difficulties and complications which confront the President, but I believe that the time is not far distant when we will have a just settlement for the peace of the world.

In addition to the duties which I have mentioned, I have availed myself of numerous opportunities to visit the different hospitals—American and French—in Paris. The American doctors have done excellent work over here and they have reflected great credit on our profession. I have scarcely seen anything of the professional work of the Navy owing to the fact that there are no American Naval hospitals in Paris. The nearest one is at Brest, which is about twelve hours' ride on the train from Paris. As a whole the French have not made as good a showing professionally as our doctors, but there are scattering instances where they have performed brilliant feats in surgery.

I haven't seen anything of Eppa Rixey, who is over here, but several officers have spoken to me in the highest terms of the work which he has accomplished.

I have enjoyed a visit from my old friend, Frank H. Hitchcock, former Postmaster General, who spent a couple of weeks here.

While calling on General Foch recently I met General Drain. The sight of him created a longing for a game of golf on the Virginia links! Although we are only about fifteen minutes from a beautiful golf course the President was able to have only two games of golf since the first day of December. His physical powers have been taxed to the limit. It is almost beyond superhuman endurance what he has been going through. In addition to doing things himself he has had to spend a great deal of his strength in pushing others onward and making them get down to work. These people over here are great on parleying and dilly-dallying. But for the President's great ability in the way of making others do things, it is hard to tell how long this Conference would have lasted.

I see a good deal of Mr. Lloyd George and Mr. Balfour, and we have become good friends. We hope sometime to have a foursome game when opportunity affords. Mr. Clemenceau, as you know, has a bullet lodged in his lung. The X-Ray shows that it is in the center of his lung. He is 79 years of age. In a conversation with him a few days ago I asked him how he was feeling. He replied, "Excellent. You know, I go to bed every night at seven o'clock, get up at three, then read until seven o'clock, a. m., when I go out in my garden and work and exercise. In this way I keep from getting old." Then, with a twinkle in his eye, he added, "You know, we doctors can't afford to get old." Mr. Clemenceau was a doctor and practiced medicine until he was forty years of age, when he entered politics.

A few weeks ago the President was taken violently sick with the influenza. He was very sick for a few days. I am happy to say that he is now fully recovered.

I shall be glad when we are homeward bound, as I am particularly anxious to see Gertrude and the boys. I suppose you have seen them. I haven't seen the second little fellow, but have received the following cable from him:

> "I salute you. I weigh seven pounds and seven ounces, but am slightly bald. Mother, Gordon, and I send dearest love. Please write to me.
>
> LIEUTENANT CARY T. GRAYSON, JR."

He is evidently a hustler because I had a cable this morning saying that he is now a month old and weighs ten pounds.

When I get back I will have lots to tell you.

With warmest regards to you both, believe me,

Sincerely yours,

(Signed) CARY T. GRAYSON.

Admiral P. M. Rixey, U. S. N.,
Navy Department,
Washington, D. C.

Instead of being censured by anyone, his services should have been recognized as of great value to his department and his country and the work so ably performed had required not only the ability to perform but the greatest tact and judgment, all of which I think he has displayed.

The only picked board of examiners in the Navy that I am cognizant of was that of Surgeon General Stokes and he was permitted by Secretary Myer to name a special board for his promotion to Medical Director.

DEPARTMENT OF THE NAVY
BUREAU OF MEDICINE & SURGERY
WASHINGTON

January 15, 1913.

My dear Doctor Rixey:

I am about to be examined for promotion, rather a delayed examination, and have asked former Surgeon General Van Reypen and Medical Director Flint if they will be willing to serve as members of a Board for the mental and professional examination, and they have kindly agreed to do so.

I am writing this to beg of you the courtesy of expressing a willingness to serve on this Board as well.

The examination can be conducted in my office and need not, I should think, go further than an examination on record.

The regular Board will examine me physically.

I have held to the point that for me to appear before a Board of my juniors in rank, even though for promotion in grade, is unmilitary and not in accordance with the law. To this the Department has yielded and consequently I am asking that you permit me to put this burden upon you. I doubt if the examination will last longer than half an hour or more. I should be greatly obliged if you could telephone a reply to the bureau as soon as possible.

With kindest regards, I am,

Yours very truly,

(Signed) C. F. STOKES.

Surgeon General P. M. Rixey, U. S. N., Ret'd.,
1518 K Street, N. W.,
Washington, D. C.

I replied that if ordered, of course, I would serve on the Board.

DEPARTMENT OF THE NAVY
WASHINGTON

January 16, 1913.

From: Acting Secretary of the Navy
To: Surgeon General P. M. Rixey, U. S. N., Ret'd.,
1518 K Street, N. W., Washington, D. C.
SUBJECT: Member of Naval Examining Board, Bureau of Medicine & Surgery, Navy Department, Washington, D. C.

1. Having been appointed Member of a Naval Examining Board to convene at the Bureau of Medicine and Surgery, Navy Department, Washington, D. C., at 2:00 p. m., January 17, 1913, you will report to Surgeon General William K. Van Reypen, U. S. N., President of the Board, for this duty.

2. Upon the completion of this duty you will regard yourself detached from all duty.

3. This employment on shore duty is required by the public interests.

(Signed) B. WINTHROP.

The examination was held and no favoritism was shown, and after it was over he is said to have remarked that he wished he had gone before the regular board of examiners. I did my duty but I considered it very unpleasant duty as I personally disliked the man and I here give my first reason. When he relieved me as Surgeon General I told him that I wished to give him a dinner and have all the Bureau Chiefs meet him at the dinner. He accepted, and the night of the dinner all the guests had arrived but the guest of honor and over the phone I was informed that he was sick. He never gave me any excuse or apology. My second reason was that I did not approve of the course he was pursuing in the Bureau and I did all I could to prevent his being reappointed, and succeeded, as I was instrumental in having Dr. Braisted succeed him as Chief of the Bureau of Medicine and Surgery.

* * * * *

This concludes my personal sketch of fifty years of a Naval Medical officer's life, during which I was an intensely interested spectator of all that was done by those in power to preserve peace, at the same time doing my duty in an humble capacity as outlined by my Commander-in-Chief, Theodore Roosevelt, on the occasion of his appointing me Surgeon General of the Navy in 1902. He impressed upon me in no uncertain way that my first duty was the personnel of the Navy, its officers and men must be fit and kept fit for any emergency which might confront our country, and every material assistance must be supplied the medical personnel to attain that end. His views in regard to other departments of the Navy and the Navy as a whole were that it was to be ready to fight at all times. He believed, with our first President, that "In time of peace, prepare for war," as the only safeguard against war. His knowledge of Naval Affairs was of inestimable value to the Navy and his great concern regarding it was shown by his endeavor to find the best man for the office of Secretary of the Navy. On an average, he appointed a new Secretary every year he was our Chief Executive.

The success of the Medical Department of the Navy in the World War shows conclusively how well it did its part. I had the privilege of serving during this war in a position that enabled me to judge of this work to my great satisfaction, especially so in regard to the prevention of disease in the great body of men called to arms. When we compare the loss of our young men in the Army and Navy from communicable diseases during the World War with that of the Spanish-American war, a tremendous credit is due the Medical Departments of the sister services and the Public Health Service, which for the World War formed a part of the Medical Department of the Navy.

The Navy at the end of the World War had become second to none, and under no consideration should it ever for a moment lose this position in the World's Navies if peace is, as it should be, our main object.

CHAPTER XIII

COMMEMORATIVE OF FIFTY YEARS' SERVICE IN THE NAVY AND PRACTICE OF MEDICINE

AT A DINNER, January 28, 1924, in commemoration of fifty years' service in the U. S. Navy and practice of medicine, the following program was followed, and may be of interest. Before dinner, grace was said by James E. Freeman, Bishop of the Episcopal Diocese of Washington. After the dinner was finished, Dr. W. H. Bell, U. S. Navy, read the regrets of those invited who were unable to attend on account of previous engagements or for other reasons, among which were the following:

NAVY DEPARTMENT
ASSISTANT SECRETARY'S OFFICE
WASHINGTON

January 15, 1924.

Dear Doctor and Mrs. Rixey:

I wish it were possible for me to be with you on the twenty-eighth. I should like so much to be a member of the party celebrating the Doctor's "golden wedding" to the service. Unfortunately, however, on that night, I am speaking in Elmira, New York.

Affectionate best wishes to you both.

(Signed) TED.

700 North Walnut Street,
West Chester, Pa.
January 19, 1924.

Dear Admiral and Mrs. Rixey:

Mrs. Braisted and I were much pleased to receive your invitation for dinner, on January 28th, in commemoration of "Fifty years service in the U. S. Navy and practice of medicine" and regret that we cannot be present owing to the distance and official engagements at that time.

We both want to congratulate you on such a splendid record of life work and a reputation that has made the name of Rixey and the Medical Department of the Navy known to the World.

We realize that your life work and endeavor has made our own and that of many others possible, and we feel for you a deep and affectionate regard.

Two names stand out, to my mind, in the history of the Medical Department of the Navy, that of our first Surgeon General Barton and that of Surgeon General Rixey whose efforts have made the Medical Department of the Navy the leading medico-military service of the world.

We who have had the honor and privilege to work with and after you, have tried, so far as we were able, to carry on and complete what was so splendidly formulated by you.

All glory and honor to our respected Chief, and we trust that those to come in the history of the Country, will more and more learn to appreciate and venerate the name of Surgeon General Rixey.

With esteem and personal regard,

Sincerely yours,

(Signed) WILLIAM C. BRAISTED.

Rear Admiral Rodman who commanded the Grand Fleet in European waters during the World War, wrote:

January 16, 1924.

Dear Doctor and Mrs. Rixey:

Mrs. Rodman and I very much appreciate your invitation to dinner on the 28th, and ordinarily would accept with a great deal of pleasure, but will be compelled to decline owing largely to Mrs. Rodman's state of health.

She joins me in hearty congratulations on having performed fifty years of service, and I can add from my own knowledge, that it is far and away above the average. And may fifty years more be added to a famous career!

Yours sincerely,

(Signed) HUGH RODMAN.

Rear Admiral Charles J. Badger, a shipmate of Dr. Rixey's, wrote:

7 Kenwin Road,
Winchester, Mass.
January 17, 1924.

Dear Admiral and Mrs. Rixey:

Your very kind invitation to dinner, January 28th, in celebration of the fiftieth anniversary of the Admiral's Naval service and Practice of Medicine has just reached me.

I wish I could help you celebrate and at the same time give you both my hearty congratulations, but as it is, I am too far away for anything but the congratulations upon so long and successful life and service.

I have been here in Winchester with Bessie and her family since last summer. Not to mention Bessie and her husband, the children are a great comfort to me and I am happier here than anywhere else, for the present at least.

Oscar is home from the Asiatic Station and with his family, one little girl and his wife—is living in my house in Cleveland Park. They want me to go there and perhaps next fall I shall do so, but I have as yet made no plans and this is a mighty pleasant place for the Grandpa.

I trust you are both well. Bessie joins me in much love and wishes for all happiness in the year just commencing.

Sincerely yours,

(Signed) Charles J. Badger.

U. S. Naval Hospital
Washington

January 25, 1924.

My very dear friend:

It is impossible for me to tell you how greatly I appreciated your very kind invitation for your commemorative dinner on January the 28th, and how I regretted having to send the formal declination, which was mailed to you several days ago. The occasion is not only one of great sentimental significance to those of your friends who may be privileged to be present, but is also, in reality, the commemoration of fifty years of most notable public service.

As one of your colleagues in the Navy Department more than twenty years ago, I have personal knowledge of the splendid work performed by you as Head of the Medical Department of the Navy. As a matter of fact, I am now personally benefiting through residence at one of the splendid hospital establishments which you initiated and developed during your period of service.

Although unable to be present in person, I shall be with you in spirit, and you and Mrs. Rixey have my most earnest good wishes for health and happiness for many years to come, in which good wishes Mrs. Capps most heartily joins.

Affectionately, your friend,

(Signed) W. C. Capps.

1600 Sixteenth Street
Washington, D. C.

January 23, 1924.

Dear Admiral:

I am so sorry that long before I knew that the fiftieth anniversary of your association with Medical Corps of the Navy was to occur on Monday next I made an engagement to be out of town, which engagement it is impossible for me to cancel. And so I am taking this occasion to express to you my own admiration and sense of personal obligation to you for what you have done for the Medical Corps of the Navy and for many a youngster who found himself in the Medical Corps through your influence and inspiration—one of whom I am.

It is a source of great gratification to your friends and admirers, as well as to yourself, that you modernized the naval hospitals, established the naval hospital ship, built up the most progressive naval medical school—surpassed perhaps by none in the world—introduced female nurses into the Medical Corps, and, indeed, turned an archaic system into the present system—of which every man who wears the uniform is so proud. We who know what opposition you encountered and the masterful way in which you overcame it, can and do appreciate beyond the general public your enduring service to the United States Navy.

This is very little of what I might say at great length, and should like to say, if I could be present at the dinner.

I do not need to tell you that in addition to my admiration of your official career, I esteem for you personally an undying affection.

Faithfully yours,

(Signed) Cary T. Grayson.

From Captain Robert M. Kennedy, M. C., U. S. Navy:

Naval Hospital
Annapolis, Md.

January 16, 1924.

Dear Admiral Rixey:

It is with deepest regret that I shall not be able to accept your very kind invitation to dinner Monday evening, January twenty-eighth, at seven o'clock, on account of a previous dinner engagement.

I should like very much to be present, especially in view of the fact that it is in commemoration of fifty years of naval service and practice of medicine.

With many thanks, and kindest regards and best wishes for Mrs. Rixey and yourself, in which Mrs. Kennedy joins me, I am.

Cordially yours,

(Signed) ROBERT M. KENNEDY.

THE JOHNS HOPKINS UNIVERSITY
SCHOOL OF HYGIENE AND PUBLIC HEALTH
BALTIMORE, MD.

January 18, 1924.

My dear Admiral and Mrs. Rixey:

I cannot content myself with a mere formal reply to your kind invitation to dinner on Monday, January 28th.

To my very deep regret I am unable to accept, as I have an important engagement on that evening which I cannot cancel. I have made an appointment with Dr. Balfour of London, recently appointed director of the new school of Hygiene there, and with a representative of the Rockefeller Foundation for a confrence on matters which are of considerable importance.

Believe me that no ordinary engagement would keep me from participating in a festive occasion in honor of your fifty years' service in the Navy and the practice of medicine. I should like to have joined with your many friends in paying my personal tribute to your useful and patriotic services and to personal and professional qualities which exemplify the best standards of our profession. Above all I should have been happy to greet you in memory of our old friendship and to renew associations which I have found so agreeable and helpful.

I beg you and Mrs. Rixey to accept my heartiest felicitations and my best wishes for years of continued health, prosperity and happiness.

Very sincerely yours,

(Signed) WILLIAM H. WELCH.

W. S. THAYER, M. D.
1208 Eutaw Place
Baltimore, Md.

January 18, 1924

Dear Admiral Rixey:

I meant to write by hand but I shall have to dictate this to tell you how really sorry I am that I shall miss your fiftieth anniversary dinner. But I have an engagement which takes me out of town that it will be impossible for me to break—at least I think so. If by any chance I can get out of it, I am going to write to ask for permission to come, for, my dear friend, I have a very deep and sincere regard for you and the work that you have done in a life which is already long. Who could fail to be touched by your ideals, your accomplishments, and last but not least, your real sportsmanship!

With love and every good wish, believe me,

Yours very truly,

(Signed) W. S. THAYER.

THE HOWARD A. KELLY HOSPITAL, INC.
1418 Eutaw Place
Baltimore, Md.

January 18, 1924.

Dear Mrs. Rixey:

What a delightful occasion that will be when my dear friend, Admiral Rixey, rounds out half a century of splendid service. I wish I could be with you and him and his friends to celebrate the occasion; I shall be prevented, however, by an absence in the West in Michigan, much to my regret.

With sincere affection, yours,

(Signed) HOWARD A. KELLY.

JOHNS HOPKINS UNIVERSITY AND HOSPITAL
Baltimore, Md.

January 23, 1924.

My dear Admiral Rixey:

I hope you will pardon the delay and this typewritten letter, but I am anxious to write you in detail why I cannot be present at the dinner to which you have so kindly invited me. I had hoped by delaying that it might be possible for me to go, but unfortunately important things have arisen which will make it absolutely impossible for me to get away, much as I would like to do so. I can't tell you how much I appreciate the great honor you have done in inviting me and there is no one in this country who would like more to meet with you and celebrate your 50 years of service in the U. S. N. and practice of medicine, in which you have been such an illustrious example of the highest type of medical man and administrator. Your work in the U. S. N. has probably done more for medical progress than any other one man in this country and I wish to assure you of my great admiration and regret that I cannot be present.

With the kindest regards and best wishes, I am,

Very sincerely yours,

(Signed) HUGH H. YOUNG.

Dr. Bell read short extracts from letters of the eight Secretaries of the Navy under whom Dr. Rixey had served during his incumbency as Chief of the Bureau of Medicine & Surgery, which clearly showed the great esteem these officials had for Dr. Rixey and for the work he accomplished. These extracts showed how well Dr. Rixey kept the good opinion of these men, while in a very diplomatic way he had to go over their heads—an absolute necessity, as most of the eight secretaries knew little of Naval affairs, due to their short terms of office as head of the Navy Department.

Dr. Bell then read letters from Secretary of the Navy, Josephus Daniels, as to Dr. Rixey's service during the World War, which showed his continued interest in the Navy. He read also the commendation from Admiral Dewey as to Dr. Rixey's achievements as Surgeon General of the Navy, and read extracts from letters of President Roosevelt already printed in this book.

After which, Dr. Bell introduced the toastmaster of the evening—Honorable R. Walter Moore, Representative in Congress from Virginia.

Mr. Moore said:

I should have spent my time today in considering what I was to say on this occasion, but instead of that I was interested in something of a Naval problem—the Teapot Dome Controversy—and it will be proper for me to detain you only a minute or two, in order to congratulate our distinguished friend upon the success that has attended his career and upon the fact that he reaches this anniversary in such a happy frame of mind.

I remember that Edmond Burke said in his great Bristol speech something that is very often quoted, but it has always seemed to me to be a mistake. His colleague, upon the ticket with him for appointment to the House of Commons had died suddenly. A great throng appeared and Mr. Burke said before the assembly: "What shadows we are and what shadows we pursue." When we think of such a life as that of our friend, here, we cannot share in any such sentiment as that. There has been nothing shadowy about his life, nothing shadowy about his purposes which he has had in view and that which he has accomplished. I know he is looking back now rather than forward, and I hope he is going to tell us something of his earlier days—something of the difficulties that he encountered and overcame. He is thinking perhaps tonight, and I trust he will say something, about that time, when in his section of Virginia just after the

Rear Admiral Presley Marion Rixey and Two of His Dogs "Tobias" and "Puff," on The Lawn at "Rixey"

close of the Civil War the men, women, and children were called upon to make the utmost sacrifices in order to rebuild the country which had unfortunately been devastated; that he will tell us something of his mother and her advice to him to go to that beautiful institution—the University of Virginia; of his receiving his medical degree in nine months—almost as remarkable as John Marshall taking his degree as a lawyer after studying about six weeks; about his entrance into the United States Navy, and the beginning of his service that has been of such very great value in every way to his country. I hope we will hear something of all of that from our friend whom we so much honor.

We thank Dr. Rixey for having us with him upon this red-letter occasion, upon this golden anniversary we congratulate him upon this gathering here tonight which is so honorably participated, and we hope that there are many years to follow of serene days and happy hours, and that he will long remain with us in order that we may do him the honor to pay him the tribute which he merits in such a very high degree. It is not for me but rather for our friends to do the talking and I trust that Admiral Rixey now will do us the favor of speaking to us.

Dr. Rixey then greeted his guests and read to them a short synopsis of his fifty years service.

My Friends: The pleasure you have given me tonight by your presence, representing not only yourselves but the host of others in official and private life whom I could not reach, cannot be estimated in words. Whatever the achievements that have been and are ascribed to me could not have been accomplished but for yourselves and those you represent here tonight. Those who have gone before, those, who as I, have grown old in the service, and you younger men who are taking up the burdens of the day—all have been most helpful in the arduous duties that have fallen to me, and my gratitude, appreciation and affection are beyond expression. Those who are not here tonight comprise so many that I cannot enumerate them—in official life there were two Presidents—McKinley and Roosevelt, their cabinets, members of the Supreme Court, senators, congressmen, Admirals of the Navy, Generals of the Army, all the way down to the apprentice boys. In private life my appreciation is equally due to those splendid men in professional life, many of them old when I was commencing my career, and last but not least, my patients whose appreciation of my efforts to care for them made hard work a pleasure.

My service for the first forty years was a wonderful experience for a farmer boy, and what comes in a measure to every young medical officer. I made good use of it in gaining experience in professional work so that my reputation as a medical man came at an opportune time to the ears of President McKinley and I became White House Physician, and in the short two years before his tragic death he was as dear to me as a brother. His voluntary promise, without solicitation, to make me Surgeon General, when a vacancy occurred, was carried out by President Roosevelt, and the prominent features of my official career began.

Fortunately for me Mr. Roosevelt was well versed in naval affairs, and I saw at once that with his "*Do or Die*" views of life I had to put my best foot forward and keep it there. He directed me to continue my duties as White House Physician. Immediately after assuming duties as Chief of the Bureau of Medicine and Surgery I asked him what kind of a Navy he wanted—"a Navy on paper, or one always ready to fight." His face turned red, his teeth came together with a click, and his right hand came down on the table with great force as he snapped out: "*It Must Be Ready to Fight at the Drop of a Hat.* You are and will be responsible for the Medical Department of the Navy. The personnel must be fit and kept fit."

Now, *Gentlemen*, this was an entering wedge, and I saw a chance for the recognition of the Medical Department of the Navy as never before, to the end that the efficiency of the Navy would be immeasurably increased. All I had to do during the seven years I was with him was to refer to his instructions to me to have his interest, and once aroused he sifted the point at issue to the finest particle. I took no trifling matters to him and was always sure I was right in any matter I referred to him. In my eight years as Surgeon General I served under *eight* Secretaries of

INTERIOR VIEW OF DINING ROOM AT "RIXEY"

the Navy, and everyone of them were dear friends and most of them my patients I always consulted them before taking a question to the President, clearly explaining what my relations with the President were and how he often questioned me as to my work. As to those needs of the Medical Department requiring Congressional action, I relied upon Congressmen, many of them patients as well as friends, and my brother, a member of the Naval Committee of the House of Representatives.

My service in the World War came very near, at its end, being my end, and my life has since never been as before.

In commemorating my half century of service to the relief of suffering humanity and as a naval officer, I want you to include that of a very dear friend of fifty years standing and my senior in point of service, and in the practice of his profession—I refer to DR. JOHN C. BOYD, of the United States Navy—a more loyal friend in all the past 50 years, a better posted or more efficient officer, I have not known. He was my best man almost 50 years ago when I was married and he has been the same ever since. For the first time tonight he has disappointed me—instead of being here to help me commemorate our long service he goes to Florida. I forgive him as I do not believe that any of us can do otherwise, as he is with us tonight in all that goes for a half century of service.

With what success we have spent the past fifty years remains for others to judge.

* * * * * * * *

It may be well to say what has sustained me most in these past years, and so I am going to read a few verses founded on the 23rd Psalm of David:

In "pastures green?" Not always; sometimes He
Who knoweth best, in kindness leadeth me
In weary ways, where heavy shadows be.

Out of the sunshine, warm and soft and bright,
Out of the sunshine into darkest night,
I oft would faint with sorrows and affright.

Only for this; I know He holds my hand;
So, whether led in green or desert land,
I trust, although I may not understand.

Beside "still waters?" No, not always so;
Oft times the heavy tempest 'round me blow,
And o'er my soul the waves and billows go.

But when the storms beat loudest, and I cry
Aloud for help, the Master standeth by,
And whispers to my soul, "Lo, it is I."

Above the tempest wild I hear Him say,
"Beyond this darkness lies the perfect day:
In every path of thine I lead the way."

So, whether on the hilltops high and fair
I dwell, or in the sunless valleys where
The shadow's lie, what matter? He is there.

And more than this: Where'er the pathway lead,
He gives to me no helpless, broken reed,
But His own hand, sufficient for my need.

So, where He leads me I can safely go:
And in the blest hereafter I shall know
Why in His blest wisdom He hath led me so.

Mr. Moore continued:

Dr. Rixey and Mrs. Rixey are among my most distinguished constituents. I am very proud to represent them, very proud to number them among the great Virginians I have known. (Mr. Moore then related an incident in the life of George Washington showing how his mother had influenced him to remain in the United States services instead of joining the British Navy.) I have mentioned this because, representing a District like this, we so naturally harp back to these historical occasions of which this country is so full. No other section of the Union is so radiant with stories of the past as this land—with its Mt. Vernon, its Monticello, its Oak Hill, and Arlington, the home of one of the most wonderful men in modern history, Robert E. Lee.

I am now going to have the pleasure of introducing one of the successors of Admiral Rixey—Admiral E. R. Stitt, the Surgeon General of the Navy at this time—a man who has probably done as much scientific and practical work applied to the principles of Medicine and Surgery and in making the world safe for democracy, as almost anyone who is in the services of the United States. I beg to introduce that distinguished gentleman, Admiral Stitt, Surgeon General and the father of bacteriology and tropical medicine in the U. S. Navy.

Admiral Stitt said:

Several weeks ago I went over the details of the Naval Medical School for the purpose of preparing a memorandum, and it was a surprise to me to see how Dr. Rixey kept that school going—there was the greatest opposition to men being taken from duty aboard the ships and other naval activities and assigned to a course of instruction at the Naval Medical School. In many ways I feel that in the establishment of that school and the continuing of his efforts in connection with the school that he did one of the greatest services for the Medical Corps of the Navy because it doesn't make any difference how well equipped the hospitals are, the main thing for accomplishment of great success is the equipment and training of the men in charge of the hospital. I think that he has furthered the professional development of the men in the Medical Corps and that the present status of the medical department of the Navy is largely due to his efforts on insisting upon such an institution.

I had the particulars brought to my desk in connection with the construction and rehabilitation of our hospitals—and started with our hospital furthest north on the Atlantic Coast, but presently I found that it was entirely unnecessary because apparently at every hospital of the U. S. Navy he had left his stamp in construction or reconstruction of hospitals. There is something I have here which I doubt very much if Admiral Rixey has figures about—I learned that he spent $4,313,744.94 in the building of these numerous hospitals and in the reconstruction of the old hospitals. You remember in 1882 the law was passed that they were to stop repairing old ships and to build modern ships. It really was not until 1904 when Surgeon General Rixey was Chief of the Bureau of Medicine and Surgery that they began to put this into effect for the hospitals of the Navy. You know that in those days we looked upon $100,000 much as we do now upon a million—and how in the world he succeeded in getting so much money from Congress as the four millions mentioned before—is something which he will have to reveal to us.

Those of us in the service know the difficulties he encountered. Our very much loved Chief Clerk of the Bureau of Medicine and Surgery, Dr. Gibson, was telling me this afternoon of the difficulties encountered when Dr. Rixey endeavored to build a modern and up to date hospital at the U. S. Naval Academy, Annapolis, Md. Those in control at the Naval Academy and in the Navy Department preferred that we simply have "sick quarters" at the Academy rather than a hospital we could be proud of. I have forgotten how many times Dr. Rixey was sent to Annapolis to select the site for the hospital—and every time he was most cordially received—but they never would allow him to select the site. In this case also, he eventually had his way, and those acquainted with the Naval Academy know that we have as well-equipped a hospital as you will find anywhere.

Now, as I think about his accomplishments I don't know that as much smooth sailing in connection with hospital affairs was effected by him as his work in the establishment of the "Female Nurse Corps," one of his greatest achievements. Before we had a female nurse corps I must say we had very efficient hospital Corps men, who so far as the medical work went gave the officers much satisfaction, but a man never can serve the food for a sick man in the way that a woman can, so that there were always complaints about the food and the service by the well-meaning hospital corpsmen, but when we had our female nurse corps it didn't make any difference what you gave the sick man—it was always pleasing to him, and for the people in command of hospitals it has made a very different matter of running the Naval hospital.

Another thing that probably very few of us have thought of is Dr. Rixey's establishment of the Medical Bulletin. I don't know what we would do today to inform the medical officers of the Navy of late advances in medical science and to give publicity to the various orders of the Department without this bulletin.

If I had the time it seems that outside of these great things that he has done for us I could keep you all for a much longer time, but I feel that I must say at least this in appreciation of how much Admiral Rixey has done for us.

Mr. Moore, the toastmaster, then introduced Bishop Freeman, who spoke at length of his acquaintance with Dr. Rixey and related several incidents of past friendship. He told of his affection for Mr. Roosevelt, and then referred to Dr. Rixey as "the man who watched over Mr. Roosevelt through his entire time in the White House."

Bishop Freeman continued:

There are two other things which made me feel interested in this great occasion. During the World War it was my privilege to come in very close contact with both the Secretary of the Navy and the Secretary

RECEPTION HALL AT "RIXEY"—FACING LIVING ROOM

of War, and while serving in the various camps and naval stations I met the men and officers of the Army and Navy at very close range during the active period of the war, and I never expect to meet a better body of men than it was my privilege to associate with. I used to return to Washington with glowing accounts of the men who were training for duty on ships and for land service—and for that reason I find here that which is exceedingly appealing to me. Then too, Admiral Rixey, in your capacity—our associations have been very happy, and I confess to you very inspiring and stimulating. I always felt, Admiral Rixey, that there was a very close connection between our professions. Let us never forget that the ministry of the Master was in a very peculiar sense a ministry to the bodies of men. He sought to reveal their souls, to make them conscious of them, but He dealt with men as He found them in every class and kind, and in ministering to their bodies He ministered to their souls—it seems to me that the highest exercise of your office is along these lines, and am I wrong in my estimate of you that there has been a decided tendency of late years to look upon the practice of medicine perhaps as something more than mere ministry to body? At least this is my estimate of you. Now, my dear Admiral, I am not here to make a speech. When you go to your pillow tonight and to your rest, it is not so much the felicitation of these your loving friends, invited to break bread with you and to enjoy this occasion, that will come to your mind, but in the quiet after this brilliant affair you will recall what you know of yourself and also what your Master could say about you. To you—Dr. Rixey—length of life, greater honors if you can have greater honors, and I doubt if you can have greater than you now enjoy, life, and strength, and the companionship of your wife for years to come. But, my dear fellow, the best thing you have is a clear conscience, a clear conscience that makes you believe, as I am confident, that you are in favor with God and man. There comes a certain stage in life when honors come to count for mighty little. A man says to himself—I have made my mistakes and I am conscious of them, but so far as I was able I tried to play the game like a man. My first and foremost obligation was to Him whose I am and Whom I serve.

My dear friend, the finest thing I can say about you is this. You have not only been a fine man in your profession, and in serving your time you have not only carried the finest honors, you have not only been a distinguished citizen of the state and the nation that you have served, but you have always thought in all the things you have done that after all, when the final assize is said and the record of life is disclosed, the best thing a man carries in this world and into eternity is a conscience.

A few lines from Shakespeare come back to me: "His life was gentle, and the elements so mixed with him that nature cried out to all the world 'This was a man.' "

General Ireland, Surgeon General of the Army, said:

When you became Surgeon General of the Navy you established a very warm friendship with the medical officers of the Army. I know of the ups and downs he had in the ministrations of his office, of the establishment of the Naval Medical School, and of many other problems which he solved under difficult circumstances. I am glad to hear Admiral Stitt say that he looks upon the establishment of the Naval Medical School as one of the accomplishments of Dr. Rixey. I consider the Army Medical School one of the greatest things for the Army. I present to you, Dr. Rixey, the congratulations of the Medical Corps of the Army, and I hope that you will enjoy many years of life as an example to all in the service and as an inspiration in the work.

Mr. Moore said:

We have with us this evening another gentleman, educated at the University of Virginia, of which Dr. Rixey is an alumnus. He is concerned with a new work—a work that we all should be giving more attention to—not only the members of the medical profession but the citizens of the country as well—and that is Public Health work which has been so much neglected up to this time. We neglect to consider the very paramount importance of what we have come to call the "Public Health Work." As was remarked a short while ago Congress has become even more "hardboiled" than ever before. Nevertheless, we have initiated this

MRS. PRESLEY MARION RIXEY IN HER ZENIA GARDEN AT "RIXEY"

work. I have the honor to introduce to you, Surgeon General H. S. Cumming of the Public Health Service, a very efficient, very loyal and devoted son of Virginia, and a graduate of the University of which we are so proud in Virginia.

Surgeon General Cumming spoke as follows:

I am sure that those who have called upon me know of my great affection for Dr. Rixey. He has been pointed out at the University of Virginia as one of its most famous graduates. I was privileged during the war to be detailed in the Office of the Surgeon General of the Navy and was thrown with Dr. Rixey a great deal, and I had the opportunity to see the confidence and affection which Admiral Braisted and all the medical officers had for him. I appreciate more than I can tell you being here tonight to celebrate this occasion, and on behalf of the officers of the Public Health Service, I wish you, Dr. Rixey, a very long life, and I hope that we will be together for many years to come.

Mr. Moore then introduced Dr. Robert Johnston, Rector of St. John's Church, where Dr. Rixey is a devoted attendant.

I feel at home here. Why I feel at home I don't know. Dr. Rixey has thrown his heart and soul into St. John's, and in his activities there as well as in the Navy he has seemed to be gifted in knowing exactly what he wants, in knowing how it should be done, and in having it done. Dr. Rixey has had the satisfaction of knowing that he hasn't wasted his time. It must be a great satisfaction to him to know that apart from the flowers of speech and apart from the possible exaggeration of his very great achievements cited here tonight, and when he has made a very liberal discount of his own limitations (which it is my duty to point out), and also for good luck and good fortune, he knows as he comes to the evening of life that there are real flowers of very deep and very sweet affection being offered to him by his friends while he is still here.

Of course, my sympathy for Mrs. Rixey tonight is marked, as it always has been. Admiral Rixey may have had great difficulties in his life which he has overcome, but I rather imagine it is due to Mrs. Rixey's patience as well that he has been able to reach this time in life, and that probably most of these great tributes laid at his feet tonight belong to her. I make this deduction from his honors tonight, at the same time wishing him continued years of happiness, health, and prosperity, in order that it may be possible for her to live with him for the rest of his life. I wish them both a great deal of joy.

Captain Bell spoke as follows:

I haven't any right up here at this table among these eloquent speakers, but in view of the fact that I am here by direction of our most gracious host, I am going to play the game as well as I can. In anticipation of this commemoration I had no advance information that I was going to be asked to say anything, but in the full belief that "good luck is good management"—I have prepared a few notes, and I am going to deliver a perfectly good extemporaneous speech in writing! Dr. Johnston's last few words gave me a comforting satisfaction in that I have the distinction, at least of those who have made remarks so far, in giving dual consideration in this paper to Dr. Rixey and Mrs. Rixey.

Dr. Rixey is a man who has infinitely more than held his own both in satisfaction of his own personal urge and to the advancement of that with which he, for the moment or as a forward visioned purpose, identified himself. He, early in his career laid his course by the compass of '76 and he has never been satisfied in his endeavors with the windward side of a sea-going pie. It behooves us all to observe on which tack the ship has been laid before selecting our half of the pie in process of baking. I am most gratified to have been included among those invited to participate in this commemoration and I am here fully conscious—agreeably conscious of its meaning. As one who labored close under the kindly but insistent lash of his leadership, I know whereof I speak.

This occasion punctuates a record of usefulness and distinction at a period in the course of an individual life (still going strong) when to pause in this delightful fashion and contemplate its past is eminently fitting. It is the golden anniversary of the marriage of that life to its best possibilities in a chosen profession, and service and in those super-

opportunities which capability and personal charm were instrumental in creating.

It is primarily an occasion for congratulation upon the grace with which our host bears the number of years, suggested by 50 years of adult pursuit, which time has settled upon his devoted head. It is primarily an occasion for congratulation upon the accomplishment which our host, as doctor and Rear Admiral, must feel. But it is also an occasion for a review of those accomplishments and a reminiscent mood of the friends here gathered about him. We will not delay expression of appreciation too long—nor shall he need to "play dead," as our poet of recent fame did, to learn "our regard and what is in our hearts for him."

Someone, I think Pope, said: "Be to my virtues not unkind, and to my faults a little blind." What more reasonable injunction and who more intelligently and sympathetically capable of observing it than friends, who are without the bias that either near relationship or ill disposition engenders. Faults we all have, as even the great with whom Dr. Rixey was privileged to associate acknowledged of themselves. Indeed, the appealing humility of such acknowledgments is one of the signs of their greatness, and Dr. Rixey has the virtue of frankly and openly recognizing this. But in appraising those traits of character commonly accounted faults, it is not the vision of them at short range and out of relation to the whole picture which gives true values. Some virtues in their practical effect become faults, some faults in their influence upon the course of events under one's control may be esteemed virtues. Certainly, in these days of inaccuracy, and neglect of the requirements of dependability and disregard of the obligations of responsible manhood, patience and the dead level of even temperament get us nowhere and in the end cease to be virtues. The antithesis of these qualities has and always has had an important place in the progress of the world's interests, and the impatience and high temper which Dr. Rixey acknowledges were the at times uncontrolled expression of the quick perception, alertness of mind and body, optimism and tireless energy which characterized his attention to professional, official and personal concerns. He worked himself as hard as he worked his staff; he exacted of himself no less than he expected of the subordinates of his corps. If at times he appeared hard in his demands it was because he saw the importance, in broadly beneficial effect, of this or that part of his program and was anxious for quick realization of these effects. I recall the pressure under which I worked as a member of his official family and how frequently I left his office fearful of my ability to do his bidding in the time proposed. A willingness to do, however, covered a multitude of sins with him and back of his apparently severe mien was a chuckle and a warmth of feeling and a large, tender heart which never permitted him to needlessly wound the sensibilities of another and which always prompted a generous consideration of those in difficulty.

His bark was never a good index of his bite, though he set his jaw firmly to a course that was just. He always had and still has a concern for the efficiency of the Navy. He always was and still is interested to see his corps deliver its full quota to that efficiency, and during his active service career he fought not only for what he considered necessary to that end but for all that was legitimately attainable and vital to the dignity and fair promise of his profession in the Navy. No indifference or delayed action upon the part of those to whom he had to appeal for enabling decisions or legislation discouraged him in his purpose or his hope of ultimate attainment. His was the "tenacity" but not always the "methods" of the bull dog and we will all agree that he lacks the physical conformation suggestive of that canine species. He returned to the task he had set himself again and again, but by different routes if variation seemed desirable. No opposition dismayed him and yet in the assertion of the desserts and rights and needs of his corps he never lost sight of or neglected the just dues of his fellow officers of the line. "They were, as now, men to be proud of and most fully did he recognize their claim to the country's gratitude and highest praise." But they and the officers of his corps were of one service, with a common end in view, and what he did in the building up of his Department toward its utmost contribution to that common end is now a matter of history. His work has made it relatively easy for his successors to carry on. To him we owe our modern hospitals, our dental corps, our nurse corps, our schools, much of Medical Department standing in relation to the rest of the service, and many other things that are of ethical as well as material benefit. The whole service has profited as is freely and generally acknowledged without distinction of branch. He did more for the corps and service in general than any Surgeon General either before or since, present company always excluded. His achievements were recognized outside of our service, and outside this country, and the crowning event of his active career in the Navy, it seems to me, was when, as Surgeon General of the Navy and also as President of the Military Surgeons of the United States, the Surgeons General of the Royal Army and Royal Navy and of the Italian Army and other high ranking officers of foreign services, attended the meeting of that organization over which he presided, in *compliment to him.*

No remarks commemorating this occasion would be complete without pointed mention of that dear companion of his joys and difficulties who has stood staunchly and wisely helpful at his side. This is an anniversary in which she shares the implied honors and the congratulations we may here extend. None knows so well as our host how much he owes Mrs. Rixey and none is more ready than he to credit her account with a partner's portion of the earnings.

So here's to them both on this eventful day,
Which punctuates the years of their felicity,
And gathers their friends in a spirit to pay
The homage their due indisputably.

WATCHING THE SUNSET FROM THE WEST PORTICO OF THE NEW HOME

May they live long and prosper,
With recurring celebration,
And may each year add lustre,
To their now brilliant escutcheon.

* * * * *

Admiral McCormick:

I come from Virginia, but from so far back in the woods that there is some superstition about it. Sometime ago—so the story has it—a flying machine landed in the corn fields near my place, and when it alighted the aviator got out and an old colored man ran to him and said—in a very excited tone—"How are you Marse Jesus? How you left your farm?"

I wish to mention the business ability of Dr. Rixey to show that his constructive work outside of the Navy has been equal to that in the Navy. He has raised fine horses, Jersey cattle, and has cultivated extensive farms, and his work has been constructive wherever he has been—both in the U. S. Navy and elsewhere. We in Virginia feel that he is one of the leading men in farming and agriculture in general, as also we in the Navy know he is a fine surgeon. It is a great pleasure to be able to call him "Doctor." We have an unbounded debt due him for the service he has performed for his country.

Dr. Sinclair Bowen of Washington then said:

Admiral Rixey, I didn't have any idea that I was to have this honor tonight. Your record has been so beautifully stated by those who know it so well that I shall not say one word about it, but there is a personal equation I would like to say something about. I first met Dr. Rixey at the home of Dr. Busey, when Dr. Rixey was paying a call. After Dr. Rixey left, he said: "There is Surgeon Rixey of the Navy who does more medical work than any man in Washington"—and he spoke of his great power for work. I never knew in my life a man who could do as much work as Dr. Rixey. When I first started to practice here in Washington I suppose I began like many others—in very moderate circumstances—in fact, most of my patients were in Willard Tree Alley and I had quite a nice practice. One day Dr. Rixey came in and introduced me to a Cabinet member, the Secretary of Agriculture. Dr. Rixey then took me around and introduced me to many of his friends—and on another occasion introduced me to Mr. Chandler—Secretary of the Navy. So I can say that Dr. Rixey promoted me from Willard Tree Alley to the Cabinet.

Dr. Ruffin, one of Dr. Rixey's close friends, then spoke:

It is a great pleasure to be here, Dr. Rixey, and I wish I could make a speech fitting the occasion. I wish to say, however, that we in private practice in Washington have an affection for you just as great as the affection of the Navy. We all appreciate your work and are just as familiar with the great service rendered to your country as your associates in the service. I felicitate you very much, and wish for you and Mrs. Rixey many anniversaries to celebrate.

Dr. Mitchell said:

I am very glad for this opportunity to say a few words about Dr. Rixey, whom I have known for twenty-five years. Captain Buckingham, many, many times told me how he not only owed Dr. Rixey his life but how he felt the greatest love for him because he had taken him as an officer sick on board ship, had brought him to his own home, nursed him, and brought him back to life; so that from that time on I always thought of Dr. Rixey only with deep affection. He has been good to me in many ways and I have had very close association with him—and we have many times talked over our aims and ambitions. He has discussed with me, and, in fact, I feel very much flattered to say that he has asked my advice on plans he had for the medical department of the Navy. I remember he discussed with me the question of bringing women nurses into the Navy—which reminds me of an expression which our good friend Mr. Dooley used again and again: "If doctors had a little more Christianity, and Christian Science had a little more science, it wouldn't matter which you called in, just so you had a good nurse." I remember his telling me of one of his first great surgical operations aboard ship—that of extracting a tooth.

I wish to express to you the great affection of the members of my profession outside the Navy, and of the great respect we have had for your ability. We have always honored your friendship, and I, for my own part, wish for you and Mrs. Rixey a long life of happiness.

Dr. Pleadwell and Dr. Dunbar presented their congratulations to Dr. and Mrs. Rixey on the occasion. Dr. Carpenter paid tribute to Dr. Rixey for the work he did as Surgeon General, and especially to the many things Dr. Rixey did for the younger men in the medical corps of the Navy.

General Drain spoke of Dr. Rixey in that phase of his career which had to do with the Washington Golf & Country Club as being as supreme as that in the Navy, and said:

He is responsible for this golf club. He was the first chairman of the Greens Committee and is a charter member of the Club. I have served with him on the board of directors for many years. During this last year, 1923, Dr. Rixey had charge of the great deal of improvements around the club—which he did in addition to his many other activities. (Addressing Dr. Rixey.) You know, old man, that I love you sincerely. I have gloried in hearing these noble men pay these tributes to you. I have been in this house often—and Mrs. Rixey and yourself have always made me feel at home, but I have never been so happy in it as I am tonight.

* * * * *

Dr. A. Camp Stanley said:

Dr. Rixey, I am not gifted in the expression of my sentiments on such an occasion as this. Speaking of recollections of Dr. Rixey's great energy, during my early years in the Navy at the Naval Hospital, after my fourth day at the hospital I was told about four o'clock in the morning that the Surgeon General was inspecting the hospital and was then in the kitchen. By the time I got to the kitchen, he was driving away from the front entrance. This is only one instance of the great strength that has driven Dr. Rixey forward during these fifty years.

I had a telegram from Dr. Boyd yesterday, asking me to express his felicitations on this memorable occasion, and to congratulate Dr. and Mrs. Rixey for him.

Dr. Bell said:

There is with us tonight one who is serving in the north, and an officer who has always been an extreme admirer of Admiral Rixey, who has with the rest of us done his utmost to make use of the advantages which Dr. Rixey was responsible for—and I would like to call upon Captain Blackwood.

Dr. Blackwood:

It is a very great pleasure indeed for me to be here, and a very unexpected one. I was making one of my trips to Washington on official business, and soon after my arrival received an invitation by telephone from Dr. Rixey to be present on this occasion. There is nothing, it seems, that I could add to the tribute already paid Admiral Rixey for his splendid work in the Navy. Admiral Rixey came into the medical corps at a time which all of us remember as a very low point. He was the saviour of the Medical Corps; he put it on its feet, and has given us the inspiration to carry on and make it all that we could wish it to be. I join with all my friends here in felicitating Dr. and Mrs. Rixey, and in wishing them many years of happiness and success.

Dr. Butler congratulated Dr. Rixey on the occasion and expressed the hope that the years to come would be as successful and happy as the fifty commemorated at this time.

CHAPTER XIV

THE WASHINGTON GOLF AND COUNTRY CLUB

UNDER this head I do not propose to write a history of the club but to show my interest and cooperation in its upbuilding from its inception to the present time. The club was organized March 7, 1908. The officers for the first year were: A. C. Yates, President; Frank Upman, Secretary; and the following directors: Joseph Taber Johnson, Frank S. Bright, Charles W. Draper, Frank P. Evans, and Otto Luebkert, as they were the incorporators and a supplemental certificate of incorporation added E. Wiley Stearns, Arthur L. Dunn, William I. Deming, Proctor L. Dougherty, and Clarence J. Blanchard, making the twelve directors four for one year, four for two years, and four for three years. There were five meetings of the Board of Directors to June 15th considering charter of incorporation, details of organization, and the numerous technical and legal forms in regard to transfer of land, etc. At the June 15th meeting of the Board, Mr. Yates resigned the Presidency, and Dr. Johnson was elected President and Mr. Yates as Vice-President. Dr. Johnson, knowing something of my ability to get work done as a farmer appointed me Chairman of the Greens Committee and I accepted it with many misgivings, but realized that each must do his share if this beautiful land was to be utilized as a play ground. Fortunately my dairy cows had given us fairly good fairways and as fast as Mr. John Davidson, Mr. Yates, and others whom I looked upon as experts would plot out the course and the location of the trees and greens, with my small force of four men(Richard Wallace, foreman, and three other colored men) they were placed in condition to play on and my report of September, 1908 states:

> "That for the above expenditures a large amount of work had been done, such as clearing up and removing stones and brush, filling gullies, mowing grass and weeds, making greens, sawing logs and posts, cutting out objectionable trees and digging

The Washington Golf and Country Club, 1910

out the stumps removing many fences and carting away the debris. A portion of the grounds including nine holes will be ready for use by the 16th instant. To prepare the permanent greens and put in shape the grounds for the remaining nine holes, there should be employed for the next three months at least eight men. In this way the permanent greens can be established this fall and everything put in fair shape for a complete course, and it is believed that two good men, with one horse, cart, mower, roller, and tools on hand, will be able to keep the grounds in fair condition and improve them steadily."

Quoting from Dr. Johnson's report at the annual meeting May 4, 1909:

"One of the chief difficulties we had to contend with was to make a small amount of money accomplish a large amount of work. If the stockholders and members of our Club could have gone over with us the original grounds purchased and seen their condition then, and take another trip with our Greens Committee today, we are sure they would agree with us that wonders have been accomplished in a marvelously short space of time, and with the expenditures on them of less than three thousand dollars; notwithstanding the fact that the hills and the valleys, the trees and the streams, the rocks and the gullies, the very beautiful views and pure fresh health-giving air were all there in great varieties and large quantities, much, very much had to be done by our energetic and devoted Greens and Grounds

Committees to bring anything like golf order out of this wild chaos and to produce an eighteen hole course, the whole of which can soon be played over."

My report as Chairman of Greens and Grounds Committee for the first year was:

"From May, 1908 to May, 1909:

Total amount appropriated	$2575.00
Total amount expended	1925.00
	$ 650.00

"The Committee is pleased to call the attention of the Club members to the work accomplished in the first year of the Club's existence; and much credit is due to those employed by the Committee, as they have labored most faithfully and seem to have taken a real interest in what your Committee was endeavoring to carry out.

"Twenty tons of lime and sixty odd bushels of grass seed have been sowed on the grounds; eighteen greens have been made and seeded. In equipment the Club has 2 good horses; 1 new wagon; 1 cart; 1 set double harness; 1 cart harness; 1 single horse harness for mower; 1 one-horse mower (side bar); 1 hand roller (300 ℔s.); 2 hand mowers, and 54 tools."

At the present writing (in 1923) this experience of mine on this committee was one that I often think of as I saw under my successors, greens, tees, bunkers, and fairways shifted as if they were checkers on a checkerboard, but not so quickly, and the amount expended in this work since the organization of the club would, I believe, have gone far towards paying off the whole of the club debt if our "foresight had been as good as our hind-sight." This, however, could not be, and I have voted for a change whenever I was convinced it was needed to make a first class golf course. The time that I gave to the golf course was from sunrise—the time that the men started to work—until just time to get to my office in the Bureau and usually I was one of the first there, and after office hours I was with the men again until sunset, and the work laid out for them during my absence had to be satisfactory to me. I was enabled to do this much for the club at this time because my duties of White House Physician had ceased with Mr. Roosevelt's administration and I was drawing out of all professional work preparatory to going on the retired list of the Navy.

After we had our first 18 holes and playing on them, our expert golfers wanted to change a tee or a green about every day, and I was too much of a farmer and not enough of a golfer to stand for it, and resigned from the committee, but was continued on the board of directors.

The first land purchased by the club of me was 75 acres for $46,377.91; to be paid as follows: $1,000 cash and 150 shares of stock ($7,500), 1st mortgage notes, 18, each $2,000, and one $1,877.91; these notes were payable one each year with interest every six months. The next important financial problem was a club house. I held a mortgage on all the land that I had sold and volunteered to release my rights under it in order that the club might borrow the money to build the club house to cost $12,500 and $1,500 for furniture—of this sum $5,000 was raised in cash by the members and $8,000 first mortgage on the club house and one acre of ground, to be paid off in five years. The second annual meeting was held in the new club house May 3, 1910. Up to this time the members had only the present little cottage, now used by the professional and the caddies. Besides the increasing demands of a new club for tennis courts and the improvement of the whole golf grounds with a professional and other absolute essentials, with $9,500 to be paid in 5 years with the interest on the whole debt for club house and grounds there was a serious problem to be met by a membership of 125 the first year, and at the meeting the second year, we had only 175 members. To meet the emergencies confronting us an intensive campaign was waged for new members and every member was urged to bring in at least one new member. The third and fourth years of the club were ones of a financial struggle with no prospect of the club being able to meet its obligation to pay me the $2,000 due each year on the purchase of the land and even the interest was not paid promptly. Most of my property was in real estate and heavily mortgaged at that time, and to meet my obligations I had counted on the club doing likewise. I saw that the club could not pay the principal due me but the interest must be paid or I could not use the club bonds to borrow money for my absolute needs. I could not expect anyone to loan money upon overdue bonds as a collateral and upon which even the interest was not paid. In October, 1912, the first crisis arose when I notified the Treasurer that interest due me must be paid or else the club would force me to foreclose the mortgage. The interest was paid.

Realizing even then the impossibility of the club paying anything on the principal due me for at least four years I agreed to take in April, 1911, its bond for $14,000 in payment of the three $2,000 bonds overdue and the four bonds to become due before April, 1915. This was done in order to have no overdue bonds. Even then to borrow $14,000 I had the greatest difficulty but by putting up all my club bonds (over $37,000) Mr. Jorden of the U. S. Trust Co., of Washington, D. C., made me the loan for three months with promise of renewal.

Thus, in order to keep the club going I deliberately placed myself in an embarrassing position and it was embarrassing to have $14,000 due every three months and it had to be renewed, and the interest paid promptly so I required the club to pay its interest just as promptly. To show how important it was that the interest on the club bonds should be paid, at one of the meetings of the board of directors I was requested by the Treasurer of the Club to allow the interest due on the bonds to go over a few months. I replied that I could not but I could loan them the money for the time specified on a club's note, so I gave my check for the amount due me for interest and took the note and was paid the interest with the proceeds of my own check.

April, 1915 arrived and the club was unable to pay its $14,000 bond. General James A. Drain had been made Secretary and I saw he was the man upon whom we must principally rely in this second crisis of the club's history. I told him that I would, as the principal creditor of the club, do all in my power to insure the future success of the club.

At the annual meeting May 11, 1915, the gravity of the situation was duly explained and discussed, and in accordance with the recommendation of the Board of Governors as expressed in the following resolution:

WASHINGTON COUNTRY CLUB
Office of the Secretary

April 8, 1915.

Resolved by the Board of Directors of the Washington Country Club, Inc.:
That it is advisable that amendments, changes, and alterations in the plan of incorporation of this corporation be made so as to provide as follows: that is to say:

1st. That the capital stock be decreased by the retirement of the entire issue thereof and that the corporation shall be hereafter without capital stock.

2nd. That for such retirement of the capital stock there shall be issued sealed obligations of this corporation of the denomination of fifty dollars each, payable to bearer fifty years after date, to bear interest at the rate of 5% per annum after twenty years from their date, one of which shall be deliverable for and be in full discharge of each share of stock now outstanding.

3rd. That the right to vote for members of the Board of Directors and for all corporate purposes heretofore lodged in the stockholders, shall hereafter be lodged in the active members in good standing, as such membership shall be defined in the by-laws.

4th. That should this corporation be at any time dissolved or terminated, the property thereof, subject to corporate debts and liabilities shall be deemed and taken to be in the then active members defined as aforesaid.

If you do not expect to attend this meeting, kindly sign the enclosed proxy and mail it in the accompanying envelope addressed to Edmund A. Varela, Treasurer.

(Signed) JAMES A. DRAIN,
Secretary.

This was approved by the membership in substance, and General Drain representing the Board came to me and stated the bonds of the club could be provided for by at least half of them being taken up by members if I would agree to the general plan outlined and would accept the club's bond of $7,500 for my 150 shares of stock, no interest on this bond until 1935, and after that 5% interest until its maturity 50 years from date. The general plan provided that the new bonds, each of $100 denomination, should be paid off $1,000 each year, and the ten bonds so paid should be determined by lot at each annual meeting. I accepted the proposition as the only way that I could see to meet this crisis and keep the club going. However, I stipulated that the $7,500 was available for membership entrance fees at any time and at face value. This stipulation was made as I believed that I could use it to the best interests of the club in that way and at the same time give me the pleasure of doing for those who had stood by the club from its inception principally on account of personal friendship for me.

This arrangement placed the finances of the club in good shape and it had a far reaching effect upon its future.

Twelfth Annual Report of The President of The Washington Golf and Country Club

Read at the Clubhouse,
May 4, 1920, at 8 p. m.

The President of this club, who served from its organization and has made the preceding eleven annual reports, has requested me to present the twelfth report. Dr. Joseph Taber Johnson, who was elected president in 1908 and who was year after year unanimously elected to the chief place in the club, had at various times during the last few years asked to be relieved. Each time his resignation was presented, the Board of Directors persuaded him to withdraw it. In December 1919, the board reluctantly yielded to his urgent request that he be allowed to resign.

The present incumbent was elected on account of the vacancy thus created, not to fill it, because that would be impossible, but to do the best he could to carry forward, as Chief Executive Officer, along the high and worthy lines set by Dr. Johnson. The warm regard and great respect felt not only by the members of the Board of Directors and by members of this club alone, but all who know Dr. Joseph Taber Johnson, are well deserved. He has always given his best, which is the very best. In accepting the resignation of Dr. Johnson, the Board of Directors unanimously voted him to be the President Emeritus of the club. He, of course, remains a member of the Board of Directors.

> There is another member of the board who has been with it from the beginning and whose intellectual, material, and moral support has at all times been of much value. This is Rear Admiral P. M. Rixey, U. S. Navy, Retired. His services to the club have been very great. During the past year he showed a further substantial evidence of his deep interest by becoming the first life member under the authorization for a limited number of that class of membership.
>
> Now that we are speaking of men, it is not amiss to say that it is believed this club has been especially fortunate in having as members of its Governing Board men of high ideals, practical purposes and consistent devotion to its welfare.

General Drain, having assumed the office of President, the success of the Club was assured, and up to this writing (in 1923) the governing body has labored faithfully for the club's best interests. With the works authorized and contemplated these beautiful playgrounds will be one of the most attractive homes for the lovers of the outdoor life in Arlington County (the future Arlington City) or any other locality in the world.

In my old age I have a great pleasure in watching the development of the Club and of having participated in its upbuilding, and the always pleasant association with its members. The trend of golf is to make good comrades and to make its devotees physically and mentally fit to meet the problems of life whether they be great or small. My love for these beautiful hills and valleys was begun twenty years before the Club was organized and during that period many happy hours I passed in company with the dearest friends in every walk of life, among them President and Mrs. Roosevelt and their children, on horseback, or strolling among my cattle making plan after plan for the future, day dreams I suppose they may be called, and I have lived to see many of those dreams fulfilled and more of them approaching that desirable end. It is beautiful to have lived and still have an active interest in all that makes living worth while.

My personal relations with the Governing Board have always been pleasant and only recently they gave a beautiful dinner with me as the guest of honor. A little later, on the occasion of a painful illness, the President of the Club brought me the following letter:

WASHINGTON GOLF AND COUNTRY CLUB
Rosslyn, Virginia

August 10, 1922.

My dear Admiral Rixey:

We missed you at the meeting of the Board of Directors last night and the Board unanimously requested me to tell you that and to say that we all hope and expect you will soon be back with us again. The Board further directed me to convey to you in the strongest possible terms the high appreciation which it has for your generous and whole-hearted assistance to the Club, in advice and counsel; in indefatigable efforts as a member of the House Committee; as the active and vigorous supervisor of much of the improvements lately made to the Clubhouse and grounds; for the loan of the tractor and tools with it; and for all the other helpful things you have done.

I wish you could have been, by radio or as a mouse in the wall, able to hear the expressions of members of the Board, of affection, gratitude and respect. It would have proven to you what you already know, that you occupy a central place in the hearts of the members of the Board.

Sincerely,

(Signed) JAMES A. DRAIN,
President.

Admiral P. M. Rixey,
Rixey Station, Virginia.

I now enjoy golf more than ever before and I get more exercise out of a game of golf than most of our members; and no matter how many strokes I have to make to get there, I have thus far made the green and holed out!

After selling the Club the 75 acres in 1908, I held about 125 or more acres adjoining the land sold and lying between it and Washington City. I held this land until 1922, hoping that the Club would find it possible to acquire it and make another shorter course of 18 holes or only 9 holes. About this time I offered to sell to the Club for $600 an acre, and if the Club had decided they wanted it, payments of principal and interest could have been made satisfactorily, as I was in better shape to assist the Club than ever before. As to my optimism in this matter I could say little towards influencing the members of the Club as I would be urging them to buy my property. After a careful investigation by a special board of twenty of the members and the Governing Board, it was deemed inadvisable to buy for the Club.

In less than a year's time I sold the land for $1,000 per acre, and I thought then that it was worth not less than $2,000, but I wished to realize from it during my life.

CHAPTER XV

ST. JOHN'S CHURCH, LAFAYETTE SQUARE, WASHINGTON, D. C.

St. John's Church Centennial

By REV. EDWARD MARSHALL MOTT
Rector, Church of the Advent

Dear old St. John's! Who knows thee but to love thee!
Standing there,
The Nation's shrines about thee, God's skies above thee,
So quaintly fair!
No other house of God such memories holdeth (We fondly dream);
No flock more precious strains of life enfoldeth, We rightly deem.
Now have a hundred fateful years departed since thou wert born;
Child of the church and always loyal hearted since thy first morn!
Thou from thy vantage ground viewest the splendor
Commemorate of noble lives, of passions true and tender, of good and great.
Those sculptured forms, Jackson, Lafayette, true patriots twain!
Kosciusko, Steuben, names that thrill men yet, Our freedoms gain.
And when thou dost thy records fair unroll, What wealth they bring
To history and the nation! The patriot soul, seeing, must sing!
When thou wast born, Democracy was a child, striving to learn
The lessons of true government undefiled, A task more stern.
A hundred years of light and shade, ere love of God and man,
Under the name St. John, men's faith to prove, Inspired thy plan.
Thou camest forth, truly memorial fame, to show the earth
That honors unadorned are not in vain! But richest worth.
The people's love, and not a monarch's fingers, Give the true sign
Of nobleness; and true glory only lingers in lives divine.
Severe thy form and classic thy design, Thou dost abide
Thru changeful eras, fit for use divine, Our praise and pride.
Thy form, the cross: man's only way to peace, Never more clear;
Above, thy dome, type of life's mysteries, Bound by thy sphere!
Thy templed entrance tells of Greece and Rome and all their story.
But Parthenon and Pantheon never were home to fit thy glory.
Not Windsor nor Versailles nor orient halls hath finer strain
Of chivalry or patriotism than thy walls' record contains.
Rank may be rank; but Christian life remains the only test
Whereby the soul, thru all the years attains the truly blest.
This, thru the years, hath been the message ever of all thy teachers;
The joy and praise, the constant glad endeavor of all thy preachers.
Dear old St. John's! Who knows thee but to love thee! Accept my lays,
And may all blessings from our God approve thee
And crown thy days.

St. John's Church, Washington, D. C.
16th and H Streets

I DEEM these verses read at the 100th anniversary of St. John's Church a fit beginning of what I have to say in regard to my personal relations with dear old St. John's Church which we all do, or should, so dearly love.

I was baptized in St. Stephen's Episcopal Church in Culpeper, Va., soon after entering the Navy but was not confirmed until a number of years after by Bishop Paret. Rev. William A. Leonard, now Bishop of Ohio, who was rector of St. John's from 1881 to 1889 was succeeded by the Rev. George W. Douglas who resigned in 1892 to take charge of an important church in New Haven, and he has since held conspicuous positions in the church. The Rev. Alexander Mackay Smith was elected rector in 1893 and remained with us until elected Bishop Co-Adjutor of the Diocese of Pennsylvania in 1902; during these twenty-one years St. John's made great progress. Dr. Mackay Smith was very popular and he earned the respect and love of the church members. Neither he nor his family ever wavered in their love of St. John's and both he, up to the time of his death, and his wife, now one of our most cherished members, ever failed in all that pertains to the welfare of this dear old church.

The Rev. Roland Cotton-Smith was our next rector with Rev. Frank H. Bigelow and Rev. Edward Slater Dunlap, Assistant Ministers. The Rev. Oscar L. Mitchell, Vicar of St. Mary's. Dr. Cotton-Smith took up the duties of rector with a zeal that more than pleased his vestry which was composed at this time of Dr. Robert Reyburn, General B. C. Card, James Lowndes, Henry E. Pellew, Commander F. A. Miller, Thomas Nelson Page, General George L. Gillespie, and myself. The church wardens were Alexander B. Hagner, Senior Warden, and Chief Justice Fuller, Junior

Warden. I believe I am the only living representative of the vestry as composed at that time.

For almost twenty years, Dr. Cotton-Smith gave the church great service and the unanimity with which we all worked was most gratifying and our next great trial came when we found our rector's health would probably make it necessary for him to reign.

It was in December, 1912, viewing his condition with much concern I wrote (with Dr. Cotton-Smith's permission) to his physician in Boston and received the following reply:

230 Beacon Street
Boston, Mass.

December 30, 1912.

Dr. P. M. Rixey,
1518 K Street,
Washington, D. C.

My dear Doctor:

In regard to Dr. Roland Cotton-Smith, I felt when I last saw him that it would do no harm to let him hold service once a week and nothing more. I particularly told him that I did not want him to enter into the work of the parish or to make any parish visits and that during the week he was to carry out his routine treatment the same as before. It seemed to me that a little serious work would be a decided help as our good friend was getting rather hipped and moreover needed all the encouragement possible. It was a clear case of over-work and over-strain mentally, but he improved so much that I feel quite sure that I am not making a mistake in allowing him to hold one service a week.

I hope that this will reach you in time, and shall be very glad to tell you anything further that you or the Parish wish to ask.

Yours very truly,
(Signed) James Marsh Jackson.

We recognized the gravity of the situation, but still hoped, especially as Mr. Dunlap was a good worker and could relieve Dr. Cotton-Smith of much of the parish work.

It must be remembered that during Dr. Cotton-Smith's term as rector more was done in keeping the church in good physical condition than had been done in the previous fifty years. The vestry prior to 1912 had been saving every dollar possible, recognizing the urgent need for repairs, and we had a surplus of $6,000 on July 31st of that year. Mrs. Lowndes had presented the church with $10,000 for a new organ and its installation cost us $1,500. It was discovered that one of the main arches in the church was weak and the supporting pillars had to be strengthened by underpinning. The bell tower was not considered safe and new timbers had to be put in. The heating plant and the ventilation of the church were not satisfactory. The above items—absolutely necessary—depleted our treasury and left us nearly $10,000 in debt. This was paid off gradually. The celebration of St. John's centennial was another task upon our rector and his sermons on that occasion will be long remembered by those who heard them. Under Dr. Cotton-Smith at this time was inaugurated the endowment fund which it is hoped will be of great benefit to the old church in caring for its future.

Then came the beautiful gift of Mrs. Berton Payne of about $100,000—to renovate the old church and this put the finances of the church in good condition and was equivalent to that amount given the endowment fund.

Ipswich,
July 19, 1919.

My dear Admiral Rixey:

The vestry met in New York on Wednesday and approved the architect's plans. It was felt by the members of the vestry that we did not want to do anything without the approval of the members who were absent. I have asked Mr. Kendall (the architect) to connect with you on his first visit to Washington to explain the plans, and I enclose a copy of the specifications. In regard to the color of the exterior, the architect says that we do not have to decide until the new plaster is placed on the church, and then we can make experiments.

I trust that you are all well.

Sincerely yours,
(Signed) Roland Cotton-Smith.

A few days later I met the architect and went over the plans and specifications.

Ipswich,
August 21, 1919.

My dear Admiral Rixey:

I have just received your letter of August 18th. After Mrs. Payne's death, of course, everything stopped until we heard from Judge Payne as to what he meant to do.

The architect received word from Judge Payne last week to go on with the work. I went to New York last Monday and saw the architect. He told me that they were to begin at once, and that he was going to Washington this week-end and would connect with you. I trust that he has done so.

I think that we are mighty fortunate in having so much done for us. It is equal to a large sum for the endowment and I think that the church is to be vastly improved without changing its character in the least.

I am glad that you are well and I am anxious to see your new house.

Sincerely yours,
(Signed) ROLAND COTTON-SMITH.

These letters show clearly how interested he was in everything pertaining to the welfare of St. John's and although in failing health he was giving up his summer leave to help forward the good work which must be completed as soon as possible so as to have the church opened again. Services were being held regularly in the Parish Hall during the summer by Mr. Dunlap or a substitute.

These unusual demands upon the rector and vestry did not help Dr. Cotton-Smith's physical condition which I had viewed with much concern for eight years, and the vestry granted him a year's leave in 1919, and during his absence we were fortunate in securing the services of Canon Douglas for the winter months. He had been our rector from 1889 to 1902. Dr. Douglas was most successful in keeping the church together and deserves the gratitude of every well-wisher of the church. He suffered personal discomfort and I fear pecuniary loss for the sake of the dear church he had previously served as rector. I personally feel under the greatest obligations to Canon Douglas for the six months he was acting rector and if it had been in my power I would have relieved him of much of the embarrassment under which he suffered. The approval of his work as acting rector has been attested by Bishop Leonard, Bishop Gailor, Bishop Parsons, Rev. Dr. Kinsolvin, and many others, a copy of whose letters are in my possession. Dr. Cotton-Smith's leave was not up until October 1st, but he evidently had St. John's on his mind and when Dr. Douglas' six months had expired he came back before his leave was up to see that we had everything in shape and much to our grief announced that he would have to retire. I personally had feared as much. Nevertheless it was a distinct shock to all of us. Our efforts to secure the right man to fill his place required a most energetic compaign and the vestry had its hands and hearts full until we finally decided to call, Dr. Robert Johnston, Rector of the Church of the Savior, Philadelphia, Pa. Before accepting he came on several times and canvassed the whole situation with the vestry. These conversations convinced me that he was not only the rector we wanted but under him the old church would go forward in doing good and we need have no fear of the parish not making satisfactory progress. Final arrangements were made and we agreed to make his salary $7,500 a year—the rectory and the church to pay all expenses of his moving to Washington. After his arrival we found that the rectory was not satisfactory for himself and family and we purchased the house, 1754 Massachusetts Avenue, N. W., and soon his family were comfortably housed and our next move was to make the vestry room at the church satisfactory, with a secretary in the vestry room during office hours. So we thought our rector was now equipped to give the church his best efforts, and they have in his first year proved most successful and the church under him is a beautiful place in which to worship. Every pew is rented and they are filled. The vestry having discovered that our rector with his large family was unable to live on his salary, decided at our February meeting after free and full discussion of the church finances to increase his salary to $9,000 a year and make it retroactive to the time of his acceptance of our call. We ran a budget system and the vestry required the Finance Committee to show in their expenditures for 1922 and their estimates for 1923 that the revenues of the church would guarantee the unusual expenses incurred in 1922 and 1923. The reports of the finance committee have shown in the last year the greatest increase in the church revenues of any period of one year since I have been a member of the vestry. This is due in part to increase in rentals of pews, but I believe our greatest asset has been our new rector. Writing me under date January 17, 1922, he said:

"If I were asked what I had in mind for St. John's, I would say (whether it be attained or not is not the question):

1. I should want to see St. John's the center of religious thought and spiritual perception and interpretation of life in Washington.
2. I should want to see St. John's sanely but truly serviceable to the diocese.
3. I should want St. John's to be a place where the tired in soul and perplexed in mind, would find comfort and help.

"To get this, a parson must be a reader and thinker, familiar with the thought of our time, and discriminating in his judgment. A parson must be a "sacrament,"—he is the sign of his message. If he is a human sign without official self importance, or without being eternally conscious of his privileges and rights, *and moves freely among the people*, he will achieve these results. If he is not a superficial religious egoist, mistaking crude autobiography for the gospel of God, and has a fundamental humility he will see some results.

"At any rate, for better or worse, my lot is cast with St. John's. And very soon it will begin to be the thing I most care for. Everything I do in Washington will be done with St. John's in view. In spite of the pessimistic talks of people in the church at large, I am beginning to see a bright day. One distinguished clergyman of our church wrote and said "You are going to ecclesiastical darkness." Our Bishop here told the wardens of this parish "Johnston has made a mistake." If work and a good will can achieve anything at St. John's, it will be achieved.

"What we have achieved here is largely due to the vestry. We have had thirteen years of intimate and close fellowship. Only one thing has been *demanded* of all, viz, that every man put his cards on the table and be frank. We have discussed and differed but never a whisper of unpleasantness. The result is the parish has been held in hand, for nothing impresses a parish more than the sense of a firm, united, alert, and efficient governing board. I am attending the vestry meetings which are to elect my successor, much against my inclination, but it is a mark of the unusual unity and confidence when these men insist on my judgment and help. It has greatly touched me.

"I shall want to talk some matters over with the vestry if I can't see daylight—but my inclination is to go very slowly and deliberately for a year and then, knowing people and being known, things will look differently.

"I am sorry to have inflicted this long letter on you. But your letter of this morning found me in the mood and I must now stop.

"Mrs. Johnston joins with me in wishing you and Mrs. Rixey all the joy in the world, and with kindest regards, I am,

Yours sincerely,

(Signed) ROBERT JOHNSTON."

And, again writing me the following day in regard to church matters he shows the strain of breaking off old relations and starting anew:

"The frightful pulling on the affections here makes it hard to think of the future—but I am sure that it is the inevitable pain of breaking up associations which have been so intimate and close. My judgment commands the course I have taken. My wise apple writes from Italy where she is spending the Christmas holidays—'I have heard rumors of St. John's, Washington; of course, you will go,' and she gives her reasons.

"I am going to do all in my power to serve St. John's. It will be my one occupation and my one absorbing task. And we are going to do it together,—the Vestry and I are going to be a unit. There are some things they know better than I. But I am going to be an apt pupil, and a quick learner.

"With kindest regards to Mrs. Rixey and you, in which Mrs. Johnston joins, I am

Yours sincerely,

(Signed) ROBERT JOHNSTON."

My intimate associations with the vestrymen of St. John's and our rectors for so many years have endeared everyone of them to me. I served many years on the Finance Committee and after General Gillespie's death I served as its Chairman. On December 6, 1915, I was elected Junior Warden to fill the vacancy caused by the death of Judge Hagner and the election of Surgeon General Gunnell to be Senior Warden—he resigned and January, 1921, I was elected Senior Warden and Admiral Stockton, Junior Warden.

As I read over the names of my associate vestrymen in my long service I have a distinct feeling of having lost very dear comrades and associates in church work, tireless, earnest, and faithful. A list of those who have gone before me includes, Dr. Robert Reyburn, General B. C. Card, James Lowndes, Henry E. Pellew, Commander Miller, Thomas Nelson Page, Judge Alex. B. Hagner, Chief Justice Fuller, Surgeon General Gunnell, General Gillespie, Colonel Cary Sanger, General Wetmough and Mr. W. C. Eustis,—each and everyone a loss to the church as well as a personal loss to me whose association with them had been most pleasant.

The vestry as composed today is Mr. William Corcoran Hill, Dr. Ralph Jenkins, Mr. Richard Harlow, Mr. W. S. Hutchins, Mr. Montgomery Blair, General W. M. Black, and myself, vestryman and Senior Warden, Admiral C. H. Stockton, Junior Warden, and Mr. W. C. Burchell, Chief Usher.

In addition to the church itself, the vestry has the care of the parish hall, the rectory adjoining it, the rectory recently purchased, St. Mary's chapel, and although the St. John's church orphanage is officered by the Bishop of Washington as President, our rector is the warden ex officio and a member of the board of trustees, ex officio.

The principal conduct of this splendid charity comes under "The Board of Ladies' Aid" composed of many of the most prominent ladies of Washington. Besides the president and warden there is a secretary, treasurer, and seven trustees—all men prominent in church work who handle its finances and when voluntary contributions are not adequate St. John's parish has always made good the deficiency besides a yearly collection taken up for the orphans. This is a charity that appeals to everyone interested in the lives of orphan children left destitute.

The vestry has had also in its keeping the following memorial and endowment funds—"Louisa Lovett Memorial Fund," "Mary Jane Jackson Memorial Fund," "Endowment Fund, Mrs. Florence L. Page—Gift Fund," "Mrs. Virginia L. Woodby Fox's bequest." The income from the above has done and is doing much good in the parish.

It is an impossibility for me to give in detail all the good work done by the parishioners of this church and I am only trying to give my personal relations with it since I have been a member. St. John's occupies the best position in the diocese for a church of its character and in all the forty years of my intimate association with it I have, as a member of its governing body, done all in my power to keep and preserve it for future generations. Much work has been done and all looking forward to the church's future. My work for the church or anything else is almost done, but I have a feeling that a church, over a hundred years old, will go on doing its splendid work under those who will come after me, and I have great faith that in time a new and commodious parish hall will be built along with a new rectory and finally before the end of another hundred years a new church built. This could not be done without additional ground, and that at present is impossible to obtain, but in the years to come the ground between the parish hall and the church may come into the market and when it does I hope St. John's will have so managed by the Grace of God to be able to perpetuate itself upon the same spot with all the most modern conveniences for church work. St. John's has been in the past, and will be in the future, a great asset for good. With the completion of our great Cathedral at St. Alban's, Washington will be well equipped to carry on the good work of our Lord and Saviour.

CHAPTER XVI

ST. MARY'S CHURCH, THE CHURCH OF OUR MOTHERS

JUST before a serious operation from the effects of which I thought my recovery was doubtful I signed a deed to William Cabell Brown, Bishop of the Protestant Episcopal Church of Virginia, to a triangular tract of land at Rixey Station for the purpose of a church to be built on it when practicable. This lot comprises about one acre in the eastern part of Langley Parish in which there was only St. John's Church in the western part of the Parish.

For the purpose of providing ways and means for the building of this new Church a committee was appointed by the Vestry of St. John's Church and it met at the office of Mr. Walter T. Weaver, July 24, 1925. The Committee was composed of five members, Rev. J. G. Sadtler, Mr. D. S. Mackall, Mr. Walter T. Weaver, Mr. B. G. Foster, and Mr. Edward Kershner, all present except Mr. Kershner.

The first act of the Committee was a resolution expressing to Mrs. Rixey and myself their grateful appreciation of the gift of the land. Next, the Committee adopted the sketch and ground plans by Mr. Fleming. The next suggestion was that Mrs. Rixey and I select a name for the Church—to be built of stone. We declined to be responsible for the name and the name was voted as St. Mary's, the Church of Our Mothers, by the Building Committee of the new Church. Finally a pledge card was selected to cover a period of five years with ten semi-annual payments, said pledges to be based on securing five thousand before they became operative.

The building Committee of St. Mary's was composed largely of the Rector and Vestrymen of St. John's and their families, most of whom resided near the site for St. Mary's. Mrs. Rixey and I pledged ourselves to give dollar for dollar for every dollar raised in Langley Parish up to

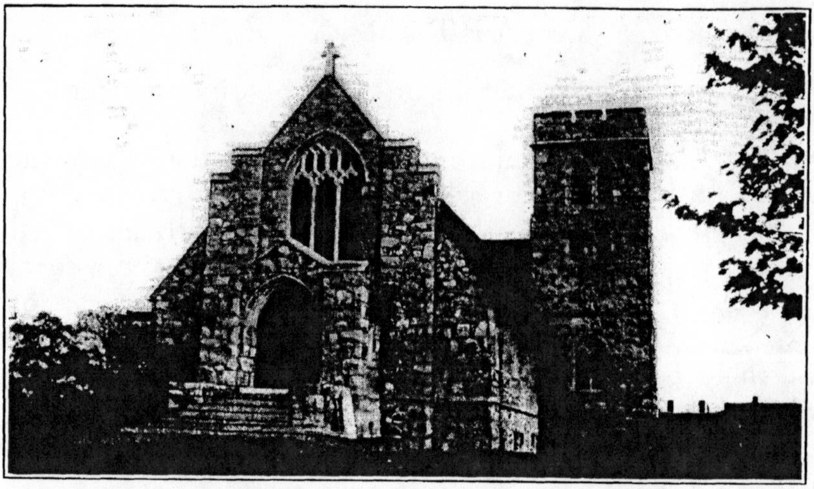

St. Mary's Church, the Church of Our Mothers

twenty-five thousand, one-half by those interested, and the other half by ourselves.

This Building Committee was organized with more lady members than men, and they were, and are today, more enthusiastic and more to be counted on in regular attendance of the meetings, which were for the most part held in our home.

My health did not seem to justify my being a member of the Building Committee, and the St. John's Vestry voted to make me an honorary member, an honor which I appreciated as much as being an honorary member of St. John's Vestry of Washington, D. C.

The Building Committee of St. Mary's as now organized consisted of Rev. Mr. Sadtler, Mr. B. G. Foster, Mr. and Mrs. W. T. Weaver, Mr. and Mrs. Kershner, Dr. E. M. Blackwell, Mr. Douglass Mackall, Mrs. Turner Smith, and Mr. Walter Campbell.

At the first meeting of this Committee held in my house I was requested to attend its meetings and accepted as an honorary member which carried, as I reviewed it, no responsibility.

After several meetings and the plan of the St. John's Committee only having been adopted by this Committee, further discussions proved to me that if the church was to be built it must be done by a subcommittee with power unlimited as to details and only governed by the funds obtainable. I suggested a committee of three, known as a construction committee, and the chairman elected by the Building Committee, and he to nominate two members. This was adopted and I was elected Chairman and chose Dr. Blackwell and Mr. B. F. Foster to form the Construction Committee.

We had only a few thousand dollars in hand, but the Building Committee's Finance Committee had in sight a loan from the Peoples State Bank of Cherrydale, Va., the promise of a loan up to fifteen thousand dollars. With this and new subscriptions we hoped to get the Church under roof.

Ground was broken in June, 1926, with the usual ceremonies, and an address by Rt. Rev. H. St. George Tucker and Mr. B. F. Foster.

The Construction began by selecting Mr. Kilgore as contractor on a percentage basis. A meeting was held every Friday at two p. m. to pay bills and outline work ahead. Dr. Blackwell was appointed Secretary, and he gave most of his time to supervising construction work, and trying to keep expenses down as much as possible. Work was carried on rapidly, and on the understanding with the Building Committee that an additional twenty thousand would be needed to complete the Church. The Construction Committee had made subcontracts for cut stone and completion of the tower, etc., at a cost of about $6,610.00, which with the balance of the loan of $20,000.00, it was thought that the building could be completed, and the Construction Committee would have spent $41,000.00, and the debt of the Church if the $20,000.00 was made would be $35,000.00.

Church services were being held in a schoolhouse for some time by the Rev. Mr. Sadtler, and it was hoped they might be continued until the new building was usable. Up to this date, about Nov. 28, work progressed rapidly with only one exception when a member of the Construction Committee appealed to the Building Committee (from a profound sense of duty) to overrule the decision of the majority of the Construction Committee as to the excavation for the building claiming that the minority members and the architect's opinion should offset the vote of the majority. The Building Committee upheld the majority vote, and the result is a building over a foot more above ground and one that has as good a foundation as if we had buried the building a foot or more under ground.

The real crisis in this Church work was late in November, at which time we were all deeply concerned about the debt which would have to be carried if the Church was finished, in addition to the $15,000.00 and subscriptions borrowed and almost expended and only a shell of a building completed, with outstanding obligation of $6,610.00. A lengthy report by Mr. B. G. Foster of the Building Committee to enclose the shell as it stood and use basement floor for services at a cost of approximately $20,000.00 was condemned. I did not think it practicable, and the danger of exposure to those of all ages attending services was too great. I had already made, in a long report in reply to Mr. Foster, an offer to assist the Committee in making this regular loan, and even offered to endorse the bond if necessary. The question what to do was a very serious one, and a sub-committee of three members was formed. Their report follows and very clearly outlines how desperate the situation was (report of Sub-Committee November 30, letter of same date to Dr. Rixey, as follows):

Washington, D. C.,
November 30th, 1926.

Dr. Presley M. Rixey,
Rixey Station, Rosslyn,
Arlington County,
Virginia.

Dear Doctor Rixey:

We the undersigned acting as a Sub-Committee are herewith presenting a copy of our report to the General Building Committee of St. Mary's Church, P. E., at Rixey Station, Virginia.

We have earnestly and conscientiously tried to reach some definite conclusion as to the problem facing us but have found it a very difficult question to solve.

We feel that it must be taken into consideration that we are an infant church with only such a small number as a congregation and none of us are sufficiently endowed with worldly goods to permit us to carry such a large indebtedness as has been suggested with our limited incomes.

While we have adopted this report and are enclosing it as the unanimous report of our Committee, we must be perfectly frank with you and say that we do not recommend, or even assume for one moment, that you should undertake this obligation unless you feel that you are fully justified in so doing. Nevertheless, we are staunch supporters and believe in the future of this church and should you so decide to undertake this work we feel sure that the members of this Committee and the congregation will give you their loyal support.

In making our report we also wish you to know that we fully realize that we are asking a great deal of you, should you decide to adopt it, and that the greater portion of the burden will fall on your shoulders, at least for the present.

Respectfully yours,

WALTER T. WEAVER
EDWARD KERSCHNER
E. M. BLACKWELL, *Chairman.*

REV. JOHN G. SADTLER, ex officio.

REPORT OF SUB-COMMITTEE, APPOINTED BY THE GENERAL BUILDING COMMITTEE, NOVEMBER 29th, 1926

November 30th, 1926.

General Building Committee,
St. Mary's—The Church of Our Mothers,
Rixey Station,
Arlington County, Virginia.

Pursuant with the desires and action of the General Building Committee of St. Mary's Church, P. E., on Monday, November 29th, 1926, your Sub-Committee, composed of Rev. Mr. John G. Sadtler, ex officio, Dr. E. M. Blackwell, Walter T. Weaver and Edward Kerschner, met at three o'clock on Tuesday, November 30th, and considered the two separate reports submitted to the General Building Committee by Dr. P. M. Rixey and Mr. B. G. Foster, in connection with the proposed plan for proceeding with the work and financing, thus finishing the construction of St. Mary's Church, P. E., at Rixey Station, Virginia.

The two reports were carefully read and after due deliberation and discussion of each report your Sub-Committee unanimously decided to make the following written report of their findings:

First—Careful consideration was given to the most kind and generous offer of Dr. P. M. Rixey made to the Building Committee in his report made on November 28th, 1926, which is a part of the minutes and records of the General Building Committee, to arrange for and to personally endorse the notes for the additional $20,000.00 loan all of which is practically required to complete the Church so that it can be used, and also his further offer to guarantee all interest payments, and protect any other endorser on either the large or small supplementary notes by supplying each endorser with an indemnity bond for the full amount of such endorsement to protect them against any loss.

Your Sub-Committee finds it very difficult to adequately express to Dr. and Mrs. Rixey their feeling of gratitude for their kind and liberal offer, especially when it is recalled how much they have already done and are doing toward this work.

Second—Mr. B. G. Foster's letter summing up the present status of the building finances and which so graphically shows how dangerous it would be to burden the Church with such a small congregation with a debt beyond that already obligated for, namely, $15,000.00, which is based on short term notes, interest and payments on principal which will soon become due, was fully and duly considered.

A discussion of this matter reveals the fact that there seems to be no possible way under the present plan by which the debt contemplated, providing the additional loan is made, could result in less than a $30,000.00 debt, with no reduction from this amount until such time as outstanding subscriptions are paid. In further connection with this matter we have discussed plans "A" and "B" as outlined in Mr. Foster's report, but it is the consensus of your Committee that Plan "A," which is the one of stopping all work, would not be satisfactory to Dr. Rixey in the form presented, and which would be lamentable in that it would result in stopping all progress on the work of completing the Church. Your Committee, therefore, sought to provide other ways and means by which some agreement could be reached, whereby the work could proceed along the lines advocated in Dr. Rixey's report.

It may not be within the province of this Sub-Committee to offer any suggestion in this matter, however, realizing that each and every member of the Committee and of the Congregation is anxious to carry on if at all possible and are anxious and willing to co-operate in every way with the furtherance of this work, we are going to suggest the following plan:

That Dr. Rixey's plan be adopted as outlined in his report before mentioned, which is substantially the plan included in Mr. Foster's report "B," subject to the following modifications:

Namely, that Dr. P. M. Rixey shall and will agree to arrange for this loan and guarantee the interest and principal to the entire amount of $20,000.00, with the understanding that he, Dr. P. M. Rixey, shall and will agree to and obligate himself and his estate to assume and pay and discharge one-half of the said principal debt and one-half of the interest of the said debt of $20,000.00 to the end that the Church of St. Mary's, P. E., shall only assume responsibility for the other one-half of the principal debt and one-half of the interest of this loan of $20,000.00, it being also understood and agreed that Dr. Rixey shall continue to duplicate and pay into the Treasury of the Church as all subscriptions are received until the amount of $12,500.00 is paid, or any part of that which may be due, and that the subscriptions to this fund which we now have or may receive, and all monies now in bank and the duplications made by Dr. Rixey shall be applied against the curtailment of the loan in the Peoples State Bank of Cherrydale, Virginia, until such loan is entirely paid off, and that all unexpended balance of the $20,000.00 loan after the Church has been completed, shall also be applied to the debt of the Peoples State Bank of Cherrydale, Virginia, until that account is fully paid.

In making the above suggestion we want it clearly understood that we believe the Church Organization will do everything within their power to support Dr. Rixey in this undertaking and will further endeavor in every way to help him in meeting such interest and payments on principal as are to be made on their portion of this $20,000.00 debt, with the proviso that no money shall be borrowed by them or money from subscriptions shall be used for making payments for interest until after the debt of the Peoples State Bank of Cherrydale, Virginia, is paid in full.

Your Committee sincerely trusts that this report may help to solve the problem of the Building Committee and is offered with this end in view.

Respectfully submitted,

WALTER T. WEAVER
EDWARD KERSCHNER
E. M. BLACKWELL, *Chairman.*

REV. JOHN G. SADTLER, ex officio.

As I read this report and letter signed by four of my best friends I realized as never before that I must be considered by them, and probably by all my friends, as of unlimited resources financially, and that they did not realize that it was constant struggle, more difficult now on account of my age and infirmities than ever before to live the life that I had always lived.

I always tried not to have those whom I have tried to help, rely upon what I could do to help them in need beyond what I may have done or committed myself to do.

The Sub-Committee's report outlined what I had offered to do in regard to the required loan, and that was the limit of prudence on my part. In my opinion the best interest of a church demands that the congregation do not rely upon any individual or group of individuals to assume its debts, but that each member of a congregation subscribe according to their ability towards the support of their Church, and after that is done the one that gives the mite is as much of a churchman as the one who gives thousands.

My proposition was finally accepted, and after some difficulty in adjusting terms, etc., Mr. Larner, President of the Bank, informed the Washington Loan and Trust Co., of Washington, he would advance the money needed.

The Church being under cover and the details of completion requiring the full membership of the Construction Committee at every meeting, and one of them being unavoidably absent, I found it necessary to ask the privilege of renaming two additional members, and selected Mrs. W. T. Weaver, and Mrs. Walter Campbell. Work from now on was pushed rapidly, and on April 3, 1927, the first services were held in St. Mary's Church.

The need of this Church in this locality was amply proven in the first year of its existence.

CHAPTER XVII

THE ROOSEVELT COWBOY SADDLE AND BRIDLE

IN MAY, 1926, I had a letter from Mr. R. W. G. Vail, Librarian of the Roosevelt House Library and Museum, stating that Archie Roosevelt had informed him he thought his father had given me the cowboy saddle and bridle and asking if I would be willing to place them in the Museum. I did not then feel I could part with this saddle and bridle, but two years later decided it would be best to have them placed in the Museum during my lifetime and wrote Mr. Vail the following letter, and his replies are also given here:

January 18, 1928.

Dear Mr. Vail:

As I wrote you some two years ago in reply to yours—the Roosevelt saddle and bridle presented to him by the citizens of Cheyenne, Wyoming are a beautiful example of cowboy saddle days mounted in gold and silver. On the eve of leaving the White House he presented them to me and for nearly 20 years I have loved them and used them. However, I have made up my mind to send them to the Roosevelt House Library and Museum and have had them polished up and boxed to ship to New York. Please give me explicit shipping directions by return mail and I will forward by express charges prepaid.

It goes hard to part with them, but after I am gone I fear something may go wrong and the Museum not get them. I also have a number of personal letters from President Roosevelt which have never been in print which the Library should have, but I am not willing to part with them yet.

Hoping to hear from you promptly,

(Signed) P. M. Rixey.

Roosevelt House Library and Museum
28th East 20th St., New York

Jan. 20, 1928.

Dear Dr. Rixey:

I was delighted to hear from you again and to know that you are about to send on the splendid Roosevelt saddle and bridle. I am sure that it will be a satisfaction to you, as it will be to us, to have them here where the school children and grown folks of this and future generations may examine them and through them, remember the friendship which you had with the Colonel. Of course, we will be delighted to have the letters, too, at such future time as you may care to turn them over to us, but I can readily understand that you would want to keep them for the time being.

You may send the saddle and bridle addressed to The Roosevelt Memorial Association, 28 East 20th Street, New York City.

I am all eagerness to see them and put them on exhibition. They will add much to the interest in our museum.

Very sincerely yours,

(Signed) R. W. G. Vail.

Roosevelt House Library and Museum

February fourteenth
1928

Dear Dr. Rixey:

The saddle is here and it is a beauty. I have never seen as fine a cowboy saddle and bridle and you may be sure that it will add much to the interest of our museum. We appreciate very much indeed your generosity in presenting us with this splendid reminder of Colonel Roosevelt's love of life in the open. It will remain a permanent reminder of his friendship with the people of the West and of his affectionate regard for his personal physician while in the White House.

Sincerely yours,

Dr. P. M. Rixey (Signed) R. W. G. Vail.
Rixey
Rosslyn, Va.

CHAPTER XVIII

LITERARY CONTRIBUTIONS

BESIDES my official contributions as written in the Surgeon's General reports from 1902 to 1910 I wish to refer here to some of the contributions published in the Youth's Companion in 1893, "The Doctor in the Navy;" in the University of Virginia's "Why go to College" under the title of "How can those of us under military age best serve our Country," published during the World War; and in the Better Health Magazine of San Francisco, Cal. under the title "Guarding the Health of our Presidents."

Under my views of "The Doctor in the Navy" I tried to show how important their duties are if we are to have the best first line of defense possible. What I wrote in 1893 is applicable to the Navy of today, only supplemented by the wonderful strides in the submarine, under the sea work and aeronautics, both of which require of the Doctor in the Navy, additional preparation and work.

Under the title, "How can those of us under military age best serve our Country," I wrote:

HOW CAN THOSE OF US UNDER MILITARY AGE BEST SERVE OUR COUNTRY?

By Dr. Presley M. Rixey, U. S. N. (Retired), Va., 1873,
Former Surgeon General of the United States Navy

The future of the young men and women of our country is bright indeed if they will look squarely at the conditions that confront them.

Before the beginning of the war, the professions and business of the United States were well supplied with men and women who had equipped themselves in times of peace for their work.

In the first year of the war we find our college graduates, young men of the greatest promise in civil life, entering the Navy, the Army and other public Services. By the thousands, they have entered the fighting branches of the Government, and, just here I wish to say that the college graduate by reason of his training and physical development, especially where athletics has had the importance in the college they deserve, had a great advantage over his brothers, enlisted men or officers, who have not. Who are to take the places of these young men who are giving their lives that those coming after them may enjoy what they have enjoyed: that freedom, the birthright of us all, for which our forefathers strove so successfully?

The answer to this question concerns every young man under military age, and it is, that everyone under that age should pursue his or her college studies until called to the colors, in order that they may fit, and worthily fit, themselves to take the places of the splendid men now serving in the front ranks; or, in case of the ending of the war, that they may be prepared to take the places in civil life of those who have given all, even in many instances life itself, that these young men and women now growing to maturity should have the opportunities and advantages they themselves have enjoyed.

Young men and women, boys and girls, you can best serve your country now by preparing to give yourselves to that country equipped mentally and physically. This can best be gained in our colleges, and I cannot too strongly urge upon the youth of our country that they take up college life with its mental and physical development with all that in them lies—it is thus they can best serve their country at this time.

The field of medicine, to which I have devoted myself for forty-five years, will offer exceptional advantages in the Army, Navy and Public Health Service or in civil life. If war should continue for several years medically trained men would, in all possibility, see active service with our soldiers, sailors and marines, even though they were undergraduates.

Such an experience would mean much to every young man so fortunate as to have served his country in this war.

As to those of our young men physically unfit for military service, medicine offers to the well-equipped men a splendid opportunity in civil life.

Under the title, "Guarding the Health of our Presidents," at the request of Better Health, I wrote an article from which I quote:

GUARDING THE HEALTH OF OUR PRESIDENTS

By Presley Marion Rixey, M. D.,
Surgeon-General, Rear Admiral, U. S. N. (Retired)

The health of the President of the United States and of his immediate personal and official family is of so much importance to all our people and indeed to the whole world that I am glad in my declining years to express, in accordance with the wishes of Better Health, my views on this subject, formed after an experience of over ten years as the official White House physician of two of our Presidents. I had the responsible honor of serving Mr. McKinley from 1898 to the date of his death in 1901, and Mr. Roosevelt from that date to his retirement from office in 1909. This experience gave me increased interest in the health of all our Presidents since that period.

Everything concerning the President's health affects society and business in a very material way and the thousands of letters and telegrams asking to be advised whenever the President is even slightly sick and offering all kinds of advice and all varieties of prescriptions for the guidance of the official physician would take up more of his time than could be spared, so that the policy has been adopted of making all acknowledgments deemed necessary through the Executive Office. And just here let me say that the White House physician should clearly have it understood that he will give out nothing in regard to the health of the occupants of the White House except through the President's secretary, and then only when it is of such importance as to demand bulletins signed by the official physician and consultants which are always given to the press through official channels. In this way the public, which has a right to the information, is kept advised in no uncertain way and nothing is given out that might unduly alarm or affect social or business life.

In the national capital of our great country are three of the finest medical establishments in the world, all kept up at Government expense—I refer to the Medical Department of the Army, the Navy, and the Public Health Service. Officially they all come under command of the President and each of these is glad and always ready to serve their commander-in-chief. From the personnel of these services the President usually selects his official physician, who is amenable to the discipline governing them. The family physician to the President remains his private family physician called by the official physician as a consultant whenever he or the President desires it. This plan has been found to work very satisfactorily.

During my term of service as White House physician I had eminent specialists in consultation on serious cases of both Presidents and various members of their families. The serious illness of his wife or child obviously interferes materially with the President's service to his country.

Many Duties and Responsibilities of White House Physicians

The President and his personal family are the first care of the official physician, and it is important that the President keep advised as to the health of his official family, that is, the members of the Cabinet and others in official life and members of Congress in whom the President might be much interested. Here the President calls in the services of the official White House physician, especially where the illness is serious, as in the case of Vice-President Hobart, Senator Hanna, and many Cabinet officers whom I visited by the President's direction. Many of these officials had consulted me and I was their attending physician and before the expiration of my ten years' service I had more than I could care for professionally besides the duties of Chief of the Bureau of Medicine and Surgery.

The official physician includes in his duties the health of the White House office force, and any emergencies which may arise, especially in the prevention of contagious or infectious diseases, and to this end a close watch must be kept upon all those who come in contact with the President and his personal and official families. Having outlined what I believe to be important in a general sense and what I deem essential in watching and caring for the health of our President, I will give a few of my personal experiences during my service as an object lesson of what may present itself to the White House physician.

While on duty caring for the health of the National Personnel in Washington, D. C., in 1898, I received an order to accompany President McKinley, members of the Cabinet, and invited guests to the Atlanta Jubilee, Tuskegee, and Montgomery, Ala., Savannah and Macon, Ga., December 13 to 20. Mrs. McKinley and ladies of the cabinet were to accompany the party. With an emergency outfit I reported to the President and was assigned a compartment in a car adjoining his. There were about fifty persons on the special train. This being the first time I had been thrown in such close contact with the members of so august an assembly, I felt the responsibility correspondingly heavy. However, as it happened, I had only to care for minor ills. At Atlanta I was called upon for the first time to attend Mrs. McKinley, and discussed with the President her condition.

This particular tour of 2187 miles was delightful, even if the responsibility was great. As an official member of the President's party, I had to participate in everything and remain always near the President. Returning to Washington I resumed my duties at the Naval Dispensary and looked upon the very pleasant experience as a thing of the past, as I thought that Surgeon General Sternberg, who had succeeded General Leonard Wood as White House physician, would continue. To my surprise, a few days later, the President sent for me and directed that in the future I was to be White House physician and that I should make two calls, 10 a. m. and 10 p. m. at the Executive Mansion, and to hold myself in readiness to accompany him and Mrs. McKinley whenever they left Washington. I realized that this, in addition to my duties at the Naval Dispensary, would be difficult, and also that the duties at the White House would have to be my first consideration. Mrs. McKinley, as was generally known, suffered with a mild form of epilepsy and other ailments since the birth of her last child, and the shock of the death of their children. I spent much time in the study of her condition and proper care in conjunction with noted specialists, and inside of the year I had her case well in hand. I was always at the call of my eminent patients and I had the greatest consideration that could be given a family physician, always welcome and invited, with Mrs. Rixey, to all the private and public entertainments. The relationship was that of the devoted family physician and his patients, and just here let me say that this continued through my whole time of service as White House physician, lasting over ten years.

The summer of 1899 was spent at Hotel Champlain, Bluff Point, N. Y., and it was the White House for the time being, all business being transacted from the President's quarters. Here I endeavored to have the President walk as much as possible and drive in an open trap. That was before the day of the automobile.

Touring With The President

The next tour of the President was to Chicago and the Northwest from October 4 to October 19, 1899. The members of this party were Mrs. McKinley, as the only lady, and most of the Cabinet. The distance traveled by special train was 5009 miles. The President or his physician were with Mrs. McKinley constantly and she stood the tour better than I expected. Before starting on a tour the President always consulted me as to how it would affect his beloved wife and he would give up the tour rather than have her run any risk to her health. The responsibility was correspondingly heavy on me; but I knew the President considered this long tour important as well as the still longer one from April 19 to June 15, 1901, from a campaign standpoint. There was an insistent demand from all sections of the country to hear him and he thought it desirable to speak personally to the larger body of the American people on the eve of his nomination and election.

I expressed my deep concern as to Mrs. McKinley being able to stand such a strenuous journey, but her anxiety to go with her husband finally prevailed and I reluctantly gave my consent. I knew that I would have every assistance the country could afford if she should be unable to continue the tour. All went well and she seemed to enjoy the immense enthusiasm which everywhere greeted the President. We had traversed Virginia, Tennessee, Alabama, Texas, New Mexico, Arizona, and arrived at Los Angeles, Calif., on the 8th of May, just ten days after leaving Washington, D. C. Mrs. McKinley was not so well and gradually developed a slow fever with a bone felon (Whitlow) forming on her left thumb. This was relieved by operation and then dysentery developed. This, in her weakened condition, was serious, and I admonished the President that his wife must have absolute and complete rest. Mr. Henry Scott of San Francisco had offered his home to the President and I advised that we go there by special train. He at once ordered that the tour be continued and his place be taken by Secretary Hay, Postmaster General Smith, Secretary Long, Secretary Hitchcook, and Secretary Wilson, who were in the party, and when they had completed the California itinerary they were ordered by the President to report to him at San Francisco.

The President, Mrs. McKinley and myself, left Los Angeles on May 12. I soon had my patient where we could make the best fight for her life. Her strength was going fast. We had made nearly half of the 10,581 miles which the tour called for, and I felt that even if Mrs. McKinley should improve she could never finish the tour as planned. I so informed the President and the rest of the tour was given up.

I immediately called in consultation Dr. Hirschfelder, Dr. Cushing, and Dr. Gibbons. More than once we almost considered our patient hopeless, but heroic efforts prevailed, and on May 25 she recovered sufficiently for us to start back to the White House.

During the time the Henry Scott home was occupied by the President it was the official White House and everything the city could do was done for its inmates. When I reported to the President that at our consultation on the 24th of May it was decided that it was reasonably safe to move his wife to Washington, he said: "That will not do, you must decide that it *is* safe."

I had informed my confreres that Mr. McKinley would object to the word *reasonable* so I called them together again and, after conscientious consideration, we eliminated the word and immediate preparation was made for the start.

I left nothing undone to make the trip safe, a special train, two trained nurses, everything that could be needed in an emergency—even a tank of oxygen was put on board. The train was to run slow or fast or be sidetracked as the patient's condition demanded. Dear Mrs. McKinley was so anxious to be home that she aided me immensely on this trip. Her condition on arriving at the White House was as good or better than when she started. Early in June, Mr. McKinley decided that he would take Mrs. McKinley to their old home in Canton, Ohio. It was made the White House for the rest of the summer and I was ordered to continue on duty with them and to live in their home. Mrs. McKinley steadily improved and was in better health when we left Canton than she had been since I knew her.

Shot in The Line of Duty

Early in September, 1901, the President's party went to the exposition at Buffalo, N. Y. Having been inaugurated for his second term in March and his wife so much improved in health, the President never seemed so happy as when he left his Canton home for Buffalo. Here the crowds of people all trying to get as near him as possible gave me great concern. At 4:07 p. m., September 6, 1901, he was shot by Leon Czolgosz. "In line of duty while receiving the people," was the heading of my official report to the Navy Department. This report is on file and is a matter of history. The hope, fear, and agony of the next seven days cannot be expressed in words. He died at 2:15 a. m., September 14, 1901. The sorrow of a whole people was tragically impressive to witness, as I did from Buffalo, N. Y., to Washington. The official funeral services at Washington and the interment at Canton, Ohio, demonstrated what a firm hold McKinley had on the affections of the American people.

During all this I was bowed down by my personal loss but not for one moment did I forget my professional charge, Mrs. McKinley. Her grief for her idolized husband was heart-rending and strong mediums had to be administered to enable her to be with her Dearest (as she called the President).

After the interment at Canton I remained in Mrs. McKinley's home until her condition warranted my leaving, about October 1, when I resumed my duties at the Naval Dispensary in Washington, and by direction of President Roosevelt I was to continue my duties as White House physician. At the same time he directed that I should go to Canton to see Mrs. McKinley as often as necessary. A trained nurse was left with her and her family physicians, Dr. Philips and Dr. Portman of Canton, were to keep me informed as to her health. In the professional care of President and Mrs. McKinley I had a patient who, on account of his invalid wife, refused to leave her to take proper exercise, and, indeed, the only exercise he did take was short walks and drives usually in a closed carriage. The result was that he had poor resistance to disease or injury, as was proven when stamina was needed following the fatal shot.

President McKinley was most appreciative of my professional services as White House physician and informed me a few months before his death that he intended to appoint me Surgeon General of the Navy when the vacancy should occur, which would be in about a year.

After his death, Mr. Roosevelt carried out Mr. McKinley's promise and I was not only White House physician and Chief of the Bureau of Medicine and Surgery of the Navy, but also had the professional care of many friends in private and official life. The duties of White House physician under the Roosevelt administration were entirely different from those of the previous one, as the President and Mrs. Roosevelt and the six children were devoted to the outdoor life, and all in good health. Deciding that the worst I would have to contend with professionally would be children's diseases or accidents, I fitted up in the White House an emergency outfit and planned to care for contagious or infectious disease if occasion should arise, in order that the official White House would not be quarantined on account of infectious disease among the children. My foresight proved of great service as cuts and bruises were frequent; but Archie's attack of diphtheria in 1907 was the only serious contagious case. The President himself was seriously injured in the collision of his automobile with a trolley car in which one of the secret service men was killed. It was part of my service to accompany the President on his outing trips, hunting, riding, walks, etc. We rode horseback from twenty-five to one hundred miles a day. We had many long walks, wading or swimming streams. The hunting trips were for all kinds of game, big game being his preference. My services on these trips were frequently required, not only for the President but for others who might be of the party. When at the close of the Roosevelt administration I was relieved of duty as White House physician I realized how great had been my sense of responsibility.

During the time of my service at the White House I was consulted by both Presidents as to important health appointments, notably in the appointment of Dr. White in regard to the appointment he still holds as the head of the St. Elizabeth's government asylum for the insane, and on the occasion of President Roosevelt's visit to the Panama Canal I assisted him in his inspection in all matters pertaining to the health of the employes of this great undertaking and I was glad to be of considerable help to General Gorgas in obtaining the necessary authority for carrying on his great work in the Panama Canal Zone. Likewise, I was consulted on all matters of sanitation and health, and after I was made Chief of the Bureau of Medicine and Surgery my position at the White House enabled me to obtain many important reforms in my own Corps and to assist the sister services of the Army and Public Health.

Doctors for Taft, Wilson, Harding and Coolidge

President Taft succeeded President Roosevelt and elected to have an Army Medical Officer to relieve me of duty at the White House, Col. M. A. Delaney. President Wilson succeeded President Taft and appointed P. A. Surgeon Cary T. Grayson of the Navy as his official White House physician. Surgeon Grayson came into the Navy during my administration of the Bureau of Medicine and Surgery and was with me occasionally at the White House and notably on the one-hundred mile ride made by President Roosevelt, Major Archibald Butt, and myself, to Warrenton, Va., and return the same day. His service was so much appreciated by Mr. Wilson that he was promoted over the heads of two grades of older medical men from the rank of Surgeon, Lieutenant Commander to Medical Director, Rear Admiral, an unprecedented action, but not more so than the unprecedented service he was called upon to render President Wilson in foreign countries as well as at home.

President Harding elected to have Dr. Sawyer as his official physician, and gave him the rank of Brigadier General in the Army, and he had Past Assistant Surgeon Boone of the Navy as his assistant.

A short time after President Harding's death I wrote to General Sawyer and suggested that he write an official report of President Harding's illness and death as he was his official physician and it would become a matter of record and of great interest to the people and profession. He replied as follows:

CHARLES E. SAWYER
Brigadier General, M. O. R. C.
Washington, D. C.

August 13, 1923.

My dear Admiral Rixey:

Accept my thanks for your very opportune suggestion and for the copy of the medical report you made in the case of President McKinley.

As soon as I have time, will be very happy, indeed, to talk to you about the details which occurred and which, I am sure, will be of much interest to you.

I trust that you are feeling well, and that everything is going well with you and your good wife. I shall take advantage of the first opportunity presenting and call upon you.

With kindest regards, I am,

Sincerely yours,

(Signed) C. E. SAWYER.

Rear Admiral P. M. Rixey,
Rosslyn, Virginia.

President Coolidge has an army surgeon, Major Coupal, as his official physician.

In conclusion I wish to emphasize the importance of the President's health while in office, and in caring for his physical well-being among many other things I suggested these simple rules: Ten minutes setting-up exercise before breakfast, one hour's walk before going to his office, from one to three hours' exercise in the open air before dinner at 8 o'clock. These simple suggestions as to exercise, accompanied by proper advice of the White House physician as to observing ordinary rules of diet and personal hygiene, will help greatly if illness or injury should come to the President.

How would you like to shake hands with thousands of persons who desire to express their admiration and affection by squeezing your hand until it swells? In my opinion the President should not shake hands on the occasion of large receptions of the people. Instead, as each one's name is called and he passes in close review the President can greet him or her as cordially without shaking hands. A good rule might be that as each person in the line approaches the President he should place his right hand over his heart instead of reaching for the President's hand. It would seem that the few thousand who would forego the handshaking would be glad to do so in order that the tax on the President's energy might be reduced to a minimum and the prevention of such a terrible tragedy as came to President McKinley.

As to the White House physician, he must always sink his own interests in that of the health of the President and of his personal and official families. In other words, his desires, pleasures, and all other duties must be subordinated and devoted to this special service.

I wrote this article to give some idea of the importance of having the Presidents' health kept in good condition. The President, Mr. Coolidge, and the only living Ex-President showed their appreciation as follows:

THE WHITE HOUSE
WASHINGTON

June 17, 1925

My dear Admiral Rixey:

I am indeed glad to have the copy of "Better Health" which you were good enough to send me, and I want to thank you for it. I was very greatly interested in reading your article.

Very truly yours,

(Signed) CALVIN COOLIDGE.

SUPREME COURT OF THE UNITED STATES
WASHINGTON, D. C.

June 20, 1925

Dear Admiral Rixey:

Thank you for sending me your interesting article on the health of our Presidents. I have read it with great pleasure. No one can speak with more authority on that subject than you.

I am glad you have told the public the facts on that important subject.

With best wishes and warm regard

Sincerely yours.

(Signed) WM. H. TAFT.

CHAPTER XIX

RULES COMPILED AS AN OBJECT OF ENDEAVOR

THE following rules were compiled by me during my long service. I commenced writing them on my first cruise and they have served me as an object of endeavor.

Never forget that there is a great first cause which rules the world; a something that we can but dimly comprehend, because it is too vast for our finite minds. It is the Infinite. It is God. It is fruitless to try "to find out God." He is "Our Father in heaven;" this is all that we poor mortals may know; it is all that the most learned man can ever know. That this great Creator is just and merciful, and rules by equal laws, we have every reason to believe; and that it is one of the Creator's laws that our lives may be influenced by earnest prayer for guidance in the right way, there is no doubt. Strong and honest prayer to our Father in Heaven for guidance in the way for our best good is sure to bring *strength and enlightenment* to the mind and thus aid us in the affairs of life and lead us in the way which is right. That we have a spiritual as well as a material nature and that this spiritual nature or soul survives the body and is happy or miserable "according to the deeds done in the body," we also have reason to believe.

Truth, unfaltering integrity, justice and honor are never to be departed from under any circumstances. Lies come from meanness, low vanity, cowardice and a depraved nature, and they always fail of their object, are found out and bring the liar into contempt. One's true character is sure to be known and justly appreciated. Never trouble yourself about popularity. Do right the best you can, deserve respect, and you will have it. It requires neither brains nor courage to break rules, regulations, or laws—they are made for good: true men keep them; thieves and burglars break them. Do each duty every day; never let them accumulate when avoidable. *Always make the most of every opportunity*, or *it were better that the advantages had never presented themselves.* Success comes of continued everyday work and not of spasmodic effort; when attained with honor it is one of the highest pleasures of life. No one is born to greatness in the United States of America —the highest position is attainable by the lowest, but he who gets it must achieve it. An idle life is a *worthless and an unhappy one.*

Never neglect duties for pleasures. Avoid late wines and dinners; they often injure the health, and without health, life has scarce a pleasure. Statistics prove that early to bed and early to rise, is a chief cause of longevity. Sleep restores the nervous forces of the exhausted mind and well may it be called: "sore labor's bath, balm of hurt minds, great nature's second course, chief nourisher of life's feast." Nothing is (or rather should be) a pleasure that injures the health.

Economy is a virtue and extravagance is a vice. Very few, in old age, regret economy in their youth while many mourn in poverty their early extravagance. Lavish expenditure never wins respect. Pay every debt you owe. "Neither a borrower nor a lender be, for loan oft loses itself and friend." Never let vanity tempt you to spend money. Keep a record of business transactions.

Study well an undertaking. It will be of use if it only disciplines and strengthens the mind; it needs training as well as the muscles. Duties well done and difficulties surmounted as they arise, grow easier continually, and finally become lasting enjoyments.

Never play cards for money. It is easy to commence, always bad, and often fatal.

Dress as a gentleman, and as becomes you, and not as becomes someone else.

Never talk about private expenses and *never be ashamed to live with economy*. On the contrary, be proud of it.

Never be anxious to display your knowledge especially to older men but always try to learn of them.

Never say to another what would be unpleasant for him to say to you.

Manners should be frank and easy, with dignity. Avoid fawning, toadying ways, as one would the foul fiend.

Be courteous and manly everywhere and to everyone. Let your manners be quiet.

Nothing is more underbred than a flurried address, and a face wrinkled all over with grinning delight. If your habitual manner is bad, you cannot have a good manner in the drawing room. Far better that one look frigid even than to degrade the countenance with silly hilarity. One may feel neglected and have his vanity wounded, but he should never let that annoy him, as in due time all will come right and he will have the consideration that he merits.

The world is so constructed that it is not in men's power to withhold respect from lofty character, real ability, and good conduct.

Youth is short and the pleasures of youth perish in manly life. Reputation, power, and the consideration which comes of ability, attainment, and good character are what a man from 30 to 70 years of age covets. Nothing but the well-spent years of early life can secure these.

Profanity is vulgar and slang not much better.

Live each year in the way which will best fit you for the next year.

Avoid becoming a bore as you would the "plague." Short visits do not bore.

After duties are done and well done, let us take our pleasures which will be all the more enjoyed.

Close study and observation of each case of disease is the secret of success. It speaks its own language, furnishes its own peculiar indications and reads it own lesson.

Avail of every opportunity to improve and do not be afraid to do systematically the regular duties of each day. Systematic exercise of the muscles of the body and extremities ought to be kept up from early childhood at least once a day if possible. It requires an effort but one is well repaid as the years roll by, especially if engaged in sedentary occupations.

Competence is very desirable; indeed is indispensable. The way to acquire it is by forethought to plan, industry to execute, and prudence to keep the earning of your work, that is what you have honestly, fairly, and really earned. The best thing in life is not money. One is here in this world to become a good man—a wise man, a just man, an affectionate man, a religious man. True manhood comprises all this and is what is carried out of this world and into the next. True manhood, that is—wisdom, justice, affection and religion, will make you acceptable to God and blessed by Him forever. One must work for one's manhood as much as for one's money and take as much pains to keep it.

Keep clear of certain vices, especially intemperance, gambling, and licentiousness.

Be cheerful, lively, even gay, and mirthful, all that belongs to your period of life.

One can enjoy life without sin, and without putting a sting into one's cup to torment the heart all life long.

Cultivate the mind by reading valuable books as you have leisure and opportunity. Forethought, industry, and prudence will help as much as in getting money. It will be found pleasant and profitable to keep a Journal of what one sees, reads, and thinks.

Become familiar with the History of America, with the lives of its great men, and also with the History of England and the lives of its great men, and next with the writing of the best authors in English and American literature.

There is no real and satisfactory happiness in life without religion. It is a restraint from doing wrong, an encouragement to do right, and a great comfort at all times. By religion is not meant any certain form or belief, nor a certain ritual for joining a church or anything of that sort, although they are all helpful; but a respect for one's own nature and obedience to its laws; a love of truth and justice, love of neighbor as one's self, and of God with all one's mind, heart, and soul. Set apart a few minutes every day to commune with your God and with yourself. Review all the actions of the day, the deeds, the words, even the thoughts and feelings, and ask if they are such as God can approve; and if not, resolve to do such things no more and in your prayer ask God for forgiveness and His help for the future.

Do not antagonize your associates. Respect the age and experience of your superiors and elders.

Don't sign petitions. Don't take sides in quarrels.

Don't permit yourself to be prejudiced against those whom you are about to meet or whom you may know but slightly. *Judge for yourself.*

Don't argue. Have your own opinions, but don't obtrude them upon others.

Never sign papers without reading and understanding them.

Don't neglect social duties.

When wrong don't hesitate to make the amend honorable.

CHAPTER XX

OUR GOLDEN WEDDING

WE CELEBRATED the fiftieth anniversary of our wedding on April 25, 1927—a beautiful and a very happy day on which we received the congratulations of so many dear friends—over five hundred present, and our home never appeared to better advantage.

A beautiful booklet bound in gold and velvet was given us by Dr. John J. O'Malley and family. On its front leaf inside is inscribed, "Love from all of us, John, Mildred, Elizabeth, and John, Jr."

"May memories of Golden Days
Your Golden Wedding bless
Recording many joyful ways
Of youthful happiness
And if December's wintry snows
Have also played their part
Though on your head the silver shows
Love's Gold is in your heart."

Mrs. Roosevelt, the widow of our beloved President, and her son, Archie, came on from Oyster Bay for the celebration, and Mrs. Woodrow Wilson, the widow of our World War President, was with us.

Besides those present, numbers of letters and telegrams were received from those of our friends who were unable to be present.

The *Washington Post* of April 25, 1927 says:

MARK GOLDEN WEDDING ANNIVERSARY WITH FETE

ADMIRAL AND MRS. PRESLEY MARION RIXEY CELEBRATE WEDDING DAY

Weddings, Golden and Silver will be celebrated this afternoon at "Rixey," the beautiful colonial home of Admiral and Mrs. Presley Marion Rixey near Rosslyn, Va. Admiral and Mrs. Rixey will be celebrating their fiftieth wedding anniversary while the former's nephew and niece, Mr. and Mrs. Charles Rixey will mark the twenty-fifth anniversary of life together. The reception begins at five o'clock and will be informal.

Mrs. Rixey was formerly Miss Earlena English, her marriage to Dr. Rixey taking place at Portsmouth, N. H. Navy Yard at the time her father, Admiral Earl English was stationed there, the ceremony being performed in the Commandant's house. That was April 25, 1877, and Dr. Rixey's best man was Dr. John C. Boyd, who with Mrs. Boyd will assist them at the celebration today. Two of Mrs. Rixey's bridesmaids, Mrs. Benson, wife of Admiral William S. Benson and Mrs. Henry B. Brown, widow of Associate Justice Brown, will also be with her.

Dr. Rixey was formerly from Culpeper, Va. and was for many years White House physician. For some years he and Mrs. Rixey have spent their time at their lovely Virginia home.

The receiving party will be as follows: Mrs. B. H. Buckingham, Miss I. C. Freeman, Bishop and Mrs. Freeman, Rear Admiral and Mrs. John C. Boyd, Mrs. Eberle, Mrs. Henry B. Brown, Mrs. Russell Smith, Rear Admiral and Mrs. Benson, The Rev. Dr. and Mrs. Ze Barney Phillips, Miss Phillips, Mrs. John F. Rixey, widow of Representative Rixey, The Rev. Dr. and Mrs. Robert Johnston, Admiral and Mrs. Robert Gleaves, The Rev. Dr. and Mrs. Rolland Cotton-Smith, Rear Admiral and Mrs. Helm, The Rev. Dr. and Mrs. Wallace Radcliffe, Mr. and Mrs. Joseph Moore, Dr. and Mrs. John O'Malley, Mrs. Earl E. Whitehorne, Mrs. John Marshall Taliaferro, Mrs. Paul Morton, Mrs. F. L. Bradman, Mrs. La Garde, Mrs. Gouvernir Hoes, Mr. and Mrs. John S. Barbour, Dr. and Mrs. Sinclair Bowen, The Rev. and Madame Vurpillot, The Rev. and Mrs. John E. Sadler, Mrs. Martha Goddard, Hon. Walton Moore, the Misses Moore of Fairfax Co., Mrs. Keith and Miss Keith of Fairfax Co., Captain and Mrs. Dunbar, Miss Dunbar, Captain and Mrs. James C. Pryor, Mrs. Hughes Oliphant, Mrs. John A. Lejeune, Mrs. Geo. Trible, the Misses Lejeune, Mr. and Mrs. Barbour Rixey, Mr. John Rixey and little Elizabeth O'Malley.

The day following the reception, the *Washington Post* of April 26, 1927, gives a short account of it, as follows:

RIXEY GOLDEN WEDDING

Rear Admiral and Mrs. Presley M. Rixey celebrated their Golden Wedding yesterday afternoon at their home "Rixey," Va. Their beautiful colonial house, which they built about five years ago, was profusely decorated with spring flowers from their own grounds.

Mrs. Rixey wore a white georgette dress, embroidered in gold and trimmed with gold flowers, she also wore beautiful gold jewelry. Her niece, Mrs. Charles Rixey, who was celebrating her twenty-fifth anniversary was gowned in silver.

A stringed orchestra played all afternoon. All the decorations on the beautifully appointed table were in yellow, a large yellow candy wedding bell being part of the color scheme. There were about five hundred guests, and hundreds of telegrams from friends unable to be present. The wives of two Presidents were there, Mrs. Theodore Roosevelt, who came on from Oyster Bay and her son, Mr. Archibald Roosevelt, and Mrs. Woodrow Wilson.

The following letters of congratulations were received from dear friends who were unable to be present.

Italy, April 8, 1927.

Dear Mrs. Rixey:

I want to thank you for the beautiful calendar, it was so kind of you to remember me, and now my sister tells me that you and Dr. Rixey are celebrating this month your golden wedding. I always think with great pleasure of the many years of happiness you have had together, and what a beautiful picture of what marriage should be, and an example to those living near you.

Your picture, with that of Dr. Rixey, in the frame you gave me is always before me, as I write I wish I could see the dear originals of this picture appear in my pink villa, what a welcome I would give them.

All good wishes for a happy Easter, and a very very happy Golden Wedding Day.

With love to you both.

Yours affectionately,

(Signed) EMILY TYLER CAROW.

Panama City, Florida.
April 20th

Dear Dr. and Mrs. Rixey:

Mother will tell you that we hoped to get North in time for the great anniversary, but that cannot be. Dick has not been very well and must stay away a little while longer. So this note is to take you my affectionate greetings and every good wish for many years more together.

I remember all the happy times we children had with you, the delight of driving out to the farm, or of having the horses meet us, and the ride up and down hill until the gates came in view, then the dogs, horses and cows, and the bull in the pen and the flowers. The fields sloping down to the woods and brook where we played for so many hours, and the wonderful luncheons and picnics, Black Betsey with Mrs. Rixey scrambling anywhere on her. Algonquin, with Archie keeping him as well in front as possible.

Mrs. Presley Marion Rixey, 1927

We shall hope to see you on our way North if we can stop over in Washington, and in the meantime, my love and greetings.

Affectionately,

(Signed) ETHEL ROOSEVELT DERBY.

Hollycroft, Mentor, Ohio.
April 15, 1927.

Dear Golden Friends:

How much we would welcome the chance of greeting you under your own roof tree on the twenty-fifth and telling you how much you are to be congratulated. That sounds strange, but it is not—you have meant so much to your friends as well as to each other, you have made your lives count for so much, and you have been dispensers of cheer in every direction you have turned. Bless you both, and may many more years together spread out happy before you, and may we be able to catch a glimpse of you both as they pass. We would so gladly welcome you here.

With love from us both, and appreciating the remembrance, believe me.

Affectionately yours,

HELEN NEWELL GARFIELD.

Caroll Hall,
Paterson, N. J.

Dear Dr. and Mrs. Rixey:

It has given me great pleasure to be remembered by you on the happy occasion of your Golden Wedding, and I wish that I could accept your kind invitation, but I am not equal to such an effort.

With love and warm congratulations, believe me ever

Faithfully yours,

(Signed) JENNIE I. HOBART.

April 11, 1927

Norfolk, Va., Naval Hospital.
April 6, 1927.

My dear Admiral and Mrs. Rixey:

First of all I, with Mrs. Holcomb want to extend to you our heartiest congratulations upon this occasion, the fiftieth anniversary of your wedding.

And to you, my dear Admiral, I want to take the occasion to tell you what an inspiration your great service for the Medical

Corps of the Navy has been to me. Last week I had been studying the old Surgeon-General Reports in connection with the history of her hospitals, and a deep consciousness took possession of me of the great service you performed by improving the character of our hospital buildings and the service in them.

I regret that Mrs. Holcomb and I will not be able to call upon you personally on the 25th, but I can assure you both that we will be with you in spirit.

Sincerely yours,

(Signed) R. C. HOLCOMB,
Captain, U. S. N.

The Toronto Apts.

My dear Mrs. Rixey:

I have thought so continuously during this week of your and Admiral Rixey's wonderful Golden Wedding Day, and I feel impelled to write and tell you what pure joy and gladness the memory of it will always be to me.

It has seemed to me, as I have thought of it, and of the character of the multitude of friends who made a little journey out to Rixey to gather about you, of the beautiful home you have made, the Church of God you have established, and the young relatives in such numbers, clustering about you in such evident love and gratitude for your love and interest in them during your beautiful fifty years, and of your open loving hospitality to all who know you, on your crowning day of your fifty years of life together, I have felt that I have witnessed a triumph of right living and a shining example of what an American home should be.

I thank you many times, dear Mrs. Rixey, for my great privilege in having witnessed the loving scene, and value so highly the living memory of Harry Hunt—so dear a memory that made you ask me out to see you on last Monday afternoon.

Always sincerely yours,

(Signed) JULIA HERRICK HUNT.

University Club, 5th Ave. & 54th St.

Dear Dr. and Mrs. Rixey:

It is with the greatest pleasure that I extend to you both my heartiest congratulations.

I find that it is impossible for me to attend the great event, but I want you to feel that I do so with the utmost regret.

I have always looked back upon your many kindnesses to me and the friendship that existed as one of the pleasantest events of my life.

With best wishes for many prosperous years ahead.

I am,

(Signed) CONRAD HEWETT.

April 20, 1927

Oyster Bay, N. Y.
April 18, 1927.

My dear Admiral:

Mrs. Loeb and I greatly appreciate Mrs. Rixey and you remembering us with an invitation to your Golden Wedding anniversary and we value the kind note which accompanied it. We had hoped to be able to accept, but an important government business matter has just developed which will keep me here.

Mrs. Roosevelt told Mrs. Loeb last evening that she was planning to be with you.

With heartiest congratulations and best wishes for many more anniversaries, believe me my dear Admiral and Mrs. Rixey.

Faithfully,
(Signed) WILLIAM LOEB.

Hingham, Mass.

Dearest Mrs. Rixey:

I wish that it were possible for Pierce and me to be with you in person as we shall be in spirit on your Golden Wedding Day. How happy it would make my John and little Helen and dear Mrs. Glover to hear about this happy occasion and to know that all the dreams that came to the young Lieutenant in his berth on ship board were realized in his lifetime. A long, useful, happy life, the beautiful home on his native soil, the building of an altar for his faith, and through it all, the loving devotion of the most loyal and loving of wives. Such bliss comes to few in this world, and to none who better deserve it.

Warmest congratulations from us all, including my sister who remembers you both with affection.

Your card said "no gifts," but a bit of gold for remembrance, to be added to other bits that may come and make some worthy memorial for the day is surely permissible. So with this goes a small box with our love.

May the skies be bright, and the sun shine, and the flowers bloom on that day which you celebrate.

Your devoted friend,

(Signed) AGNES LONG—PIERCE LONG.

April 26, 1927.

My dear Mrs. Rixey:

I just must drop you a few lines to tell you what a lovely party you did have yesterday, and how everyone did enjoy it.

We all felt a little uneasy about Dr. Rixey, as we left him lying on the bed and we feared he was more than exhausted. I truly hope he is feeling quite well and refreshed today.

I am sure you both will bear ever in mind the bright memory of your Golden Wedding anniversary, which was indeed all that one could wish it to be, perfect in every detail. I shall never forget the very happy and festive occasion, nor will my good General, for having been happily married for thirty-one years we really could feel and understand how very near and dear you are to each other. As the years go by the love and admiration and affection seems to grow.

It is our wish to you and Dr. Rixey that you may still have many, many happy useful years still ahead of you and climb on up to the very top of the mountain together, being blessed as you go with the same kind friends and good wishes and affection of all that know you.

I must add that Laura and Eugenie were thrilled also with the lovely party.

With many fond wishes and love to you and Dr. Rixey.

I am as always,

Affectionately yours,

(Signed) ELLIE M. LEJEUNE.

1325-16th St.

My dear Friends:

I am so sorry I cannot be present at the Golden Wedding, but I do not want to be forgotten at the feast, and although my little gift arrives a little early, I send it for in the confusion of packing up it might be overlooked. You must consider it as coming from your old Rector as well, as the words are his, written to me on our 25th anniversary.

Let us all celebrate the diamond wedding.

Ever sincerely, with many happy memories of the past.

(Signed) V. S. MACKAY-SMITH.

Paris, France,

April 18, 1927.

Admiral and Mrs. Presley M. Rixey,
Rixey, Rosslyn, Va.

My dear Friends:

The kind invitation to your golden wedding anniversary has been forwarded to me here, and I sincerely regret my inability to be with you on the happy occasion.

Please accept my most hearty congratulations, and believe me, with cordial good wishes always,

Yours very sincerely,
(Signed) JOHN J. PERSHING.

London, 6 Grosevenor Sq.
April 30, 1927.

Dear Admiral and Mrs. Rixey:

Mrs. Petherick and I were pleased to receive the card announcing your golden wedding, which you so kindly and thoughtfully sent us, and although it is rather late, we desire to send you our warmest congratulations and good wishes. Long may you live, and happy may you be.

It is delightful to me to feel that I have known you all these years, even before your marriage, and that I have always retained your kind friendship.

Hoping this will find you both quite well, and with kindest regards and best wishes.

Always yours sincerely,
(Signed) C. J. PETHERICK.

Theodore Roosevelt,
Oyster Bay, Long Island.

Dear Admiral and Mrs. Rixey:

I was heart broken when the Doctor here told me I could not come to Washington for the Golden Wedding. Unfortunately I was laid low with carbuncles and boils. I have had a series which have lasted about six weeks. All I need is a potsherd and ashes to pass as a modern Job.

It is difficult to think of you both celebrating fifty years of married life. When the panorama of events slide by it seems as if those fifty years you have seen together contained much that was all important in the world. Fifty years ago Germany had just crushed France, England had a House of Lords that played an important part in the Government, Japan was a little nation of unimportance, China was an Empire, there was no radio, airplanes, and the west in our country was frontier.

Affectionate love to you both,

(Signed) THEODORE ROOSEVELT.

April 27, 1927.

Sagamore Hill, April 10th.

Dear Dr. Rixey:

It is just like you and Mrs. Rixey to ask us to stay with you at that busy time, but unfortunately we cannot have the pleasure. Ethel and the Doctor are having a holiday in Florida, and their children are under my care, so I shall arrive in Washington in time for the party and leave by a later train.

The boys will write you themselves.

All my congratulations to you and dear Mrs. Rixey, and great anticipation of the 25th.

Affectionately yours,

(Signed) EDITH KERMIT ROOSEVELT.

White Oaks Farm
Marion, Ohio.

My dear Mrs. Rixey:

It would be a great pleasure to be with you on Monday, April 25th, and to extend personally my heartiest congratulations and good wishes. However, it will not be possible for me to do so. May I extend to you and Dr. Rixey my sincere and hearty greetings on this the Golden Wedding Anniversary. "Look down, you gods and on this couple drop a blessed crumb."

Most sincerely,

(Signed) (MRS. CHARLES E.) MARY E. SAWYER.

San Diego, Cal.

Dear Dr. and Mrs. Rixey:

The Spears send you all their love and congratulations and we are only sorry we cannot be with you on the Golden Wedding Day. It surely would be a great joy to see you. You both have accomplished so much together and it was undoubtedly the help and support from one to the other that has made your lives so successful, so full of joys and accomplishments. We treasure you as our dearest friends, and long may you both enjoy good health and prosperity.

Devotedly,

(Signed) ELEANOR L. SPEAR AND RAYMOND SPEAR.

April 26
2215 Wyoming Ave.

My dear Mrs. Rixey:

I was very sorry that I could not come to wedding reception yesterday, but at the last minute I was prevented by guests who were leaving that afternoon.

With kind regards, and hoping you and Admiral Rixey will have many more.

Sincerely yours,

(Signed) HELEN H. TAFT.

Annefield,
Berryville, Va.

Dear Mrs. Rixey:

Thank you so much for your very kind invitation to your Golden Wedding reception. I think it was so sweet of you to remember us. I do so wish that we might be with you and Dr. Rixey that day, but I am afraid it will not be possible as we expect guests to be with us at that time, and the roads up are in an almost impassable condition. Tuesday we motored down from mother's and instead of coming through Falls Church, Fairfax, and Middleburg which usually takes two and one half hours, we had to go way around by Leesburg, taking almost four hours.

But even if we cannot get to you on the twenty-fifth, we send a great deal of love and very heartiest congratulations on your fifty happy years.

May you have many more of them.

Affectionately yours,

(Signed) GLADYS ALDEN WATKINS.

147 East 61st St.

Dear Mrs. Rixey:

How I wish I could be present in person to give you both my warm congratulations on your Golden Anniversary.

I always think of you with loyal affection because of the faithful regard in which my dear brother, Theodore Roosevelt, held you.

May the day be beautiful, and may many friends and their interest make it all that your heart could desire.

(Signed) CORINNE ROOSEVELT ROBINSON.

A few of the telegrams received as follows:

New York, April 25, 1927.

Rear Admiral and Mrs. Presley Rixey,
Rixey, Va.,

Mrs. Cortelyou has written explaining our inability to join you this afternoon. We send affectionate greetings and heartiest congratulations upon your anniversary, and every good wish for the future.

(Signed) GEO. B. & LILY M. CORTELYOU.

Newport, R. I., April 25, 1927.

Admiral and Mrs. Presley M. Rixey, R. F. D. No. 1, Rosslyn, Va.

May all days be golden.

(Signed) PRESS AND LILLIAN.

Schofield Barracks
April 19, 1927

Admiral and Mrs. Presley M. Rixey, Rosslyn, Va.

Loving congratulations and best wishes for you both on your Golden Anniversary.

(Signed) CAPT. AND MRS. CHURCHILL.

Wilmington, Del.
April 25, 1927.

Admiral and Mrs. P. M. Rixey, Rosslyn, Va.,
Via Washington, D. C.

Accept best wishes. Your old friends.

(Signed) RICHARD AND LAURA SYLVESTER.

Chicago, Ill., April 25.

Adm. & Mrs. Presley Rixey, Rixey, Rosslyn, Va.

Mrs. Dawes joins me in affectionate greetings to you both on this anniversary.

(Signed) CHARLES G. DAWES.

New York, N. Y.

Adm. Rixey, Rixey Station, Va., via Washington, D. C.

Deeply disappointed that I am unable to be with Mrs. Rixey and you this afternoon. Hoped to be able to go until this morning when important meeting obliged me remain. Am thinking of all the delightful times we have had at Pine Knot and in Washington, and wishing I could be with you today.

(Signed) KERMIT.

Portsmouth, Va.

Adm. & Mrs. Rixey, Rixey, Rosslyn, Va.

Capt. and Mrs. McLean extend heartiest congratulations and best wishes.

(Signed) N. T. McLean.

Trenton, N. J., April 25, 1927.

Rear Adm. & Mrs. Presley M. Rixey, Rosslyn, Va.

Congratulations and wishing you a great deal of happiness.

(Signed) Louise Hewett.

Caldwell, N. J., 25th.

Rear Adm. P. M. Rixey, Rosslyn Station, via Washington, D. C.

Sorry I cannot be with you today, have been ill. Wish you both long life together.

(Signed) H. B. Whitehorne.

Wycoff, N. J., 25th.

Rear Adm. & Mrs. Presley M. Rixey, Rosslyn, Va.

Love and congratulations. Sorry we cannot be with you.

(Signed) Inglis & Beulah.

Newport, R. I., 24th.

Rear Adm. & Mrs. Rixey, Rosslyn, Va.

Your kind invitation received. Many pleasant memories. Thanks for thinking of us. Adm. Sims joins me in best wishes to you both.

(Signed) Anne H. Sims.

Richmond, Va., 25th.

Rear Adm. & Mrs. Presley Rixey, Rosslyn, Va.

Love and congratulations. We regret very much not being with you today.

(Signed) Helen and Walton Rixey.

Wilkes Barre, Pa., 25th.

Adm. P. M. Rixey, Rixey, Rosslyn, Va.

Exceedingly sorry unable to leave home today. Long life and much happiness to yourself and Mrs. Rixey.

(Signed) Rev. J. J. Curran.

New York, N. Y., 25th.

Rear Adm. & Mrs. Presley M. Rixey, Rixey, Rosslyn, Va.

Congratulations and best wishes. Regret unable to be present.

(Signed) Mrs. William Cary Sanger.

Boston, Mass., 25th.

Rear Adm. & Mrs. Presley M. Rixey, Rosslyn, Va.

Very best of wishes to you both on your Golden Anniversary. (Signed) WALTER BOYD.

Barnstable, Mass., 25th.

Adm. & Mrs. Presley M. Rixey, Rixey, Arlington Co., Va.

Warmest congratulations Bride and Groom. Rejoicing with you in spirit.

(Signed) DR. & MRS. PHILLIPS, MISS PHILLIPS.

New York, N. Y., 25th, 1927

Adm. & Mrs. Presley Rixey, Rixey, Rosslyn, Va.

Congratulations, love and best wishes for many happy returns. From (Signed) WM. & HELEN PRALL.

Richmond, Va., April 25th.

Adm. & Mrs. Presley M. Rixey, Phone Rosslyn, Va.

Hearty congratulations and best wishes. Many regrets we will be unable to be present today, being detained here in Richmond. (Signed) CAPT. & MRS. GIBBONS.

Bremerton, Wash.

Adm. & Mrs. P. M. Rixey, Rixey, Rosslyn, Va.

Regret my absence, sincerest congratulations, best wishes and many happy returns. (Signed) T. W. RICHARDS.

Washington, D. C., 25th.

Adm. & Mrs. P. M. Rixey. Phone, Rixey Station, Rosslyn, Va.

Mrs. Mead and I wish to congratulate you upon your fiftieth anniversary. We have just returned from Atlantic City to find your invitation which we will be pleased to accept.

(Signed) STERLING V. MEAD.

Paterson, N. J., April 25.

Rear Adm. & Mrs. P. M. Rixey, Rosslyn, Va.

Congratulations on anniversary. May both be in good health celebrate Diamond.

(Signed) MARY E. & W. J. LOCKWOOD.

Annapolis, Md., 25th.

Adm. & Mrs. Presley M. Rixey, Rixey Station, Rosslyn, Va.

Regret exceedingly am unavoidably detained in Annapolis today on official business connected with Board of Visitors to Naval Academy and Naval Hospital. Many congratulations and best wishes from us. (Signed) KENNEDYS.

CONCLUSION

IN CLOSING these memoirs of an active life I am grateful for the discretion I have displayed in my intimate relations in official affairs, especially in regard to the White House and its inmates.

I now realize it more than ever before as I read Major Archibald Butts' letters written in the last two years of President Roosevelt's administration to his mother and sisters, now being printed in the *New York Herald*. As aide to the President, Major Butts was very active and his service was most acceptable and pleasing to both the President and Mrs. Roosevelt. I did not see so much of this young man except on official occasions as I had to be very active in administration of the Bureau of Medicine & Surgery in addition to being White House Physician. The day of the hundred mile ride to Warrenton, Va., and return, we were together, he as the aide to the President and Dr. Grayson as my aide. I felt the greatest responsibility for the success of this ride as I inadvertently had gotten the President to decide to make it himself. I had recommended the different physical tests for the Army and I had advised a similar one for the Navy. The result was a great protest from those who were not physically fit and from those who loved the life of ease. The President was much annoyed although he recognized the importance of my advice. In order to put his mind at rest in regard to the one hundred mile ride in three days I proposed, with his consent, to make the one hundred miles in *one* day, and if he was not satisfied I would repeat it for three days. He replied: "*We* will do it. We will ride it in one day." As far as he was concerned I couldn't get him to change his mind and on January 13, 1909, the ride was made as described in the preceding pages of this book.

Major Butts has put in writing a personal criticism of that which, as a member of the President's official family, he has seen and heard in his official capacity. I am sure that he would never have approved of this criticism being made public, even at this late date.

In regard to my long life, I believe I have achieved success, have lived well, laughed often and loved much; I have gained the respect of intelligent men and the love of little children; I have filled my niche and accomplished my task. I hope I will leave the world better than I found it, and that it will never be said that I have lacked appreciation of Earth's beauty or failed to express it. I have tried to look for the best in others and have given the best I had.

APPENDIX

APPENDIX

ADMIRAL RIXEY'S death on June 17, 1928 came as a great shock to his relatives and many friends, for while he had been in feeble health for several years he was still very active. Only a few hours before the end he was busy at his desk putting the finishing touches to his autobiography; his morning had been spent superintending the building of a large bungalow adjoining his home, and the afternoon in visiting the graves of departed friends in Arlington Cemetery and looking over the grounds of the new Army-Navy and Marine Country Club.

The love and esteem in which Admiral Rixey was held by all who knew him, finds expression in more than five hundred letters and telegrams of sympathy to Mrs. Rixey from all parts of the world, a few copies of which are presented here:

The *Washington Post* of June 18, 1928, says:

ADMIRAL RIXEY BURIAL TOMORROW

FORMER SURGEON GENERAL OF THE NAVY TO BE LAID AT REST IN ARLINGTON

With full military honors, the body of Rear Admiral Presley Marion Rixey, U. S. N. retired, who died early yesterday morning at his home in Rixey Station, outside of Cherrydale, Va., will be buried tomorrow morning in Arlington National Cemetery.

Funeral services will be held at eleven o'clock in St. John's Episcopal Church, Sixteenth and H Streets. Rev. Dr. Robert Johnston, pastor will preside.

Pallbearers Named

Rear Admiral Cary T. Grayson today announced the active and honorary pallbearers as follows:

Active—Rear Admiral E. R. Stitt, Surgeon General of the Navy, Rear Admiral W. L. Capps, Rear Admiral C. J. Badger, retired, Rear Admiral Cary T. Grayson, Maj. Gen. John A. Lejeune, Commandant of the Marine Corps, Maj. Gen. M. W. Ireland, Surgeon General of the Army, Maj. Gen. Charles P. Summerall, Chief of Staff of the Army, Dr. Robert M. Kennedy, Naval Medical Corps, and Lieut. Comdr. G. W. Calver.

Honorary—Richard Harlow and N. L. Burchell, Vestrymen of St. John's Church, Representative R. Walton Moore of Virginia, John S. Barbour, J. George Hiden, Dr. Camp Stanley, Dr. Howard F. Strine, Dr. W. Sinclair Bowen and Frank Upman.

Few medical officers of the Navy had served with so much distinction as had Admiral Rixey, who was former surgeon general of the Navy and for ten years White House physician during the administrations of Presidents McKinley and Roosevelt.

Retired in 1910

In 1910 he retired from active service but was recalled in 1917 when the United States became engaged in the World War. He served during that time as inspector general of medical activities of the Navy, as a member of the Bureau of Medicine and the Council of National Defense.

Admiral Rixey was seventy-five years old. He died suddenly after an attack of acute indigestion. Last year Admiral and Mrs. Rixey observed their golden wedding anniversary. With him at his bedside were Mrs. Rixey and Mrs. John J. O'Malley, wife of Comdr. O'Malley of the Naval Medical Corps.

The Paris Edition of the *New York Herald*, says:

PRESLEY M. RIXEY, U. S. NAVY, RETIRED, DIES IN VIRGINIA

FORMER SURGEON-GENERAL. SERVED AS PHYSICIAN TO MCKINLEY AND ROOSEVELT. ACUTE INDIGESTION

Veteran Medical Officer had gone into seclusion at home in Arlington.

(By special cable to the Herald)

Washington, June 18, 1928.

Rear-Admiral Presley Marion Rixey, retired, former Surgeon General of the United States Navy and official physician to President McKinley and President Roosevelt, died this morning at his country home at Arlington, Va., from an attack of acute indigestion. Admiral Rixey was seventy-six.

Admiral Rixey was appointed Surgeon General of the Navy with the rank of Rear Admiral on February 10, 1902, and held the position until February 25, 1910. He spent eleven and one-half years on active sea duty and twenty-five and one-half years on shore duty.

He was attached while on shore to the Navy Yard at Norfolk, Va. and the Naval Dispensary at Washington.

From 1898, he served as official physician to President McKinley until the President's death, and to Mrs. McKinley until the time of her death. He was also President Roosevelt's physician from 1901, and was physician at the White House for ten years to 1909, in addition to other duties. He retired from service in 1910 and took up the occupation of farming for the next seven years.

He re-entered active service in 1917 with the Bureau of Medicine and Surgery, in the Council of National Defence, and as inspector general of medical activities in the Navy until September, 1918. He was decorated by Alfonso XIII of Spain for services rendered officers and men of the Santa Maria following the explosion of that vessel.

He was a former president of the Association of Military Surgeons of the United States.

TELEGRAMS

Easthampton, N. Y.

Mrs. Presley M. Rixey, R. F. D. No. 1,
Rixey, Arlington Co., Va., June 18, 1928.
My heart goes out to you in tender sympathy and love as I mourn the loss of my husband's friend and mine.

(Signed) JENNIE T. HOBART.

June 18, 1928.

9 Radio Via RCA SS Homeric CD Chatham 18
Mrs. Rixey, R. F. D. No. 1, Rosslyn, Virginia.

Deepest sympathy.

(Signed) KATE BOYD.

Boston, Mass., June 19, 1928.

Mrs. P. M. Rixey, Arlington Co., Va.

Our tenderest sympathy to you in your great sorrow.

(Signed) BISHOP AND MRS. FREEMAN.

Mrs. Presley Marion Rixey,

Yarmouthport, Mass., June 19, 1928.
Rixey Station, Va., Route, Rosslyn, Va.

Our tenderest love, deepest sympathy and constant prayers for you in this overwhelming sorrow.

(Signed) DR. AND MRS. Z. B. PHILLIPS.

Hingham, Mass., June 19, 1928.

Mrs. Presley M. Rixey, Rosslyn, Va.

Pierce and I join in tenderest sympathy for your great loss.

(Signed) AGNES LONG.

New York, N. Y., June 18, 1928.

Mrs. P. M. Rixey, R. F. D. No. 1, Rosslyn, Va.
Very deepest sympathy in your loss. Mother sailed Saturday for Europe. She will be greatly distressed.

(Signed) BELLE AND KERMIT ROOSEVELT.

Boston, Mass., June 18, 1928.

Mrs. P. M. Rixey, R. F. D. No. 1, Rosslyn, Va.
Clarendon, Va.

My sympathy to you in the loss of one I too shall miss so much.

(Signed) WALTER BOYD.

Kansas City, Mo., June 17, 1928.

Convey to Mrs. Rixey deepest sympathy. How little we thought we would be plunged into sorrow so soon when we talked together last Sunday. I am here with Dr. Small who is in hospital with fractured hip.

We unite in grief with you.

(Signed) ELIZABETH K. CRAVEN.

New York, N. Y., June 18, 1928.

Mrs. Presley M. Rixey,
Rixey, Arlington Co., Va.

Mrs. Cortelyou and the family join me in deepest sympathy with you in your great sorrow.

(Signed) GEO. B. CORTELYOU.

Evanston, Ill., June 19, 1928.

Mrs. Rixey, Rixey, Rosslyn Station, Va.

Mrs. Dawes and I send you our deepest sympathy in the death of your noble husband whom we mourn as a personal loss.

(Signed) CHARLES G. DAWES.

New York, N. Y., June 19, 1928.

Mrs. Presley M. Rixey, Rosslyn Station, Va.

On my return from Kansas City today found the distressing news of our beloved friend's death. It seems as if one of the last links between father and those old days in Washington has been broken. Much love and deepest affection from all.

(Signed) THEODORE ROOSEVELT.

Port Huron, Mich., June 18, 1928.

Mrs. P. M. Rixey, Rixey, Va., via Rosslyn Station, Va.

Have just learned of Admiral's death. My deepest sympathy and prayers.

(Signed) E. S. DUNLOP.

Blue Ridge Summit, Penn., June 17, 1928.

Mrs. P. M. Rixey, Rosslyn, Va.

Alice and I send love to you. I expect to get in town 18th. If there is anything I can do please let my office know.

(Signed) CAMP STANLEY.

San Francisco, Cal., June 17, 1928.

Mrs. Presley M. Rixey, Rixey Station, Va.

Love and deepest sympathy.

(Signed) ELIZABETH GOLDSBOROUGH ADAMS.

Letters of Sympathy

War Department
Office of the Chief of Staff
Washington, D. C.

June 20, 1928.

My dear Mrs. Rixey:

While any words appear to be useless in your great sorrow, I wish to assure you of my profound sympathy and my own sense of a great personal loss in the death of Admiral Rixey.

While my personal association with him unfortunately was relatively short, his reputation and his character were familiar to me over a long period of years. My attachment to him, therefore, cannot be measured by the associations which I was privileged to enjoy. His great public services, his intense human sympathy, his altruism and unselfish devotion to the good of his fellowmen made him one of the outstanding characters of his generation. He attracted all to him by his personality, his magnetism and his kindliness, and he commanded respect and admiration because of his superior intelligence, his professional attainments and his lofty patriotism. His influence must survive and the example of his life will point the way to his contemporaries and those who follow them. Not only ourselves but the country must mourn a loss which cannot be replaced.

With my warm regards and with my earnest desire that you will afford me the privilege of serving you should occasion require, I am

Faithfully yours,

(Signed) C. P. Summerall.

Mrs. P. M. Rixey,
Rixey, Arlington County,
Virginia.

Hiden, Rickers and Button
Attorneys and Counsellors at Law
Culpeper, Virginia

June 19, 1928.

My dear Mrs. Rixey:

Everything today passed off as it should. It was a beautiful and touching service, and I want you to know how deep my sympathy is for you. I hope to see you soon again, and I want to assure you of my lasting friendship. When I can render you any service it will be a pleasure to have you command me.

With the best wishes,

Always faithfully your friend,

(Signed) J. G. Hiden.

DEPARTMENT OF THE NAVY, BUREAU OF MEDICINE AND SURGERY
Washington, D. C.

June 18, 1928.

My dear Mrs. Rixey:

As Superintendent of the Navy Nurse Corps, and as one of the first nurses to be appointed when Admiral Rixey finally succeeded in establishing the Corps, I wish you to know our deep sympathy is with you in your great loss.

I had a chat with Admiral Rixey but a few weeks ago in Admiral Grayson's office, when he expressed his interest in and admiration for the Corps. It gave us a warm glow to learn he had not, in his busy life, forgotten us. The Navy Nurse Corps will ever hold the name of Admiral Rixey near the hearts in love and appreciation.

Very sincerely yours,

(Signed) J. BEATRICE BOWMAN,
Superintendent, Navy Nurse Corps.

Mrs. P. M. Rixey,
Rixey, Arlington County,
Virginia.

DEPARTMENT OF THE NAVY, BUREAU OF MEDICINE AND SURGERY
Washington, D. C.

June 18, 1928.

My dear Mrs. Rixey:

It seems almost impossible to realize that those of us in the Medical Corps of the Navy shall no longer have Admiral Rixey to turn to for advice and encouragement.

It is to him, always forceful, always alert to institute any measure which might be of benefit to the sick of the Navy, we owe the splendid group of modern hospitals which were such a godsend for the country during the late war, and which are now serving its unfortunate disabled veterans. Not only did he strive to make available in the Navy facilities equal to those offered by the latest type of civil hospital of the period when he was Surgeon General of the Navy, but, realizing that hospital facilities without the men trained to make use of them were as naught, he established the Naval Medical School, an institution which has served us to this day for the training of our medical officers in service specialties, and for keeping them abreast of the advances of the medical profession in civil life.

Doctor Rixey will always be remembered for his forceful personality, his deep interest in the advance of his corps, and his insistence that every member of that corps carry on with high purpose. As we come to full appreciation of our loss, we realize yours, and sympathize with you deeply.

I am, with sincere sympathy,

(Signed) E. R. Stitt.
Surgeon General, U. S. Navy.

Mrs. Presley M. Rixey,
Rixey, Virginia.

Washington Golf and Country Club
R. F. D. No. 1
Rosslyn, Virginia

June 19, 1928.

Mrs. P. M. Rixey,
Route No. 1,
Rosslyn, Virginia.

My dear Mrs. Rixey:

Under instruction from the Board of Directors of the Washington Golf and Country Club, I beg to tender to you the deep sympathy of the Board and of our entire membership in the sorrow which has come to you. The character of Admiral Rixey has been woven into the fabric of our organization to such an extent that his loss is simply irreparable. I do not believe that we have ever really sensed the deep love and affection which we held for him until now and words are simply inadequate to express to you the depth of our feeling at his loss.

Very sincerely yours,

(Signed) A. G. Rice,
Secretary.

Washington, June 17, 1928.

My dear Mrs. Rixey:

I cannot express to you how grieved we are to learn from this morning's paper of your great bereavement in the death of your husband, our very dear friend, Admiral Rixey.

I had known him so well, from our earliest days in Washington and found him always the same kindly, genial friend, that his death comes as a grave personal sorrow to me, as it will to many.

At such a time little can be said to assuage your grief, but the knowledge will live with you forever of a life's work so well and faithfully done, of the affection in which he was held by all who knew him and the genuine sorrow his passing is to his friends among whom we are happy to feel ourselves included.

Mrs. Dorn joins me in most sincere expressions of earnest sympathy, and I remain,

Faithfully yours,

(Signed) Edward J. Dorn.

UNITED STATES GOVERNMENT DISPATCH AGENCY
6 Grosvenor Gardens, S. W. I.

London 25, June, 1928.

Mrs. P. M. Rixey,
Rosslyn, Va., Route No. 1.
My dear Mrs. Rixey:

I was intensely grieved and sorry to hear of the death of your dear husband, and I desire to convey to you my sincere and deep sympathy in your great and irreparable loss.

It was my privilege and pleasure to have known him, and to have retained his friendship for a great many years, and I, therefore, feel I have lost a good and valued friend.

Hoping you will keep well under your heavy affliction, and with warmest regards and best wishes.

Always yours sincerely,
(Signed) C. J. PETHERICK.

PEOPLES STATE BANK

Cherrydale, Va., June 18, 1928.

Mrs. P. M. Rixey,
Rosslyn, Va., R. F. D.
Dear Mrs. Rixey:

It was with profound sorrow that we observed in Sunday's paper, the death of your husband, the late Admiral P. M. Rixey.

Our relations with Dr. Rixey have been most pleasant since the organization of our bank. We prized his friendship towards our institution very highly, and feel that we always had a friend in Dr. Rixey. Our relations in business, as well as social life, will indeed be a benefaction to us. We regarded his counsel and experience as a great asset to our bank, and community, and by vote of our Executive Board, the secretary was instructed to write you a letter of sympathy in this, your hour of bereavement.

Not only our community, but our State and Nation has lost a valuable public servant. Though he can not be present with us in body, we are sure that the good work he rendered while here will live on for untold ages, for the good of our community and country.

We, therefore, convey to you our deepest sympathy, both as an Executive Board and personally, and if we can be of any service, we trust that you will not hesitate to call upon us.

Very sincerely yours,
(Signed) A. B. HONTS,
Secretary.

WAR DEPARTMENT
General Dispensary, U. S. Army
Boston, Mass.

34th St. Paul Street
Brooklyn, Mass.
June 20, 1928.

My dear Grayson:

Just a few moments ago I read of the passing of Admiral Rixey and I want to send our sincere sympathy to you and through you to Mrs. Rixey.

I have always admired him, and he has often written me about various things since I left Washington. Indeed only a few months ago he sent us an invitation to their golden wedding. Everybody who had the honor and pleasure of knowing him loved him. A real man with a big heart has left us. I will never forget how he showed me the numerous details of things at the White House when I relieved him in 1909. Many times I dropped in to see him at his home in Virginia, but I never found him seventy-five years old—more like fifty years. We will all think of him as a loyal friend and a most efficient Navy Officer.

With very kind regards, I am

Very truly yours,

(Signed) M. A. DELANEY.

PEOPLES STATE BANK
Cherrydale, Va., July 6, 1928.

Mrs. P. M. Rixey,
Route No. 1,
Rosslyn, Va.

Dear Mrs. Rixey:

At the regular monthly meeting of the Vestry of the Church of St. Mary, the Registrar was instructed, by unanimous action of the Vestry, to send you reassurance of the sympathy of all the members of that body, of your recent sorrow.

We all realize that but for Dr. Rixey, our beautiful church would not be here today, and it will forever stand as a fitting memorial to him, and be to those who knew him, and therefore, loved him, a constant reminder of his wonderful simplicity and nobility of character.

We wish again to assure you that we, individually and collectively, wish you to have our most sincere sympathy.

Yours very truly,

(Signed) CLEGGE THOMAS,
Registrar.

300 Goodwood Road
Roland Park,
Thursday.

Dear Mrs. Rixey:

It was only on Tuesday that I heard of your great sorrow, and I want to send our belated messages of deep sympathy and love. All who knew your dear husband will miss him, but the memory of him we will always have.

Words are so inadequate, but I am thinking of you, and Norman joins me in many messages.

Always sincerely,
(Signed) ISABELLA H. JAMES.

LAW OFFICES OF B. G. FOSTER
805 G. Street, N. W.
Washington, D. C.

June 20, 1928.

Dear Mrs. Rixey:

Mrs. Foster and I want to add a word to the many messages of sympathy you must have received. Though we had not become really acquainted with Dr. Rixey as a neighbor until his later and less active years, that acquaintance had ripened with genuine and indeed affectionate friendship.

It has been an inspiration to have been associated with him in the building of the church. I am proud to feel that I have had his regard and confidence. I will especially prize in my remembrance our last evening's visit together when we consulted over his autobiography and he read and told me so much of his interesting life and experiences, and of his plans.

We shall all miss him very greatly. But surely his good works remain and will stand as the finest kind of a monument to that inner and truer greatness which we were fortunate enough to know.

With genuine sympathy,

Sincerely,
(Signed) BERTRAM G. FOSTER.

THE SECRETARY OF THE NAVY
Washington, D. C.

June 19, 1928.

My dear Mrs. Rixey:

We have heard of the death of your husband, Rear Admiral Presley Marion Rixey, Medical Corps, United States Navy, Retired. We regret and deplore his death and desire to express to you our heartfelt sorrow at his loss. We share with you in the sense of personal bereavement and trust that you may be comforted and your grief assuaged by God who holds the eternal destiny of man in His hands.

Sincerely yours,

(Signed) CURTIS D. WILBUR,
Secretary of the Navy.

Mrs. Presley M. Rixey,
Rosslyn, Virginia.
Route No. 1.

U. S. NAVAL HOSPITAL
San Diego, Cal.

June 22, 1928.

Dear Mrs. Rixey:

Eleanor and I send you our deepest sympathy and love in your great bereavement.

The Doctor stood out in the Navy as having done more for the Medical men individually and more for taking care of the sick than anyone else. We all admired and loved him.

Washington will not be the same for me, I valued his friendship for me more than I can tell. We in the Navy are all proud of what Dr. Rixey really accomplished.

We have the Doctor's photograph in our drawing room and see it every day so we have felt that he has been near us ever since we left Washington.

Please always consider me one of your "boys" and if I can ever be of any service please command me.

Again Eleanor and I send you our warmest love.

Affectionately,

(Signed) RAYMOND SPEAR.

Commanding Officer
UNITED STATES NAVAL HOSPITAL
Newport, Rhode Island

Dear Mrs. Rixey:

The sad news of the Admiral's death has just reached us through the press and Mrs. Bell and I feel a deep sympathy for you in your great loss. Your faith will be your consolation, of course, but also the fullness and richness of your life together will be a continuing delight in recollection. His was a life of distinction and constructive usefulness in many directions and his Corps and Service can never forget his outstanding personality. Succeeding generations will continue to enjoy and profit by the great benefits with which he was able to endow them during his active career.

We feel sure that you will find compensating happiness in a consciousness of all this and in the devotion of your friends and family.

Sincerely yours,

(Signed) WM. H. BELL.

SUMMERFIELD
Blue Ridge Summit, Pa.

June 25, 1928.

My dear Mrs. Rixey:

I want you to know how greatly I appreciate your giving me the opportunity to take part in the final honors to Admiral Rixey, a friend of more than fifty years and one whom I have always held affectionately in mind.

I know that there is no comfort for you in words at this time, but later it will be a comfort to realize how prominent a place in the respect and affection of a multitude of people and how universally he will be missed.

The Bryans and I came to Blue Ridge Summit last Saturday where we expect to remain until school begins next September.

I know that Bessie would send you her love, as I do mine, were she here as I write.

Always sincerely yours,

(Signed) CHAS. J. BADGER.

ALL SOULS MEMORIAL CHURCH
Cathedral and Connecticut Avenues, N. W.
Washington, D. C.

June 20, 1928.

My dear Mrs. Rixey:

Is it presumptuous of me to write you a line at this time? In view of the gracious hospitality that you and Admiral Rixey have extended to me, I think not. I am thinking of the "sweet and strong" impression he made on me, and his love of God's great out of doors. And now he is living an unfolding life in the "spacious fields of eternity." For you it is hard—so hard—, let your friends help you a bit—and the friend of friends so much more.

Mrs. Sterett joins me in this word of friendship and understanding.

Yours sincerely,

(Signed) H. H. D. STERETT.

U. S. MARINE BARRACKS
Washington, D. C.

Monday.

My dear Mrs. Rixey:

General Lejeune joins me in sending to you at this sad time our deepest sympathy and affection. Indeed we were both greatly shocked and grieved to read of the Admiral's death, as he was always so full of life and interest. It is indeed hard to associate death with one whom you have "loved long since and lost for awhile." I recall to my mind your "Golden Anniversary" and I did so hope and pray that you both would be spared to each other for many long years yet to come. But one who has lived such a long and useful life, so full of human interest, and love for his neighbor and his God, can but reap his full reward in the presence of his Master.

I will see you soon and endeavor to express more fully my sympathy for you at this time.

Laura and Eugenie join me in love and sympathy.

I am

Most cordially yours,

(Signed) ELLIE M. LEJEUNE.

June 22, 1928.

My dear Mrs. Rixey:

I can't express how deeply I sympathize with you in the passing away of Dr. Rixey.

Those who knew him cannot help but feel keenly the loss of such a splendid man.

A life so fully lived in the service of others, has left behind many friends whom I hope will be a source of comfort to you in your great loss.

Most sincerely yours,

(Signed) EVA LAKE.

Reserve Hill,
Rosslyn, Virginia, Route 1
June 19, 1928.

Mrs. P. M. Rixey,
Rixey Station, Va.

Dear Madam:

Permit me to express my sympathy in the great loss you have so suddenly suffered.

Little did I think that my meeting with the Admiral a week ago would be the last one.

Not being at all well myself and not taking any interest in the reading of daily papers, I did not learn of the sad occurrence until late last night.

It will always be a bright spot in my memory that I could call this great good man my friend, and I hope you will bear the great loss you have sustained with fortitude and in the best of health.

Very respectfully yours,

(Signed) GEO. N. SAEGMULLER.

170 Marlborough Street,
Boston, Mass.
June 23, 1928.

My dear Mrs. Rixey:

I wish to express my sincere and heartfelt sympathy for your deep sorrow. You and Dr. Rixey and Cousin Cassie have been so wonderful to me since the time when I was trying to enter Annapolis, and I have had so many good times with you, that I feel as though I had lost a second member of my family.

It is a privilege to have known anyone like Dr. Rixey, and I shall always be proud of the fact that he was a friend of mine, and be grateful for his very many kindnesses.

Very sincerely yours,

(Signed) ROB LOWELL.

Wildcliff
Seal Harbor,
Maine.

Dear Mrs. Rixey:

I want you to know with how much sympathy I am thinking of you, since Helen told me, on my way through Washington Monday, of dear Dr. Rixey's death.

Though I have not seen either of you for quite a long while, I have always remembered you with much love, and the happy days when we went to St. Johns.

I cannot think of one of you without the other, and can so well realize how dreadful it is for you to be parted, and how you will miss him.

Helen gave me the news just as I was catching the train, and Charles Marlatt was at the station to see me off. I was talking to him, leaning from the step of the train, and said, "I feel so awfully sorry about Dr. Rixey's death;" a colored porter who had just brought in some luggage for a lady, turned to me, as I said it, and said, "You don't feel nearly as awful as I feel over that news." I said, "Oh, you knew him?" and he answered, "Deed I did Mam, and I just loved him." The train started, and he jumped off, and I had no chance to find out any details. But I wanted you to know it, for I'm sure Dr. Rixey had helped him, or talked with him sometime or other, for there was really love in his voice. I know he is only one of the very many who will miss dear Dr. Rixey.

With much love, and very deepest sympathy, believe me,

Always affectionately,

(Signed) VIRGINIA BOY-ED.

Hingham, Mass.
June 29, 1928.

Dearest Mrs. Rixey:

The sad news that came by wire yesterday was not entirely unexpected as Pierce had told me of your anxiety and his frail health. But nothing can prepare one for such a blow, and I cannot think of you as going on without the presence of the dear Doctor. For a long time you will be comforted by the feeling that strength has come to him in place of the weakness of these latter days. Then, too, the sense of his spiritual presence about you will, I hope, be very evident. Both to Mrs. Roosevelt and me, the constant sense of nearness was very comforting. And the faith that you both had in the nearness of the divine presence will be with you always.

You know that many, many hearts are saddened today at his passing, and at the hour of the service at St. John's many more people than the church can hold will be with you in spirit.

After you are somewhat rested from this great strain, I shall write again, hoping to know your future plans.

Pierce is so glad that he had that pleasant meeting this spring.

With warmest affection.

Your loving friend,

(Signed) Agnes Long.

Villa "Lea Breeze"
Le Moulleare
Arcachon, France
June 20, 1928.

My dear Mrs. Rixey:

I learned today of the passing of our dear lifelong friend, and my heart is heavy indeed. I write to say how deeply I feel for you in your bereavement. Though we boys have not seen you and the Doctor very often in late years (the last time was in the spring of 1926) we have never failed to feel very close to you both and to always speak of you with affection.

The closest friend of my father and mother, an unfailing friend to me, I will always cherish the memory of Doctor Rixey as the highest type of man I ever knew. I remember him particularly at my own Father's funeral when he held me kindly by the arm and spoke words of courage to me.

I pray that his last moments were peaceful.

When I return to America I will go to see you, and together we will recall the memory of the dear friend I loved with all my heart.

With deepest sympathy and affection.

As ever yours,

(Signed) Douglas Wise.

1233-31st Street, N. W.
Washington, D. C.

June 17, 1928.

My dear Mrs. Rixey:

We had not heard of Admiral Rixey's illness and were shocked and distressed to get the news of his death from the morning papers. Our hearts go out to you, dear Mrs. Rixey, in sympathy. Mrs. Kean said, "what a beautiful couple they were."

Admiral Rixey became a good friend of mine very soon after I came here for duty with General O'Reilly in 1902, and his cordial friendship never varied in twenty-six years. Often I did not see him for long periods, but when I did he always gave me the same cordial and friendly greeting and asked me why I did not come to see him (we have no car, so it was difficult to do so).

I hope and pray dear Mrs. Rixey that God will give you strength and resignation to bear this terrible blow, and we both send you our deep and affectionate sympathy.

Sincerely your friends,
(Signed) RANDOLPH AND CORNELIA KEAN.

U. S. NAVAL MEDICAL SUPPLY DEPOT
Sands and Pearl Streets
Brooklyn, N. Y.

June 18, 1928.

Dear Mrs. Rixey:

It was with much sorrow I read in the N. Y. paper this morning of your husband's death. Outside of my warm personal feeling for him I can never forget your sweetness and sympathy to me in Mrs. Lowndes' last illness, nor can I forget Dr. Rixey's kind offer to help me. Those things, dear Mrs. Rixey, make a lasting impression. And now, in your sorrow I know so well how you suffer. Nothing I can say can help you, but I do want you to know you have my heartfelt sympathy in these long and sad days.

Please believe me

Very truly yours,
(Signed) C. H. T. LOWNDES.

NEWPORT HOUSE AND ANNEX
Bar Harbor, Maine

July 17, 1928.

My dear Mrs. Rixey:

The news of the Admiral's death reached me only a short time ago. He has meant so much to me for so many years; I feel in his death the sense of a great personal loss, as if he had been a near relative.

He was strong and tender, with a determined will, and yet very gentle. I looked to him for guidance and he never failed me. The memories of the great days in Washington are penetrated by the pleasant thoughts of you and Dr. Rixey. Your friendship, your hospitality, and all your kindnesses.

He was a Christian gentleman, and was prepared to meet his God. No two people ever lived more closely and completely together, and I know what the loss must mean to you. But such a relationship can never be destroyed. Death has no dominion over it.

Mrs. Smith and I send you our deepest love.

Your friend,

(Signed) ROLAND COTTON-SMITH.

THE ENGLISH SPEAKING UNION
Deartmouth House
37 Charles Street, Berkeley Square, W. 1

Darling:

I have just heard about the dear Doctor's falling asleep, and am writing to express my very deepest love and sympathy for you in your great sorrow. I only wish I were near you, and just as soon as I return I shall come to you and do all I can for you. I only heard of it today at luncheon, and it was a terrible shock. The Admiral was a magnificent man, fine, sweet and brave, and lion-hearted. He knew no fear and lived a beautiful life, and we all loved him. At these times there is so little to say. Both life and death are a great mystery, but it will not be so very long before we all meet in the Spirit World, and how glorious that will be.

I saw Mrs. Stanley's mother this afternoon after luncheon and we talked about you, for we all love you very tenderly. Bless your dear heart; just as soon as I am in Washington I shall look you up and kiss your dear sweet self.

A heart full of love and sympathy.

Devotedly ever,

(Signed) MARY BOWEN.

WILLIAM PRALL
Roadside
Lenox, Mass.

June 18, 1928.

Dear Earlena:

How can I tell you of the grief Helen and I felt when we learned that dear Presley had passed to his reward. And what must your own grief be. After more than fifty years spent in the love and companionship of a man so kind, so good, so full of interests, your life will be vacant, and time will hang heavy on your hands. There is one consolation: he was as good as mortal man can be, and he was in every way prepared "To meet his Captain face to face when he crossed the bar." May he rest in peace, and may perpetual light shine upon him.

I wish I could be with you tomorrow, but Helen is still in bed with a lingering fever from influenza, and she is afraid to have me go to Washington and Rixey alone.

She joins me in heartfelt love and sympathy for you in your irreparable loss, and with prayer that our Heavenly Father will love and will keep you always in his mercy.

As ever, I am your devoted and affectionate cousin,

(Signed) WILLIAM PRALL.

LAW OFFICE OF B. G. FOSTER
Washington, D. C.

July 31, 1928.

Mrs. P. M. Rixey,
Rosslyn, Va.

Dear Mrs. Rixey:

At the regular meeting of the Vestry of Langley Parish and St. John's Church, McLean, Virginia, held July 27, 1928, the following resolution was unanimously adopted:

> The death of Admiral Presley M. Rixey constitutes a genuine loss in many fields of human endeavor, but in none is it more keenly felt than in the church of which he was a strong, active, and abiding member.
>
> Always interested in the general work of Langley Parish, of which he was a member, his activity finally culminated, in association with Mrs. Rixey, in giving the land and making it possible to build and equip within the lower portion of the Parish, the very beautiful church of St. Mary—"The Church of Our Mother."
>
> It stands a monument not alone to his initial munificence, but to his tireless effort that only ended with his death, and above all to his absolute faith that it could and should be done.

The Vestry requests that the Registrar in addition to making this record in the minutes of the Vestry, send a copy hereof to you, with the genuine sympathy of each member.

In accordance with the wishes of the vestry I transmit the above.

As you already know it expresses my own deep regret and sincere sympathy.

Sincerely,

(Signed) BERTRAM G. FOSTER,
Registrar Vestry
Langley Parish & St. John's Church.

Greenbrier, Ohio. Sept. 4, 1928.

Dear Mrs. Rixey:

You may well imagine my astonishment and sorrow when the belated news of your dear husband's death came to me. I had been away from here, and on my return I learned of his departure. Since then I have been taking a cure at Hot Springs, Virginia and now on this late date I am able to write and tell you of my sincerest sympathy.

I don't know your address, and so have put this double direction on the envelope. I had looked forward with the greatest interest to coming over and calling on you in your Virginia home. Dr. Rixey had written generously inviting me to be your guest for at least a little while during the General Convention. But this was out of the question, as my duties are and will be very engaging in the House of Bishops. But the generous and hospitable thought gave me much pleasure. And now—he is gone home, and I shall not see his pleasant smile, nor feel his hearty genuine hand-shake. I think of him, as a good Christian, a skillful physician, a faithful officer of the Navy, and a dear, devoted husband and friend. I know what your sorrow is. I have passed through the deep valley. But Christ will be with you and sustain you, and comfort you. God bless you, is my prayer.

I shall try and find you when in Washington next month. I am booked to preach in St. John's on October 21st, and that will be a joy, though only a few now are left of my beloved friends and parishioners, and you are one of them.

Affectionately,

(Signed) WILLIAM A. LEONARD.

RESOLUTION

Whereas, Rear Admiral P. M. Rixey, United States Navy, died on June 17, 1928, in the fullness of years and service, causing profound sorrow to all who knew him.

And Whereas, he had from 1902 to 1926 been a vestryman of St. John's Church, and from 1921 until the date of his death been the Senior Warden of the Church, serving in both positions with that fidelity and wisdom which endeared him to those associated with him in Parish affairs.

Be It Resolved, that the members of the Vestry, both for themselves and the entire church membership give recorded expression of the deep feeling which is entertained at the loss which St. John's Church has sustained through the death of Admiral Rixey.

And Be It Resolved, that this resolution be spread upon the minutes of the Vestry meetings of the Church and a copy thereof be transmitted to Admiral Rixey's widow.

AN APPRECIATION

By Rear-Admiral Cary T. Grayson, Medical Corps, U. S. Navy (ret'd)

DOCTOR RIXEY'S buoyancy and enthusiasm for life made his career always colorful, vivid and interesting. He was ever crusading, challenging what he felt to be wrong, fighting for what he saw as the right. This spirit led him into many of the experiences which he describes in his book. His courage was unfailing, and his chivalry an inspiration to those under his banner.

In the Medical Corps of the Navy he has become a tradition of efficiency and gallant leadership.

His generosity of nature and greatness of heart were superlative. His kindness was unlimited. The number of people he befriended in his long and extraordinary active life is beyond reckoning. He had an enormous capacity for friendship. His great house in the country on the Virginia hills overlooking the Potomac and the fair city of Washington was a mecca for his host of friends.

Seated by the open fire, dogs around his feet, at the appearance of a friendly step he would throw back his head in a hearty laugh of welcome—such a jovial greeting—and call to the incomer "Come in, boy, come in. Why didn't you bring all the family? Where are those boys? I wanted to take them for a ride on my saddle with me. Anyway, you'll have to stay for supper. We have birds and an old ham."

So he would gather in his friends—the great and the humble, the rich and the poor, his country neighbors and his city associates. His was the democracy which only a great gentleman feels and dares to show for his fellowmen.

Into his three score and ten years was crowded more of living than most of us can hope for. His tremendous vitality, his physical prowess, and his prodigious activity were only the outward expressions of a great restless, and ambitious spirit. This spirit was tempered by a deep religious belief, a pleasure in the familiar things of home, and a great love of the land.

He had his wish—to lead an active life, to spend his last days serenely among the hills which were so dear to his eyes, and to return in peace and in faith to the soil from which he sprung.

INDEX

INDEX

Printed in the United States
141146LV00005B/99/A

9 781417 928958